ASIAN DEVELOPMENT OUTLOOK 1999

Special Chapter
**Economic Openness:
Growth and Recovery
in Asia**

Published for the Asian Development Bank
by Oxford University Press

OXFORD
UNIVERSITY PRESS

Oxford University Press is a department of the University of Oxford.
It furthers the University's objective of excellence in research, scholarship,
and education by publishing worldwide in

Oxford New York

Athens Auckland Bangkok Bogotá Buenos Aires Calcutta
Cape Town Chennai Dar es Salaam Delhi Florence Hong Kong Istanbul
Karachi Kuala Lumpur Madrid Melbourne Mexico City Mumbai
Nairobi Paris São Paulo Singapore Taipei Tokyo Toronto Warsaw
with associated companies in Berlin Ibadan

Oxford is a registered trade mark of Oxford University Press

First published 1999
This impression (lowest digit)
1 3 5 7 9 10 8 6 4 2

Published in the United States
by Oxford University Press, New York

This book was prepared by the staff of the Asian Development Bank,
and the analyses and assessments contained herein do not
necessarily reflect the views of the Board of Directors
or the governments that they represent. The Asian Development Bank
does not guarantee the accuracy of the data included in this publication
and accepts no responsibility whatsoever for any consequence for their use.
The term "country" does not imply any judgment by the Asian Development
Bank as to the legal or other status of any territorial entity.

Published for the Asian Development Bank by
Oxford University Press

British Library Cataloguing in Publication Data
available

Library of Congress Cataloguing in Publication Data
ISBN 0-19-592010-4
ISSN 0117-0481

Printed in Hong Kong

Published by Oxford University Press (China) Ltd.
18th Floor Warwick House East, Taikoo Place, 979 King's Road, Quarry Bay
Hong Kong

Foreword

The *Asian Development Outlook 1999* is the 11th in a series of annual economic reports on the developing member countries of the Asian Development Bank. Developments in the world economy provide the backdrop against which this *Outlook* reviews the recent economic performance of the Bank's developing member countries, assesses their economic prospects, and examines relevant short- and long-term policy issues.

The year 1998 saw the further unfolding of the Asian financial crisis that erupted in mid-1997. Last year's *Outlook* discussed the genesis and complexities of the crisis, its economic impacts, policy options for the affected economies, and lessons for the relatively unaffected ones. In 1998 the consequences of the financial crisis were particularly apparent in the real sectors. All those countries directly affected—namely, Indonesia, Republic of Korea, Malaysia, Philippines, and Thailand—suffered varying degrees of economic contraction. The marked negative growth in East and Southeast Asian developing economies as a group (excluding the People's Republic of China) was their poorest performance since World War II. Net private capital flows to emerging Asia, which had exceeded $100 billion in 1996, turned negative for two successive years as foreign investors lost confidence and withdrew their capital from these economies. Domestic investors also suddenly became cautious. The People's Republic of China and South Asia, which were less exposed to international short-term capital flows and their wide fluctuations, performed relatively better. Growth in the states of Central Asia slowed, while the performance of the Pacific economies improved from the previous year.

To help hasten economic recovery in the countries hit by the crisis, the Asian Development Bank is extending substantial assistance for structural reforms in such critical areas as finance, trade, and industry. Meanwhile, the economic crisis has had a massive impact on the social sectors. Unemployment levels and inflation rates rose significantly in 1998. These have set back the remarkable achievements in poverty reduction and social and human development during the last two decades. Overall, the absence of or weakness in social protection systems in the affected countries has made the social impact more severe than it might have been. To help the affected economies address this problem and to maintain the social cohesion needed for economic growth and stability, the Asian Development Bank has been attaching special importance to assistance to the social sector. For example, the Bank has provided a Social Sector Program loan to Thailand in March 1998. It was the first social sector loan approved by the international financial institutions since the outbreak of the crisis. Similarly, in Indonesia, the Bank provided a Social Protection Sector Development Program, which included the development of an innovative loan and scholarship scheme to help parents of secondary school students keep their children in school. The Bank is prepared to extend similar types of assistance to other countries to ease the social pain stemming from the crisis. In both its analytical work and operations, the Bank is paying special attention to the social costs of the crisis.

For many emerging economies, the financial crisis has provided a challenge and an opportunity to rectify their banking systems, capital markets, and corporate sectors and to bring them up to international standards. While integration with international financial systems can potentially bestow immense benefits, the crisis has provided a chance for circumspection and highlighted the need to proceed more cautiously with capital account liberalization. On balance, these appear to be healthy reactions, as one important lesson of the crisis seems to be that robust banking and corporate sectors are a precondition for full opening of the capital account. However, viewing the crisis as a reason for turning inward would be ill-advised, because the net benefits from openness are potentially immense. A further key lesson is that good governance in both the public and private sectors is critical for sustained and equitable economic growth. Signs that the needed policy reforms in the affected economies are on track are encouraging, and this appears to be a major part of the explanation why the financial turmoil may have stabilized. I believe that the worst of the financial crisis is over and that the affected economies have largely bottomed out. This gives us reason to expect that 1999 will see notable improvements in economic performance. Of course, this expectation is contingent on developments in other parts of the global economy, especially in Japan, the United States, and Europe.

In the long run, it is important to note that the basic factors that have uplifted the economies, such as high propensities to save, emphasis on education and diligence, and generally prudent economic management, still prevail. In addition, overall economic fundamentals will be strengthened by the ongoing reforms in the financial and corporate sectors and governance, both in public and private sectors. I am confident that the region will overcome the current difficulties before long and will be back on a more solid and sustainable growth path.

Part I of this year's *Outlook* comprises two chapters. The first chapter briefly surveys the recent growth experience of and short-term prospects for the world economy, and then focuses on the Asian and Pacific region. The second chapter provides an in-depth examination of the Asian financial crisis. It touches on the evolution of the crisis and interprets it by examining competing views. It also discusses the policy response and debates whether the stabilization and structural policy measures the crisis-affected economies adopted actually helped or hindered their recovery. It then addresses the question of whether a new international financial architecture is called for. Part II discusses each of the 37 developing member countries of the Asian Development Bank, analyzing their recent economic performance and assessing their near-term prospects. This section pays considerable attention to policy and development issues. Part III deals with the critical issue of the implications of the financial crisis for economic openness. It discusses the current policy issues relating to openness, along with policies required for facilitating economic recovery in East and Southeast Asia and for sustaining growth in the long run. Finally, it examines how Asia should shape its agenda for the new millenium round of multilateral trade negotiations.

Tadao Chino
TADAO CHINO
President

Acknowledgments

The preparation of the *Asian Development Outlook 1999* has benefited from the support of and valuable contributions from many individuals, both inside and outside the Asian Development Bank. Special thanks are due to the following Bank staff for comments on various parts of the *Outlook*: Yoshihiro Iwasaki, Kazi F. Jalal, Rahul Khullar, Jeffrey Liang, Jayant Menon, Brahm Prakash, and S. Ghon Rhee. The following individuals provided critical support, guidance, and advice on various matters relating to the preparation of the *Outlook*: Basudev Dahal, Shoji Nishimoto, and G. H. P. B. van der Linden. The help and support of the following in preparing the country reports in Part II are deeply appreciated: Nihal Amerasinghe, Thomas Crouch, T. L. de Jonghe, Khaja H. Moinuddin, Bruce Murray, Filologo Pante, Jr., Kazu Sakai, Cedric Saldanha, Werner Schelzig, and Marshuk Ali Shah. Isidoro David and Bishnu Dev Pant offered support with data-related matters. Ian Gill, Tsukasa Maekawa, Lynette Mallery, Robert H. Salamon, and Karti Sandilya of the Office of External Relations provided advice and assistance in publicizing the *Outlook*. The prepress work was done by the Printing Unit under the supervision of Raveendranath Rajan. The assistance of the resident missions, Office of Administrative Services, and Office of Information Systems and Technology in the preparation of the *Outlook* is also gratefully acknowledged.

Many scholars, policymakers, and economists from international organizations also participated in the *Eleventh Workshop on the Asian Economic Outlook* to discuss the background materials for this issue. In particular, we would like to acknowledge the contributions of the following individuals, who either presented papers or acted as designated commentators: Juanjai Ajanant, Masahiro Aoki, Uri Dadush, Emmanuel de Dios, Farid Harianto, Moon Soo Kang, Peter Lloyd, David Nellor, and Cayetano Paderanga, Jr. In addition, the contributions of the following Bank staff who acted as discussants at the workshop are acknowledged: Robert Boumphrey, David Green, and Richard Vokes.

A number of individuals from outside the Bank prepared background papers for Part II of the *Outlook*, namely: Mohamed Ariff, Iwan Aziz, Lok Sang Ho, Bruce Knapman, Eshya Mujahid-Mukhtar, Nguyen Van Quy, Aniceto Orbeta, Jr., Chirathep Senivongs, Shankar Sharma, Sang Dal Shim, Myat Thein, and Chung-Shu Wu.

Giancarlo Corsetti, Dean DeRosa, Arvind Panagariya, and T. N. Srinivasan prepared the background papers for Parts I and III, and Andrew Balls and Zanny Minton-Beddoes were the principal economic editorial consultants for these parts.

Several international institutions shared their research material and data with the *Outlook* team. In particular, we would like to acknowledge the contributions from the International Monetary Fund and the World Bank, who shared their research on global economic prospects and the financial crisis in developing Asia and participated in the *Eleventh Workshop on the Asian Economic Outlook*.

JUNGSOO LEE
Chief Economist

The Team

A team drawn from the Economics and Development Resource Center of the Asian Development Bank prepared the *Asian Development Outlook 1999*. M. G. Quibria led this core team, assisted by Rana Hasan, Rajiv Kumar, Ernesto Pernia, Pradumna Rana, and Christopher Walker, along with Elizabeth Leuterio, who was responsible for coordination. The other members of the core team included Biswanath Bhattacharyay, Dilip Das, Madhushree DasGupta, Christopher Hnanguie, Sailesh Jha, Haider Ali Khan, Soo-Nam Oh, Reza Siregar, Emma Banaria, Charissa Castillo, Modesta de Castro, Emma Murray, Aludia Pardo, and Cherry Lynn Zafaralla. The core team was assisted by the following members of the Programs Departments and the Office of Pacific Operations, who prepared most of the country reports in Part II of the *Outlook*: Shiladitya Chatterjee, Hua Du, Ziba Farhadian-Lorie, Klaus Gerhaeusser, Cindy Houser, Neeraj Jain, Yun-Hwan Kim, Seung Beom Koh, Srinivasa Madhur, Alessandro Pio, Sultan Hafeez Rahman, Robert Siy, Yumiko Tamura, Min Tang, Myo Thant, Hong Wang, Lan Wu, Tao Zhang, and Joseph Zveglich. Charito Arriola, Catherine E. Cruz, Franklin de Guzman, Marichu Duka, Carmela Espina, Loretta Jovellanos, and Ma. Olivia Nuestro provided additional support for the preparation of Part II. John S. L. McCombie and Alice Dowsett were the principal editors for the *Outlook*. The work was carried out under the overall direction of Myoung-Ho Shin, Vice-President (Region West) and the supervision of Jungsoo Lee, Chief Economist.

Many others inside and outside the Asian Development Bank wrote background papers, provided helpful comments, and participated in the *Eleventh Workshop on the Asian Economic Outlook*, held in Manila on 27 November 1998 to discuss the background papers. Contributors and participants are listed in the Acknowledgments. The statistical database and country tables were prepared by staff from the Economic Analysis and Research Division in collaboration with the Statistics and Data Systems Division. Charissa Castillo and Anicia Sayos were responsible for the *Outlook* data management and Statistical Appendix preparation. Ma. Teresa Cabellon and Socorro Fajardo provided secretarial and administrative support, with the assistance of Zenaida Acacio, Ma. Lourdes Antonio, Patricia Baysa, Rochie Ignacio, Eva Olanda, Nilo Sandoval, and Anna Liza Silverio. Noli C. Galang handled the interior layout and Alex McLellan designed the cover and dividers. Mercedita Cabañeros was responsible for typesetting, assisted by Ma. Lourdes Maestro and Edmond Sid M. Pantilo. Charissa Castillo and Cherry Lynn Zafaralla coordinated production. Edith Laviña and Joy Quitazol provided substantial research and technical assistance.

Contents

PART III ECONOMIC OPENNESS: GROWTH AND RECOVERY IN ASIA 177

BOXES

TEXT TABLES

TEXT FIGURES

Acronyms and Abbreviations

ADB	Asian Development Bank
ADE	Asian developing economy
AMF	Asian Monetary Fund
ASEAN	Association of Southeast Asian Nations
CPF	Central Provident Fund (Singapore)
EU	European Union
FDI	Foreign direct investment
FY	Fiscal year
GATS	General Agreement on Trade in Services
GATT	General Agreement on Tariffs and Trade
GDP	Gross domestic product
GNP	Gross national product
HKMA	Hong Kong Monetary Authority
IMF	International Monetary Fund
MAS	Monetary Authority of Singapore
MEA	Multilateral environmental agreement
NAFTA	North American Free Trade Agreement
NIE	Newly industrialized economy
NPRT	Nauru Phosphate Royalties Trust
NTB	Nontariff barrier
OECD	Organisation for Economic Co-operation and Development
Lao PDR	Lao People's Democratic Republic
PRC	People's Republic of China
RBP	Restrictive business practice
R&D	Research and development
SOE	State-owned enterprise
WTO	World Trade Organization

Definitions

The classification of economies by major analytic or geographic groupings such as industrial countries, developing countries, Africa, Latin America, Middle East, Europe, and transitional countries follows the classification adopted by the International Monetary Fund. Latin America, however, refers to the Western Hemisphere in that classification and transitional countries include Kazakhstan, Kyrgyz Republic, Mongolia, Tajikistan, and Uzbekistan, which for the purposes of this *Outlook* are included in Asia.

For the purposes of this *Outlook* the following apply:

- **Newly industrialized economies (NIES)** comprise Hong Kong, China; Republic of Korea; Singapore; and Taipei,China.
- **East Asia** comprises the NIEs, the People's Republic of China, and Mongolia.
- **South Asia** comprises Bangladesh, Bhutan, India, Maldives, Nepal, Pakistan, and Sri Lanka. Note that in Part III of this *Outlook* South Asia refers only to Bangladesh, India, Nepal, Pakistan, and Sri Lanka.
- **Southeast Asia** comprises Cambodia, Indonesia, Lao People's Democratic Republic, Malaysia, Myanmar, Philippines, Thailand, and Viet Nam. Note that in Part III of this *Outlook* Southeast Asia consists only of Indonesia, Malaysia, Philippines, and Thailand.
- **Central Asian republics** comprise Kazakhstan, Kyrgyz Republic, Tajikistan, and Uzbekistan.
- **The Pacific** comprises Cook Islands, Fiji, Kiribati, Marshall Islands, Federated States of Micronesia, Nauru, Papua New Guinea, Samoa, Solomon Islands, Tonga, Tuvalu, and Vanuatu.
- **Developing Asia** refers to the 37 developing member countries of the Asian Development Bank discussed in this *Outlook*.
- **Other non-Asian developing economies** refer to Argentina, Brazil, Chile, Colombia, Egypt, Mexico, Morocco, Turkey, and Venezuela.

Billion is 1,000 million.
Trillion is 1,000 billion.
Tons are metric tons, equal to 1,000 kilograms or 2,2204.6 pounds.
Unless otherwise specified, the symbol $ means United States dollars; dollars are current US dollars.

This *Outlook* is based on data available up to 15 March 1999.

Part I
Developing Asia and the World

Economic Developments and Prospects

The growth of the world economy fell sharply in 1998, partly because of the Asian financial crisis, and partly because of economic problems in Brazil, Japan, and Russia. Asia's economies endured a difficult year as growth rates in many once dynamic economies became negative or barely remained positive. Inflation rose in Southeast Asia, where steep depreciations reduced the value of local currencies. Current account balances improved dramatically in the crisis-affected countries, but this reflected reduced imports rather than increased exports. The crisis had only a mild impact on the People's Republic of China (PRC) and South Asia, and the PRC succeeded in maintaining the external value of its currency. Japan continued in recession, partly because of the slowdown in the rest of Asia. By contrast, the industrial economies of Europe and North America grew strongly and inflation remained modest.

The world economy moved down two divergent tracks in 1998. Many developing economies contracted as currency chaos buffeted markets on several continents. Contrary to the experience of recent decades, the more open and dynamic developing economies fared badly, with many subject to investor panic and large capital outflows. Even economies such the Republic of Korea (henceforth referred to as Korea) and Thailand, with recovering financial markets, experienced severe contractions. And Japan, the world's second largest economy, was dragged into recession, partly because of the slowdown in the rest of Asia. In marked contrast, Europe and North America continued to grow strongly. In the United States low inflation and seemingly limitless faith in the expansion of corporate earnings drove equity markets to record heights. European stock exchanges registered even stronger gains in a flood of optimism leading up to monetary integration under the euro.

After many years' progress, globalization took a step backward in 1998. Total world trade measured in

value terms actually fell from 1997 to 1998, after several years of near double-digit annual increases. World capital flows contracted dramatically as investors in the industrial countries shied away from the turbulence in the developing countries. Net private capital flows to developing economies came to less than one fifth of their record levels of only two years before. The near failure of a sophisticated hedge fund in the United States raised a warning flag that caused governments and international investors to reexamine their strategies for managing risk in a world of fluid, short-term capital flows. In a few cases governments cited the volatility of international capital flows in moving to reverse years of financial liberalization.

Despite these developments, few now doubt the inevitability of increasing integration in world trade and finance. Even after the upheavals of 1997 and 1998, most governments still regard those trends as desirable. However, economic turbulence has brought about a healthy awareness of the risks involved in integration and the problems inherent in relying heavily on short-term, private capital to fund development. During such times the ready availability of official capital flows becomes especially crucial for counteracting the damaging consequences for the developing countries of short-term, private capital volatility.

THE WORLD ECONOMY

World output growth fell sharply in 1998, from a strong 4.2 percent in 1997 to 2.2 percent. The slowdown had several causes, including the crisis-induced contraction of many Asian developing economies, the Russian devaluation and default, the fiscal problems and currency instability in Brazil, and the deepening recession in Japan. Spells of turmoil in Russia, Asia, and Latin America reverberated throughout world trade and financial networks as international flows of private capital slowed. But despite the often negative tone of world markets in 1998, growth in Europe and North America was generally robust.

Oil prices dropped by 30 percent in 1998, providing large terms of trade benefits for most industrial economies and compensating in part for the loss in export demand from crisis-affected Asian countries. The impact on developing economies varied considerably, with major exporters such as Mexico, Saudi Arabia, and Venezuela suffering large fiscal shortfalls and current account deficits. Non-oil commodity prices also fell sharply, by about 15 percent on average, with the negative impact of those price drops falling disproportionately on developing countries.

A worldwide trend toward conservative monetary policy contributed to a continuing drop in inflation. In the industrial countries, the average inflation rate was only 1.4 percent. In the developing economies inflation rose slightly from 1997—due largely to currency depreciations—but even at 10.2 percent was still well below historical averages. While Canada, the United Kingdom, and the United States benefited from fiscal tightening because of favorable revenues from economic expansion, Japan and several crisis-affected Asian economies experienced countercyclical fiscal expansions, and world budget deficits increased slightly on average.

International capital flows continued to drop precipitously as private lenders moved to reduce their exposure to the turbulence prevailing in many developing economies. Net private capital flows to developing economies were about $29 billion in 1998, down from a peak of $177 billion in 1996. With lenders less willing to provide financing through trade credits or other loans, developing countries' trade declined in dollar terms while current accounts moved into surplus. Taking up the slack in world demand represented by those current account surpluses, consumers in the United States began to spend some of their large stock market gains. That brought US household savings rates down below zero, and increased the US current account deficit to 2.7 percent of gross domestic product (GDP).

Reflecting the cutback in the supply of capital to developing economies, credit spreads on emerging market bonds (the premium that emerging market bond issuers pay to lenders to cover perceived credit risks) increased from about 6 percent at the beginning of 1998 to almost 17 percent immediately following Russia's debt default in August. They closed the year near 10 percent, well above their 1996 and 1997 levels. Equity markets in Asia, Latin America, and most of the transitional economies also had a poor year, although markets in Korea, the Philippines, and Thailand rallied strongly from their losses in 1997. The US stock market registered double-digit gains for the eighth straight year, raising concerns that future earnings are unlikely to justify present valuations. Stock markets in the European countries destined to participate in the euro common currency rallied strongly, possibly in anticipation of lower domestic interest rates.

Currency issues took center stage as Asian economies were adjusting to being forced off fixed exchange rates. The Russian ruble collapsed, Malaysia imposed capital controls, and Brazil's real came under heavy attack. In January 1999 Brazil ultimately failed to defend a crawling peg against the dollar, despite financial support from the International Monetary Fund and a strong political commitment to do so. By contrast, developing economies with a "hard money" currency board—Argentina and Hong Kong, China—seemed better able to adapt to market turbulence. At the other end of the spectrum, however, economies such as Mexico and Thailand that had recently moved to floating exchange rates also seemed to weather external shocks reasonably well. These developments lend support to arguments that attempts to maintain independent monetary policy and open capital flows while fixing exchange rates are destined to fail.

Industrial Countries

With the exception of Japan, growth in the industrial countries was strong in 1998. The United Kingdom and the United States maintained growth rates of 2.5 and 3.9 percent, respectively, despite some reduction in external demand because of recession in Asia and Latin America. Compensating for that loss in demand in the United States was the supply-side effect of foreign investors using the US market as a safe haven. Growth in the countries participating in the euro common currency ("Euroland") varied from 1.5 percent in Italy to 3.8 percent in Spain. France and Germany grew at about 3 percent, the average for Euroland. Elsewhere, Australia managed 4.5 percent growth despite the Asian crisis. Meanwhile Japan's troubles with weak domestic demand and banking sector insolvency worsened, contributing to an economic contraction of 2.8 percent.

Inflation remained moderate in the United States, despite strong growth, a rising stock market, and historically low unemployment of 4.6 percent. Low commodity prices and gains in labor productivity helped keep consumer prices from rising. In Europe, tight monetary policies imposed in preparation for the euro's advent kept consumer price inflation generally below 2 percent. Reversing a persistent deflationary trend, consumer prices in Japan rose slightly, but are expected to fall in 1999.

Trade and capital flows among the industrial countries maintained the pattern of recent years. The United States was once again the world's largest capital importer, with a current account deficit of about $210 billion, or 2.7 percent of GDP. Stock market gains fueled surging consumer demand in the United States, effectively canceling out the national savings gain from a balanced government budget. Despite a rising yen, Japan generated a current account surplus of $120 billion (3.1 percent of GDP) that financed a large share of the US deficit. European current accounts averaged a 1.6 percent of GDP surplus, with Germany running close to a balance.

The industrial economies generally fared well in the face of the Asian financial crisis. For a time that did not seem to be a likely outcome. Russia's default in August prompted a wave of panic selling in both developing and industrial country stock markets, as investors shunned assets deemed to be risky, but US Federal Reserve intervention in September and October calmed the markets. On the trade side, estimates indicate that lower Asian demand for industrial country exports reduced output in the United States and Europe by 0.5 percent. The impact on Japan has been somewhat greater.

Transitional Economies

Lack of concrete progress in macroeconomic stabilization and structural reforms continued to be the main stumbling block for sustainable growth in the transitional economies. In addition, the financial crisis in Russia and weak world prices of primary commodities, especially oil, adversely affected most of these economies. GDP contracted by just under 1 percent in 1998 for the transitional economies as a whole. Output declined by around 1.5 percent in the Czech Republic. Hungary, Macedonia, and Poland, however, performed relatively well. The devaluation of the Russian ruble in August 1998 triggered large fluctuations in the value of the Polish zloty and the Hungarian forint.

Most of the transitional economies have embarked on macroeconomic and structural reforms, but progress remains limited. Russia urgently needs fiscal discipline, wherein current expenditures would be largely financed by current tax revenues rather than by debt. The devaluation of the ruble in mid-August 1998 also contributed to the recent widening of Russia's fiscal imbalance. The government's ability to restructure its external debt, which amounts to about $160 billion, will help determine how quickly market confidence returns to the domestic economy.

The transition to a stronger market orientation remains a major challenge for other post-Soviet economies. Most continue to be highly dependent on Russia's performance. The decline in trade with Russia, the drying up of new financing, and the need to repay maturing external debt created uncertainties for the successful implementation of Ukraine's 1999 budget. Belarus, Moldova, and the Baltic countries have been facing similar constraints.

Worsening external terms of trade contributed to deteriorating current accounts in many transitional economies. Estonia, Lithuania, and the Slovak Republic reported the worst imbalances. The Russian debt default in August reduced the transitional economies' access to external financing. However, the crisis in Asia has provided opportunities for some transitional economies to attract international private capital. Poland managed to attract close to $7 billion in private capital in 1997 and early 1998, and Hungary managed to issue Eurobonds at favorable spreads.

THE DEVELOPING ECONOMIES

For nearly all the developing countries 1998 was a bad year. The Asian developing economies experienced their slowest growth in a decade, with economies in East and Southeast Asia actually shrinking. However, the PRC and most South Asian economies managed substantial growth. The fall in oil and commodity prices had negative effects on the economic performance of many of the non-Asian developing economies dependent on these products for their exports. The Russian default led to a major reassessment of the risk associated with international lending. This led to a fall in international capital flows and was associated with the slow growth in many Latin American countries.

The Non-Asian Developing Economies

The non-Asian developing economies continued to grow, but generally at a slower rate than in 1997. The fall in oil prices contributed heavily to slowdowns in the output growth rates of the Middle Eastern and some of the Latin American countries. The devaluation of the Brazilian currency in early 1999 and associated uncertainty about that country's exchange rate policy has increased concerns about the prospects for developing economies this year.

Africa. With the notable exception of Morocco, most African economies experienced growth slowdowns in 1998. The region grew by about 2 percent, compared to more than 3 percent in 1997. The growth outlook for 1999 is similar to 1998.

The sharp fall in key commodity prices (both oil and non-oil commodities) had adverse effects. For example, the fall in world copper prices delayed the crucial privatization of Zambia's copper mines, and depressed oil prices subjected Angola, Gabon, and Nigeria to large terms of trade shocks. The damage from those shocks is likely to continue into 1999. The outbreak of hostilities in Eritrea, Ethiopia, Sudan, and most of the countries in West Africa increased political and economic uncertainties in the region.

Domestically, banking sector reform is urgently needed in most African countries to facilitate the development of capital markets throughout the continent. In addition, overly lax monetary policies have left some countries with ballooning inflation rates and weakening domestic currencies.

A major challenge currently facing African governments is poverty reduction, as nearly half of Africa's population lives in absolute poverty (defined by the World Bank as an income of $1 a day). With population growing at an annual rate of about 2.9 percent over the last decade, African countries are going to have to grow at least twice as fast as they have in recent years if they are to achieve any significant reduction in poverty.

For 1999, the prospects for faster growth will likely be influenced by the recovery of the East Asian economies. That will have a bearing on at least three important external factors for Africa: private capital flows, terms of trade, and export markets.

Latin America. Major Latin American economies experienced slow growth or outright contraction in 1998 as private capital flows dried up. Brazil's economy, by far the largest in Latin America and the world's eighth biggest, shrank 1.9 percent as investors alarmed by Russia's collapse moved money offshore. Lower external demand and pessimism about the region kept growth in Argentina and Mexico at 4.2 and 2.6 percent, respectively, well below expectations at the beginning of the year. Colombia managed slightly positive growth, while Venezuela's economy, facing a currency crisis, contracted by almost 5 percent. The growth outlook for Latin America as a whole is poor in 1999, with little or no growth expected on average.

Russia's default and the ruble's collapse in August focused investors' attention on Brazil, and they did not find the picture encouraging. Despite a fiscal austerity package implemented in late 1997, Brazil's budget deficit of about 7 percent of GDP was still expanding. At the same time the current account deficit, equivalent to 4 percent of GDP, was falling only slowly. Equity prices plunged and spreads on Brazilian sovereign and corporate debt rose to levels suggesting imminent default. To stem capital outflows and protect the Brazilian currency's sliding peg against the dollar, the central bank tightened monetary policy severely. The aggressive monetary stance resulted in short-term interest rates of 49 percent in an environment of virtually zero inflation, effectively stifling growth.

Stock markets throughout Latin America dropped sharply, dashing investors' hopes that the region could steer clear of the uncertainty surrounding Asia's crisis-affected countries. Measured in US dollar terms, the three largest equity markets of Argentina, Brazil, and Mexico all dropped by about 38 percent. Chile fared slightly better and Venezuela slightly worse. Nervousness about currency values, which was based on concerns about rising debt stocks and perennial current account deficits, was one reason for the drop. Sovereign bonds also suffered large losses during the year.

Yet despite the equity and bond market losses, regional currencies were generally stable in 1998. The central bank's austere monetary stance held depreciation of the Brazilian real to the planned rate of 7.6 percent in 1998 (that sliding currency peg collapsed in January 1999). In Argentina, monetary and fiscal austerity, along with well-planned sovereign bond sales and an innovative financing arrangement to protect bank solvency, helped the central bank maintain the peso's one-to-one parity with the US dollar. As a result of those policies, consumer price inflation in South America's two largest economies was near zero. Mexico's peso, which has been floating since the 1994 crisis, depreciated by 18.6 percent, touching off consumer price inflation at the same level.

Poverty remains a major problem in Latin America, despite per capita income levels that are generally well above those in developing economies in Africa, Asia, and the Middle East. Poverty in Latin America tends to be unevenly distributed, both within and between countries. Particularly impoverished areas include Haiti, Central America, the Andean region, and northern Brazil. Rising unemployment in Brazil in 1998 worsened the situation of the poor, but in the last five years Brazil's poor have been surprise beneficiaries of the hard money Real Plan, as real cash incomes rose with the defeat of inflation. Those gains may be at risk with the sudden devaluation of Brazil's currency in early 1999.

The Middle East. Average GDP growth in the developing countries of the Middle East slowed from 4.5 percent in 1997 to 3.3 percent in 1998, hamstrung by the 30 percent fall in the price of oil during 1998. Egypt and Turkey led the region with growth rates of around 5 percent, while major oil exporters such as Iran, Kuwait, and Saudi Arabia had growth of only zero to 2 percent. The growth slowdown did little to relieve the region's chronic high unemployment rates, which are still well over 10 percent in most Middle Eastern countries. With continued low oil prices expected over the medium term, regional growth is not likely to accelerate in 1999.

The adverse oil price move also had a significant impact on current account positions, pushing Saudi Arabia from near balance to an 8.0 percent of GDP deficit, and Egypt from balance to a 3.4 percent deficit. To cover the resulting financing gap, net private capital flows to the Middle East increased some 200 percent from the previous year, to about $25 billion. However, private sector interest in the region remains relatively low given the size of regional economies. Foreign direct investment, often the most dynamic catalyst for economic modernization, actually fell from the previous year to $3.9 billion.

With a strong legacy of state ownership, most countries in the region have been slow to privatize leading industries. At the same time trade barriers have remained relatively high. These impediments have kept the region from fully capitalizing on its oil income and moving on to a more dynamic growth path.

The Asian and Pacific Developing Economies

The slowdown in Asian growth that began with the export deceleration of 1996 and worsened with the 1997 currency crisis turned into a widespread regional contraction in 1998. Growth in the developing economies of East and Southeast Asia (excluding the PRC) was the lowest since World War II, averaging -6.9 percent in the economies of Southeast Asia and -1.4 percent in the newly industrialized economies (NIEs) (see table 1.1). Private capital flows to emerging Asia, which reached $105 billion in 1996, turned negative as foreign investors scrambled to move money out of supposedly risky markets. That forced central banks into monetary contractions, reducing domestic demand and exacerbating an already large bad debt problem.

Although currencies remained depreciated well below their precrisis levels, export dollar receipts did not respond to the exchange rate stimulus as governments and investors had hoped.

The richer and traditionally more dynamic Asian economies generally fared the worst during the year. Southeast Asia remained at the center of the crisis, with Indonesia suffering a huge contraction and Malaysia and Thailand hit by substantial declines. Of the four NIEs, only Taipei,China weathered the storm

Table 1.1 Selected Economic Indicators, Developing Asia, 1996-2000
(percent)

Item	1996	1997	1998	1999	2000
Gross domestic product growth					
Developing Asia	7.4	6.2	2.6	4.4	5.1
Newly industrialized economies	6.3	6.0	-1.4	2.3	4.3
PRC and Mongolia	9.6	8.7	7.8	7.0	6.5
Central Asian republics	1.1	3.5	0.4	—	—
Southeast Asia	7.1	4.0	-6.9	0.8	2.8
South Asia	7.2	4.7	5.7	5.5	5.8
The Pacific	3.1	-3.4	0.1	—	—
Inflation rate					
Developing Asia	7.3	4.6	6.5	3.7	4.1
Newly industrialized economies	4.3	3.5	3.8	1.1	2.3
PRC and Mongolia	8.4	2.8	-0.8	2.0	3.0
Central Asian republics	42.3	21.6	10.1	—	—
Southeast Asia	6.6	5.6	21.0	8.3	6.4
South Asia	9.5	7.3	13.0	7.6	7.2
The Pacific	8.6	4.0	8.6	—	—
Current account balance[a]					
Developing Asia	-1.3	0.5	3.6	2.5	1.4
Newly industrialized economies	0.3	1.7	9.2	4.9	2.8
PRC and Mongolia	0.9	3.2	2.5	0.9	0.4
Central Asian republics	-6.0	-4.2	-7.2	—	—
Southeast Asia	-5.5	-3.3	5.2	4.4	3.2
South Asia	-2.3	-2.2	-2.0	-3.1	-2.5
The Pacific	4.4	-1.1	-1.6	—	—
Debt-service ratio					
Developing Asia	14.2	16.0	19.2	17.7	13.5
Newly industrialized economies	—	—	—	—	—
PRC and Mongolia	6.7	9.8	—	—	—
Central Asian republics	15.7	22.2	—	—	—
Southeast Asia	15.6	17.6	17.0	15.9	11.1
South Asia	30.2	29.6	29.0	25.3	23.9
The Pacific	10.7	12.2	0.6	—	—

— Not available.

a. Share of GDP.

with little damage. Korea suffered a major contraction, while Hong Kong, China and Singapore were unable to avoid the impact of the regional slowdown on their trade- and financial services-based economies. The less open economies of the PRC and South Asia were not so exposed to international short-term capital flows and did relatively better, given their inherent protection from short-term shocks. Growth in the Central Asian states slowed, while the Pacific economies as a group grew faster than in 1997.

Currency devaluations drove up inflation rates in several crisis-affected Asian countries. Across Asia, the average rate of consumer price inflation rose to 6.5 percent from 4.6 percent in 1997. The rupiah's sharp depreciation in late 1997 sparked high double-digit inflation in Indonesia. More moderate depreciations in Korea, Malaysia, Philippines, Singapore, and Thailand also prompted increases in inflation. Elsewhere—notably in Hong Kong, China—monetary contractions implemented to defend the currency exerted deflationary pressures. Average inflation should moderate to about 4 percent in 1999 as the shock of the late 1997 depreciations dies out.

Current accounts improved throughout the region as capital flowed out. From approximate balance in 1997, Asia's aggregate current account moved to a surplus of 3.6 percent of GDP in 1998. Most of that improvement came from import reductions, while overall exports failed to increase as expected. In some cases, the elimination of credit lines to Asian exporters was to blame (see box 1.1). Unfavorable shifts in terms of trade also reduced export values. Assuming that net private capital outflows from Asia are near zero and that import demand recovers only slowly, the region's aggregate current account should remain in surplus in 1999.

Weak and ill-regulated banking systems contributed heavily to Asia's initial vulnerability to capital flow reversals. Although many of the worst hit countries—including Korea, Thailand, and to some extent Indonesia—have instituted significant financial sector reforms since the crisis began, the ratio of nonperforming loans to total lending continued to rise in 1998. The regional nonperforming loan ratio of 20 to 30 percent represented an equivalent share of output, as financial leverage in Asian economies remained at about 100 percent of GDP.

The Newly Industrialized Economies. The crisis engulfed emerging Asia's richest economies in 1998, spilling over to the financial centers of Hong Kong, China and Singapore. Steep drops in regional trade, tourism, and financial activity slowed both economies, and prompted Hong Kong, China's monetary authority to intervene in the equity market. Korea took firm steps to pull its way out of the late 1997 financial chaos, causing the won to stabilize and then strengthen. Taipei,China reaped the benefits of a strong financial system, a large stock of foreign reserves, and flexible factor markets in resisting the regional contagion.

Aggregate growth for the NIEs was negative, and two of the four economies suffered recessions in 1998 (see figure 1.1). Only Taipei,China managed substantial growth. Korea's recession turned out to be worse than anticipated at the end of 1997, and annual output fell by 5.5 percent. GDP growth in Hong Kong, China was sharply negative, while Singapore managed positive growth of 1.5 percent. Attempting to stimulate

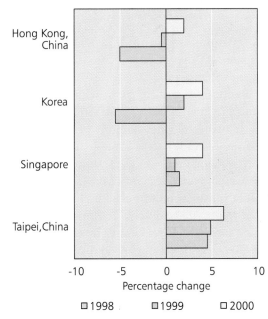

Figure 1.1 Real GDP Growth, Newly Industrialized Economies, 1998-2000

Percentage change

☐ 1998   ☐ 1999   ☐ 2000

Source: Appendix Table A1.

Box 1.1 The Importance of Letters of Credit for Reviving Trade

The steep currency depreciations of the crisis-affected Asian economies did not lead to a rapid, export-led revival as one might have expected. One reason for this was the problem exporters faced in obtaining export credit facilities after the crisis began. To meet external demand for their goods, producers must have adequate funds to finance a steady stream of raw materials and other key inputs, some of which are imported. If the domestic banking sector is facing severe liquidity constraints, letters of credit become an important source of capital for domestic producers. In 1997 alone, major Asian economies received more than $155 billion in officially supported export credits, more than double the corresponding value in 1990 (see the table).

The recent crisis in Asia worsened economywide credit ratings, which had an adverse effect on credit flows. In East Asia only the PRC, Indonesia, and Thailand

managed to accumulate more credit financing in 1997 than in 1995. The South Asian economies, in general, also received less export credit in 1997. Reports of rejected letters of credit from Asian importers increased significantly in 1998. For example, their counterparts in Australia, Japan, and the United States rejected the letters of credit from Indonesian importers of basic materials for making newsprint during the first half of 1998. Although the domestic production capacity of newsprint is still large enough to meet domestic demand, a shortage is inevitable, because the basic materials still have to be imported. Domestic prices of newsprint and related products increased tremendously in 1998.

Recognizing the need to revive the export sectors of the crisis-affected economies, a number of major trading partners have expressed their commitment to

extend more credits. The United States, for instance, pledged to use its agricultural credit guarantees to finance trade between Asian and domestic markets. The US Department of Agriculture extended $1.5 billion in export credit to Korea in fiscal year 1998, most of which was used to purchase US feed grains, meat, cotton, and soybeans. Also in 1998, the US Department of Agriculture offered a $10 million export credit facility to the Philippine government. Other countries such as Australia, the PRC, and Japan, as well as international private banks, have also been active in extending more credit support to the crisis-affected economies.

Active domestic government intervention to increase credit facilities is also increasingly feasible in some Asian economies. While the Malaysian government more than tripled its export credit facilities in mid-1998, the Indonesian Ministry of

---

their economies, Hong Kong, China; Korea; Singapore; and Taipei,China resorted to monetary and fiscal expansions.

Reduced export demand helped explain the contractions in Hong Kong, China and Korea in 1998. In these two economies outflows of foreign capital forced up domestic interest rates, thereby reducing domestic demand, but investment increased in Taipei,China, partly because of opportunities arising from the privatization of public utilities and expansion in the airline industry. The private sector accounted for all of Taipei,China's investment growth, about 20 percent over the previous year.

Inflation in the NIEs rose in 1998, primarily because of price increases in Korea stemming from the won's steep depreciation. Hong Kong, China and Singapore actually had lower inflation in 1998 than in 1997, largely because of the steep drop in asset prices. Taipei,China also experienced asset price de-

flation. (See box 1.2 for a discussion of the effect of the Asian crisis on land prices.)

The NIEs' export performance in 1998 was not encouraging. Weak demand from other crisis-affected Asian economies was largely to blame. Weak global demand for electronic products also hurt exports from the NIEs. But currency depreciations and reduced domestic demand caused imports to fall even further, resulting in trade surpluses and pushing current accounts (Hong Kong, China excepted) into surplus.

Bad loans increased because of the impact of high interest rates on weak financial institutions, especially in Korea. The two regional financial centers saw massive stock market swings, with Hong Kong, China's Hang Seng Index and the Singapore Straits Times Index dropping by more than 30 and 40 percent, respectively, in 1998. Financial links to affected countries were key to those stock market drops. As an example, Singapore's four largest local

Industry and Trade announced its intention to set up an export financing agency in late 1998. The Korean government, through its state-run Korea Export Insurance Corporation, is also committed to playing a more active role in increasing exports. The Korean government has asked for $1 billion in US farm export credits for fiscal year 1999.

However, beyond pledges by partner countries to extend more officially guaranteed credit facilities and local government efforts to provide more official commitments, any revival in Asian exports will depend largely on efforts by exporting countries to implement economic reforms and improve their credit ratings. In recent years, most export credit finance has been provided by the importer, the exporter, or the private insurer. These creditors are exposed to the commercial risk of the recipient not being able to raise the foreign exchange for payments and to the country risk of a currency crisis. The factor foreign creditors cite most

often to explain their reluctance to cover private sector buyers in developing countries is the lack of adequate legal protection. Another important factor is the lack of well-developed and well-regulated local private banking systems. A domestic bank in which there is international confidence can greatly

assist foreign creditors by providing them with independent assessments of the creditworthiness of interested applicants. Until economies lower these risk factors through comprehensive banking reforms, the rapid revival of domestic export sectors remains uncertain.

Officially Supported Export Credits, 1990 and 1995-1997
($ billions)

Country	1990	1995	1996	1997
Korea	12.1	8.9	6.1	7.4
PRC	10.1	44.1	44.9	47.5
Bangladesh	0.6	0.9	0.8	0.8
India	10.2	13.6	13.8	13.5
Pakistan	4.4	8.4	9.3	8.5
Sri Lanka	1.0	1.7	1.5	1.4
Total	16.2	24.6	25.5	24.2
Indonesia	15.5	33.0	32.6	34.2
Malaysia	2.4	8.3	6.7	6.4
Philippines	7.0	14.1	12.9	14.1
Thailand	5.4	19.4	19.7	21.9
Total	30.2	74.8	71.8	76.5
Grand total	68.6	152.4	148.4	155.6

Source: Asian Development Bank database.

banks had loan exposures as high as $35 billion to Indonesia, Malaysia, Philippines, and Thailand before the crisis.

World capital flows will continue to exert a major influence on the NIEs in 1999. Recovery of the Japanese economy and a stronger yen would help stimulate recovery in this group of economies. The web of close trade and investment ties in the region also makes recovery in the NIEs partly dependent on Southeast Asia. For 1999 Korea is expected to have growth of 2.0 percent, while Hong Kong, China is likely to experience a further contraction of 0.5 percent of GDP. Singapore should post 1 percent GDP growth, while growth in Taipei,China is projected to remain stable at about 5 percent in 1999.

If exchange rates stabilize as expected in 1999, inflation in the region should drop. Projections indicate that inflation in Korea and Taipei,China will be around 2 percent. Singapore will have near zero

inflation and Hong Kong, China will undergo deflation. Current account balances should remain in surplus in 1999.

The PRC and Mongolia. The PRC's growth slowed in 1998, largely because of a drop in foreign export demand. Nevertheless, the PRC still fared substantially better than most of its neighbors (see figure 1.2). Domestic investment demand remained strong, as the country's exchange restrictions allowed the economy to resist the high domestic interest rates forced on many other Asian countries by world capital flows. Domestic consumption grew more slowly than in previous years. Government spending stayed under control, with the consolidated budget deficit remaining close to balance.

Foreign investment stayed strong, and domestic savings remained over 40 percent of GDP, providing the PRC with adequate investment capital to maintain positive growth. The country made limited progress on its structural reform agenda in 1998, with little privatization of state-owned enterprises and few deregulation initiatives. However, some financial reform took place in 1998, as evidenced by the introduction of a new loan classification scheme for commercial banks. The central bank also expanded its supervision role and encouraged state-owned banks to write off their bad debts, which may amount to 20 percent of total domestic loans outstanding. The Asian crisis gave the PRC little incentive to reduce trade barriers or eliminate its still extensive exchange restrictions.

Export growth, which averaged 20 percent over the last five years, registered a mere 0.5 percent increase in 1998. The slowdown reflected sharply lower demand from Japan and the rest of Asia. Although the drop in export demand reduced the PRC's trade surplus from the previous year, it still managed a surplus on the current account for the fifth consecutive year. Foreign direct investment inflows were the second largest in the world after the United States. The PRC's unwillingness to rely on short-term capital and its strict regulations controlling its capital movements helped save it from the large capital outflows experienced throughout Asia. This contributed to an increase in the reserve stock to $145 billion, also the second largest in the world after Japan.

Protection from unfettered capital movements and the surplus on the current account gave the central bank freedom to hold the exchange rate fixed while reducing interest rates twice during the year. That successful defense of the yuan in the midst of sharp regional depreciations earned praise from market participants and increased the PRC's standing as an economic power. The central bank also slashed reserve requirements from 13 to 8 percent of deposits. Despite the slightly expansionary monetary stance, inflation was dormant at zero percent as aggregate demand failed to keep pace with the growth of production capacity and the urban labor force. Notwithstanding the fiscal stimulus of the second quarter, domestic demand remained subdued and that helped contain inflation.

The outlook for the PRC in 1999 is positive, with continued growth in the 7 percent range expected. Inflation will remain under control and the current account will stay positive. The combination of large

reserves and stringent restrictions on foreign capital movements means that the PRC is unlikely to face a financial panic of the kind that struck so many of its neighbors. Over the next few years, however, to maintain high growth rates the PRC will need to accelerate the pace of privatization and financial reform.

Mongolia's GDP grew strongly in 1998, despite lower international prices for the country's two main exports, copper and cashmere. The lower export receipts affected government revenues, leading to a budget deficit exceeding 10 percent of GDP. The central bank's tight monetary stance contributed to a reduction in inflation from 17.5 percent in 1997 to 6.0 in 1998. Economic reform has proceeded swiftly since 1991 as the government has slashed trade protection and strengthened macroeconomic management, but Mongolia still needs to privatize several state-owned enterprises and strengthen its financial sector. Growth in 1999 is expected to remain relatively strong.

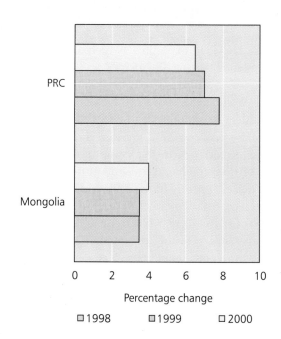

Figure 1.2 Real GDP Growth, PRC and Mongolia, 1998-2000

Percentage change

□ 1998   □ 1999   □ 2000

Source: Appendix Table A1.

The Central Asian Republics. Aggregate growth in four Central Asian member countries of the Asian Development Bank slowed in 1998 (see figure 1.3). Progress on macroeconomic stabilization, structural reform, and better cotton and wheat harvests boosted Tajikistan's growth, despite the impact of a long-running civil war. Kazakhstan suffered a 1.5 percent contraction, hurt by the drop in Russian demand stemming from the financial crisis in that country. Growth slowed in Uzbekistan as the depreciation of the Russian ruble lowered world prices of some major Uzbek exports, namely, gold and other nonferrous metals. A decline in export revenues also reduced growth in the Kyrgyz Republic. In 1998 Tajikistan and Turkmenistan became the latest Central Asian republics to join the Asian Development Bank.

Tighter monetary policies had some beneficial effect on the region's high inflation rates. These dropped in every member country except the Kyrgyz Republic. With the exception of the Kazakhstan all

Figure 1.3 **Real GDP Growth, Central Asian Republics, 1997-1998**

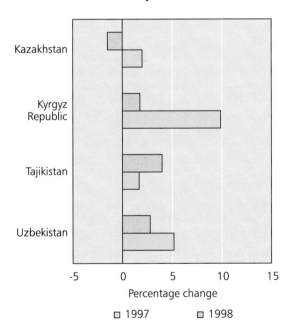

Percentage change

□ 1997   □ 1998

Source: Appendix Table A1.

the Central Asian republics suffered from rising budget deficits. Kazakhstan managed a fiscal contraction through vigorous implementation of tax and budget reforms.

In the difficult transition from centrally planned to market economies, Kazakhstan and the Kyrgyz Republic have made significant progress in privatization, agrarian reform, governance, and banking reform. Tajikistan and Uzbekistan still face difficulties in restructuring and privatizing enterprises and reforming financial institutions. Nevertheless, all these nations will need to make further progress on structural reform and macroeconomic stabilization to achieve sustained growth. All will need some relief from external shocks as well, because economic ties left over from the former Soviet Union make this group of countries highly dependent on events in Russia.

The Southeast Asian Economies. Southeast Asia's economies remained at the vortex of the Asian financial crisis in 1998. Civil unrest and an unexpected change of government in Indonesia heightened the sense of instability as the subregion's largest country struggled to regain its economic footing. The first to be struck by speculative attack in 1997, Thailand moved decisively to reverse capital outflows in 1998 through financial and other structural reforms. Malaysia chose a different path, introducing capital controls and expanding the government's economic role in an attempt to shield the domestic economy from the volatility of international capital flows. Having participated less in the economic boom than its neighbors, the Philippines was proportionately less affected, while the countries of Indo-China were even less affected, but did suffer export demand shocks.

After 4 percent growth in 1997, the region contracted by about 7 percent, underperforming even the most pessimistic expectations for the year (see figure 1.4). More than $30 billion fled Indonesia, Malaysia, Philippines, and Thailand in 1997 and 1998. Indonesia continued to bear the brunt of the crisis as exports and investment collapsed, reducing output by 13.7 percent. Thailand implemented a series of financial reforms, but still suffered an 8 percent contraction. Malaysia at first appeared to avoid the worst effects of the crisis, but capital outflows late in the year brought growth down to -6.2 percent.

Box 1.2 **Is Any Air Left in Asia's Property Bubble?**

Coming after more than a decade of booming Asian real estate markets, the regional financial crisis was supposed to be the needle that popped a major property bubble. With foreign investors in retreat for more than a year, interest rates climbing, currencies sliding, and local demand for commercial property in recession, speculators should have vanished and property owners should have been unlikely to charge rents and prices beyond what the market would have borne. In the event, although prices in some cities may have further to fall, this story has turned out to be generally right. Prices in many Asian cities are now much closer to economic fundamentals than before the crisis.

Asia has long been known for spectacularly high land valuations. During the Japanese economic boom of the 1980s, one square meter of land in Tokyo's central business district cost over $200,000, more than 20 times as much as a corresponding patch in New York City. The Imperial Palace grounds in downtown Tokyo were supposedly worth more than all the land in Canada. And while Japanese land prices have converged with those of some other major Asian cities in the

1990s, most of the movement has consisted of large price increases in the cities of Hong Kong, Singapore, Mumbai, Taipei, and elsewhere. Even in 1998—well into the financial crisis—prime downtown land in the city of Hong Kong and in Tokyo was selling for more than $100,000 a square meter.

There are some good reasons for land to be expensive in rich countries. These economies have high levels of human and physical capital, which increases land productivity and boosts rents. While this is true of Hong Kong, China; Japan; and Singapore, it is also true of many developing countries. Thus a further factor is at work. Population densities in East and Southeast Asia are far higher than in Africa or the Americas, and even in most of Europe. More people forced to live on less land raises the amount people are willing to pay per square meter.

On top of those normal market influences, government policies often force up land prices. In many Asian cities the government acts as a monopoly land supplier. Tax policies may favor holding land if property taxes are low, but capital gains and other transaction taxes are high. The effect may be to keep the market

illiquid and prices high. Finally, macroeconomic policies and conditions may contribute to a land price bubble. In Asia, and in Hong Kong, China in particular, the combination of a fixed exchange rate and a strong inflow of foreign investment seems to have pushed up land prices in the period before the financial crisis.

How far did land prices fall during the Asian crisis? In dollar terms, office rental rates in 12 Asian commercial centers fell by an average of 34 percent, ranging from a 6 percent drop in the city of Taipei to a 65 percent fall in Bangkok. Currency depreciation certainly played a part in the fall in dollar prices. Thus Indonesia, the country that experienced the steepest depreciation, had the second sharpest drop in rents. As shown in the following figure, local currency changes were less consistent than changes in dollar rents. Rental increases (in domestic currency terms) in Jakarta and Seoul seem to reflect the impact of inflation that accompanies a sharp depreciation.

Exchange rates cannot explain all the changes. Market inefficiencies account for some of the differences between major cities. If rents are not

---

In the Philippines tight monetary policy to defend the peso constrained investment demand, while poor agricultural performance caused by bad weather limited growth from the supply side. However, the Philippines' relatively low level of financial leverage (about 60 percent of GDP) and continued strong export demand helped save it from some of the worst effects of the crisis. Growth in the Lao People's Democratic Republic and Viet Nam slowed from the previous year, as the former was hurt by the baht's

depreciation and the dropoff in Thai investment, and the latter suffered from a fall in foreign direct investment from the NIEs. Cambodian growth fell from 2 to zero percent.

Inflation in 1998 increased fourfold from the previous year, driven by currency devaluations and, in some cases, food price increases arising from the impact of the El Niño drought. Indonesia, stricken by shortages of basic products and import price increases, contributed most to the regional price increase. Fiscal allowed to fall with declining demand, either because of regulations or because large landowners restrict supply, then substantial commercial space may go unoccupied. Occupancy rates close to 50 percent in Shanghai and Hanoi suggest that markets in those cities are not allowed to clear. In contrast, the combination of high occupancy rates and falling rents in Tokyo, Hong Kong, Singapore, Mumbai, and Manila indicates reasonably efficient rental markets.

However, even efficient markets may contain asset bubbles. To see whether they do, one of the best indicators is yield, that is, the ratio of the annual rent on a piece of land to its price. If investors are pricing real estate correctly, yields should be roughly equal to interest rates on short-term bonds plus expected capital gains, as investors will be able to substitute between land and other interest-paying investments. A low 4 percent yield on Tokyo office space corresponds to Japan's low short-term domestic interest rates, while a yield in Manila of 12.5 percent approximates Philippine interest rates of about 15 percent.

Other markets appear somewhat distorted. While property yields in Jakarta are relatively high at about 10 percent, they are well short of interest rates approaching 40 percent, possibly reflecting expectations of an interest rate drop.

How much further could prices drop? For several years Hong Kong's land prices have been the highest in the region and about double those of Singapore, Hong Kong's rival as a regional financial center. During the past year that gap has contracted as city of Hong Kong prices dropped faster despite the depreciation of the Singapore dollar over the period. However, property yields in Hong Kong are still only half of domestic short-term rates, indicating that prices may still have further to fall. Other cities with low occupancy rates or low yields relative to interest rates are Jakarta, Hanoi, and Shanghai, but while prices in these and other cities could still fall further, real estate valuations in many Asian cities are now much more in line with economic fundamentals than before the crisis. That may be bad news for lenders and property owners in the short run, but a blessing for Asian economies over the next several years.

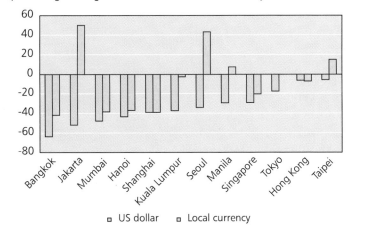

Rental Rates in Central Business Districts, Selected Asian Cities
(percentage changes in dollars and in local currency from 1997 to 1998)

□ US dollar   □ Local currency

Sources: J. P. Morgan, Colliers Jardine, and Jones Lang Wootton data.

constraints limited the ability of governments to cushion the effects of depreciation, resulting in higher food, gas, and electricity prices.

Exchange rate stabilization remained a major economic objective for Southeast Asian countries in 1998. The Indonesian rupiah, Malaysian ringgit, Philippine peso, and Thai baht all dropped to their lowest levels during the first half of 1998. They recovered much lost ground by the end of the year, but remained volatile. The crisis also prompted two moderate devaluations of the Vietnamese dong and devaluations in Cambodia and the Lao People's Democratic Republic.

The situation of the corporate and banking sectors continued to deteriorate, particularly in Indonesia and Malaysia. Nonperforming loans rose and more financial institutions found themselves insolvent. At the end of 1998, of Indonesia, Malaysia, Philippines, and Thailand, Indonesia had the highest level of nonperfoming loans at 35 percent or more of loans outstanding, followed by Thailand at upwards of 30 percent, Malaysia at 25 percent, and Philippines at 10 percent or more

In some cases, tight monetary policy exacerbated loan default problems. Short-term interest rates in Indonesia rose as high as 60 percent, forcing bank and corporate defaults. In Malaysia, the central bank's policy of limiting domestic credit expansion to 12 to 15 percent resulted in a complete lending freeze by several domestic banks. Despite widespread defaults, Thailand also tightened its monetary policy.

The crisis created a dilemma for the region's monetary authorities. Defending the currency required maintaining relatively high interest rates, but that worsened the financial condition of banks and firms. Through the end of the year Indonesia held to high interest rates, while Malaysia and Thailand gradually lowered their key rates, albeit for different reasons. Malaysia's currency controls allowed the central bank to lower rates without prompting further attacks on the currency. Thailand, by contrast, gained some breathing space from investors by implementing financial and structural reforms. Viet Nam also tightened its already stringent capital restrictions, requiring certain companies to convert 80 percent of their foreign exchange holdings into domestic currency.

The economic slowdown caused a significant import contraction, which bolstered current accounts throughout Southeast Asia. For the first time in a decade the aggregate current account for the region registered a surplus. While export revenues weakened as some creditors refused to roll over trade loans, export volumes started to pick up in the second quarter of 1998, possibly pointing the way to an export recovery.

The foregoing discussion of changes in macroeconomic indicators does not adequately convey the full extent of the social costs of the crisis that the population of Southeast Asia has incurred. These are discussed in box 1.3.

The outlook for 1999 depends on the fate of current reform initiatives and the mood of world capital markets. Restructuring and recapitalization of banks and firms will be high on the priority list. Even though fresh capital from several donor countries and multilateral institutions will be disbursed in 1999, the sharp reduction in the availability of private capital will keep the overall supply of foreign exchange to the region well below precrisis levels.

Of Indonesia, Malaysia, Philippines, and Thailand, Malaysia and Philippines are the countries most likely to grow in 1999, albeit at a modest rate. Indonesia continues to have the most uncertain prospects within the group. On the assumption that currencies will stabilize and aggregate demand will remain weak, inflation rates should drop. With the exception of Indonesia, Cambodia, and the Lao People's Democratic Republic, Southeast Asian countries will experience single-digit inflation. Reduced domestic demand will bring continued positive improvements to trade and current account balances in 1999.

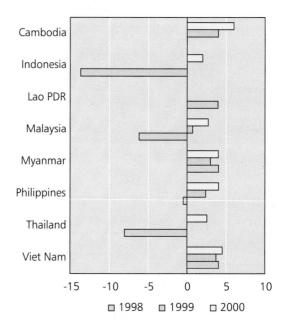

Figure 1.4 Real GDP Growth, Southeast Asia, 1998-2000

Note: 1999 and 2000 forecasts for Lao PDR are not available.
Source: Appendix Table A1.

South Asia. Together with the PRC, South Asia managed to evade the main impact of the Asian financial crisis (see figure 1.5). India's growth was slightly higher than in 1997, while growth picked up in Pakistan in 1998. As a result of the impact of massive flooding on

Box 1.3. The Social Impact of the Asian Economic Crisis

The Asian financial crisis is causing turmoil throughout the affected economies in such areas as employment, prices, human development, poverty, and social capital. The social consequences of the crisis vary across countries according to the extent of the downturn and dislocation. While the poor and vulnerable groups (such as women, children, and migrant workers) are invariably most at risk, the impact of the crisis is pervasive, hurting all social classes, particularly middle- and lower-middle-income ones. The damage is proportionately more severe in urban centers than in rural areas.

Unemployment rates are on the rise. In Indonesia the rate rose to 5.5 percent in 1998, up from 4.7 the previous year. In Thailand it reached 5.3 percent, compared with just above 1 percent in 1997. The unemployment rate in Korea more than doubled to 6.8 percent, while in the Philippines it climbed to 9.6 percent. However, these figures probably underestimate the true extent of the problem, as underemployment is also likely to have increased markedly. Standards of living are falling as inflation outstrips any increase in nominal incomes. For example, in Indonesia the increase in food prices contributed a large portion of the 58 percent rise in the consumer price index in 1998.

The crisis has reduced household expenditure in a number of important social areas, including health and nutrition, education, and family planning. Although social services are subsidized, households still have to incur costs, either directly or indirectly, when they use these services. With reduced incomes and higher prices for such items as medicines and school supplies, households tend to cut down far too

much on their consumption of these important items. Investment in human resources takes time, which becomes scarcer as household members work longer hours to cope with falling incomes. The quality and quantity of government-provided services are declining because of budget reductions and massive shifts of clients from private to public providers.

Thus observers cite notable enrollment decreases or dropout increases, particularly at the secondary level. Estimates indicate that in Indonesia more than 6 million students have dropped out of school and in Thailand about 250,000 students have dropped out. In Malaysia private hospitals and clinics have reported a fall of up to 50 percent in the number of patients seeking treatment. In Indonesia many people are shifting from modern medical care to traditional healers and to self-treatment, while higher drug prices are adversely affecting the treatment of AIDS patients in Thailand. Also in Indonesia, with the higher cost of contraceptives, the government's family planning program is imposing steeper user charges. Consequently, a large number of women are dropping out of the program, which is likely to lead to a rise in the birth rate and a substantial increase in the number of abortions.

The crisis is setting back the spectacular strides made in the fight against poverty during the last two decades. The World Bank (1998a) estimates that a 12 percent GDP shrinkage in Indonesia in 1998 would raise the incidence of poverty from 11 percent in 1996 to 14 percent in 1999, with a larger relative increase in urban centers than in rural areas. Another study (Warr 1998) comes to roughly the same conclusion, and sees poverty in Thailand climbing

from 6.2 percent in 1996 to 7.6 percent in 1998. The increases in the incidence of poverty correspond to about 6 million Indonesians and 1 million Thais falling below official poverty lines. These are huge numbers that require urgent policy attention, but are far less than claimed by earlier reports. If these later estimates are correct, there are some grounds for encouragement, as reductions in poverty brought about by years of broadly based economic growth may not be completely reversed all that quickly.

The environment is also suffering from serious degradation because of the crisis. Household attempts to obtain additional income often lead to increased environmental destruction, such as deforestation, erosion, and overfishing. In Thailand, the devaluation of the baht has provided a strong stimulus to agricultural exports, resulting in expansion and intensification of shrimp farming and, hence, destruction of wetlands and increased salinity of rice lands. An increase in illegal logging has also occurred in Thailand and in neighboring Cambodia and Myanmar.

Finally, in many countries the informal norms and social relationships that enable people to cooperate in pursuit of a common benefit are breaking down as a result of the crisis. This is seen in an increase in crime and violence, including domestic violence, and in a weakening of community cooperation and participation.

The adverse social consequences of the crisis are clearly severe and require urgent action on the part of governments to provide adequate social safety nets; however, the only long-term solution is to ensure a return to broadly based and sustained growth.

Source: Pernia and Knowles (1998).

agricultural and manufacturing output, Bangladesh's 5.7 percent growth was slightly lower than expected for the year. Sri Lanka managed a fairly robust 5.3 percent growth rate, down slightly from the previous year.

Inflation in the region was fairly high in 1998. In India it rose from 1997, driven by shortages of some agricultural goods. The decline in Pakistan's reserves associated with sanctions because of the nuclear tests prompted a 20 percent depreciation of the Pakistani rupee. That contributed to a price rise of 7.8 percent, despite the overall slowdown in economic activity. Aggravated by supply shocks, inflation in Bangladesh was 7 percent, slightly above the levels of recent years. Reserve outflows associated with the nuclear test shock to South Asia prompted accelerated depreciation of the Sri Lanka rupee, leading to inflation of 9.4 percent.

Restrictions on trade finance lines imposed as part of the nuclear test sanctions reduced the amount of capital available to fund current account deficits in the region. Export growth slowed, but imports grew little as the fall in world oil prices reduced India's import bill for oil by 25 percent. India's current account deficit expanded slightly to 1.8 percent of GDP. With new reluctance from foreign lenders to provide financing, Pakistan had little choice but to reduce its current account deficit by half, to about 3 percent of GDP. Bangladesh, relatively unaffected by either the Asian crisis or the impact of nuclear test sanctions, continued to run a current account deficit of about 1 percent of GDP. Sri Lanka's current account deficit was 3.1 percent of GDP in 1998.

Pakistan's budget deficit contracted slightly despite the loss of aid flows that had made up as much as 6 percent of government expenditures in previous years. The still large deficit weakened market confidence in the country. Pakistan's high level of foreign debt ($31 billion, or about 100 percent of GDP) and low foreign exchange reserves (about $1.3 billion) placed it in continuous danger of default throughout 1998. The result was depreciation, stagflation, and the need to negotiate new loans from the International Monetary Fund.

India also had a large budget deficit, yet its more positive external position and conservative monetary policy helped it increase its reserves to the relatively comfortable level of $22 billion, or about 15 percent

of GDP. Despite a network of licensing rules and regulations that remains extensive, India made some progress in structural reform. That gave a supply-side boost to the economy.

Severe flooding struck most of Bangladesh in 1998, damaging rice production and reducing livestock herds. The flooding took out much of the country's infrastructure, destroying more than 6,500 bridges and washing out 11,000 miles of roads. Food production in this largely agricultural country fell by about 10 percent as a result. Although the flooding had a strong adverse impact on fiscal accounts, emergency loans from aid donors bridged much of the gap.

Aggregate growth in South Asia in 1999 is forecast at 5.5 percent, about the same as in 1998. In the short run, weather fluctuations of the kind that the La Niña phenomenon might cause will have a large impact on actual growth results in South Asia. Over the longer run, growth will depend on accelerated progress in privatization, deregulation, and trade liberalization. Inflation will fall to 7.6 percent, assuming that governments do not resort to printing money to

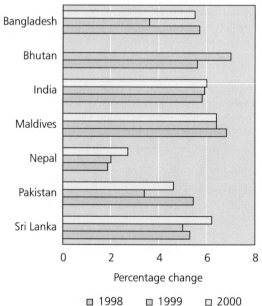

Figure 1.5 Real GDP Growth, South Asia, 1998-2000

Percentage change

☐ 1998   ☐ 1999   ☐ 2000

Note: 2000 forecast for Bhutan is not available.
Source: Appendix Table A1.

finance their large budget deficits. With continued slow growth and the reduction in world capital flows, current account deficits will be fairly low at 3.1 percent of GDP.

The Pacific. Most Pacific countries were mired in slow growth even before the Asian financial crisis, and the crisis itself affected them little. However, Papua New Guinea, the largest economy in the group, was an exception on both counts: it managed to achieve relatively strong growth despite falling commodity demand from Asia. Elsewhere in the Pacific, the shock waves from Asia hit Solomon Islands the hardest, while Fiji, Nauru, and Vanuatu felt moderate adverse effects. The remaining countries had limited direct exposure to Asia, and so received little damage from the crisis.

Higher export revenues explained Papua New Guinea's growth following a recession the previous year. Those revenues reflected an increase in mineral output that more than compensated for falling commodity prices. Fiji suffered negative growth in the face of increased competition from Asian exporters and a drop in world sugarcane demand. Vanuatu also had negative growth, partly because of civil unrest and a drop in foreign demand for beef and timber. Kiribati, and Tuvalu grew at about 2 percent. The economy of Solomon Islands, which sends two thirds of its exports to Asia, contracted by 10 percent. The economies of Cook Islands, Marshall Islands, Federated States of Micronesia, and Tonga also contracted.

In Papua New Guinea a currency depreciation prompted by the Asian crisis and by the depreciation of the Australian dollar pushed inflation to 10 percent, a steep rise from the previous year. Currency depreciation also led to higher inflation in Fiji, while tight monetary policy kept Vanuatu's inflation under control. Most Pacific nations continue to run large budget deficits, and economic prospects for the group in coming years will depend heavily on progress in fiscal reform.

RISKS AND UNCERTAINTIES

The financial and exchange rate crisis remains the main source of uncertainty in Asia. While some currency and equity markets staged partial recoveries in 1998 and current accounts moved into surplus, conditions continued to deteriorate in most economic sectors. For example, bad loan rates kept rising in 1998 as corporate failures exacerbated banking sector problems, even as many Asian countries initiated significant financial sector reforms. At the same time policymakers faced narrowed sets of alternatives. Many felt forced to choose between growth and stability.

The speed and volatility of the Asian crisis makes it difficult to forecast how long it will take for fresh portfolio capital and banking credit to begin flowing again to developing economies. The danger of predicting a rapid recovery became clear in August, when Russia's devaluation and default prompted a new round of capital flight and stock market drops around the world. International bond markets again demanded huge spreads for emerging market debt over "safe" issues, and bank credits contracted. As in 1997, shocks from the financial markets quickly spread to economies at large as governments tightened their fiscal and monetary policies to constrict the capital outflows. As long as international capital markets remain shaky, developing countries in Asia and the world will be vulnerable to investor panic. That high level of uncertainty makes forecasting returns on investment difficult, which means that Asian businesses will feel compelled to scale down their investment plans for the near future. If firms find themselves in a tight spot now, Asian financial institutions are even worse off, with many carrying large, and sometimes increasing, bad debt loads on their books. Eager to avoid extending those bad debts, banks have tightened their lending standards. This newfound conservatism in the face of uncertainty, while arguably beneficial in the long run, is likely to restrain growth over the short and medium term. Even when the recovery is established, when, or even whether, East and Southeast Asia can ever return to the high average annual growth rates of the 1980s and early 1990s is not clear.

Financial markets in Asia itself are not the only source of uncertainty in the region. Integrated global capital markets transmit financial contagion almost instantaneously around the world. Long distance trading relationships make the impact of a devaluation in one part of the developing world quickly felt elsewhere. Since the beginning of the crisis instances have occurred (such as the attack on the Hong Kong dollar in October 1997) when a selling round in Asia spread to other regions, and returned back to Asia in the form of new rounds of asset selling and capital withdrawal.

Brazil and Russia are two developing economies outside Asia with demonstrated potential to disrupt Asian markets. While the initial impact on Asia of Brazil's large devaluation in January 1999 was less severe than many had feared, continuing financial turmoil in Brazil and the rest of Latin America could increase volatility in Asian currency markets. Worse, if Brazil were to default on its sovereign debt, risk premiums on emerging market debt would rise again and capital flows to many developing countries would evaporate. On the other side of the world, Russia's economic situation, exacerbated by banking sector insolvency, fiscal breakdown, and monetary irresponsibility, continues to deteriorate. Financial markets have already absorbed one round of bad news from Russia, but further economic shocks or political unrest would likely have a negative impact on Asian markets.

Developments in the industrial countries are also likely to affect Asia's prospects for recovery. As they appeared to do in mid-1998, Asia's troubles could prompt a slide in US stock prices. A large enough stock price drop would damage consumer confidence and reduce US import demand. With the United States the first or second largest market for many export-dependent Asian countries, a US recession could spark another round of contagion in the region. A recession in Europe could have the same impact, though perhaps a smaller one. Asia's crisis-driven trade surplus could also provoke a protectionist response in the United States or Europe, with potentially severe consequences for Asian exporters.

Arguably, there is more positive potential in Japan's trade and financial relationship with Asia. If Japan were able to pull itself out of its current recession, higher growth would raise import demand, which would provide a large trade boost to the region. Perhaps more important, given the large volume of Japanese lending to the region before the crisis, substantial progress in resolving Japan's banking difficulties under the current financial sector rescue package would increase the flow of private capital to Asian banks and firms. In addition, the Miyazawa initiative to create a $30 billion Asian recovery fund may increase official capital flows to make up for lost private capital.

The economic crisis has had far-ranging political effects, and political uncertainties remain. Salient among these is the possibility of social unrest leading to change in regimes, as happened in Indonesia. But even when a government's survival is not at stake, political forces arising from the crisis may determine policy. For example, to cushion the social costs of recession, inflation, and unemployment, governments have been tempted to resort to higher subsidies, increased regulation, and other direct government interventions. Such responses are inevitable and, in some cases, desirable. However, governments need to be careful that emergency measures do not slow the adoption of needed structural reforms or, in an extreme case, lead to fiscal insolvency.

The Financial Crisis in Asia

How has the Asian financial crisis developed over the last 12 months? What caused the crisis? Did it result from basic structural weaknesses in the affected countries or was it merely the result of investors panicking? Did the policy response by the International Monetary Fund (IMF) ameliorate or exacerbate the situation? This chapter closely analyzes these important questions. It concludes by showing that whatever the answers, a fundamental need is to strengthen the international financial architecture and proposes a necessary, minimum set of reforms within the existing institutional setting.

The collapse of the Thai baht in July 1997 marked the beginning of Asia's financial crisis. It began modestly enough. After a series of speculative attacks, Thailand was forced to let its currency float on 2 July, but within weeks what had been a local financial crisis became a regional problem. Equity markets and currencies throughout Southeast Asia were under pressure as contagion raged and foreign capital fled. Within months Indonesia, the 4th most populous country in the world, and the Republic of Korea (henceforth referred to as Korea), the world's 11th largest economy, were engulfed in crisis.

Financial turmoil spread with a ferocity that none foresaw. Asia's once vibrant economies, used to decades of rapid growth, were plunged into deep recession. For many countries the economic hardship has been similar to that suffered during the Great Depression of the 1930s. In many Asian economies, this economic collapse has forced an unprecedented reappraisal of policies ranging from corporate governance to exchange rate management. In addition, the crisis managers, particularly the IMF, have come under criticism. Intense debate continues about whether IMF policies helped or hindered economic recovery. Finally, Asia's crisis has spawned wide-ranging discussion about the basic design of today's international financial system. Suggestions for reform and blueprints for improving the international financial architecture abound.

These debates are far from settled. This chapter reviews the progress achieved so far in a number of areas. Given that Indonesia, Korea, Malaysia, Philippines, and Thailand suffered the most severe adverse impacts as a result of the crisis, the analysis in this chapter largely focuses on these countries, collectively referred to as the crisis-affected countries. While other countries in the region also suffered in varying degrees because of the spillover effects of the crisis, terms such as Asian crisis and Asian policies refer to this former group of countries. After an account of the crisis in 1998, the chapter critically examines competing explanations of what caused Asia's turmoil, and points out that no simple interpretation suffices. The causes of Asia's problems were complex, and understanding them fully will require a new generation of academic models. It then reviews some of the priorities that Asia's governments now face and analyzes the debate about policy responses to date. Here too the truth is more complex than many commentators allow. Finally, it addresses the global architecture debate. It analyzes the various proposals for international financial reform and discusses what is likely to emerge from what could be the biggest reappraisal of international finance since the Bretton Woods Conference of 1944.

THE EVOLUTION OF THE CRISIS IN 1998

Asian financial markets began 1998 on a pessimistic note. With confidence eroded by Korea's near default in December 1997, the region's financial markets reached record lows in January 1998 (see figure 1.6). However, by early February markets had bounced back, largely on the hope that foreign confidence in the region was returning. On 2 February, for instance, Hong Kong's Hang Seng Index rose 14 percent, its second largest one-day point gain ever, while other regional exchanges saw strong rallies. But this optimism did not last long, partly because of turmoil in Indonesia, and partly because of increasingly poor economic performance in Japan.

Indonesia's economic crisis began to worsen sharply in February. Mixed policy signals, galloping inflation, and a vast debt overhang scared investors and sent the rupiah plummeting. That same month the Suharto government proposed establishing a currency board, but eventually abandoned the idea under strong pressure from various quarters. Political uncertainties and civil unrest compounded the country's difficulties. Eventually, the combination of soaring prices, civil protests, sharply rising unemployment rates, and widespread corporate defaults precipitated a major political crisis. On 21 May President Suharto resigned; however, this did little to rally the markets.

Japan's woes compounded the region's troubles. In early February 1998, the Japanese government

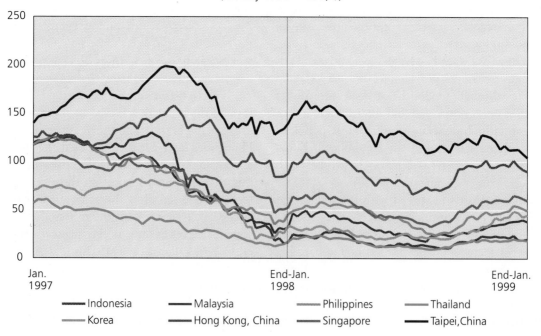

Figure 1.6 Weekly Composite Stock Price Indexes, Selected Asian Economies, January 1997-January 1999

(January 1996 = 100; $)

Indonesia   Malaysia   Philippines   Thailand
Korea   Hong Kong, China   Singapore   Taipei, China

Source: Based on data from BLOOMBERG.

declared the economy "stagnant" in a monthly report that offered the bleakest assessment of the country's business climate in more than 20 years. Responding to the turmoil in Asian markets in mid-February, the government unveiled a long-awaited package of stimulus measures designed to support the stock market and boost the economy. It proved insufficient. The economy continued to contract, despite an increase in the fiscal stimulus measures in April. Moody's rating agency revised Japan's sovereign debt rating downward, and by 12 June the yen had declined to an eight-year low of ¥145 to the US dollar.

The tumbling yen triggered declines in other Asian currencies in June (see figure 1.7), including the Malaysian ringgit, the Thai baht, the Korean won, and the New Taiwan dollar (which hit an 11-year low). Stocks throughout the Pacific Rim fell sharply as investors worried that falling currencies would worsen the region's economic difficulties. Hong Kong's Hang Seng Index and Seoul's composite index tumbled to their lowest levels since February 1995 and June 1987, respectively.

Worried by the regional impact of a plummeting yen, Japan and the United States turned to official intervention. On 17 June, in coordination with the Bank of Japan, the United States spent an estimated $2 billion to bolster the value of the yen. News of the intervention—which represented a marked change of American policy toward the yen—had the desired effect. It soared to ¥138 to the US dollar, and Asian markets rallied.

Unfortunately, the rally did not last. By mid-August the yen had fallen to a new low of ¥147 to the dollar. Pressure on the Chinese yuan and the Hong Kong dollar mounted as investors feared a new round of regional devaluations. Another major shock hit financial markets on 17 August: the Russian central bank devalued the ruble and the government effectively defaulted on its internal debt. This action had a dramatic and deleterious impact on all financial markets. Investors fled all types of risk, from emerging market bonds to noninvestment-grade corporate bonds in developed markets.

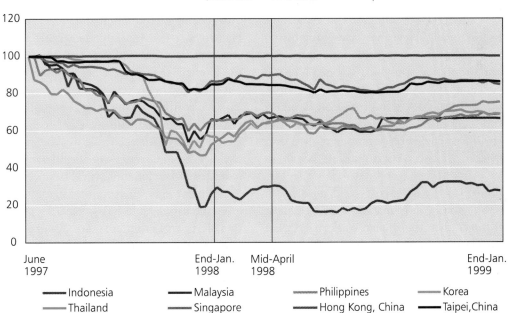

Figure 1.7 Weekly Nominal Exchange Rate Indexes, Selected Asian Economies, June 1997-January 1999
(end-June = 100; $/lc)

Source: Based on data from BLOOMBERG.

As capital fled policymakers were forced to resort to unorthodox responses. The Hong Kong, China authorities intervened directly in the stock market to counter what they viewed as market manipulation, and spent an estimated $15 billion of public funds on the Hong Kong Stock Exchange. On 1 September Malaysia's government decided to impose exchange controls to counter speculative attacks on the ringgit.

As investors fled to the safety of cash and treasury bonds, interest rate spreads widened on all debt instruments, and highly leveraged hedge funds that specialized in arbitraging risk hit trouble. The near collapse of the Connecticut-based hedge fund, Long Term Capital Management, and its rescue organized by the Federal Reserve Bank of New York, showed that by the end of September 1998 the crisis had moved well beyond Asia.

By this time financial markets were clamoring for a coordinated G7 interest rate cut to calm the panic. Although no coordinated move took place, the US Federal Reserve cut interest rates three times, by a total of 0.75 percent, between September and December 1998, and European central banks cut their benchmark rates. Markets were also reassured by the decision to enhance the IMF's capital base or "quotas" in October, which had been held up by political opposition in the US Congress.

Since October 1998 conditions in Asia have improved substantially. Japan has made progress on the much needed reform of its banking sector and is implementing the fiscal stimulus package. The yen strengthened dramatically to ¥113 to the US dollar by the end of December. Buoyed by progress in Japan, by interest rate cuts in the industrial countries, and especially by the gradual implementation of their own reform programs, other Asian markets began to recover.

October was a particularly good month: on average, the region's equity markets rose by almost 18 percent. Since then the Korean stock market has been the strongest performer (see figure 1.6), though it is still far from its precrisis levels. As stock markets rebounded, currencies also strengthened. Between the end of September 1998 and January 1999 the Indonesian rupiah rose by just over 20 percent, the Korean won by 18 percent, the Philippine peso by 15 percent, and the Thai baht by 7 percent.

By the beginning of 1999 one could say that the Asian economies seemed to have stabilized. In Korea and Thailand especially, the bitter economic medicine was beginning to work. Attention was shifting from immediate crisis management to accelerating recovery. Debt restructuring, corporate workouts, and banking reform moved to the top of the agenda. In this regard, the announcement of a $30 billion assistance package from Japan under the Miyazawa Plan improved the region's economic prospects. While emerging markets remained fragile—as evidenced by the collapse of Brazil's currency, the real, in late January 1999—the worst in Asia seemed to be over.

INTERPRETING THE CRISIS

As Asia's crisis deepened, so the search for explanations intensified. What exactly caused these once vibrant economies to fall victim to such a financial disaster? The issue is not simply one of academic interest, because the appropriate policy responses depend in large part on an understanding of what caused the crisis.

Competing Explanations: Panic versus Fundamentals

Two general interpretations dominate the debate. One blames poor economic fundamentals and policy inconsistencies. The other argues that Asia fell victim to a financial panic, where negative sentiment became self-fulfilling.

According to the "fundamentalist" view, the Asian crisis (along with most other financial crises) was caused by basic economic weaknesses. Proponents of this view argue that Asia's healthy macroeconomic indicators—low inflation, fiscal balance, low stock of government debt, high rates of domestic saving and investment (see table 1.2)—painted a misleading picture. They argue that in reality, Asia's economies suffered from serious structural problems as well as policy inconsistencies. They point out that warning signals existed: for instance, in Thailand the current account deficit was dangerously large and rising fast. Moreover, benign macroeconomic indicators, such as a healthy budget balance, could mask real economic weakness. Many Asian governments provided implicit guarantees to the banking system, which often engaged in lending practices that favored financially unqualified borrowers. These implicit guarantees led banks to lend recklessly. This, in conjunction with poor corporate governance in many of these economies, created a large stock of nonperforming loans, thereby risking the banks' collapse. This meant that the governments' implicit guarantees created a sizable "contingent fiscal liability."

By contrast, the panic interpretation views the self-fulfilling pessimism of international lenders as the root cause of the crisis. The most sophisticated version of this argument interprets Asia's crisis as a classic bank run. In a bank run, if enough investors are suddenly seized with panic and demand immediate payment, then financial intermediaries are forced to destructively liquidate long-term assets at a great loss. In the classic model of a panic, the central bank can

Table 1.2 Macroeconomic Indicators, Selected Asian Economies, 1990-1997
(percent)

Economy	Growth rate			Inflation rate			Fiscal balance/GDP		
	1990-1995	1996	1997	1990-1995	1996	1997	1990-1995	1996	1997
Korea	7.8	7.1	5.5	6.6	5.0	4.5	0.2	0.5	-1.4
Indonesia	8.0	7.8	4.9	8.7	7.9	6.6	0.2	0.2	0.0
Malaysia	8.9	8.6	7.7	3.7	3.5	4.0	-0.4	0.7	1.8
Philippines	2.3	5.8	5.2	10.6	9.1	6.0	-1.1	0.3	0.1
Singapore	8.6	6.9	7.8	2.7	1.4	2.0	9.4	6.8	3.3
Thailand	9.0	5.5	-0.4	5.0	5.9	5.6	3.2	2.4	-0.9
Hong Kong, China	5.0	4.5	5.3	9.3	6.3	5.9	1.6	2.2	6.5
PRC	10.7	9.6	8.8	11.3	8.3	2.8	-1.0	-0.8	-0.7
Taipei,China	6.4	5.7	6.8	3.8	3.1	0.9	-5.0	-6.6	-6.3

Economy	Savings/GDP			Investment/GDP			Current Account/GDP		
	1990-1995	1996	1997	1990-1995	1996	1997	1990-1995	1996	1997
Korea	35.6	33.7	33.1	36.8	38.4	35.0	-1.2	-4.7	-1.8
Indonesia	31.0	27.3	29.9	31.3	30.7	31.3	-2.5	-3.4	-1.4
Malaysia	36.6	42.6	43.8	37.5	41.5	42.0	-5.8	-5.0	-5.3
Philippines	16.6	18.5	20.3	22.4	23.1	23.8	-3.7	-4.7	-5.3
Singapore	47.0	51.2	51.8	34.9	35.3	37.4	0.6	15.4	15.4
Thailand	34.4	33.7	32.9	41.0	41.7	35.0	-3.9	-7.9	-2.0
Hong Kong, China	33.6	30.7	31.8	29.6	32.1	35.4	—	—	—
PRC	40.8	40.5	41.5	38.8	39.6	38.2	1.2	0.9	3.2
Taipei,China	26.9	25.1	24.8	24.0	21.2	22.0	4.2	4.0	2.7

— Not available.

GDP Gross domestic product.
PRC People's Republic of China.

Sources: Statistical Appendix Table Nos. A1, A7, A8, A9, A16, and A23.

prevent such a destructive bank run by acting as lender of last resort and providing liquidity to the market. However, in the international version of a bank run, if a country's exchange rate is fixed and foreign exchange reserves are limited in relation to short-term external debt, as was the case in some Asian crisis-affected countries, no mechanism for stemming panic is available. In Indonesia, Korea, and Thailand short-term external debt exceeded international reserves immediately before the crisis (see table 1.3), and indeed, for more than two years prior to the crisis.

Economic fundamentals, such as inflation, unemployment, and the budget deficit, are unimportant in this interpretation, although fears about economic weaknesses might cause the initial investor shift from optimism to pessimism. What matters is the maturity structure and currency denomination of external and internal debt. If, for instance, a large proportion of a country's debt is denominated in foreign currency and is of a short maturity, as it was in much of Asia, the risks of a crisis arise.

Which Explanation Fits Asia Best?

At first sight, the past stellar economic record of the Asian economies does not support the fundamentalist interpretation. However, closer inspection clearly shows that these countries' economic success was built on a particular kind of economic strategy that emphasized export orientation, centralized coordination of production activities, and implicit (or even explicit) government guarantees of private investment projects, as well as a close operational relationship and interlinked ownership between banks and firms. Widely referred to as Asian industrial policy, this strategy allowed firms to rely heavily on bank credit. By international standards, firms in crisis-affected countries were extraordinarily highly leveraged. In Korea and Thailand, for instance, the average debt-to-equity ratios in 1996 were above 200 percent. In Hong Kong, China; Indonesia; and the Philippines debt-to-equity ratios were lower, but nevertheless high by international standards (see table 1.4).

The financial sector was also exhibiting significant problems. Weak prudential regulation, lax and inexperienced supervision, low capital adequacy ra-

Table 1.3 Short-Term External Debt and International Reserves Prior to the Crisis, Selected Asian Economies, Second Quarter of 1997

Economy	Short-term debt ($ billions)	International reserves ($ billions)	Debt-reserve ratio
Korea	70.18	34.07	2.06
Indonesia	34.66	20.34	1.70
Malaysia	16.27	26.59	0.61
Philippines	8.29	9.78	0.85
Singapore	196.60	80.66	2.44
Thailand	45.57	31.36	1.45
Taipei,China	21.97	90.02	0.24

Sources: Short-term debt: Bank for International Settlements data; reserves: IMF (1998a); staff estimates.

tios, lack of adequate deposit insurance schemes, distorted incentives for project selection, and sometimes outright corruption all rendered the region's financial systems weaker than they appeared.

For many years, most Asian economies kept their financial systems relatively closed. Foreign borrowing was limited and capital inflows were controlled. These controls ensured that the region's financial sectors remained immune from external shocks despite their domestic fragility. Most important, controls prevented domestic fragility from being translated into external vulnerability in the form of short-term, unhedged foreign debt. This changed during the 1990s. As international capital markets were gradually opened and domestic markets were deregulated, supervision and regulatory oversight did not improve in tandem. For example, Thailand's now infamous finance companies grew rapidly during the 1990s with virtually no regulatory oversight.

The 1990s also saw a dramatic increase in foreign borrowing. While Asian companies maintained their strong bias in favor of debt financing, foreign debt financing became increasingly important (see table 1.5 for corporate debt composition in selected Asian economies in 1996). The pegged exchange rate elimi-

Table 1.4 Selected Indicators of Corporate Financing, Selected Asian Economies, 1996

Economy	Debt-to-equity ratio		Ratio of short-term debt to total debt	
	Mean	Median	Mean	Median
Hong Kong, China	1.56	1.42	0.60	0.64
Indonesia	1.88	1.83	0.54	0.57
Japan	2.21	1.92	0.58	0.59
Korea	3.55	3.25	0.57	0.59
Malaysia	1.18	0.90	0.64	0.70
Philippines	1.29	0.93	0.48	0.49
Singapore	1.05	0.81	0.58	0.59
Taipei,China	0.80	0.74	0.59	0.61
Thailand	2.36	1.85	0.63	0.67

Note: Data are derived from a sample of 5,550 Asian firms.
Source: Claessens, Djonkor, and Lang (1998).

Table 1.5 Corporate Debt Composition, Selected Asian Economies, 1996
(percent)

Economy	Foreign debt		Domestic debt	
	Short-term	Long-term	Short-term	Long-term
Indonesia	20.5	19.6	31.4	28.5
Korea	29.4	17.0	27.7	25.8
Malaysia	32.1	11.0	35.7	21.2
Philippines	19.7	21.3	25.5	33.5
Taipei,China	22.3	19.2	23.9	34.6
Thailand	29.6	12.3	32.0	26.1

Note: Data are derived from a sample of 5,550 Asian firms.
Source: Claessens, Djankov, and Lang (1998).

nated exchange risks in borrowing in dollars. At the same time international investors were falling over themselves to lend: interest rates in the industrial countries were low, prompting a search for higher yields elsewhere, and optimism about Asia's prospects was high. Between 1991 and 1996 overall borrowing doubled in Malaysia and Thailand and grew by one third in Korea (World Bank 1998a). The fundamentalist interpretation of the crisis links this extraordinary optimism among foreign investors to their belief that the borrowing was ultimately guaranteed, either by Asian governments or by international institutions. The panic interpretation regards the optimism as rational, based on the correct judgment that these economies were fundamentally sound.

Although specific characteristics varied, a pattern of increasing vulnerability to external shocks emerged in all the region's economies prior to the crisis. First, short-term borrowing to finance long-term projects became increasingly important, especially in Korea, Malaysia, and Thailand. This created a sizable maturity mismatch in the balance sheets of domestic

financial institutions. Second, domestic banks lent to domestic firms in local currency, while borrowing short term in foreign currencies without hedging. This created a significant currency denomination mismatch. Third, the easy availability of credit fueled investment in increasingly risky assets. In some countries the credit boom was translated into bubbles in real estate and property. In other countries financial resources were directed toward overinvestment in narrowly specialized industries such as electronics or large, prestigious projects with unclear benefits. These poor and risky investments, in turn, worsened the quality of the portfolios of domestic financial institutions, thereby increasing the risk of panics and subsequent crises.

At the same time, several factors combined during the 1990s to worsen the fundamental economic outlook for the region. The rapid appreciation of the US dollar since 1995, to which most of the region's currencies were pegged in some way; the increasing competition from the People's Republic of China (PRC) in export markets; and the prolonged slowdown of the Japanese economy were all reflected in slower export growth, rising current account deficits, depressed stock markets, and widespread corporate difficulties long before the outbreak of the crisis. In 1996, for instance, 20 of the largest 30 Korean conglomerates had rates of return below the cost of invested capital, and in the first months of 1997, 7 of the 30 largest conglomerates were effectively bankrupt.

As these financial difficulties emerged, some governments played an increasingly active role in reassuring international investors about their willingness to back domestic financial firms. A case in point is the collapse of the large Thai finance company, Finance One. In the months preceding the crisis, the Bank of Thailand repeatedly confirmed to foreign investors its willingness to "back Finance One all the way" (*Financial Times* 12 January 1998).

In the first half of 1997, despite the worsening financial environment, capital inflows did not slow down, but increasingly took the form of short-term, interbank loans that could be readily withdrawn and could count on formal guarantees in the interbank markets. However, once the crisis began, international banks suddenly stopped lending and began to call in their loans. A huge amount of private foreign capital fled the region in the second half of 1997. Between them, Indonesia, Korea, Malaysia, Philippines, and Thailand received a net capital inflow of about $76 billion in 1996, but suffered a net capital outflow of around $36 billion in 1997. This implies a difference of approximately $112 billion, or about 12 percent of the countries' combined gross domestic product (GDP). Commercial banks withdrew about $26 billion from the crisis-affected countries in 1997, after lending them about $63 billion in 1996.

The suddenness and speed with which capital fled the region in the second half of 1997 gives credence to the panic interpretation of the crisis. However, as this section has shown, it was the region's structural weaknesses that initially created the vulnerability to crisis.

Academic Theories of Currency Crises

The competing interpretations of Asia's crisis are mirrored in debates between academic economists. Economists have developed an entire literature that tries to analyze currency crises using formal models. These models of currency crises fall into two broad categories, appropriately called "first generation" and "second generation" models.

First generation models (also known as exogenous policy models) show how fundamentally inconsistent domestic policies lead an economy inexorably toward a currency crisis. In the most popular version of this model, a currency crisis in a country with a fixed exchange rate is caused by an excessively large budget deficit. To finance the budget deficit, the government prints money. At the same time, the central bank is committed to defending the exchange rate; however, it can only do so as long as it has the necessary foreign exchange reserves. As the government continues to print money to finance the budget deficit, reserves will fall because the private sector is willing to hold all the new money the government prints, and therefore exchanges some local currency for foreign currency. At some point a currency crisis occurs. The analysis does not focus on predicting whether or not the currency will collapse—because eventually it certainly will—but on the timing of a speculative attack on the currency. Deteriorating economic fundamentals and inconsistent policies are the cause of the crisis.

By contrast, second generation models (also known as endogenous policy models) stress that a currency crisis can occur even when macroeconomic policies are apparently consistent with a fixed exchange rate policy. These models show how a spontaneous speculative attack on a currency can cause a crisis, even if fiscal and monetary policies are consistent. In these models, rational governments choose their macroeconomic policies and choose whether or not to retain a fixed exchange rate on the basis of a calculus of costs and benefits. The benefits of maintaining a fixed exchange rate include reduced inflationary pressure and a stable environment that facilitates trade and investment. The costs of a fixed exchange rate can include high interest rates and high unemployment (if wages are rigid).

Self-fulfilling expectations play an important role in this model. If the public does not believe that a government will maintain its fixed exchange rate, then domestic bondholders will demand a higher interest rate in anticipation of a currency devaluation. Labor unions might demand higher wages, thereby rendering domestic industries uncompetitive. Such actions would raise the government's costs of maintaining a fixed exchange rate, encouraging it to abandon the peg. The public's concern about a devaluation would become a self-fulfilling prophecy.

The second generation models do not imply that every country can be a victim of speculative attacks. Countries are only vulnerable when economic fundamentals—such as foreign exchange reserves, the government's fiscal situation, and the political commitment to defend the peg—are sufficiently weak. When a country's fundamentals are obviously strong, a crisis will not occur. When they are extremely weak, it will certainly occur. In between a currency peg might survive, or it might fall victim to a speculative attack. Box 1.4 explains the logic behind such sudden losses of confidence.

The fundamentalist interpretation of Asia's crisis is closely related to the first generation of currency models. The implicit (and later explicit) government guarantees to failing banks implied a large fiscal burden to Asian governments. To the extent that such a rising fiscal burden raised the likelihood that governments would eventually resort to printing money to finance growing deficits, the currency crisis is exactly what first generation models would predict. The panic interpretation of the crisis is derived from the second generation models. These models underscore the idea that a regime of fixed exchange rates that is not perfectly credible is intrinsically unstable and subject to sudden swings in market sentiment.

POLICY RESPONSES TO THE CRISIS: AN OVERVIEW OF THE DEBATE

The principal responsibility for dealing with the Asian crisis at an international level was assumed by the IMF, the institution charged with safeguarding the stability of the international financial system. The IMF's goal was to quickly restore confidence in the three hardest hit Asian economies—Indonesia, Korea, and Thailand —through a combination of tough economic conditionalities and substantial financial support. In 1997 the IMF approved $35 billion of loans for these countries, and in addition, mobilized commitments worth $77 billion from the Asian Development Bank (ADB), the World Bank, and bilateral sources. In 1998 the IMF arranged further loans worth $6.3 billion for Indonesia.

The IMF's economic strategy had two key components. The first, in keeping with its usual practice,

concentrated on macroeconomic policy, the main component of which was to be tighter monetary policy. Higher interest rates were designed to defend exchange rates, and so stem (or reverse) the capital outflows. Modestly tighter fiscal policy was designed to support current account adjustment and provide the funds that would be necessary to bail out sick banking systems. The second, complementary, component of the strategy was substantial structural reform. The IMF demanded deep reform of the region's banking systems, the breakup of monopolies, the removal of barriers to trade, and substantial improvements in corporate transparency. This marked a significant departure from past IMF practice, when conditionalities had been more closely confined to macroeconomic policies alone. The IMF saw the structural reforms as essential for a long-term solution to Asia's financial crisis.

Both components of the IMF's strategy have come under heavy fire. Some critics have gone so far as to argue that the policies the IMF initially imposed, far from ameliorating the situation actually made the region's problems worse. Not surprisingly, such accusations have led to a vigorous defense of its actions by the institution and its supporters.

Two difficulties plague any evaluation of the IMF's policies. The first is the insoluble problem of the counterfactual. Knowing precisely what would have happened if the IMF had adopted a different approach is impossible. The second difficulty is that the IMF's targets and tactics changed over time. As the situation in Asia progressively worsened, the IMF eased its approach and required less fiscal contraction. In Indonesia, for instance, it relaxed its initial requirement of a budget surplus in 1997 to allow for a sizable budget deficit. Similar, if less dramatic, relaxation occurred in the cases of Korea and Thailand. The crucial question is whether these changes in policy were an implicit admission of initial misjudgments by the IMF, or whether they simply represented a flexible response to changing conditions.

Did Tight Monetary Policy and High Interest Rates Exacerbate the Crisis?

In crisis-affected countries, the IMF recommended a sharp increase in interest rates to restore confidence, stem capital outflows, and stabilize the currency. The

Box 1.4 **The Logic behind Confidence Crises**

The logic of self-fulfilling, speculative attacks and bank runs can be illustrated by a simple example. Suppose that a country pursues a fixed exchange rate, but its monetary authorities have only 10 units of international reserves to defend the exchange rate. For simplicity, suppose that before the speculative attack, 1 unit of domestic currency is exchanged for 1 unit of foreign currency. There are two identical agents (or speculators) who can attack the currency. Each can use at most 6 units of domestic currency. Thus no agent alone can deplete the international reserves of the country and force the central bank to abandon the defense of the peg. Nonetheless, the stock of reserves is low enough to make the country vulnerable to a joint speculative attack by both agents.

Attacking the currency involves a fixed cost equal to 1 unit of domestic currency. Clearly, if one of the agents decides to attack, the payoff will depend on the behavior of the other agent in the economy. A lone, and therefore unsuccessful, attack is costly to the agent. Conversely, a joint attack will yield a net payoff equal to the amount of reserves that each agent can buy at the existing exchange rate—say half the central bank's stock of reserves— times the size of the devaluation, minus the fixed cost. For an exchange rate depreciation to take place, there must be a sufficiently large speculative movement in the foreign exchange market. The size of the depreciation, of course, depends on underlying economic fundamentals.

The figure shows the agents' possible payoffs, expressed in units of domestic currency. Each cell reports the payoff from the various combinations of the two actions the agents can take, that is, whether or not to attack the currency. If both

		Agent II	
		Attack	Not attack
Agent I	Attack	Agent I gains 2 Agent II gains 2	Agent I loses 1 Agent II gains 0
	Not attack	Agent I gains 0 Agent II loses 1	Agent I gains 0 Agent II gains 0

agents decide to attack the currency and the currency is devalued by 60 percent, then the net payoff to each agent (that is, the payoff after paying the transaction cost) is 2 units. If the attack is unsuccessful, the speculating agent ends up with a net payoff of -1 unit. The figure shows that two outcomes are likely as follows:

■ If one agent attacks the currency, it also pays the other agent to attack, as both will make net payoffs of 2 units. Thus one possible outcome is a simultaneous speculation leading to a collapse of the currency. (This is shown in the upper left-hand cell of the diagram.)

■ By the same logic, if one agent does not attack the currency, then it does not pay the other agent to speculate, as this would merely give the latter a net loss of 1 unit. In other words, the attacking agent would simply incur the fixed cost. (These are the cases shown in the bottom left-hand and the upper right-hand cells.) Thus, the outcome would be no attack on the currency (the bottom right-hand cell).

Consequently, the actual outcome depends on whether or not the agents coordinate their expectations. Note that in both cases discussed above, the fundamentals— the size of the international reserves, the "firepower" available to the agents, and the size of the devaluation when the peg is abandoned—are the same.

This provides a simple example of how an otherwise sustainable currency peg can be vulnerable to self-fulfilling speculative attacks. Note that in this example, no attack would ever take place if the international reserves in the central bank were more than 12 units (so that the firepower of the speculator would be relatively low), while the currency would certainly collapse if international reserves were less than 6 units. However, neither this example nor the more sophisticated economic literature provide any explanation of how agents coordinate their decisions, nor do they explain the factors that swing market confidence.

More important, for a given state of fundamentals, the likelihood of a speculative attack increases if information is incomplete. In this environment, even news events that are unrelated to economic fundamentals can shift agents' expectations and help trigger speculative attacks (the trouble in the province of Chiapas before the 1994 Mexico crisis is a case in point). The theory reaches the important conclusion that more information, or greater transparency, decreases the likelihood of a self-validating crisis, and thus ensures currency and financial stability.

Sources: Morris and Shin (1998); Obstfeld (1996).

IMF maintained that because of the time needed for other (structural) reforms to take hold, the only way to stabilize a crisis situation quickly was to raise interest rates with sufficient resolve.

Critics of the IMF argue that this approach was misconceived and counterproductive. They point out that high interest rates forced highly leveraged corporations into bankruptcy. Widespread bankruptcies in the corporate sector led to bank insolvencies as the banks' corporate customers failed to repay their loans. These bankruptcies weakened the financial system and encouraged capital flight, and thus caused a further decline in the exchange rate. All this had a tremendous negative impact on the real sector of the economy. Given this negative spiral, the critics claim that a more appropriate policy response to the crisis would have been a looser monetary policy, that is, a fall rather than a rise in interest rates. Lower interest rates would have made it easier for firms to maintain production, thereby restoring investors' confidence that the economy would recover quickly, and would thus have caused currencies to appreciate. That would have created a virtuous circle. Many of the critics point out that Japan followed just such a policy when dealing with its domestic crisis.

The IMF, however, feared that a lower interest rate policy would cause a vicious downward spiral. As currencies plummeted, so the real burden of debt denominated in foreign currency would rise. Because the Asian firms had high leverage ratios, a much higher foreign debt burden could have forced insolvencies and caused even larger collapses in production. Unlike Japan, which is a net foreign creditor, the size of foreign debts was a much greater concern in Asia's crisis-affected countries.

Some of the critics who advocated lower interest rates to reflate the domestic economy and relieve the financial situation of heavily indebted firms acknowledge that a lower interest rate might not have strengthened the exchange rate or brought back departed capital. In that case, the only remaining alternative would have been for countries to suspend service on their external debts and impose exchange control measures. Such actions could have had an extremely detrimental and long-lasting effect on the countries' ability to access international capital markets. With the exception of Malaysia, which imposed selected exchange controls in September 1998, this option was not pursued.

Available empirical evidence does not necessarily support the view that interest rates were persistently high. Indeed, several of the crisis-affected countries pursued low interest rate policies well into the crisis. Despite continued worsening of the foreign exchange market, Korea maintained official ceilings on interest rates through December 1997, and Indonesia reduced its interest rates in September 1997 as the rupiah was declining. The real interest rate in Indonesia remained negative until mid-1998. Malaysia, another country that was affected by the crisis but did not seek IMF assistance, waited until December 1997, when its currency value had fallen by 40 percent, before it tightened its monetary policy. Supporters of the IMF's position further point to Indonesia as an example of the disastrous consequences of loose monetary policy. Indonesia manifestly failed to tighten its monetary policy in late 1997. The result was a collapse in the exchange rate, galloping inflation, and the bankruptcy of much of the corporate sector. Korea and Thailand, which eventually adopted a tight monetary policy—even though it was not extremely tight in degree or duration in relation to that in other countries elsewhere outside Asia in the past that were faced with exchange rate instability—succeeded in stabilizing their economies. In these economies interest rates began to fall during 1998 while exchange rates strengthened. Moreover, a recent IMF analysis (IMF 1999) indicates that the costs of tighter monetary policy may have been lower than many suggest. It estimates that in Korea and Thailand, the effects of the monetary tightening may account for less than a quarter of the expected decline in economic growth rates between 1997 and 1998.

Did the IMF Force Unnecessary Fiscal Adjustment?

Unlike many other crises that have required IMF intervention, the Asian crisis was not caused by profligate government spending. Thus fiscal imbalances were not a major concern in the initial IMF programs. Nonetheless, the IMF's approach in the crisis-affected countries was to demand a tightening of fiscal policy based on two arguments. First, it argued that in the presence of rapid capital flight these countries needed to reduce domestic demand in order to reduce their current account deficits. Tightening fiscal policy was an effective way to do this. Second, and more subtle, was the argument that government spending needed to be cut to make room for the expected expenditure necessary to bail out insolvent banks. Some estimates suggest that the cost of bailing out financial institutions in some crisis-affected countries could eventually reach 20 to 30 percent of GDP, which under reasonable assumptions about the interest rate would entail an annual cost of about 3.0 to 3.5 percent of GDP (see table 1.6). Eventually, the Asian economies would need to run budget surpluses high enough to cover this cost. Therefore beginning a modest tightening of fiscal policy early on was prudent.

Critics, however, claim that the fiscal tightening simply exacerbated the enormous economic contraction that was already taking place in the region. In the face of collapsing output, they argue, fiscal expansion, that is, a small budget deficit, would have been more appropriate. Even if the region's economies needed to run surpluses over the long run to pay for their banking bailouts, worsening a severe recession with immediate fiscal tightening was unnecessary. In short, they charge, the IMF failed to gauge the severity of the crisis and the fiscal conditions it imposed made matters significantly worse.

This is an easy criticism to make with hindsight. Clearly the fact that the IMF relaxed its fiscal targets over time suggests that its priorities changed as the region's economic outlook worsened. However, it is hard to blame the IMF for failing to gauge the depth and likely persistence of the region's problems. Few policymakers or commentators foresaw the depths of the crisis.

Even if running a looser fiscal policy had made more sense for Asia's governments, fiscal flexibility was severely constrained by the lack of access to international credit at reasonable rates. If international institutions and industrial countries made more liquidity available, Asian countries' fiscal flexibility would improve significantly.

Did the Closure of Insolvent Banks Precipitate Runs on Solvent Banks?

Given the parlous state of the financial sector in the crisis-affected countries, there is little doubt that many banks in Indonesia, Korea, and Thailand needed to be restructured, merged, or simply closed. The IMF believed that speedy and concerted action in this direction would, by weeding out the bad financial apples, help restore investors' confidence. In all three countries, therefore, the operations of a number of clearly insolvent financial institutions were suspended or the institutions were closed early on. In Thailand 58 finance companies were suspended in July and August 1997, in Korea 14 merchant banks were suspended in December 1997, and in Indonesia 16 banks were closed in November 1997.

The IMF's critics charge that this abrupt closure of insolvent banks panicked the public and precipitated a run on sound banks. Concerned that their banks might be closed next, depositors withdrew their money from healthy banks in a classic banking panic. Although only Korea had a formal deposit insurance scheme prior to the crisis, the general perception in all three countries was that government guarantees covered most of the deposit base. When this perception turned out to be false, panic ensued.

Indonesia is the most dramatic example of this. The closure of 16 banks—which between them con-

Table 1.6 Cost Estimates by the IMF of Bank Restructuring in Asia, Selected Asian Economies
November 1998

Economy	Debt issues		Interest payments	
	$ billions[a]	Percentage of GDP	$ billions[a]	Percentage of GDP
Indonesia	40.0	29.0	5.4	3.5
Korea	60.0	17.5	6.4	2.0
Thailand	43.0	32.0	4.0	3.0
Malaysia	13.0	18.0	0.9	1.3
Philippines	3.0	4.0	0.3	0.5

a. At the exchange rate of 30 November 1998.
Sources: IMF (1998b,e).

tained less than 3 percent of total deposits—led to a near collapse of the entire banking system as investors switched funds from private banks to the state banks, which they considered to be safer. Thus, the critics argue, the IMF's policy made matters much worse.

Clearly in Indonesia the decision to close banks did precipitate a public panic. However, the IMF's supporters argue that the lack of clear government policy caused the panic, not the bank closures themselves. The Indonesian government promised only a small deposit guarantee, did not publicize it widely, and did not explain publicly how depositors in banks that had not yet been closed would be treated. Similarly, the IMF's defendants point out, the closure of banks in Korea and Thailand did not result in such severe runs. That is true, but it is also true that the financial institutions that were closed in these countries were mainly merchant banks that did not take personal deposits.

Was the IMF too Intrusive?

Some critics question the IMF's insistence on far-reaching structural reforms in Asia's economies. They have suggested that the IMF went well beyond its mandate of ensuring prudent macroeconomic policies. Instead it was intervening excessively in the domestic affairs of sovereign governments by demanding large-scale restructuring in the corporate and financial sector, as well as improvements in governance, labor markets, and competition policy.

The IMF's proponents argue that this critique does not sit well with the facts of the Asian crisis. If reckless monetary and fiscal expansion was not at the root of the Asian financial crisis, as those who view the IMF as being too intrusive also accept, devising a response focusing on these areas made no sense. However, if, as is widely acknowledged, structural weaknesses in corporate governance and the financial system lay at the core of Asia's problems, then the IMF's loan programs would have had little chance of success if they had not addressed structural reform. Providing large-scale financial assistance to support the region's currencies would have been irresponsible if the root cause of the problem was left unaddressed. Continued financial and corporate weakness would have undermined macroeconomic policy, investors

would have continued to flee, and the IMF's ultimate goal—a quick return to economic growth—would have been impossible. The IMF's demands were intrusive, but necessary.

Did IMF Bailouts Increase Global Moral Hazard?

While much of the criticism directed at the IMF has focused on its strategy in Asia, some criticize the very existence of IMF support. This argument is based on the concept of moral hazard. Moral hazard implies that investors and borrowers behave imprudently because they believe they will be bailed out if their investments go sour. IMF loans, argue some critics, exacerbate moral hazard in two ways: they absolve governments from the consequences of profligate policies, thereby encouraging them to continue the profligacy in the future, and they reward reckless investors. Because the IMF's loans to the crisis-affected Asian countries were unusually large, the critics argue that they set a dangerous precedent that will increase moral hazard worldwide.

Although multibillion dollar support packages clearly run some risk of changing investors' incentives, three reasons support the view that the critics have exaggerated the moral hazard argument. First, most investors in Asia, whether foreign or domestic, suffered substantial losses. Typical investors in Asia have seen the value of their investments reduced to a third or a quarter of their precrisis value. Second, it is hard to believe that governments relish the tough conditions the IMF imposes on them. Many governments that turn to the IMF later lose power, as they are forced to implement politically unpopular changes. Third, the costs of not intervening in Asia's crisis would have been extraordinarily high. Investors would have fled even more quickly, countries would have been forced to default on their debts, and the region (and perhaps the world) could have been plunged into an even more serious crisis.

THE NEXT STEPS

As the region's economies began to stabilize during 1998, the full impact of the crisis on corporate and banking sectors gradually became apparent. Large parts of the corporate and financial sectors in the crisis-affected countries were either insolvent or in deep financial trouble. Statistics provided by private sector analysts paint a considerably gloomier picture than official estimates. Analysts at the Deutsche Bank, for instance, have estimated that the ratio of nonperforming loans to total loans is as high as 60 percent in Indonesia and is above 30 percent in PRC, Korea, Malaysia, and Thailand (Deutsche Bank Research various issues). At these levels, if nonperforming loans were written off against bank capital the net worth of the whole banking system would be negative. To recapitalize these banks in order to reach the minimum 8 percent capital adequacy ratio recommended by the Basle standards would cost between 20 and 30 percent of GDP (World Bank 1998d).

A simulation analysis on the effect of the devaluation and of credit and interest rate shocks undertaken by the World Bank (1998a) shows that on average, firms in the crisis-affected countries lost about half of their equity value. One firm in three had loans that exceeded its equity value. Given these figures, it is clear that improving the health of the financial and corporate sectors must be a top priority across the region.

The need to restore the appropriate conditions for viable financial institutions and firms to operate normally as quickly as possible dominates the short-run agenda. That means drawing a distinction between viable and nonviable firms; restructuring domestic and foreign debt; allocating losses between creditors, debtors, and taxpayers; and reorganizing corporate control, in particular, through mergers and acquisitions.

Exactly how these various steps occur will depend crucially on each country's legal and regulatory framework. Both financial and corporate restructuring involve many complex issues. The World Bank (1998a) lists four principles for bank restructuring. First, only viable institutions should stay in business, and losses should be allocated transparently while minimizing the cost to taxpayers. Second, financial discipline should be strengthened and moral hazard minimized by ensuring that shareholders take losses first, followed by creditors, and only lastly by deposit holders. Third, the restructuring process should maintain credit discipline on existing borrowers and pro-

vide incentives for new investors to provide fresh capital to the bank. Fourth, the restructuring process should be speedy, to restore normal credit flows and confidence in the banking system quickly.

So far, the crisis countries have had varying success in financial restructuring. Most have introduced legislation to strengthen prudential regulation and improve banking supervision. Throughout the region, disclosure requirements, auditing standards, loan classification, and provisioning rules are being improved. All the crisis countries have created financial restructuring institutions, such as the Indonesian Bank Restructuring Agency and the Thai Financial Sector Restructuring Authority. All have provided substantial public money for bank recapitalization, and all have closed down some insolvent institutions. Nonetheless, they still have a long way to go before their financial sectors are fully restructured.

Unfortunately, progress in corporate restructuring has been much slower than in the financial sector. The region's firms are heavily indebted both to local banks, and in some cases to foreign banks. In Indonesia, in particular, corporate foreign debt is huge, though virtually all firms have stopped servicing their debt. Corporate indebtedness is slowing down production and investment dramatically (because insolvent firms cannot borrow), and it is also preventing a speedy solution to the region's financial restructuring (because most banks' loans are to local firms).

However, corporate restructuring in the region is plagued with problems. Most important is the weakness of bankruptcy law and its enforcement. Even though the crisis-affected countries have revamped their bankruptcy laws in the past year, they do not have enough trained people to implement them. Second, the sheer logistics of restructuring hundreds of companies are formidable. Although some of the region's governments have promoted voluntary debt restructuring between firms and banks—by, for instance, removing tax disincentives and legal barriers—few formal institutions to organize corporate restructuring exist.

The sentiment that existing shareholders should lose control of the firms is widespread. However, some argue that such a view skirts two important considerations. First, insiders possess knowledge specific to the firm, and removing them would remove an important asset of the firm. Second, the crisis-affected countries face a shortage of domestic equity capital. As banks are largely in public hands, surrendering corporate control to creditor banks would be equivalent to nationalization. These concerns may be exaggerated, but experience suggests that reforming corporate governance is a long and difficult process, strongly opposed by those currently in control. Because existing owners have better information, and often strong political ties, dramatic and rapid corporate restructuring is unlikely.

Slow corporate restructuring has negative implications for the cost and sustainability of financial sector restructuring. As most financial sector assets are corporate liabilities, the existence of insolvent firms undermines the rationale for injecting new capital into banks. There is little justification for propping up banks if their debtors are all bankrupt. The result may simply be more fiscal transfers to cover new losses later on. In this respect, unfortunately, the experience of Mexico and Eastern Europe is not particularly encouraging. There bank restructuring took longer and cost the taxpayer more than anyone had envisaged.

STRENGTHENING THE INTERNATIONAL FINANCIAL ARCHITECTURE

The severity of Asia's financial crisis, the speed with which it spread, and the shortcomings of the international response have all contributed to a wide-ranging debate on the basic rules and institutions that govern global finance. How can this global financial architecture be improved so that crises can be avoided and can be better managed when they do occur?

Background

Recent efforts to improve the global financial architecture began at the Halifax Summit of the G7 leaders in 1995. In the wake of Mexico's financial crisis, policymakers already felt that global institutions and rules needed to be updated to cope with a modern world of integrated capital markets. The existing Bretton Woods architecture had originally been designed for a world where capital mobility was limited (box 1.5). Even though it had evolved over the years, financial markets had changed far more profoundly.

As official discussions on an international financial architecture have proliferated since 1995, so an increasing number of organizations have become involved (box 1.6). In addition, a number of individual academics and other commentators have put forward their own reform proposals. The result is a plethora of ideas. However, few concrete changes have occurred. This is partly because international institutions and policymakers have been preoccupied with the immediate task of crisis management, but mainly because the issue of international financial reform is extraordinarily complex.

US Deputy Secretary of the Treasury Lawrence Summers recently referred to the "integration trilemma" (Summers 1999). He noted that in the years ahead the central task of international political economy will be to reconcile as well as possible the three goals of greater integration, proper public management, and national sovereignty. In effect, policymakers would like the international financial system to fulfill a number of goals. They would like to foster capital market integration, they would like international financial markets to be regulated and supervised just as national markets are regulated and supervised, and they would like to maintain national sovereignty. Unfortunately, these three goals are incompatible: maintaining national sovereignty in a world of free capital means forfeiting market regulation and support. Conversely, to create regulations and a lender of last resort at the international level implies overriding national sovereignty. The only way that a country can regulate and support its financial markets while maintaining national sovereignty is by controlling capital flows.

This incompatibility of goals is particularly striking in the area of exchange rate management. Policymakers want the benefits of capital market integration, they want exchange rate stability, and they want each country to be able to pursue its own macroeconomic policy. Unfortunately, these three goals are at odds. They form what economists Obstfeld and Taylor (1998) have called the "open economy trilemma."

To understand why, consider figure 1.8. Each corner of the triangle represents one of the policymakers' three goals, and each side of the triangle indicates a possible regime. "Adjustment" means

Box 1.5 **The Existing Bretton Woods Financial Architecture**

The IMF and the World Bank were set up at the Bretton Woods Conference in 1944 to prevent a repeat of the international financial problems that had occurred during the Great Depression. The IMF was to oversee the Bretton Woods system of fixed exchange rates and the World Bank was to provide capital for postwar reconstruction, and later for projects in developing countries. Plans for a third institution, the International Trade Organization, foundered in 1947 when the US Congress refused to accept it. In its place, the "provisional" General Agreement on Tariffs and Trade took on the role of reducing international trade barriers through a series of eight multilateral negotiating rounds. Eventually, on 1 January 1995, the World Trade Organization came into existence.

The World Bank's goal was to provide foreign exchange and technical assistance for development projects, particularly physical infrastructure such as bridges and dams. During the past 50 years its role has broadened to include virtually all aspects of the development process. Later a number of regional banks were founded, including the ADB. Their regional proximity and smaller size led them to be more innovative in some respects.

The IMF oversaw the Bretton Woods exchange rate regime. The aim of the Bretton Woods system was to enable countries to achieve full employment and balance-of-payments equilibrium simultaneously. Temporary deficits were to be covered from a country's own reserves and, if necessary, by loans from the IMF. Only fundamental balance-of-payment problems, that is, ones that could not be corrected without excessive unemployment or inflation, were to be corrected by exchange rate changes. The IMF's Articles of Agreement called for convertibility of current account transactions only. Article VI, section 3, gives members the right to apply controls on capital flows. In 1997 the Interim Committee—the advisory body that oversees the IMF—recommended that the Articles of Agreement be amended to extend jurisdiction to issues relating to orderly liberalization of capital markets.

The Bretton Woods system depended on countries' willingness to hold their reserves in US dollars. This, in turn, was conditional on their expectation that they could convert dollars into gold at a fixed price. In the mid-1960s, as US inflation rates rose, partly because of the cost of the Viet Nam War, confidence in the dollar's convertibility began to erode. The system collapsed after President Nixon abandoned the US dollar's convertibility in 1971 and the fixed exchange rate regime broke down.

After the breakdown of the Bretton Woods regime, the IMF formally began to oversee the new "system" of floating exchange rates. In practice, its focus moved to the developing world. It played a central role during the debt crisis of the 1980s, coordinating lender banks and providing adjustment finance. In the 1990s it has assisted formerly communist economies in their transition to market economies and has played a central role in combating financial crises.

---

that a country can pursue independent macroeconomic policies. If the economy is slowing down, for instance, the country can adjust by reducing interest rates. "Confidence" denotes the ability to protect exchange rates from destabilizing speculation. With confidence, trade and investment flows are encouraged. "Liquidity" refers to the ability to borrow money from abroad through the free flow of capital. For countries to have this liquidity, international capital flows must be free. Unfortunately, it is only possible to achieve two of these goals at once.

Suppose a country wants a stable exchange rate as well as liquidity (that is, free access to international capital). To achieve these goals it must either establish a currency board or join a monetary union. That, in turn, means giving up the policy independence associated with a flexible exchange rate. In a world of freely mobile capital, fixed, but adjustable, exchange rate pegs are unsustainable, because they would immediately be tested by currency speculators. The only way a country can maintain confidence (currency stability) and adjustment (the ability to run an independent macroeconomic policy) is by restricting capital flows. That was the combination chosen by policymakers under the original Bretton Woods regime. For the first 25 years after the Bretton Woods agreement, the glo-

Box 1.6 Too Many Architects Spoil the Blueprint?

At the last major restructuring of the international financial system in 1944—the Bretton Woods Conference—all the major participants were comfortably housed in a single rural hotel in New Hampshire. The views of just two people, John Maynard Keynes representing the United Kingdom and Harry Dexter White for the United States, dominated the conference. A comparable conference today would probably need every hotel room in a medium sized American city. With so many different agendas and vested interests, discussion on any proposals (if, indeed, any agreement could be reached) would take far longer than the deliberations at Bretton Woods.

Today a number of official groups are involved, all of which have their own ideas on how to proceed. The best known of these is the G7, which consists of the seven most influential industrial countries, and whose current membership was determined at a summit meeting in 1976. This group has become the focal point for international cooperative

efforts. Indeed, it was the G7 that coined the term financial architecture in 1995, and the G7 finance ministers have worked regularly on this issue. The most recent initiative of the G7 in this regard is the creation of a financial stability forum.

The G10 is an older group, set up in 1962, and includes 11 industrial countries (Switzerland joined later, but the name was not changed). It consists of central bank governors and finance ministers, and consequently focuses on international financial matters. The group is closely related to the Basle Committee on Banking Supervision, and both groups are based in the offices of the Bank for International Settlements. Europe tends to dominate the group, with 8 of the 11 members being European countries.

The G22 is an ad hoc group of countries set up by the United States in April 1998 and includes a number of emerging market countries. At its first meeting three working groups were set up to examine issues of enhancing transparency and accountability, strengthening financial systems, and managing

international financial crises. These working groups delivered their reports in October 1998. At the request of several small European countries, the G22 was expanded to become the G26; however, it has not met formally again.

Despite their overlapping memberships, the various groups bring a wide range of different views and perspectives to the discussions of the international financial architecture. While these different viewpoints no doubt enrich the discussions, whether this plethora of architects will eventually contribute to a more solid architecture or merely generate too much dissension and divergence about the blueprint remains to be seen.

Note: The G7 consists of Canada, France, Germany, Italy, Japan, the United Kingdom, and the United States. The G10 includes the G7 plus Belgium, the Netherlands, Sweden, and Switzerland. The G22 comprises the G7 and 15 emerging market economies (Argentina; Australia; Brazil; PRC; Hong Kong, China; India; Indonesia; Korea; Malaysia; Mexico; Poland; Russia; Singapore; South Africa; and Thailand). The G26 consists of the G22 plus Belgium, Netherlands, Sweden, and Switzerland, that is, the four countries included in the G10 but not in the G7.

---

bal financial architecture was based on a system of fixed exchange rates and strict capital controls.

During the 1960s, however, private investors gradually began to evade these capital controls, and international capital movements increased. As capital mobility increased, countries were forced to choose between the ability to maintain macroeconomic policy independence and exchange rate stability. The breakdown of the Bretton Woods system of fixed exchange rates in the early 1970s shows that industrial countries chose to maintain independence by forfeiting fixed exchange rates. Since then, the world's major currencies—the US dollar, the yen, and the European

currencies—have all floated. However, in recent years, some European industrial countries have shifted in the opposite direction. They have solved the open economy trilemma by giving up exchange rate flexibility entirely and creating a single currency, the euro.

In developing countries capital flows remained tightly controlled for much longer. However, in the 1980s, and particularly in the 1990s, the trend toward greater capital mobility has spread worldwide. Thus ever more countries face the choice between exchange rate stability and policy independence. Most have moved toward exchange rate flexibility. In 1976, for instance, 86 percent of developing countries pegged

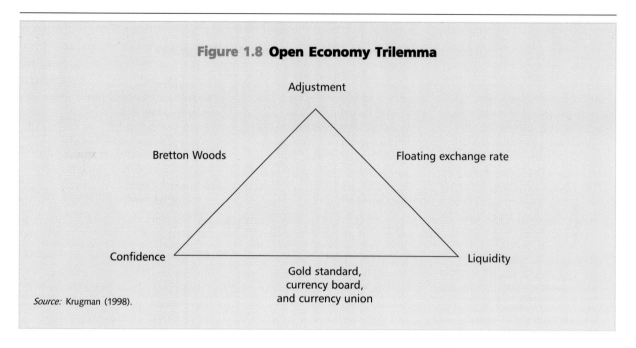

Figure 1.8 Open Economy Trilemma

Source: Krugman (1998).

their currency to a single currency (such as the US dollar or the French franc) or to a basket of currencies. Twenty years later only 45 percent of developing countries still had pegged exchange rates.

The Asian financial crisis, as well as recent crises in Brazil, Mexico, and Russia, hit countries with pegged exchange rates and heavy inflows of foreign capital. They were a direct result of the open economy trilemma. Thus at the heart of the debate on improving the international financial architecture is the thorny question of which of the three goals to give up.

Proposals for Strengthening the Architecture

Proposals for strengthening the international financial architecture abound. These proposals differ significantly in terms of their nature and scope. Some proposals are radical and demand a total overhaul of the existing structure, some are conservative and relatively easy to implement within the existing structure, some suggest more forceful responses to the crisis from the international community, while others would rely more on the market for crisis resolution. The following section reviews a set of salient proposals.

Controlling Capital Flows. One group of financial reform proposals hopes to solve the open economy trilemma by controlling capital mobility. Some commentators question the very goal of free capital flows, arguing that free trade alone should be the main objective of development and growth policies. They often put forward two arguments to support this view. First, countries can reap the benefits of free trade in goods and services without simultaneously opening up their financial markets to foreign competition. According to this view, capital mobility is an optional extra. Second, several commentators argue that the theoretical benefits of free capital flows, such as increased investment and more efficient use of funds, do not occur in reality, because the efficiency gains that a country reaps from opening up to foreign capital are more than offset by increasing uncertainty and greater risk of financial crises. Because financial markets are plagued by imperfect information and a tendency to overshoot, they bring developing countries more risks than rewards. Some economists claim that there is no empirical evidence that countries perform better with capital mobility than without.

As Part III of the *Outlook* shows, these arguments sit uneasily with both economic theory and facts. History shows that countries that try to pursue free trade while maintaining capital controls suffer a number of problems as people try to evade the capital controls. Importers, for instance, often overinvoice their shipments to smuggle capital out of the country. As economies develop and become more open, capital controls not only foster corruption, but also restrict the growth of trade.

Increasing global integration increases uncertainty. However, this also occurs as trade is liberalized. Terms of trade shocks—the sudden rise or fall in a key export or import price—are potentially as unsettling as the contagious spread of financial crises. Moreover, the claim that there is no empirical evidence of any measurable impact of capital account liberalization on a country's welfare is overstated, although the empirical work in this area is nascent.

Market integration is an ongoing multilateral process. While analyzing the costs and benefits for a single economy is possible, the ultimate benefits of integration will depend on policies followed by all countries and their evolution over time. While one country might not suffer too much by slowing down or reversing its capital mobility, the negative impact of many countries doing this could be much higher. For all these reasons, reforms of the financial architecture that are based on a broad move away from capital mobility make little sense.

However, this does not imply that all capital account liberalization is good. The record of financial crises, especially in Asia, shows that ill-planned liberalization of capital flows—without the appropriate market reforms—can result in financial instability and imply large economic costs. The Asian crisis showed that when countries open up their capital accounts without effective supervision and regulation of financial intermediaries, they become more vulnerable to crisis, because the access to foreign capital magnifies the weaknesses and distortions of the domestic financial system.

This suggests that financial liberalization must be carefully sequenced. A number of architectural reform proposals are designed to assist that process. Some concentrate on improving market regulation, bank supervision, and transparency standards. Others concentrate on minimizing the risks associated with capital flows, focusing on measures to discourage short-term borrowing in foreign currency, which is widely regarded as the most dangerous form of foreign capital.

The goal is not to proscribe international financial transactions, but simply to increase their relative cost. This can be done in a number of ways. The most widely supported is to tax foreign borrowing. Chile is the most well-known example of this approach. Until 1998, any company that borrowed abroad had to place 30 percent of the proceeds at the central bank for one year. This unremunerated reserve requirement was the equivalent of a hefty tax on short-term borrowing. Over a longer-term horizon it became much less punitive. In addition, only Chilean companies with a credit rating equivalent to that of the sovereign government could borrow abroad. Alternative ways to discourage short-term borrowing include placing limits on open foreign currency positions by domestic banks and instituting high-risks weights in the capital requirements for foreign currency loans to domestic firms.

These proposals raise a number of questions. First, should the rules apply only to banks or also to the broad corporate sector? Banks are clearly the most vulnerable institutions, but a regulation narrowly focused on banks might simply shift the foreign borrowing to firms. Second, how can such rules be effective in a financial system that lacks adequate supervision and regulation? Third, how can such prudential regulations be implemented without jeopardizing a country's broad commitment to liberalization? Finally, and most important, do they work? Evidence from Chile suggests that the main effect of the controls was not on the level of incoming flows, but on their distribution across assets of different maturities. In other words, while overall capital inflows were not affected, short-term inflows were effectively discouraged (Valdes-Prieto and Soto 1997).

While prudential controls on capital inflows may help prevent a crisis, they are not much use once a crisis occurs. However, some commentators suggest that different capital controls—this time, controls on outflows—may be an important component of crisis resolution. Imposing controls on capital outflows allows policymakers to sever the links between domestic interest rates and exchange rates. Thus they can lower interest rates and stimulate the domestic economy without incurring the cost of a currency devaluation. While capital controls themselves do not solve the fundamental economic problems underlying a currency crisis, their proponents argue that they can give policymakers time to address the relevant reform issues. (See Part III for more discussion on this issue.)

Such a strategy carries considerable risks. First, there is the risk of a strongly negative market reaction. Once a country resorts to controls on capital outflows, investors will worry that politicians could introduce them again. They will therefore demand higher returns to invest in that country again. Worse, the introduction of capital outflow controls could unsettle markets more broadly and have negative consequences for the market access of other developing countries.

Second, capital outflow controls are not often implemented and managed by benevolent governments, but by partisan policymakers in a distorted environment. They create the incentives for corruption and reduce the pressure for politicians to introduce politically unpopular structural reforms. If "temporary" controls on capital outflows remain in place for long, the negative implications for a country quickly rise. For all these reasons, proposals to sanction the broad use of capital outflow controls are unlikely to find much support among international financial architects.

Improving Regulatory Standards. One of the main causes of the Asian financial crisis was poor regulation and supervision of financial institutions. Hence it is not surprising that much of the effort to improve the international financial architecture has concentrated on finding ways to improve international standards of financial regulation and supervision.

Two of the G22 working group reports were concerned with these issues: one concentrated on transparency and accountability (G22 1998c), the other on strengthening financial systems (G22 1998b). The report on transparency contained a variety of suggestions ranging from the uncontroversial (for instance, that private firms should adhere to national accounting standards) to the ambitious (that wide-ranging data on the international exposure of financial institutions and firms should be compiled and published). The report on strengthening financial systems enumerated major weaknesses in many domestic financial sectors, such as inadequate risk management, faulty deposit insurance schemes, and mismatched assets and liabilities. It found that international consensus existed in many areas of banking supervision and securities regulation, but that in some areas best practices and standards needed to be defined, and noted that standards should be defined in a collaborative manner so that both industrial and developing countries have a voice.

The Basle Capital Accords are widely regarded as a model for international supervisory standards. Although originally agreed on by the G10, the Basle standards for minimum capital adequacy for banks are now widely accepted. To ensure that banks are adequately capitalized, the Basle standards are specified against banks' risk-adjusted-assets rather than their total assets. The Basle Capital Accords provide a framework for classifying assets according to their risk categories, specifying different risk weights for different risk categories, and calculating risk-adjusted-assets. Since 1997 they have been supplemented by a broader set of core principles of banking supervision.

One way to encourage countries to adopt such standards is through IMF surveillance. The G22 working committees, for instance, recommended that the IMF issue a transparency report along with its regular Article IV economic assessment of member countries. Another approach is to improve coordination between regulatory bodies, or even to introduce a system of peer review, whereby national regulators could supervise each other. Improved regional surveillance would be another option. In this connection, the Asian Development Bank has established a Regional Economic Monitoring Unit to support the recently initiated regional surveillance activities of the ASEAN.

Another set of reform proposals focuses on improving existing regulatory standards. Some suggestions concentrate on tightening the rules on foreign borrowing in developing countries. Others focus on changing the incentives lending banks face, in particular, by updating the Basle capital adequacy accords. Regulating lending banks has two positive effects. The first is realism: regulators of borrowing banks (in developing countries) are generally less sophisticated than those of lending banks (in industrial countries). The second effect is that better regulation might improve the incentives facing lending banks.

The existing Basle capital standards contain several perverse incentives. For instance, risk weightings for short-term loans are considerably lower than for long-term loans, which gives lending banks a clear incentive to supply short-term rather than long-term loans to emerging markets. The ongoing revision of the Basle capital standards may well contain changes to these risk weightings. The Basle supervisors are also considering the issue of banks' internal risk assessment for regulatory purposes. As the banks themselves should have the strongest incentive to act with prudence, some economists and policymakers have argued that the greater use of banks' own methods of risk assessment (value-at-risk models) can be extremely useful for this purpose. Also under discussion in this regard is the need for regulatory purposes of increased reliance on market discipline through the mandatory issuance of subordinated debt, that is, debt that has a "junior" claim on a firm's assets in the event of bankruptcy.

Compared with banking regulation, the problem of regulatory standards becomes much more severe when it comes to auditing and accounting, insolvency codes, and corporate governance. In these areas, a number of private sector bodies are active. The International Accounting Standards Committee, a committee with members from more than 100 countries, formulates international accounting standards. The International Federation of Accounts and the International Organization of Supreme Audit Institutions formulates auditing standards and issues auditing guidelines. Committee J of the International Bar Association has been concerned with bankruptcy laws and insolvency guides. The International Corporate Governance Network deals with issues of corporate governance. While all these organizations have done much useful work, much remains to be accomplished in improving standards in these areas.

To improve regulatory standards in the financial and corporate sectors internationally, some have suggested that the international financial organizations should work in harmony with these private sector entities. The international financial organizations should recognize these standards, urge adoption by their memberships, and monitor compliance. This decentralized approach to regulatory reform has much to recommend it.

More radical regulatory reform ideas include the creation of global regulatory institutions. Proposals include a world financial authority that would be the equivalent of the World Trade Organization for financial institutions and a board of overseers of international financial markets. In each case, given that the goal is to create a global supervisor and regulator consistent with global capital markets, countries would have to surrender substantial amounts of national sovereignty. That requirement renders these ideas unrealistic, at least for the moment.

Finally, in this regard, a recent institutional innovation of the G7 has been the creation of the Financial Stability Forum. This forum, which will bring together central bankers, finance ministers, financial regulators, and representatives of multilateral organizations, has an ambitious mission, that is, to assess the issues and vulnerabilities affecting the global financial system and to identify and oversee the actions needed to address them. It is too early to say what role the forum will play in the evolving international financial architecture. However, if it can create a mechanism for improving information sharing, surveillance of and agreements on standards, codes of conduct, and transparency requirements, then it would significantly increase the efficiency of global financial markets and reduce systemic risks. To achieve this objective successfully, the forum will need to expand its membership to emerging economies.

Rethinking Exchange Rate Regimes. The Asian crisis has shown that pegged, but adjustable, exchange rates are difficult to sustain in a world of increasing capital mobility. Sooner or later they are likely to be tested by a speculative attack, forcing—at the very least—high interest rates and budget cuts. The Asian crisis has also reinforced another traditional argument against fixed, but adjustable, exchange rates: by creating an illusion of permanent currency stability, they reinforce the incentive for financial institutions and firms to borrow from abroad without hedging.

Given these problems, the consensus now among economists is that only the extremes of exchange rate management are likely to succeed. Today's conventional wisdom suggests that countries must either rigidly and irrevocably tie their currency to another by adopting a currency board or entering into a currency union, or they must allow their currency to float.

Three related arguments support flexible exchange rate regimes. First, countries with floating currencies are less likely to suffer sudden crises of investor confidence. By definition, they will not waste precious reserves defending an exchange rate peg. Empirical studies confirm that serious currency crises are generally associated with the collapse of a fixed exchange rate regime. On average, countries that see a sudden depreciation of a floating currency suffer less macroeconomic distress.

Second, a flexible exchange rate regime allows the government more room to act as a lender of last resort to the financial sector. Countries committed to defending a currency peg cannot provide domestic liquidity freely without risking a loss of reserves. Countries with a flexible rate need not worry about losing reserves, because the exchange rate will simply depreciate as more domestic liquidity is created. This flexibility does not mean that countries with a flexible exchange rate can prevent financial crises generated, for instance, by large capital outflows. In fact, if the burden of external debt is high, the scope for increasing liquidity domestically may be limited.

Third, a flexible exchange rate allows a country more autonomy in regard to its macroeconomic policy. This is the classic argument in favor of floating rates (see the earlier discussion of the open economy trilemma). However, exaggerating this benefit, especially for developing countries, is easy. A developing country with significant policy autonomy may have trouble gaining credibility in international financial markets. Too often in the past governments have used their discretion to pursue imprudent, inflationary policies. Countries with floating exchange rates often have to keep interest rates high to maintain investors' confidence. Mexico's experience in mid-1998 makes the point. The peso fell by 20 percent in response to turmoil in Asia and Russia, yet Mexican interest rates were considerably higher than those in Argentina, a country with an extremely tough currency board.

The choice of currency regime will depend on a country's size, history, and geographical location. In Europe, for instance, it is likely that more countries will ultimately adopt the euro. In Latin America, Argentine policymakers are talking seriously of dollarization. In Asia, the future is much more uncertain, and the political and practical hurdles to any regional currency union are high. Yet the costs of excessive volatility and competitive devaluation are an important concern in Asia's highly open economies.

Some economists have recently advocated the need for strong coordination of exchange rates among Asian currencies. According to this view, recovery from this crisis could be strongly facilitated if the crisis-affected countries could re-adopt a dollar exchange rate target, as they did before mid-1997. While exchange rate policy does have international spillover effects, it does not mean that explicit coordination is required to achieve stability. In addition, the root causes of the current crisis were largely domestic and structural. Therefore any attempt at international exchange rate coordination without first addressing those structural problems will be based on shaky foundations and is likely to be counterproductive.

Finally, the crisis-affected countries differ significantly in terms of their history of exchange rate regimes. Before the crisis hit, exchange rate regimes in Asia were not identical. Indonesia and Korea had adopted a more flexible system (close to a crawling peg) than Malaysia and Thailand. Although the postcrisis period has seen a general movement toward greater exchange rate flexibility, the diversity in exchange rate regimes continues. This suggests that Asian economies are unlikely to see complete uniformity in exchange rate management soon.

Creating an International Lender of Last Resort. A number of reform proposals focus on preventing contagion in international financial markets by creating an international lender of last resort. The argument in favor of an international lender of last resort is based on an analogy with the role central banks play in national economies. When a banking panic hits a domestic financial system, the central bank can limit contagion by providing liquidity to the system. In a world of integrated capital markets, many argue that a similar institution is needed at the international level. By providing limited liquidity in return for policy conditionality, the IMF already plays a similar, if highly circumscribed, role. Most advocates of an international lender of last resort suggest that the IMF should play this role.

However, the proposal to create an international lender of last resort is plagued with conceptual and practical difficulties. Conceptually, scholars do not agree on exactly what a lender of last resort does. The classic definition stems from Bagehot (1873): the lender of last resort should lend freely, at a penalty rate, on good collateral in a time of financial panic.

Thus the lender of last resort must be able to distinguish between healthy and insolvent institutions, intervening only to stop unwarranted panics and leaving insolvent institutions to fail.

Extending these conditions from banks to countries and from national authorities to international institutions is extremely difficult. The first problem is that of distinguishing between illiquidity and insolvency. An international lender of last resort should provide limitless liquidity in the case of the former, and demand restructuring and adjustment in the case of the latter, but as the Asian crisis highlighted, distinguishing between the two is extremely difficult.

The second problem is that of moral hazard. National central banks put in place prudential regulations on domestic financial institutions to limit reckless behavior. They also retain the power to close or merge insolvent or weak financial institutions. Neither capacity exists at the international level. As yet, no binding global rules of financial behavior exist, and the IMF certainly cannot close down a recalcitrant country.

The final issue is that of resources. If necessary, a domestic central bank can provide limitless liquidity simply by printing money (unless it is constrained by a fixed exchange rate regime). The IMF has no capacity to issue fiat money. Its resources are limited, and despite the recent capital increase and introduction of the New Arrangements to Borrow (an emergency credit line from donor countries to the IMF), they are insufficient to make it a credible lender of last resort. To fulfill this role the IMF would need a substantial increase in its resources. Whether this would be politically feasible is unclear.

Some observers suggest that only countries that meet a stringent set of requirements, especially as concerns their banking systems, should have access to IMF funds (Calomiris 1998a). To those countries that fulfill the requirements, the IMF should lend without policy conditionality, but should demand collateral in the form of government bonds. One academic suggests that only countries that have complied with an agreed risk control strategy should qualify for IMF funds (Dornbusch 1998). These suggestions suffer from the problem that few countries would fulfill the requirements. Given the contagious nature of financial crises, it is unlikely that large countries would be left unaided even if they failed to meet the criteria. More-

over, by announcing that a country no longer fulfilled the criteria for assistance, the IMF might actually precipitate a crisis. More modest proposals suggest that this risk can be reduced by charging countries with lower financial standards higher interest rates for assistance (Fischer 1999).

A proposal put forward by the United States in September 1998, and subsequently endorsed by the G7, moves the IMF cautiously in the direction of being a lender of last resort. The goal is to set up a contingency financing facility, where countries in good economic health can set up a precautionary credit line with the IMF to reduce the chances of being hit by financial contagion. Although the idea is still under discussion, the difficulty of distinguishing between unwarranted panic and fundamental economic problems will make this facility extremely difficult to implement.

Finally, Japan has recently proposed the creation of regional currency support mechanisms to complement the role and function of the IMF. The mechanisms are institutions that would provide liquidity in times of financial crisis. These mechanisms, which could be established in Asia, the Western Hemisphere, and Eastern Europe, could be regionally funded by countries that are economically interlinked with each other by trade, investment, and so on, and are engaged in policy dialogue with each other. Nonregional countries with political and economic interests in the region could also participate. This idea of regional currency support mechanisms, which found an earlier articulation in the proposal for establishing an Asian Monetary Fund (box 1.7), is in the initial stage of discussion and development.

"Bailing In" the Private Sector. Another popular goal among the architects of international financial reform is that of bailing in the private sector. The idea is to minimize moral hazard and spread the burden of financial crisis by ensuring that private investors and banks bear some of the cost.

One approach that Argentina and Mexico have successfully pioneered is to set up private sector credit lines before a crisis. Argentina has negotiated $6.7 billion worth of repurchase arrangements with international banks. Against the collateral of domestic bonds, these arrangements give Argentina access to capital

Box 1.7 **Is There a Case for an Asian Monetary Fund?**

In September 1997, before the full international implications of the Asian crisis had become apparent, Japan proposed the establishment of a new Asian Monetary Fund (AMF). Far from undermining the role of the IMF, the AMF could act as a regional complement to the IMF in the way that, for example, the ADB complements the work of the World Bank. The sources of this complementarity are essentially fourfold:

■ The Asian crisis has demonstrated the need for an early warning system. While the problems of one or two of the Asian countries were anticipated before July 1997, the extent of the meltdown and contagion took international institutions by surprise. Thus ways to provide forewarning of impending problems are needed, and could be most effectively undertaken at the regional level, through the AMF, as the participating countries would have detailed knowledge of problems in their area.

■ Once a problem has been identified in a country, the government of that country needs to address it speedily. Given the damage that contagion can produce, regional peer pressure through the AMF could be an effective method of ensuring that this is done.

■ Given its informational advantage and regional location, an AMF would likely be more receptive—hence geared to early action—to a regional crisis than a global institution.

■ The resources the IMF initially made available were insufficient to head off the Asian crisis and additional packages had to be hastily assembled as the crisis unfolded. The AMF could provide such a line of defense on a permanent basis.

The initial proposal for the AMF suggested funding of $100 billion, half of which was to come from Japan and the remainder from PRC; Hong Kong, China; Singapore; and Taipei,China. The argument was that such a sum would provide sufficient liquidity to forestall speculative attacks on the region's currencies. Unlike the IMF's loans, the AMF's assistance would not come with economic conditions attached.

Despite strong support from Malaysia, the proposal did not get far. Only two months after it had first been suggested, it was turned down at the fifth Asia-Pacific Economic Cooperation meeting in Manila. One objection was the fear that financial support without any conditions attached would raise the risk of moral hazard. Another risk was lack of coordination and of potential conflict with the IMF.

Nevertheless, during the IMF/ World Bank Annual Meeting in 1998, Japan returned with a more modest revised proposal, the Miyazawa Plan. This proposed a $30 billion package for the region. Half of the money was to facilitate short-term trade financing, the other half was to promote economic recovery through medium and long-term projects. Japan suggested that the Japan Export-Import Bank, the World Bank, and the ADB could all participate in the undertaking. In addition to the $30 billion assistance plan, at the October 1998 Asia-Pacific Economic Cooperation meeting, Japan and the United States, with the support of the ADB and the World Bank, launched the Asian Growth and Recovery Initiative that envisages a package of $10 billion for the crisis-affected countries.

In the face of increasing instability of global financial markets, the need for regional institutions to dampen financial contagion is being increasingly acknowledged. Western Europe has a comprehensive regional financial infrastructure in the form of the Economic and Monetary Union. However, no such institutions exist in Asia, in the Western Hemisphere, and in Eastern Europe. Along with similar institutions for the Western Hemisphere and Eastern Europe, the AMF could play a potentially important role as a complement to the IMF in providing funds to crisis-affected countries and developing an early warning system. The implementation of such regional institutions as the AMF as part of the newly emerging financial architecture will help both to enhance the efficiency of global financial markets and to minimize their systemic risk.

---

in the event of a financial crisis. They are, in effect, a limited form of private lender of last resort. Such arrangements have considerable potential, particularly if multilateral development banks guaranteed some portion of the risk involved, and thereby encouraged more private banks to participate in such schemes.

More controversial are proposals to forcibly bail in private investors once a crisis has struck. One proposal, advocated by the G22, is to encourage "lending into arrears" by the IMF. Since the 1980s the IMF has been able, in certain circumstances, to lend to a country that was in arrears on its commercial bank debt. Now this idea has been extended to countries that are in default to other private creditors, including bondholders. Provided that the country is willing to undertake strong policy adjustment and is making good-faith efforts to work with creditors to solve its financial problems, the IMF can lend to the country. This effectively sanctions a default. The goal behind this approach is to encourage recalcitrant creditors to negotiate, and thereby to promote orderly and responsible debt restructuring rather than chaotic default.

The G22 working group also recommended that bond contracts be modified to facilitate restructuring. By including so-called collective action clauses, such as the collective representation of creditors, designating a trustee to speak for creditors, binding majority decisions, and formulas for sharing the costs of workouts in all sovereign bond offerings, involving the private sector in the resolution of financial crises would be easier. While an orderly workout is clearly superior to a disorderly one, the risk involved in changing bond contracts is that the market for such bonds will shrink and the cost of funds will rise.

More radical proposals along similar lines include imposing "haircuts" (mandatory losses) on investors if they flee during a financial crisis. One proposal suggests a mandatory debt rollover option with a penalty on all foreign currency lending (Buiter and Sibert 1998). This option would entitle the borrower to extend or roll over the debt at maturity for a specified period, say three or six months, at a penalty rate. The penalty would have to be big enough to ensure that the borrower would not want to exercise the rollover option under orderly market conditions. If crisis conditions still prevailed when the rollover period expired, the option could be exercised again at an even higher penalty. This proposal would only be useful when otherwise solvent borrowers are unable to roll over their foreign currency debt because of a liquidity crisis or credit crunch. It only helps when a country is solvent, willing to pay, but prevented from doing so because international financial and credit markets are temporarily closed to it. Given the difficulty of distinguishing between insolvency and illiquidity, it is not clear that a market for such options would emerge. This proposal, too, might simply raise the cost of capital for borrowing countries.

The most radical ideas for bailing in the private sector focus on creating an international bankruptcy court. Just as domestic bankruptcy courts can prevent creditor grab-races; decide on a hierarchy of claimants; and allow an insolvent, but viable, firm access to new financing, so some commentators suggest there should be an international bankruptcy court to restructure countries' debts. This idea stands little chance of being implemented. First, it would demand a huge surrender of national sovereignty. Second, national bankruptcy codes differ enormously, and reaching international agreement on a single code is highly unlikely.

Toward an Agenda of Minimum Necessary Reforms

Massachusetts Institute of Technology economist Rudiger Dornbusch has noted that in the aftermath of every crisis, whether a war or a currency collapse, a soul-searching effort to build a better world ensues. This is a great occasion for bad ideas or impractical ones (Dornbusch 1998). The Asian financial crisis is just such an occasion: it has prompted scores of proposals for a new international financial architecture.

Many of these ideas are interesting, yet impractical. Many are innovative, but often inconsistent with each other. The reason is that different reformers choose different combinations of national sovereignty, financial market regulation and support, and capital mobility. Given these incompatible goals, international policymakers are unlikely to agree on radical changes to today's financial architecture. Nonetheless, effective reforms can take place within the existing institutional system. These include the following:

■ *Negotiating minimum international standards of financial practice.* Despite considerable progress at creating international norms, auditing and accounting practices still vary considerably across countries. This makes it difficult for lenders to gauge the financial conditions of borrower banks and corporations. Differences in corporate governance practices, investor protection laws, and laws relating to insider trading in securities markets also make international capital markets less transparent and more dangerous than they need be. While individual countries should implement reforms in these areas as they deem appropriate, minimum international standards would help prevent national problems spilling over to the international level.

■ *Introducing prudent regulation of capital accounts.* While developing countries should aim for integration into the international financial system, this should not imply a reckless rush to capital account convertibility. The gradual and cautious removal of capital controls may be appropriate for countries whose domestic capital markets are underdeveloped and whose capacity to regulate excessive risk taking by domestic institutions is limited. For many developing countries, Chilean-style taxes on capital flows may be helpful.

■ *Reforming exchange rate regimes.* Large unexpected swings in the exchange rate can bring serious financial distress to domestic banks and corporations with unhedged debt exposure. This problem can be minimized in two ways. First, a floating exchange rate will induce banks and corporations to hedge their foreign currency debt. Second, a currency board or currency union will permanently eliminate unexpected currency fluctuations. International financial institutions, particularly the IMF, can push the agenda of an appropriate exchange rate regime without any fundamental institutional change.

■ *Creating the framework for an orderly restructuring of problem debts.* Debt restructuring today is a difficult, protracted process. Modest changes—including clauses for majority voting and the provision of a trustee to represent and coordinate creditors—could easily be introduced. If industrial countries included such provisions in their bond contracts, they could become standard practice, then developing countries would not incur a price penalty when they introduced them.

■ *Encouraging private sector credit lines.* Given the IMF's limited resources and the conceptual difficulties surrounding the notion of an official international lender of last resort, limited credit lines with the private sector appear promising. Argentina's contingency finance arrangements with private banks seem to have served it well. With multilateral guarantees this approach might prove useful for more countries.

These modest proposals do not constitute a new Bretton Woods. They do not call for a massive new bureaucracy nor a huge investment of public funds. However, they could help to reduce the risk of financial crises and reduce their severity should they occur. That alone would bolster, rather than hinder, the process of financial integration from which both industrial and developing countries have so much to gain.

Part 2
Economic Trends and Prospects in Developing Asia

Newly Industrialized Economies

Hong Kong, China
Republic of Korea
Singapore
Taipei,China

Hong Kong, China

The regional economic crisis has taken a sharp toll on economic activity in Hong Kong, China, with GDP falling by around 5 percent. Given the well-developed banking system, the economic downturn affected banks' profitability rather than their solvency. Developments in the regional and global economy will continue to be the key factors determining the prospects of this small, open economy.

RECENT TRENDS AND PROSPECTS

Amidst the regional economic crisis, high domestic interest rates, and depressed asset markets, the economy contracted by around 5 percent in 1998, its worst performance in recent decades. The sharp slowdown in economic activity came on the back of GDP growth of 5.3 percent in 1997, and resulted in an unemployment rate of 5.7 percent toward the end of the year, the highest level in 23 years, and stagnant earnings. The sectors that suffered the most were construction, real estate brokerage, retail trade, and restaurants. A drop in manufacturing orders toward the end of the year also led to an increase in manufacturing unemployment.

The high interest rates needed to defend one of the region's only currencies to avoid devaluation against the US dollar raised the costs of borrowing. As a result, higher mortgage payments and a deterioration of corporate balance sheets affected consumption and investment expenditures, respectively. Sharp declines in share and property markets further eroded consumer and investor confidence. The fall in retail sales of around 17 percent compared with 1997 illustrates the extent of the decline in consumer spending. Investment spending also suffered, albeit to a smaller extent, as a result of sluggish expenditures on machinery and equipment and on new building activity. The completion of the Airport Core Program, one of the largest public infrastructure projects in the world, also contributed to the slowdown in investment.

The all-important stock and property markets were depressed for much of 1998. The Hang Seng Stock Index, which achieved a peak of more than 16,000 in mid-1997, was down to a five-year low of around 6,600 in August 1998. However, it then began to pick up, starting with the $15 billion intervention by the Hong Kong Monetary Authority (HKMA) in the stock market. The property market also saw substantial declines, with apartment prices and rentals and commercial property and office rentals all significantly below their 1997 peaks. However, as in the case of the stock market, market sentiment improved somewhat, at least with respect to the residential property market, toward the latter part of the year. This was mainly in response to the introduction of various incentive schemes that lowered the costs of purchasing homes and the government's loosening of property controls.

The economic slowdown and the declines in share and property values took their toll on the banking sector. Nonperforming loans climbed to about 7 percent of banks' portfolios toward the end of the year, more than triple their precrisis level in mid-1997. The mortgage default rate climbed to about 0.8 percent, from about 0.3 percent before the crisis. However, as banks in Hong Kong, China are, on average, well capitalized, with capital in the range of 15 to 20 percent of their assets, the main impact of the increase in nonperforming loans was on their profitability and not their solvency. Net profits of the listed banks declined by an average of one third in the first half of 1998, in comparison with a year earlier.

Inflation declined steadily during the year, averaging about 2.8 percent. This was due not only to subdued imported inflation, but also to low inflation from domestic causes. The former resulted from a generally strong US dollar, to which the Hong Kong dollar is pegged; modest inflation in countries that are the major exporters to Hong Kong, China; and declines in international commodity prices. The low domestically induced inflation was because of declining property prices and rentals and negligible pay increases.

Bolstered by the huge fiscal reserves that the government has accumulated over the years, the budget for 1998-1999 was designed to be expansionary. A number of direct and indirect tax concessions were introduced, which were intended to benefit virtually all taxpayers. The government also brought in a mortgage interest allowance, which allows homeowners to deduct up to almost $13,000 against interest payments on their mortgages each year for a total of five years. This measure, along with a moratorium on land sales, through which the government earns much revenue, was aimed at stimulating the beleaguered housing market. While initial expectations were for a modest budget surplus, the final outcome was a deficit of $4.2 billion because of the sharp contraction of the economy.

On the trade front, total exports of goods declined by 7.5 percent in nominal terms in 1998. The lack of import demand in Japan and other East Asian economies that were hard hit by the regional financial crisis accounted for much of this decline. A weaken-

Table 2.1 Major Economic Indicators, Hong Kong, China, 1996-2000
(percent)

Item	1996	1997	1998	1999	2000
GDP growth	4.5	5.3	-5.1	-0.5	2.0
Gross domestic investment/GDP	32.1	35.4	30.2	30.5	31.5
Gross domestic savings/GDP	30.7	31.8	30.5	31.0	31.0
Inflation rate (consumer price index)	6.3	5.9	2.8	-1.5	1.0
Money supply (M2) growth	10.9	8.3	11.8	8.5	9.0
Fiscal balance/GDP	2.2	6.5	-2.5	-1.5	0.0
Merchandise exports growth	4.0	4.0	-7.5	0.5	2.5
Merchandise imports growth	3.0	5.1	-11.6	-0.5	3.0
Service exports growth	11.5	-0.3	-10.5	-0.8	3.5
Service imports growth	6.3	5.0	-2.2	0.5	2.0

Sources: Government of the Hong Kong Special Administrative Region; staff estimates.

ing in exports to the People's Republic of China (PRC) also contributed to this poor performance. However, with the economy in contraction, import demand declined sharply by 11.6 percent in nominal terms in 1998, leading to a substantial fall in Hong Kong, China's visible trade deficit.

As regards service trade, exports declined in particular because of subdued demand for trade-related and other business services in the region. However, tourism revived somewhat in terms of the number of visitors to Hong Kong, China toward the end of the year. This was led not only by tourists from the PRC, but also from Europe and North America. Imports of services also declined during the year, and as the value of service exports once again exceeded the value of service imports, the outcome was a surplus on invisible trade.

Given the extent of Hong Kong, China's openness and its small size, its economic prospects depend critically on developments abroad. With regional economies showing signs of stabilizing, the prospects for Hong Kong, China's external trade may be brighter than before. This will be especially so if the US dollar, and thus the Hong Kong dollar, weakens against both regional and European currencies. Key factors also include whether the PRC is able to revive its domestic demand through the policy of low interest rates and to make serious progress in its financial reforms, and whether the anticipated weakening of the US economy over the coming year is modest.

On the domestic front, much will depend on whether the easing of domestic interest rates, seen toward the latter part of 1998, can continue. The lowering of interest rates has been made possible primarily by interest rate cuts in the industrial countries, especially the United States, and by improved market confidence in the Hong Kong dollar. Property prices have dropped significantly from their bubble levels and will help make Hong Kong, China more competitive. Meanwhile, the government is going ahead with major infrastructure projects, particularly the northwest corridor railway link, and this will give some boost to investment. As long as real interest rates can come down significantly, a resumption of growth toward the latter half of 1999 should be possible. However, the economy is likely to see a mild contraction during 1999 as a whole.

ISSUES IN ECONOMIC MANAGEMENT

The impact of the regional economic crisis on Hong Kong, China's economy has been especially severe. This is largely due to unfortunate timing, as the onset of the regional crisis came around the same time that asset prices in Hong Kong, China were hitting unprecedented peaks. Repeated attacks on the Hong Kong dollar by investors anticipating a devaluation led to a sharp increase in interest rates in Hong Kong, China. (Under the currency board arrangements of Hong Kong, China's linked exchange rate system, the sale of Hong Kong dollars reduces the money supply, thereby putting upward pressure on interest rates.) Funds flowing to share and property markets were choked off, and stock and property prices began to fall.

As the economy had begun to lose its competitiveness because of rapidly increasing property prices, the downward adjustment in property prices has been a necessity. However, prices, especially rentals, are still far above those found in Singapore, a comparable economy. While one should not expect parity in property prices and rentals in these two economies— among other factors, Hong Kong, China's greater population density would naturally translate into higher prices and rentals—there is still some room for a reduction in prices, and even more so in rentals.

As regards the downward adjustment of share prices, concerns were expressed that the process was partly driven by market manipulation. The HKMA pointed out that certain investors, including some international hedge funds, sold Hong Kong dollars with the express purpose of putting upward pressure on interest rates. Because the increase in interest rates is likely to have an adverse effect on corporate profits and share prices, investors who have taken a short position in stock index futures could profit from a downturn in share prices induced by this prior sale of Hong Kong dollars.

Citing the desire to deter such activities, the HKMA spent approximately $15 billion to buy shares in the 33 companies that constitute the Hang Seng Stock Index. The increase in share prices that resulted from the intervention would have inflicted losses on investors who were shorting stocks, and may deter this form of speculation in the future. Nevertheless, some have seen the intervention as an unwelcome sign of interference by the authorities in an economy that has benefited greatly from its wholehearted embrace of market forces. With about 7.3 percent of all shares in the benchmark index, the government is now the second or third largest shareholder in these companies. This has not only raised the possibility of conflicts of interest—for example, the government influences property prices by its decisions on the release of land for new construction and is now a major shareholder in three of the city's four largest property developers—but has also raised concerns that by reducing the number of shares in circulation, the government has made it easier for speculators to influence stock prices using small trades. However, selling the shares is not simple, because if not done carefully and under the right circumstances, it may induce panic selling among the public as the sales of the government's shares send share prices down. Acknowledging these problems, the government has set up an independent body to look into the disposal of its shares. How the situation will be resolved remains to be seen, but one idea that has been discussed is to sell the shares to the public in the form of a mutual fund.

A related response by the government to high and volatile interest rates has been to introduce measures to strengthen the operations of Hong Kong, China's currency board. While some of these measures have been lauded, concerns have been raised in relation to others, particularly those involving the restructuring of the discount window, initially introduced in 1992. The new discount window will enable the HKMA to inject liquidity into the banking system more smoothly and effectively in times of large, volatility-inducing capital outflows. Hong Kong, China banks will now be able to borrow overnight funds using government bonds as collateral. As the bonds used as collateral (Exchange Fund bills and notes) are fully backed by foreign reserves, the injection of liquidity into the banking system does not entail a departure from the discipline of currency board arrangements.

The banks are expected to use around $4 billion of their Exchange Fund bills and notes to acquire end-of-day liquidity through the discount window. A result is that currency speculators will now have to spend substantially more than previously to create a serious liquidity problem in the banking system and put upward pressure on interest rates. Thus the HKMA

has moved to dampen interest rate volatility at the expense of some increase in the volatility of its foreign reserves. This has given rise to the concern noted earlier. The consequent increased fluctuations in foreign reserves could affect confidence in the currency board arrangements.

However, the possible increase in the volatility of foreign reserves is small relative to the HKMA's total foreign currency assets, which amounted to almost $90 billion at the end of 1998. Therefore, the main challenge for the HKMA seems to be to ensure that the public understands that the new arrangements do not entail any compromise on its commitment to maintaining the currency peg. In this regard, the HKMA's decision to improve the transparency of its currency board operations and its campaign to explain the inner workings of its currency board arrangements to the public are steps in the right direction.

POLICY AND DEVELOPMENT ISSUES

Guided by the principle of keeping government small and efficient, government spending is one of the lowest among economies at comparable levels of development. Moreover, adherence to the Basic Law, which states that the government should strive to achieve fiscal balance, has made budget deficits an exception, and the general trend has been one of fiscal surpluses and healthy fiscal reserves. However, a contracting economy, combined with measures to stimulate spending, have led to a fiscal deficit of $4.2 billion (2.5 percent of GDP) for fiscal year 1998 (which runs from 1 April through 31 March). Given the extraordinary circumstances that the Hong Kong, China economy finds itself in, a flexible interpretation of the Basic Law is the appropriate response.

However, the government must resist any tendency toward complacency on fiscal matters. The calls for government intervention in developing high-technology sectors triggered by the economic slowdown of 1994-1995 are sure to intensify once the current crisis has passed. There are also some calls for fiscal incentives to encourage small and medium enterprises. Unless great care is exercised in using government funds, considerable wastage could result, as has been the case in a number of economies that have followed interventionist industrial policies.

The need for fiscal restraint is especially important because of the expected increase in the share of the elderly population. Official projections indicate that the old-age dependency ratio (the ratio of those age 65 and older to those age 15 to 65) will increase by just over 4 percentage points during the next 20 years, increasing the pressure on social safety nets. Some estimates indicate that the fiscal pressures created by the need to service an aging population could lead to a public debt-to-GDP ratio that exceeds 20 percent in about 40 years. Such estimates serve to underscore the importance of careful scrutiny of proposals to encourage certain sectors of the economy.

Republic of Korea

The Republic of Korea (henceforth referred to as Korea) has made considerable progress in addressing its economic and financial crisis. While the external position has stabilized and the economy is expected to register modest growth in 1999, to sustain economic recovery the government must continue with its ongoing reforms.

RECENT TRENDS AND PROSPECTS

During 1998, with significant assistance from the International Monetary Fund, the World Bank, and the Asian Development Bank, Korea made considerable progress in stabilizing its external position. However, a severe contraction in output has accompanied its improved external payments situation. GDP declined by 5.5 percent, a dramatic reversal from the average annual growth of about 8 percent achieved during the last three decades. The industrial sector, which accounts for about 45 percent of GDP, registered negative growth of 7.5 percent in 1998, compared with an increase of 5.6 percent in 1997, while output in the agriculture sector decreased by 6.9 percent and in the service sector by 3.5 percent.

This substantial reduction in output was caused by the severe contraction of both domestic and external demand. Weaknesses in the corporate and financial sectors, the difficult external environment resulting from the Asian crisis, and the tight fiscal and monetary policies implemented in the early part of 1998 to stabilize the exchange rate all led to a severe

decline in aggregate demand. The economic uncertainty that prevailed after the onset of the crisis, the unpredictably severe credit crunch, and the deterioration in expected household incomes further exacerbated the unfavorable environment for investment and consumption. External demand fell mainly because of the economic turmoil in Asia, as the region accounted for about half of Korea's exports prior to the crisis.

Following the implementation of financial and corporate reforms, increased unemployment accompanied the economic contraction. The unemployment rate more than doubled from 2.6 percent in 1997 to 6.8 percent in 1998. Accompanying this deterioration of conditions in the labor market, manufacturing wages fell by a fifth.

The tight fiscal and monetary policy stance the government adopted until mid-1998 helped stabilize the exchange rate, but precipitated the severe economic contraction. Having achieved its stabilization aim, the government could subsequently relax its restrictive fiscal and monetary stance to stimulate domestic demand and promote economic recovery. As a result, interest rates dropped substantially, with the overnight call rate down to 6 to 7 percent in December 1998 from 21 percent 12 months previously. The benchmark market interest rate, that is, the three-year corporate bond rate, also declined sharply from 24 percent to about 8 percent during the same period.

Reflecting the more accommodative fiscal stance, total fiscal expenditures, including net lending, rose by about 18 percent in 1998 to some 28 percent of GDP. The increased current expenditures included spending on financial sector restructuring, unemployment benefits, job creation, and social safety net improvements. The higher fiscal expenditures resulted in a budget deficit of around 5 percent of GDP, up from the initial target of 1.7 percent.

The inflation rate averaged 7.5 percent in 1998, higher than the 4.5 percent registered in 1997. The rate peaked in February 1998 at 9.5 percent, largely because of the rapid depreciation of the won during the preceding months. Subsequently, the stabilization of the exchange rate; the relatively lower import prices, particularly for oil; and the deterioration in domestic demand all caused the inflation rate to fall. Although lowering the inflation rate was an important concern, the government's monetary policy was focused on facilitating the recovery of the real sector by mitigating the collapse in credit through lowering interest rates without causing undue pressure on the exchange rate.

The trade balance moved into a substantial surplus, equivalent to 14 percent of GDP. This, however, merely reflected the depth of the recession, as the demand for imports collapsed much more than the decline in exports. While exports actually experienced a growth in volume terms of 30 percent, in value terms they declined by 4.9 percent in marked contrast to 30 years of continuous growth. A number of factors account for this poor performance, including the recession in Asia; the depreciation of the Japanese yen in the first half of 1998; a cyclical decline in the world prices of industrial products in which Korea specializes, including semiconductors, chemicals, and steel; and a domestic credit squeeze that reduced the amount of trade financing available to firms. The dollar value of imports plunged by a massive 36.1 percent in 1998, compared with a drop of 2.2 percent in 1997.

The balance of payments improved in 1998 because of the current account surplus coupled with substantial assistance from the multilateral institutions. Consequently, official foreign exchange reserves increased to $52 billion by the end of 1998, up from $20 billion in December 1997.

Korea's external debt position, which was $152 billion by the end of 1998, improved only marginally, but this masks the significant progress made in reduc-

Table 2.2 Major Economic Indicators, Republic of Korea, 1996-2000
(percent)

Item	1996	1997	1998	1999	2000
GDP growth	7.1	5.5	-5.5	2.0	4.0
Gross domestic investment/GDP	38.4	35.0	29.0	27.3	28.8
Gross domestic savings/GDP	33.7	33.1	42.3	34.1	31.7
Inflation rate (consumer price index)	5.0	4.5	7.5	2.0	3.0
Money supply (M2) growth	15.8	14.1	27.9	20.0	20.0
Fiscal balance/GDP	0.5	-1.4	-5.0	-5.0	-4.8
Merchandise exports growth	4.3	6.7	-4.9	2.0	6.0
Merchandise imports growth	12.3	-2.2	-36.1	15.0	18.0
Current account balance/GDP	-4.7	-1.8	13.2	6.8	2.9

Sources: Bank of Korea data; Ministry of Finance and Economy data; staff estimates.

ing the share of short-term debt in total external debt from 40 percent in December 1997 to 21 percent in December 1998. The won began to stabilize in March 1998. By the end of December 1998 it had appreciated by 22 percent over its December 1997 level.

Although the performance of the Korean economy depends on the recovery of international investor confidence as well as on global economic conditions, the crucial factor for economic growth is for the government to implement its economic restructuring plan prudently. The economic outlook for 1999 is for improved performance compared with 1998. Considering Korea's relatively favorable external financial position, the government has some leeway for continuing to ease monetary and fiscal policy in 1999 so as to stimulate domestic demand. The economy is showing signs of bottoming out, and the worst of the economic crisis appears to be over. GDP is projected to grow by 2 percent in 1999, a significant improvement from the large economic contraction experienced in 1998. Estimates indicate some improvement in consumption and investment. Despite this recovery in GDP, the unemployment rate will be higher than the 6.8 percent recorded in 1998, because the *chaebol* restructuring will result in layoffs, and because of new entrants into the labor force. Although the economy will start to recover, the corresponding increase in employment will be realized only after a lag.

With the stabilization of the Korean won, consumer prices are expected to rise by only 2 percent in 1999. The overall deflationary trend in the world economy, the excess capacity in domestic industries, and the increase in unemployment will also subdue inflationary pressures.

The current account surplus is anticipated to fall to $25 billion in 1999 from the $40 billion recorded in 1998. Exports will increase slightly in 1998, but imports will increase much faster because of the pickup in domestic demand. Trade will continue to show a positive balance, estimated at $31 billion in 1999.

ISSUES IN ECONOMIC MANAGEMENT

Turning the potential for economic recovery into actual economic recovery depends on how effectively the government addresses both the macroeconomic and the structural weaknesses of the economy. In ad-

dition to continuing the reforms in the financial and corporate sectors, the key issues for the government in the short term include providing a social safety net program to offset the rising social costs of the economic crisis and adopting policies that will stimulate aggregate demand without destabilizing the exchange rate and prices.

The government has started to tackle these issues. It has eased fiscal and monetary policies to boost domestic demand and alleviate the prevailing credit crunch. Nominal interest rates are now lower than their precrisis levels, and real interest rates are even lower. The 1999 budget also plans for a fiscal deficit of about 5 percent of GDP. The government is committed to spending more on social safety net programs and financial sector restructuring; however, it needs to ensure that these measures do not have a serious adverse impact on external payments and are not allowed to delay the introduction of the more critical reforms in the financial and corporate sectors.

POLICY AND DEVELOPMENT ISSUES

The key development challenges for Korea in the medium to long term are the restructuring of the financial and corporate sectors. While the government has made a good start, it should emphasize four areas, namely: recapitalizing financial institutions, resolving the corporate debt situation, laying off labor as part of corporate restructuring, and improving governance standards.

Restructuring the Financial Sector

Since the onset of financial market turmoil in the fourth quarter of 1997, the government has moved rapidly to improve governance in the financial sector by strengthening the policy, legal, and regulatory framework. It established the Financial Supervisory Commission in April 1998 to supervise and restructure the financial sector. As a result, a number of nonviable financial institutions were suspended or closed, and some financially weak banks were merged, restructured, or recapitalized. In addition, international standards and norms were introduced for loan classification, loan loss provisioning, capital adequacy, and information disclosure. A timetable has been set for the banks to meet the Bank for International Settlements standard for capital adequacy ratios, with a figure of 6 percent to be achieved by March 1999, 8 percent by March 2000, and 10 percent by the end of 2000.

The huge volume of nonperforming loans is handicapping the recapitalization of the financial sector. Official estimates for 1998 placed the level of nonperforming loans in the range of $76 billion to $92 billion, or about 20 percent of all loans by financial institutions. As banks and nonbank financial institutions implement the new loan classification system, the share of nonperforming loans in their portfolios could increase significantly, implying a commensurately greater need for increased resources for their recapitalization. Financial restructuring will then require additional sources of financing beyond what the government planned. Given the current climate, financial institutions may find raising the necessary funds on their own difficult, and the government must be prepared for the additional demands that will be placed on the budget. Moreover, the government will also have to bear the interest costs of bonds to be issued by the Korea Asset Management Corporation to purchase nonperforming loans and by the Korea Deposit Insurance Corporation to finance the recapitalization, together with the contingent liabilities for guaranteeing the bonds so as to protect depositors.

Restructuring the Corporate Sector

The corporate restructuring program has two broad objectives: reducing corporate debt and improving corporate governance. Reducing corporate debt-to-equity ratios will be achieved through a combination of asset sales, debt retirement, debt-equity swaps, and new equity issues. The government has issued guidelines requiring the larger conglomerates or *chaebols* to reduce their debt-equity ratio from about 500 percent at the end of 1997 to about 200 percent by the end of 1999. To achieve this, the corporate sector will have to raise a substantial amount of resources through asset sales and new issues of equity. Success will depend on the government developing mechanisms to facilitate this debt-equity conversion. The government's effort to review the tax and regulatory framework to remove barriers to the debt-equity swaps is an encouraging beginning. It must also improve the legal framework to ensure transparent and easy accessibility to bankruptcy procedures. This is vital, because corporate restructuring will result in a sharp increase in the number of companies filing for bankruptcy. While Korea's insolvency laws are basically sound, further improvements are desirable to complement the other restructuring measures. These include steps to improve corporate governance, and involve enhancing management accountability and information disclosure, resolving cross-debt guarantees between companies and their subsidiaries, improving the financial structure, and streamlining the business activities of large corporations to focus on core businesses.

Corporate restructuring may face resistance from labor because restructuring will necessarily involve retrenchment. The government will have to ensure that sufficient measures are taken to alleviate the social costs this will entail, otherwise the resulting loss of public confidence may well undermine the necessary reforms.

For these reforms to be fully effective, sufficient expertise with the appropriate financial and accounting training will be needed. The business culture will also have to change to one that fully realizes the need for transparency and openness and appreciates the benefits of more sound accounting and auditing practices.

Singapore

Falling external demand raised unemployment and sharply reduced Singapore's growth in 1998. However, the government cushioned the impact with expansionary fiscal and looser monetary policies and a negotiated wage reduction. Singapore's high savings levels and institutional strengths position the country for early recovery from the Asian crisis.

RECENT TRENDS AND PROSPECTS

Singapore managed low, but positive, growth of 1.5 percent in 1998, well down from its 1997 growth rate of nearly 8.0 percent, but exceeding expectations in the face of the regional financial crisis. Steep currency depreciations elsewhere in Asia caused global demand to shift away from Singapore's electronics sector, which accounts for 70 percent of total non-oil exports, and output in that industry declined moderately from the previous year. Output in other key export industries, particularly chemicals and petroleum refining, also fell with declining external demand. However, stimulative government spending led to an increase in construction output.

The year's decline in regional trade flows reduced demand for the shipping services provided by Singapore, Southeast Asia's main transportation hub. Tourism, a key component of Singapore's service economy, also declined as fewer travelers journeyed to Asia in the midst of the regional recession. The country's financial and business services sector, now producing 28 percent of GDP, did better, expanding slightly as some international banks bolstered their Singapore operations.

Low growth raised the unemployment rate to 4.5 percent, its highest level since the 1986 recession. The depreciations experienced by neighboring countries had pushed up Singapore's relative labor costs, making some exports and services less competitive. To reduce unit labor costs, in August the government persuaded workers and employers to agree on a broad wage reduction. To facilitate the wage cuts while countering their expected negative effect on domestic demand, the government also cut required contributions to the national pension fund from 40 to 30 percent of wages.

After years of large fiscal surpluses, Singapore ran a budget deficit of 0.3 percent of GDP in 1998. Low growth caused revenues to fall short of expectations by about 1.3 percent of GDP, and stimulative property and corporate tax rebates increased the tax shortfall. The government bolstered the fiscal stimulus of the tax cuts by increasing expenditure in mid-year, primarily on public works. Given the need to maintain a moderate fiscal stimulus, the government expects to run a budget deficit of 3.5 percent of GDP in 1999.

Singapore's trade balance, usually positive, swung strongly into the black in 1998. Although exports fell by about 6 percent, imports dropped by 9 percent. While the trade balance improved, the services balance declined as regional demand for shipping and other services fell. In the end, Singapore registered an 18 percent of GDP current account surplus. International trade is the mainstay of Singapore's economy: in recent years total annual trade (imports plus exports) has amounted to about three times domestic output.

As did most of its neighbors, Singapore experienced substantial capital outflows in 1998, equivalent to about 13 percent of GDP. Most of those flows took the form of internal transfers from foreign banks operating in Singapore to head offices overseas. However, its large current account surplus enabled Singapore to maintain its stock of foreign reserves at around $73 billion, up $2 billion from 1997. On a per capita basis Singapore continues to hold the world's highest level of foreign reserves. In contrast to many

Asian economies, foreign debt poses little problem for Singapore.

The Singapore dollar appreciated slightly against the US dollar in 1998, rising 1.7 percent on the year. During the first nine months of 1998 the Monetary Authority of Singapore (MAS) appeared to be pursuing a policy of sterilized intervention as it accumulated foreign reserves with little increase in the monetary base. Nevertheless, during this time the Singapore dollar slid by 6 percent against the US dollar. In September the Singapore dollar began to appreciate, apparently in response to the yen's appreciation and a looser monetary stance in the United States. Presented with a more positive external environment, the MAS shifted to a more expansionary monetary policy. Short-term interest rates dropped dramatically and capital outflows increased. Given the low level of demand, however, the relaxation in monetary policy has so far not provoked inflation. Consumer prices actually fell by 1.5 percent during the year.

Based in the region's trade and financial center, Singaporean banks have considerable exposure to crisis-affected Asian countries. Loans from Singaporean banks to Indonesia, Korea, Malaysia,

Table 2.3 Major Economic Indicators, Singapore, 1996-2000
(percent)

Item	1996	1997	1998	1999	2000
GDP growth	6.9	7.8	1.5	1.0	4.0
Gross domestic investment/GDP	35.3	37.4	34.0	34.5	34.5
Gross domestic savings/GDP	51.2	51.8	52.2	50.0	49.0
Inflation rate (consumer price index)	1.4	2.0	-1.5	0.5	2.0
Money supply (M2) growth	9.8	10.3	30.3	12.0	12.0
Fiscal balance/GDP[a]	6.8	3.3	-0.3	-3.5	0.0
Merchandise exports growth	6.4	-3.1	-5.6	2.0	5.0
Merchandise imports growth	5.4	0.1	-9.0	4.0	5.2
Current account balance/GDP	15.4	15.4	18.2	15.5	14.5

a. Excluding grants.

Sources: Ministry of Trade and Industry (1996); Singapore Department of Statistics (1998); International Monetary Fund; staff estimates.

Philippines, and Thailand amounted to about $22 billion in 1998. Of that total, 18 percent constituted delinquent loans by MAS standards, thereby accounting for most of the banking sector's bad loans. That rate may continue to go up in 1999. In equity markets Singapore stocks suffered a moderate decline in 1998, with the Straits Times Index falling 6 percent in US dollar terms.

Property prices in the central business district fell 25 percent from the third quarter of 1997 to the third quarter of 1998. Although property prices rose steadily in the 1990s, Singapore avoided the type of property bubble that occurred in Hong Kong, China, and was therefore less susceptible to a large price drop. To prevent property speculation during the mid-1990s, the government imposed high taxes on turnaround sales, limited financing for housing purchases, and increased supply by releasing housing to the market.

Given the lingering impact of the Asian crisis, growth is expected to be about 1 percent in 1999. Nonperforming loans to crisis-affected countries may still increase. Wage reductions could bring about a sharp drop in domestic demand. Continued negative growth in Indonesia and Malaysia would reduce the volume of trade and demand for shipping, insurance, financial, and other services further still.

Over the longer run, however, the outlook for Singapore is good. The country's strong net debt and foreign reserves positions should limit further potential downturns. When market sentiment swings back toward Asia, Singapore should be one of the first economies to receive favorable attention from foreign investors. Eventually, Singapore's fiscal and monetary conservatism and flexible approach to economic management should bring the economy back to steady growth.

POLICY AND DEVELOPMENT ISSUES

Despite the shock from the Asian financial crisis, Singapore remains a rich economy with advanced institutions, but adjusting to the world after the crisis will require changes even in areas where Singapore has been successful. Three of those are the management of the Central Provident Fund (CPF), the administration of Singapore's exchange rate regime, and the development of financial markets.

National Savings and the Central Provident Fund

A crucial medium-term development issue for Singapore will be its treatment of savings. Singapore's remarkably high domestic savings rate of about 50 percent is due in large part to government policies. The government's fiscal conservatism is one of those policies. However, workers' required contributions to the CPF, which in 1998 amounted to 40 percent of wages with workers and employers each contributing 20 percent, may be even more important for national savings. In 1999, as noted earlier, employers' share will be cut to 10 percent to lower the cost of labor to employers and raise labor demand.

The CPF is intended first as a pension fund, but also has a major role in Singapore's economy as a source of funds for housing purchases, medical care, and insurance. In contrast with pooled pension plans, such as the US Social Security system, contributors to the CPF maintain savings in individual accounts. Recent modifications to the CPF have included increased flexibility in the use of funds for housing purchases and greater availability of a wide variety of investment vehicles for individual savers. At the end of 1998 the CPF held accumulated savings of about $50 billion.

Both the diversification of investment vehicles and the cut in the required contribution are encouraging signs of flexibility in the management of the CPF. Even as Asia recovers from the crisis and Singapore's growth accelerates, Singapore's current account surplus, supported by CPF savings, is likely to remain in double digits. Over time that surplus could become a problem, both economically and politically, which will in turn probably necessitate further changes in the operation of the CPF. Those changes could include either further reductions in the level of required contributions or even greater flexibility in workers' use of their CPF accounts.

Postcrisis Exchange Rate Regime

The MAS sets the exchange rate for the Singapore dollar through a managed float system, targeting a basket of currencies to maintain price stability while sustaining medium-term economic growth. Although the MAS does not announce the composition of either the reference basket or of its foreign exchange reserves, it admits to watching the Singapore dollar's trade-weighted exchange rate with a view to maintaining export competitiveness. However, given the importance of the external sector to Singapore's economy, the MAS tends to view the exchange rate primarily as a bulwark against inflation.

This strong currency policy has served Singapore well in the past, contributing to the city's development as a financial center, but after the crisis a reassessment may be necessary. With growth expected to be stagnant in 1999 considerable pressure for further depreciation is likely. Against this the MAS will have to weigh the need to retain investors' confidence in the relative stability of the currency.

Strengthening Singapore's Position as a Regional Financial Sector

The MAS has set its sights on making Singapore a full rival to Hong Kong, China as a financial center for emerging Asia, and Singapore is already host to a wide array of financial markets. After Hong Kong, China, Singapore's stock market is the largest and most liquid in emerging Asia and a natural focus for foreign investors in the region. In addition to the stock market Singapore has a futures exchange (the Singapore International Monetary Exchange), a commodity exchange (Singapore Commodity Exchange), and an active over-the-counter swaps market. Singapore is also the fourth largest foreign exchange trading center in the world, and the center for the offshore Asian dollar market.

One financial area where the government recognizes some room for improvement is the domestic bond market. This consists primarily of government debt, the supply of which is relatively small because of Singapore's recurring budget surpluses. Singapore issues debt through the MAS primarily to establish a benchmark yield curve. Most government bonds are held by the CPF, and the secondary market for these instruments is relatively illiquid.

Despite its widely recognized strengths, Singapore still has a reputation for regulated financial markets. Among the remaining impediments to the internationalization of Singapore's markets are restrictions on foreign borrowing in local currency and on foreigners' use of swaps, options, and forwards for obtaining credit in Singapore dollars. Singapore also maintains some restrictions on foreign issuance of debt denominated in Singapore dollars. Otherwise, foreigners generally have full access to equity, credit, currency, and derivatives markets.

To counter the perception of over-regulation and promote a reputation for friendliness toward international banks, the MAS has recently taken several substantive steps. These include the reduction (though not the elimination) of restrictions on trading the Singapore dollar offshore, and approval for a contract based on the value of Hong Kong's Hang Seng Index to be traded in Singapore's futures exchange. In 1999 the futures exchange and stock exchange will merge, foreign brokers' access to the stock exchange floor will be improved, and some deregulation of brokerage commissions will take place. The MAS has also established a new Office of Financial Sector Promotion to provide investor-friendly supervision for the markets. While these measures are encouraging, many investment banks remain skeptical about Singapore's long-term commitment to the internationalization of the Singapore dollar, and await further capital account liberalization.

Taipei,China

Despite a slowdown because of the Asian financial crisis, macroeconomic performance remains good. A crucial factor in maintaining a rapid, sustainable rate of growth is to continue developing high-technology industries. This requires encouraging both domestic research and development and foreign direct investment. The government is undertaking necessary reforms and prudent liberalization of the banking and financial sector to sustain economic growth.

RECENT TRENDS AND PROSPECTS

The Asian financial crisis slowed Taipei,China's economic growth to 4.8 percent in 1998. The industrial sector was badly hit, registering a decline of 3.6 percent against its good performance in 1997. The main source of growth was domestic demand, with services as the leading sector, but even in the service sector, growth fell by three percentage points compared with 1997. As in the past, agricultural output continued to decline.

Both inflation and unemployment rose somewhat, but are still modest by international standards. Inflation rate reached 1.7 percent, while the unemployment rate was close to 3.0 percent. With the increase in the size of the labor force, many more people were unemployed than in 1997. Nevertheless, some sectors, such as labor-intensive manufacturing activities and fisheries, experienced a labor shortage.

Gross domestic investment as a percentage of GDP increased slightly in 1998 compared with 1997. The main reason was an increase in investment in the transportation and telecommunications sectors and the building of the sixth light oil cracker plant. However, the lackluster performance of the stock market and a generally pessimistic business outlook depressed the growth of investment in the second half of 1998. At the same time, public enterprise investment declined while government investment rose by less than 1 percent. However, buoyant consumption growth, which was up 7.7 percent on its 1997 level, boosted aggregate demand. The growth in private consumption was the direct result of an earlier boom in the stock market, an increase in domestic tourism, and expenditures in local elections.

Following the decrease in both government expenditures and revenues as a percentage of GDP, the fiscal deficit also declined to 5.9 percent of GDP in 1998 compared with 6.3 percent in the previous year. A revised income tax law integrating corporate and individual taxes in a unified framework went into effect on 1 January 1998 and is expected eventually to improve the efficiency of the tax system.

The relatively low short-term interest rates and reduced reserve requirements indicated that monetary policy was fairly benign. While the money stock grew only slightly, bank loan growth still maintained a healthy pace, thereby forestalling a severe credit crunch.

Both exports and imports declined. The decline in exports, despite an approximately 20 percent depreciation in the New Taiwan dollar against the US dollar, was a result of the reduction in regional demand caused by the Asian crisis. As imports declined less than exports, the current account surplus as a percentage of GDP declined to 1.8 percent. Even so, the international reserve position remains strong. However, Taipei,China clearly cannot rely on external demand alone to sustain a high rate of growth in the immediate future.

GDP growth is expected to remain roughly the same in 1999 as in 1998, but is expected to increase to over 6 percent by 2000. This increase is largely predicated upon a boost to domestic demand through government spending on several large-scale infrastructure projects. These include the controversial $13.4 billion high-speed railway project and extensive housing construction. Consequently, the fiscal deficit is expected to remain high, at more than 6 percent of GDP, in 1999 and 2000. After 2000 revenue collection should increase faster than expenditure, and in the longer term the budget deficit will shrink.

While the central bank's anti-inflationary stance will nominally remain in force, the lower reserve ratio and the unwillingness to tighten the money supply to prevent depreciation of the exchange rate will effectively mean a looser monetary policy. With prudential regulations in place, such a monetary stance should prevent a credit crunch in the next few years.

With the domestic stimulation of aggregate demand, the depreciation of the New Taiwan dollar, and the continuing rise in the price of goods produced solely for the home market, the inflation rate is likely to increase, but only minimally, to less than 2 percent in 1999 and to 2.6 percent in 2000.

Given the rising labor productivity and the low growth in unit labor costs, low domestic production costs are likely to persist in most sectors. The weaker yen may affect the competitiveness of some exports, but it will also lower the costs of imports from Japan, the single most important source of imports. This will also help keep export prices low. Investment in East and Southeast Asia should assist in providing direct access to these regional markets. Exports are expected to experience robust growth in 1999 and 2000. For these reasons the current account is expected to improve to a surplus of $7.8 billion in 2000.

Table 2.4 Major Economic Indicators, Taipei,China, 1996-2000
(percent)

Item	1996	1997	1998	1999	2000
GDP growth	5.7	6.8	4.8	4.9	6.3
Gross domestic investment/GDP	21.2	22.0	22.7	22.4	23.0
Gross domestic savings/GDP	25.1	24.8	25.1	24.8	25.3
Inflation rate (consumer price index)	3.1	0.9	1.7	1.9	2.6
Money supply (M2) growth	9.1	8.0	8.4	8.6	8.9
Fiscal balance/GDP	-6.6	-6.3	-5.9	-6.4	-6.3
Merchandise exports growth	3.8	5.4	-9.4	9.5	10.5
Merchandise imports growth	-0.1	9.7	-5.6	6.8	11.2
Current account balance/GDP	4.0	2.7	1.8	2.5	2.3

Sources: Wu (1998); staff estimates.

ISSUES IN ECONOMIC MANAGEMENT

The effects of the Asian financial crisis have weakened demand for Taipei,China's products abroad. Consequently, stimulating domestic demand through an appropriate mix of monetary and fiscal policy has become more important than in the past. As the inflation rate is quite low, public investment projects will not lead to an overheating of the economy; however, given the inevitable delays and lags in these projects, stimulating private consumption through tax cuts is also necessary. The government should also encourage private investment by broadening the scope of investment tax credit laws. An increase in the growth of money supply to accommodate the demand for credit, especially from small and medium enterprises, is also desirable.

A small depreciation of the exchange rate that is not offset by tightening monetary policy would help keep exports competitive. Maintaining the openness of the domestic market to foreign goods while aggressively promoting exports will be crucial for regional free trade. Taipei,China has been following a cautious policy of gradual capital account liberalization. In the wake of the Asian crisis, the government is closely monitoring capital account transactions, a practice that is likely to continue in the future.

POLICY AND DEVELOPMENT ISSUES

Despite the turbulence caused by the Asian crisis, the continuing structural transformation of the economy will ultimately result in an economy based on high technology. Light and labor-intensive manufacturing activities are declining in importance, while high-technology sectors are expanding. In the changing global trade and financial environment, promoting specific industries in which the economy will have distinct competitive advantages continues to be a major challenge and policy objective. Although calling this approach a full-blown industrial policy is misleading, tax advantages and other forms of preferential treatment for export-oriented, high-technology industries are significant.

At the same time, the government should keep in mind that dynamic small and medium firms have contributed significantly to past growth. However, recent growth has also led to the establishment of some large firms in high-technology industries. It is critical that structural shifts do not lead to a sudden demise of the dynamic small firms. A combination of innovative firms of all sizes, where the small and medium enterprises play an important role in providing dynamism, may be the best structure.

Recently Taipei,China has entered into new electronics manufacturing areas while the two main producers, Japan and the Republic of Korea, remain deep in recession. More than 14,000 electronics companies in Taipei,China produce about 10.5 percent of GDP. Through these companies, Taipei,China has achieved a leading position in the global electronics and computer-related markets. Its firms occupy dominant positions in manufacturing motherboards, scanners, and monitors. It is also achieving success in producing logic and memory chips and liquid crystal display screens.

In the long run, however, Taipei,China must sustain rapid innovation through undertaking domestic research and development and taking advantage of foreign investment. An important lesson in light of the changing comparative advantages of the Asian developing countries and the decline in the competitive advantage of traditional, low-technology commodities is that domestic efforts to create research and development facilities are crucial, even in an open economy. This needs to be reflected through increased support of innovation activities in centers such as the science-based industrial park in Hsin-Chu City. Given its substantial foreign exchange reserves and rising productivity, Taipei,China stands a good chance of sustaining such efforts. The main reasons that it needs to focus even more attention on this area are the current business pessimism, the increased competition from industrial economies, and the uncertainties of developing profitable niches in high technology.

To maintain the momentum of structural transformation, a further area that needs attention is the liberalization of financial and capital markets in the face of the continuing turmoil in the region. Capital markets are being liberalized with the introduction of new financial instruments and the entry of new financial institutions. However, an ad hoc committee of Ministry of Finance and central bank representatives has suggested strengthening financial institutions along with carrying out further liberalization. Increased prudential regulation, bank supervision, and other aspects of internal regulation are being emphasized. The authorities are also considering improving the system of making provision for losses and establishing a system for quickly writing off bad debts. Historically, Taipei,China's financial liberalization has been a gradual process. In the past, observers criticized the pace as too slow, but given the problems that excessively rapid liberalization has caused elsewhere in the region, this may, in retrospect, have been to Taipei,China's advantage.

The strengthening of financial sector regulation has prevented a contraction in credit from causing systemic banking and corporate crises to date. The financial problems in much of Asia have made the government somewhat cautious with respect to the free play of market forces in the financial sector. Nevertheless, a more liberalized financial system should remain on the long-term policy agenda. Reforms already under discussion include allowing commercial banks to become involved in investment banking by entering the securities and bond markets. The authorities also launched a domestic futures exchange, thereby giving companies the option to hedge risks

without going offshore. In addition, the government has taken steps to privatize state-run banks, at the same time requiring private banks to maintain a somewhat higher risk-weighted capital ratio.

Enhancing competition in financial markets consequently remains a major objective. The strategy for making Taipei,China a regional financial and economic center—the so-called Asia-Pacific Regional Operations Center plan—is still in operation. For this plan to succeed, the government will need to undertake a number of policy reforms and development of the physical infrastructure and institutional framework. The financial reforms should facilitate the economy's continuing transformation to high-technology production.

As in the past, relations with the People's Republic of China remain a highly sensitive area fraught with uncertainty. Taipei,China is aiming to achieve stable relations, and even direct trade and transport links, with the People's Republic of China. Positive developments in this direction should improve the general business climate. Given political stability, even with the adverse effects of the Asian crisis, Taipei,China should be able to transform its economy and in the near future join the league of industrial countries with advanced technologies.

People's Republic of China and Mongolia

People's Republic of China
Mongolia

People's Republic of China

In contrast to much of Asia, the economic performance of the People's Republic of China (PRC) continued to be robust. The recently initiated fiscal stimulus package should enable the economy to maintain a good growth momentum. Although the Asian crisis has not had a major direct effect on the PRC, the government should give high priority to addressing the economy's structural vulnerabilities.

RECENT TRENDS AND PROSPECTS

Despite the unprecedented economic crisis in Asia in 1998, the PRC's economic growth continued to be robust in 1998. Notwithstanding a major slowdown in exports and severe floods along the Yangtze River that adversely affected agricultural production, GDP grew by 7.8 percent, a percentage point lower than in 1997.

Even as many industries suffered from excess capacity, the industry and construction sector, which accounts for about half of GDP, registered still robust growth of 8.9 percent, albeit slightly less than in 1997. The service sector continued to exhibit significant growth, expanding by 9 percent in 1998. This sector is continuously benefiting from the growth and transformation of the economy, which is generating increased demand for financial, accounting, legal, trade, and other services. The growth in agricultural output was, however, modest at 2.5 percent, compared with 3.5 percent in 1997.

The registered urban unemployment rate in mid-1998 was about 3 percent, but this figure may not be reliable. Adjusting registered unemployment for those laid off because of enterprise reforms and civil service redundancies brings the figure closer to 8 percent. Official data on rural unemployment and underemployment are not available, but rural areas have substantial surplus labor.

Although the Asian crisis has not had a major impact on the PRC's overall economic performance, it did have an adverse effect on exports in 1998. Largely because of the severe recession in Asia, exports stagnated, growing by only 0.5 percent despite increased exports to North America and Europe. This export performance stands in marked contrast to the growth of 21 percent achieved in 1997. Imports declined by 1.5 percent in 1998, compared with growth of 2.5 percent in 1997. This reflected the large extent of excess capacity and accumulation of inventories in many domestic sectors. As a result, external trade registered a surplus of $44 billion and the current account showed a surplus of $25 billion, representing 2.5 percent of GDP.

Notwithstanding a significant slowdown of foreign capital flows to emerging markets in the

Table 2.5 **Major Economic Indicators, People's Republic of China, 1996-2000**
(percent)

Item	1996	1997	1998	1999	2000
GDP growth	9.6	8.8	7.8	7.0	6.5
Gross domestic investment/GDP	39.6	38.2	39.0	40.0	40.0
Gross domestic savings/GDP	40.5	41.5	41.5	41.0	40.5
Inflation rate (consumer price index)	8.3	2.8	-0.8	2.0	3.0
Money supply (M2) growth	25.3	17.3	15.3	17.0	17.0
Fiscal balance/GDP	-0.8	-0.7	-1.2	-1.2	-1.2
Merchandise exports growth[a]	1.5	21.0	0.5	-5.0	1.9
Merchandise imports growth[a]	5.1	2.5	-1.5	5.0	6.0
Current account balance/GDP	0.9	3.2	2.5	1.0	0.5
External debt/GDP	14.2	14.5	14.1	14.0	14.0

a. Based on customs data.

Sources: State Statistical Bureau (1998); staff estimates.

aftermath of the Asian crisis, foreign direct investment of $45 billion in the PRC was slightly higher than in 1997. By December 1998 official foreign exchange reserves, at $145 billion, exceeded the $138 billion external debt. Despite much speculation about a possible devaluation of the yuan, the comfortable external payments position and strong macroeconomic fundamentals enabled the government to avoid devaluing the currency. This was a major contribution to containing the Asian contagion.

The government followed a strategy of stimulating domestic demand by easing monetary policy and implementing a fiscal stimulus package that increased public investment, particularly for infrastructure. This was a key factor in helping the PRC achieve a robust growth rate in an environment where external demand was weak.

The government's efforts to promote more effective allocation of credit involved abolishing the centrally directed credit plan. Under this plan the People's Bank of China, the central bank, fixed both the aggregate and the sectoral allocation of bank credit. As of January 1998, banks were allowed to allocate credit based on their commercial judgment rather than on the central bank's directives. The reserve requirements against deposits for banks were reduced from 13 to 8 percent in March 1998. Interest rates were lowered four times, with the prime rate declining from 5.7 percent in December 1997 to 3.8 percent by December 1998.

The fiscal stimulus package announced in the second quarter of 1998 consisted of Y200 billion ($24 billion, or about 2.5 percent of GDP in 1998) of additional public investment to be implemented during 1998 and 1999. Half of this investment was financed by issuing special Treasury bonds and the remainder by bank credit. The package covered mainly infrastructure investments, with more than 85 percent of the financing going toward projects in irrigation, forestry, urban infrastructure, transport, and communications. The authorities gave about Y50 billion of the proceeds from the issue of the special Treasury bonds to local governments to finance local infrastructure projects.

As a result of these measures, public investment, which increased at an annualized rate of 10.3 percent in the first quarter of 1998, grew faster in the subsequent three quarters. Gross domestic investment also registered an increase of approximately 14 percent in 1998, substantially more than in 1997.

The investment boom had the desired effect of increasing GDP growth in the latter part of 1998. The fact that the government's investment stimulus package affected production that did not rely heavily on imports contributed to the decline in imports.

The PRC's growth prospects for the next two years depend on a number of factors, including implementation of the remainder of the public investment stimulus package and changes in the world economy.

Export prospects are likely to remain weak for several reasons as follows:

■ The crisis in Asia will continue to adversely affect demand for the PRC's exports, as about 60 percent of exports are shipped to Asia (with Hong Kong, China; Japan; and the rest of Asia each taking a 20 percent share).

■ The substantial depreciation of the currencies of many Asian countries that compete directly with about 30 percent of the PRC's exports may eventually erode the competitiveness of some of the PRC's exports.

■ The recent growth projections for most of the industrial countries indicate a general economic slowdown.

Recognizing the difficult external environment confronting exports, the government has developed a set of incentives for exporters, including tax rebates,

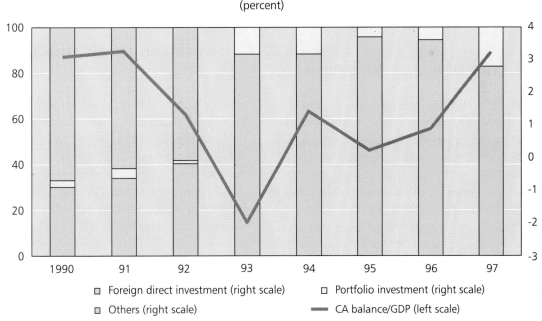

Figure 2.1 **Long-Term Capital Inflows and Current Account Balance, People's Republic of China, 1990-1997**
(percent)

Sources: People's Bank of China; State Statistical Bureau.

tariff breaks on imported capital goods, and preferential credit for exporters. While these measures should have a positive effect on exports, given the difficult conditions in world markets, the PRC's exports are projected to decline by about 5 percent in 1999.

As the economy continues to experience slower but still robust growth, the excess capacity in domestic industries and the scope for relying on inventories as substitutes for imports will decline. Also, as other Asian countries regain economic stability, their export capabilities should improve. These factors should lead to an increase in imports. Coupled with weak export prospects, this is likely to result in a decline in trade and current account surpluses during the next two years.

In 1999 as in 1998, continued implementation of the investment stimulus package and reconstruction in the areas affected by the floods will cushion some of the adverse effects of weak external demand. The PRC should continue to achieve robust GDP growth given that a portion of the Y200 billion public investment package still remains to be spent in 1999, and the government will continue its expansionary monetary and fiscal policy. In the absence of any unexpected internal or external shocks, GDP is forecast to grow at an annual rate of about 7.0 percent in 1999 and 6.5 percent in 2000.

ISSUES IN ECONOMIC MANAGEMENT

The immediate challenge facing macroeconomic management is to maintain a robust, but sustainable, growth rate through prudent use of monetary and fiscal policies. A critical need is to create enough employment opportunities to reduce unemployment and to absorb the growth in the labor force. A number of factors make this a priority issue.

The continuing state-owned enterprise (SOE) reforms and the reduction in size of ministries and departments are expected to contribute to a worsening of the unemployment situation, especially in urban areas. By June 1998 about 12 million workers had been laid off from SOEs, and another 10 million are expected to be laid off as SOE reforms proceed. About 4 million government employees were made redundant as part of the reduction in size of the civil service initiated in 1998. Given these layoffs and the natural

growth of the labor force of about 1.2 percent per year, even with an annual GDP growth rate of 7 percent, the unemployment rate is likely to increase in the next few years. The worsening unemployment situation could be a source of social unrest, which might slow down the much needed structural reforms in the financial and enterprise sectors. The government is aware of this danger, and plans to accelerate the development of improved social safety net programs and pensions. It has also initiated measures to retrain and redeploy laid off workers. Virtually every city has employment centers that provide counseling services, and most cities have established retraining centers or programs. Further strengthening of these initiatives will help ameliorate the social costs of enterprise reforms.

A significant part of the PRC's growth in 1998 was investment-led. Considering the country's infrastructure needs, the continuing program of fiscal expansion focusing on infrastructure investment is sound. The key challenge for the next year or so is to implement the remainder of the public investment stimulus package efficiently and to ensure that the funds are allocated to sound projects. With the PRC's small public debt, there is some scope for fiscal expansion without endangering macroeconomic stability.

POLICY AND DEVELOPMENT ISSUES

The PRC's cautious approach to external sector liberalization and its sizable dependency on foreign direct investment rather than on the volatile forms of short-term capital, helped the country avoid the crisis other Asian countries experienced. Nonetheless, some of the structural weaknesses in the Southeast and East Asian economies are also evident in the PRC, particularly in its financial sector and SOEs. Reform of the pension system is another area that the government will address in the medium term, with Asian Development Bank assistance. The urgent requirement for pension reforms arises from the need to finance the pension liabilities of the SOEs, which are being restructured, liquidated, or privatized.

During the last two decades, the PRC has made considerable progress in establishing the foundations for a modern financial system. Nevertheless, weaknesses persist. The key issues that the government needs to address include introducing prudential norms and risk management practices to strengthen the financial soundness of the banking system, developing the institutional capacity of the central bank to manage and supervise the financial sector, developing the regulatory framework for nonbank financial institutions, and reforming and developing capital markets.

Four state commercial banks dominate the financial sector. Strengthening these banks is a crucial component of the financial sector reform strategy. The official estimate of nonperforming loans of these banks is about 20 percent of their outstanding loans, or $170 billion. About 30 percent of these ($50 billion) are considered to be unrecoverable. If internationally practiced norms are applied, the proportion of nonperforming loans may be even higher. For example, private credit rating agencies such as Standard and Poors believe that the actual extent of nonperforming loans of the PRC banking system is much higher than official estimates. Whether the official figures or those of the rating agencies are used, recapitalizing the banks will be a challenging task.

In 1998 the government took a major policy initiative to increase the capital adequacy ratios of the four state banks to 8 percent. Special state treasury bonds worth Y271 billion (about $32 billion) were issued to provide funds for their recapitalization. The government also initiated measures to introduce stricter prudential norms and internationally comparable risk management methods in the banks. Successful implementation of these measures will require extensive training in modern financial accounting and banking techniques, such as asset-liability management, credit and risk evaluation, liquidity management, and risk-based provisioning. It will also require management information systems to support quick, informed decisionmaking at all levels of bank management and to ensure that regulators have access to necessary information on a timely basis.

In the nonbank financial sector, the government has shown the political will not to provide government funds to bail out some of the ailing institutions. The government plans to address the problems among the 240 or so trust and investment companies by closures and mergers, so that they do not threaten the remainder of the financial sector. Trust and investment companies account for about a quarter of the

assets of the nonbank financial sector. In 1997 the China Agribusiness Development Trust and Investment Corporation, the PRC's second largest nonbank financial institution, was closed because of insolvency resulting from fraudulent and illegal activities. This was followed in 1998 by the closure of the China Venturetech Investment Corporation, the Hainan Development Bank, and the Guangdong International Trust and Investment Corporation. These closures sent the right signals that the government is serious about restructuring the financial sector. The legal framework for the capital market was significantly improved with the passage of the new Securities Law in December 1998, for which the Asian Development Bank had provided technical assistance.

Many of the problems in the financial sector are related to ailing SOEs that have large amounts of loans from the financial sector, especially from banks. While some SOEs are profitable, many are having difficulties servicing their loans. Some similarities are apparent between these enterprises and the *chaebols* of the Republic of Korea, especially in terms of their governance structure, their dominant role in the economy, and their relationship with the banking sector. These enterprises needed to be restructured and reformed to improve industrial efficiency and prevent further deterioration of the position of financial institutions. The role of boards of directors and the standards of accounting, auditing, and information disclosure need to be strengthened to improve enterprise governance.

The government's long-term goals for SOE reforms include concentrating state resources in a core group of 1,000 companies that will dominate the major sectors and compete on a global scale, and reducing the government's role in commercial decisionmaking by separating the business operations under ministries from their policy and regulatory functions.

The financial sector cannot be completely reformed unless the SOEs, which account for a major share of the nonperforming loans, are restructured and reformed. Neither of these is possible unless the SOEs are absolved of their excessive social commitments (for instance, pensions, health, education, and housing) and these are financed in some other way.

In recognition of these emerging imperatives, in 1997 the government announced major initiatives to restructure the country's pension system. These initiatives aim at moving the defined benefit, pay-as-you-go pension system currently in place in both SOEs and other enterprises toward a multipillar, fully funded system (comprised of mandatory, defined benefit social pension; a mandatory, defined contribution, funded individual pension; and a voluntary supplementary insurance scheme).

The government will face many challenges in reforming the pension system. A few of the more important include financing the transition to the new pension system, regulating the system, managing the funds, and extending the coverage of the reformed pension system. The initiatives the government has taken to develop a multipillar pension system is a major step in reforming the country's social security system.

Mongolia

During 1998 overall economic performance remained positive, but diminished because of the negative impact of the Asian and Russian crises, as well as political uncertainties. Real GDP grew by 3.5 percent, the tugrik maintained some degree of stability compared with major Asian currencies, and inflation continued its downward trend. The return of political stability would contribute to Mongolia's economic growth and development.

RECENT TRENDS AND PROSPECTS

In 1998, for the second year in a row, Mongolia achieved growth accompanied by lower inflation. The 3.5 percent economic growth achieved in1998, while down from 4.0 percent in 1997, was nevertheless remarkable given the adverse impact of the Asian and Russian crises. The agriculture and industry sectors, which together account for about 71 percent of GDP, contributed substantially to offsetting the negative impact of depressed world prices for copper, gold, and cashmere, Mongolia's main exports.

The fall in the inflation rate was a major success. The consumer price index rose by 6.0 percent in the 12 months ending December 1998, compared with 17.5 percent during the previous year. Factors that contributed to this reduction included the relative stability of the tugrik compared with the currencies of Mongolia's major Asian trading partners. It was also aided by the government's continued tight monetary policy. Among the components of the retail price index, while the costs of housing, utilities, and household items declined throughout the year, the prices for foodstuff, transport, and communications rose sharply.

The trade and current accounts both deteriorated during the course of the year, moving into deficit. The continuing depressed state of international prices for Mongolia's main exports more than offset their increased production volumes. The overall result was a 17.5 percent reduction in export earnings. At the same time, the value of imports increased by 7 percent, mainly as a result of the tugrik's stability, which was due to the Bank of Mongolia's exchange rate policy. Consequently, Mongolia incurred a trade deficit of $107 million in 1998, compared with a surplus of $30 million in 1997. The current account balance moved from a surplus of about $13 million in 1997 to a deficit of $124 million (12.1 percent of GDP) in 1998. Mongolia's policy of prudent borrowing at concessional terms has meant that the ratio of debt service to export earnings remained at around the 1997 level of some 6 percent in 1998, but is expected to decline somewhat in the next few years.

The World Bank estimates that 36 percent of households—particularly those headed by women—

are now below poverty line. Although the official un-employment rate is about 7 percent, a more realistic figure that takes hidden unemployment into account is around 20 percent. Unemployment and poverty are now forcing the government to focus on developing better social protection systems. It is also being com-pelled to consider adopting policies aimed at alleviat-ing poverty directly by increasing incomes and promoting employment opportunities for women.

Fiscal performance in 1998 was disappointing. The government's deficit widened to 10.3 percent of GDP, compared with 8.6 percent in 1997. A major rea-son for this was a decline in tax revenues brought about by the dwindling earnings of the major export compa-nies. Moreover, the government's efforts to cut cur-rent expenditure were insufficient. The greatest adverse impact on the budget was due to reduced in-come taxes and dividend payments from the Erdenet copper mines, the largest contributor to the state bud-get. To partially offset this, the government has taken a number of revenue measures. The most important of these was to increase the value-added tax rate from 10 to 13 percent, to raise the petroleum excise tax

from 3 to 7 percent, and to introduce an export duty of 13 percent on gold exports.

On a more positive note, the Bank of Mongolia remained committed to maintaining a tight monetary policy aimed at keeping inflation under control. In compliance with parliamentary guidelines for ex-change rate policy in 1998, the Bank of Mongolia in-tervened in the market to maintain fluctuations in the exchange rate to within a range of 5 percent of the rate against the US dollar at the end of 1997.

The future development of Mongolia's economy depends critically on continued political stability. As-suming that this is achieved, noninflationary growth should continue, albeit at a slower pace. With contin-ued commitment by the Bank of Mongolia to control inflation, the inflation rate should remain in single digits for the medium term.

The reform and restructuring of Mongolia's banking system will put further pressure on the gen-eral budget. However, reforms in the management and financing of the public sector could result in savings in the form of increased efficiency and better cash management. The overall fiscal deficit as a propor-

Table 2.6 Major Economic Indicators, Mongolia, 1996-2000
(percent)

Item	1996	1997	1998	1999	2000
GDP growth	2.4	4.0	3.5	3.5	4.0
Inflation rate (consumer price index)[a]	58.7	17.5	6.0	9.5	5.0
Money supply (M2) growth	25.8	32.5	-1.7	—	—
Fiscal balance/GDP	-8.2	-8.6	-10.3	-8.9	-7.4
Merchandise exports growth	-12.8	34.3	-17.5	8.4	9.3
Merchandise imports growth	4.5	5.4	7.0	0.8	6.5
Current account balance/GDP[b]	-10.0	1.3	-12.1	-7.6	-7.0
Debt service/exports	11.8	6.3	6.2	4.3	4.6

— Not available.

a. End of period.
b. Excludes official transfers.

Sources: Bank of Mongolia (1998); International Monetary Fund data; staff estimates.

tion of GDP should remain relatively high, at least through 1999, before beginning to show any noticeable improvement.

Export earnings should improve in 1999 as world demand for most commodities is expected to pick up, leading to a recovery in their prices. However, the strong inflow of cheap imports has strengthened calls within the government to reimpose some trade restrictions. Taking all factors into consideration, the trade balance should show some improvement in 1999 and beyond.

ISSUES IN ECONOMIC MANAGEMENT

Mongolia's short period of democracy has reached a critical phase. The achievement of political maturity is crucial to social development and economic growth. Frequent changes in the government, together with a confrontational attitude on the part of the political parties, have led, especially in 1998, to a virtual paralysis of government machinery. It has hampered the progress of economic reforms in both the private and public sectors, and thereby reduced the potential growth rate.

The political instability, specifically, frequent changes in government priorities, has also adversely affected the flow of bilateral and multilateral assistance. The new government that took office in December 1998 has indicated its commitment to continued reforms. The hope is that with a greater degree of political consensus, the reform process can recoup the lost ground.

A further issue central to Mongolia's efforts to achieve economic stability is the importance of adhering to the requirements of a solid, medium-term adjustment program as developed under the International Monetary Fund's Enhanced Structural Adjustment Facility arrangement. The required measures under the Enhanced Structural Adjustment Facility to consolidate the fiscal deficit and to move decisively on the plans for financial sector reforms will go a long way to enhance economic stability.

POLICY AND DEVELOPMENT ISSUES

The government's major policy aim must be to consolidate the reforms already implemented to facilitate Mongolia's transition from a centrally planned to a market economy. The legal and institutional framework required for the efficient operation of a market economy needs further strengthening. Successful achievement of the Enhanced Structural Adjustment Facility objectives are of great importance in this regard. The adoption and implementation of the Public Sector Management and Finance Act would also go a long way toward imposing strong discipline on the government's finances, and would also provide the required governance framework for a market economy.

The banking sector reforms should be dealt with as a priority to regain the lost confidence in the sector. Fiscal adjustment should also be undertaken to regain control over the budget deficit and reverse the upward trend in the nation's debt to GDP ratio. Improved efficiency in government management and financing would also help reduce the drain on resources caused by the fiscal deficit and improve the domestic savings-investment balance.

After years of the government's development strategy giving high priority to providing physical infrastructure, the new government's intent to pay more attention to human development and the social aspects of economic growth is extremely welcome. The government will need to give high priority to addressing the problems of high unemployment and poverty. These are concentrated within the provincial capitals and have resulted from the closure of a number of state-owned enterprises that have lost their competitiveness in the changed circumstances of an open market economy.

Central Asian Republics

Kazakhstan
Kyrgyz Republic
Tajikistan
Uzbekistan

Kazakhstan

The precipitous fall in major commodity prices and the Russian crisis have both had a significant impact on Kazakhstan's economy, with negative growth obtained in 1998 and likely to persist in 1999. The present situation highlights Kazakhstan's long-term need to diversify from its dependence on raw material exports and trade with Russia.

RECENT TRENDS AND PROSPECTS

External shocks had a major negative effect on the economy during 1998. These stemmed from the precipitous fall in the prices of Kazakhstan's main export commodities, such as oil, metals, and grain, and the Asian and Russian crises. Given that about 40 percent of Kazakhstan's trade is with Russia, the crisis that broke out there in August had a particularly serious impact. As a result, GDP contracted by an estimated 1.5 percent in 1998, despite the positive growth achieved in the first part of the year.

With a record low harvest of 6.9 million tons of grain, the agriculture sector registered a decline of 10 percent. The main cause was the severe summer drought in the northern grain producing regions. Livestock production in cattle, sheep, and horses continued to decline, while chicken and hog production showed a modest increase. A continued decrease in the use of fertilizers and tractors and in the total acreage cultivated was also apparent.

The industrial sector, which accounts for one fifth of GDP, shrank by 1.6 percent during the first ten months of 1998. Ferrous and nonferrous metallurgy and the oil industry continued to grow, although the decrease in the demand for oil from Russia kept oil production only slightly above its 1997 level. Almost all other industrial subsectors experienced no real growth, and production of chemicals and machine building fell drastically. As in 1997, construction activities grew strongly because of the establishment of the new capital in Astana. The service sector grew modestly.

After accounting for hidden unemployment, official statistics gave total unemployment in 1998 as 6.9 percent. Considering the present severe economic difficulties, the number of unemployed is likely to increase substantially, even if official statistics may not always reflect the situation. Similarly, poverty is expected to rise, and 30 percent of the population are already below the poverty line.

In 1998 total government revenues, 88 percent of which come from tax revenues, amounted to 13.6 percent of GDP, and total expenditures were about 18.4 percent of GDP, with the budget deficit equal to 5.8 percent of GDP. This deficit was financed mostly by receipts from privatization and by foreign sources.

Faced with a deteriorating fiscal situation, especially since the second quarter of 1998, the government took measures to strengthen tax collection and administration and made two rounds of spending cuts to stay within its fiscal target. However, delays in payments of wages and pensions to public sector workers occurred.

The central bank continued to follow tight monetary policy to curb inflation further. The tenge continued its real appreciation against the US dollar until the outbreak of the Russian crisis. In defending the tenge the central bank spent $600 million, or about 30 percent of its reserves, and raised its refinancing rate in two stages from 18.5 percent in July 1998 to 25.0 percent in November 1998. As a result, the tenge depreciated by 8.5 percent for the year. Inflation amounted to 1.9 percent for the year.

For the first ten months of 1998 total trade turnover was up by about 10 percent compared with the same period last year, with $5.1 billion in exports and $6.5 billion in imports. Although the volume of exports increased, their value fell by more than 12 percent, mainly reflecting weak world prices for oil, metals,

and grain, which constitute about 75 percent of Kazakhstan's exports. Major imports consisted of oil, oil products, and investment goods as in previous years. As the Russian ruble dropped sharply in value relative to the tenge, the trade deficit with Russia is expected to have grown during the last part of 1998. At 6.7 percent of GDP in mid-year, the current account deficit was significantly higher than in the past, and was expected to remain high through the end of the year. To date the government has financed the current account deficit without difficulty through large capital inflows. Attracted by Kazakhstan's huge oil and gas potential, foreign direct investment grew by 28 percent per year during 1994-1997, reaching $1.32 billion in 1997 and an anticipated $1.3 billion in 1998. Consequently, Kazakhstan's external debt situation remains under control.

ISSUES IN ECONOMIC MANAGEMENT

Currently, the government's main focus is controlling the economic crisis. It has revised the budget for 1999

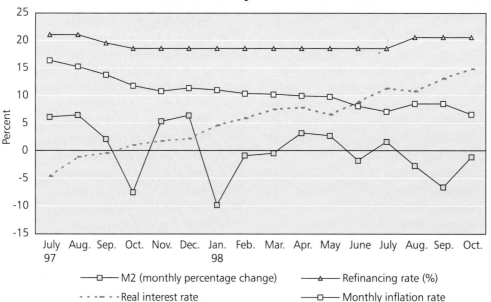

Figure 2.2 Money Supply, Interest Rates, and Inflation, Kazakhstan, July 1997-October 1998

Sources: National Bank of Kazakhstan; State Committee for Statistics and Analysis.

to reflect the deteriorating fiscal and economic conditions in January 1999. The thrust of the revised budget is to cut current and capital expenditure further and to strengthen tax collection and administration. In addition, it will continue to follow a tight monetary policy to keep inflation under control. While the relative appreciation of the tenge against the currencies of Kazakhstan's major trading partners, especially the Kyrgyz Republic and Russia, has helped keep inflation in check, imports from these countries have risen substantially. By February 1999, Kazakhstan had unilaterally imposed temporary tariffs (lasting six months) of up to 200 percent on imports from its neighbors. Finding a more permanent solution to the problem of excessive imports will present the government with a serious challenge. The current account deficit may continue to widen, and foreign direct investment is unlikely to reach the high level achieved in the past few years. As the economic recession persists, unemployment and the poverty level are both likely to rise.

POLICY AND DEVELOPMENT ISSUES

Kazakhstan possesses many favorable conditions for long-term development. The single most serious constraint to its oil exports is the need to construct a new pipeline. When the participating parties eventually resolve the problems concerning pipeline construction, this will enable Kazakhstan gradually to realize the vast wealth potential of its oil reserves. The government has also started thinking seriously about long-term development strategies, including how best to use its oil wealth. To achieve future sustained prosperity, however, the government must deal with the restructuring of the economy on a high priority basis. Restructuring should include both enforcing bankruptcy proceedings and accelerating the privatization process.

Despite the progress achieved to date, especially in privatizing small and medium enterprises, a large and increasing number of enterprises are inefficient. According to government sources, 52 percent of all enterprises were unprofitable in 1997, a 7 percent increase over 1996. In addition, proportionately more large state-owned enterprises are incurring losses.

In a market economy, a persistently loss-making enterprise goes through bankruptcy proceedings in the process of reallocating resources toward more efficient uses. In Kazakhstan, however, such reallocation rarely happens. For example, in 1997, 273 enterprises started bankruptcy proceedings, but only 71 of them were actually closed down. As the loss-making enterprises are unable to pay all their bills, arrears accumulate between enterprises and in tax, wage, and pension payments. In 1997 total tax arrears almost doubled from a year earlier, to an equivalent of 2.7 percent of GDP. Total debts payable among enterprises, another good indicator of the dire state of the enterprise sector, reached an all time high of about 60 percent of 1997 GDP by mid-1998. Of this total, 77 percent was accumulated by large enterprises. After a steady decline in 1997, the total sum of unpaid wages increased again in 1998, and amounted to about 1.5 percent of 1997 GDP by the first half of 1998. The government has had no success in attempting to clear these arrears.

To restructure, bankruptcy proceedings should be applied more rigorously and quickly to liquidate nonviable enterprises. Other enterprises, especially large state-owned enterprises, should be privatized rapidly. Although privatization has so far provided badly needed revenues for the budget, the main objective of privatization is to turn unprofitable enterprises into profitable ones by changing their incentives and governance structure. Thus problems associated with past practices, such as keeping the controlling ownership in the hands of the state or of existing management, should be rectified.

One objective of privatization should be to attract foreign investors, as progress in restructuring is closely associated with greater foreign participation. In 1997 more than 60 percent of the large increase in oil production was attributable to the Tengiz oil field, which has considerable foreign capital and management participation. The production of steel and other major metals under foreign management contracts also experienced large increases. As of 1 June 1998, the 103 industrial enterprises under the control of external management registered a production increase of 108.7 percent, in contrast to the rest of the industrial sector, which is mostly stagnant and inefficient. In particular, policies that allow majority foreign participation in large, or even blue chip, companies should be continued.

Restructuring through bankruptcy and privatization will also provide a strong impetus to capital market development. A deepening capital market will, in turn, promote the growth of the financial sector. Together they will better fulfill the crucial role of financial intermediation, which is critical for economic growth and development. This will be particularly important for the success of the ongoing pension reform. Without further deepening of the capital market, private pension funds would have no valuable domestic assets to invest in, and would have no possibility of earning a sufficiently high return to make the pension program viable in the long run.

Kyrgyz Republic

The Russian financial and economic crisis has slowed economic growth considerably, and will continue to affect the Kyrgyz Republic through 1999. Stringent fiscal and monetary discipline is crucial for maintaining macroeconomic stability and continuing the necessary structural reforms.

RECENT TRENDS AND PROSPECTS

Real GDP grew by 1.8 percent in 1998, much slower than the 9.9 percent growth rate achieved in 1997. This economic slowdown was mainly attributable to two external shocks: the heavy rainfall in May and June, which caused considerable damage in the south; and the Russian crisis that erupted on 17 August and whose adverse impacts are still working their way through the economy.

Despite the heavy rains, the agriculture sector grew by 4.1 percent. Grain production rose by 6.5 percent and animal husbandry increased moderately by 2.0 percent. The progress made in agriculture, which accounts for more than 40 percent of GDP, is primarily attributable to the supply response to the continued improvements in the policy environment. As of the end of 1998, nonstate production accounted for more than 85 percent of the sector's total production. In October land ownership was legally privatized, and this, together with other positive policy measures, is expected to give a major impetus to long-term growth in agriculture.

Industrial production increased by 4.6 percent in 1998. The Kumtor gold mine was the major reason for this good performance, as most other industrial production continued to decline. However, nonferrous metals and the food industry also expanded during the year. The transport sector grew by 4.0 percent and the service sector by 8.4 percent.

The official unemployment rate for 1998 was 6.2 percent, which was higher than in 1997. If hidden unemployment is accounted for, the actual rate could be as high as one fifth of the labor force. Given the massive fall in real income after independence and the recent relatively modest growth, the population's welfare will not improve significantly for some time. Poverty is widespread, with about half of all households currently falling below the official poverty line. This figure reaches 70 percent in rural areas.

In 1998 national investment was 14.7 percent of GDP, 58.0 percent of which came from the private sector. With private sector savings at 1.4 percent of GDP and government dissaving at 3.4 percent, the resource gap increased to 16.7 percent of GDP from 13 percent in 1997. This gap was financed by external sources.

The fiscal situation continued to improve early in the year, before the Russian crisis hit and made it considerably worse. The consolidated budget deficit was 9.9 percent of GDP (including public investment projects), higher than in 1997. Even though the government did not meet its total revenue target, tax collection surpassed expectations because of strong performance in indirect tax collection. Since the outbreak of the Russian crisis in August 1998, financing deficit spending has become increasingly difficult. Expenditure management also suffered a major setback as sizable arrears on wages and pensions built up to 1.1 percent of GDP.

Consistent with tight monetary policy, inflation declined and the som continued its gradual real appreciation against the US dollar until the fourth quarter of 1998. The Russian crisis then caused the som to plummet, and it lost about 50 percent of its value against the dollar between August and the end of the year. Consequently, inflation accelerated during the last three months of 1998 and reached 18.4 percent for the December to December period, higher than forecast. In an effort to prevent further depreciation of the som, interest rates were raised, with the yields on three-month Treasury bills reaching an all time high

of 144 percent at the end of November, before they fell at the end of the year.

In 1998 the current account deficit more than doubled from that in 1997, and the trade deficit jumped to $151 million from just $15 million a year earlier. The main reasons for this increase in the trade deficit were a 28 percent decrease in exports to Commonwealth of Independent States countries and a 47 percent increase in imports, particularly of consumption goods from countries of the Organisation for Economic Co-operation and Development. While export performance may improve over the medium term with the Kyrgyz Republic's formal accession to the World Trade Organization in December, its immediate prospects look less promising. The Russian crisis and the ensuing economic downturn in Russia and neighboring countries will continue to dampen Kyrgyz export growth, because 55 percent of Kyrgyz exports go to these former Soviet republics. With limited foreign direct investment, the country has continued to rely primarily on external assistance on concessional terms to maintain its external balance.

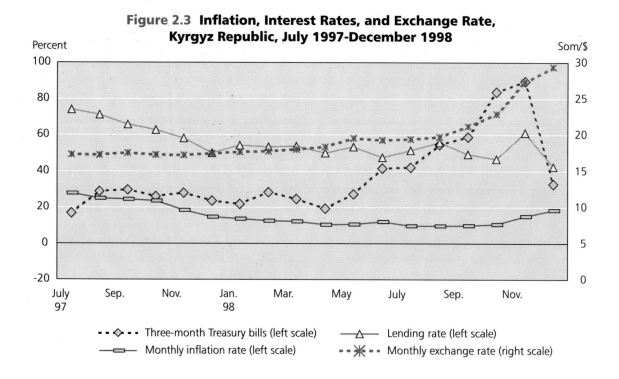

Figure 2.3 Inflation, Interest Rates, and Exchange Rate, Kyrgyz Republic, July 1997-December 1998

- - ◇ - - Three-month Treasury bills (left scale)   —△— Lending rate (left scale)
—□— Monthly inflation rate (left scale)   - - ✳ - - Monthly exchange rate (right scale)

Sources: National Statistical Committee for Kyrgyz Republic; National Bank of the Kyrgyz Republic; International Monetary Fund (1999a).

The Russian crisis has severely affected the Kyrgyz economy and will continue to do so next year. As a result, growth for 1999 is only expected to be about 3 percent, much lower than earlier projections. Similarly, inflationary pressures will increase as the effects of the som's depreciation feed through the economy.

ISSUES IN ECONOMIC MANAGEMENT

The contagion effect of the Asian crisis, and even more so of the Russian crisis, almost dried up the domestic market for Treasury bills, and will likely keep interest from both domestic and international sources in som-denominated assets low for some time. This will increase the government's difficulties in financing its deficit. Given this situation, the government must exercise extreme prudence in fiscal management to avoid incurring a large deficit; accumulating arrears, especially on social expenditures; and undertaking external borrowing on nonconcessional terms. In addition, it should continue to follow a tight monetary policy to curb further inflation. Although the som is still under pressure to depreciate further, the monetary authorities should intervene only cautiously to preserve international reserves. The next few months will be crucial for the economy. Any major slippage in fiscal and monetary management could have grave implications for macroeconomic stability and affect the ongoing program of structural reforms.

POLICY DEVELOPMENT AND ISSUES

Beyond their immediate impact, the Kyrgyz Republic's resilience to external shocks such as the Russian crisis depends principally on the progress it makes in economic transition. Even though it has achieved considerable progress in macroeconomic stabilization and structural reforms in recent years, the government cannot afford to become complacent. In particular, it needs to address the interrelated issues of fiscal reform, privatization, and enterprise restructuring.

While it should continue to rationalize expenditure, the government should also continue its efforts to generate more revenues. In contrast to its much improved collection of indirect taxes, the collection of direct taxes, such as those on income and profits, is still weak. One major cause of this is lax tax administration. Despite a reformed tax code, the lack of a system of rules and regulations to implement the laws is mainly responsible for the irregularities and weaknesses exhibited in tax collection and enforcement. Such problems shrink the tax base and reduce revenues.

However, the more fundamental problem behind the low tax revenues is the underlying unprofitability of the enterprise sector. For the first nine months of 1998, roughly half of all enterprises either showed no growth or did not produce at all. The accumulation of unsold products, which is up to 40 percent in some sectors, also reflects enterprises' inefficiency. Consequently, arrears between enterprises and on wages and unpaid budget credits rose. Budget subsidies increased, underscoring the financial weaknesses of the state-owned enterprises.

Thus accelerating the process of privatization and restructuring the state-owned enterprises is crucial. The successful completion of these and other measures, such as reforming the pension system and strengthening the governance structure, will place the economy firmly on a market basis and will dramatically improve the prospects for future growth.

Tajikistan

While Tajikistan has achieved progress in restoring economic stabilization and growth, the Russian crisis is threatening economic recovery. The government needs to continue its reform efforts and to lay solid foundations for sustained economic development.

RECENT TRENDS AND PROSPECTS

After independence in 1991 Tajikistan was plunged into a serious economic crisis, with GDP contracting by 60 percent from 1991 to 1996. This was due to a civil war that lasted from 1992 until 1997, the effects of the breakup of the former Soviet Union, and a series of heavy floods. A serious consequence was that fiscal deficits rose sharply to, on average, one fifth of GDP per year from 1992 to 1994 because of the increase in the government's military expenditures, the reduction in revenue collection, and the cessation of budgetary support from Moscow. The banking system financed these deficits, which resulted in hyperinflation that exceeded 2,000 percent in 1995. The balance of payments deteriorated because of the decline in domestic production and the collapse of the inter-republic trade and payments system.

In the face of such a devastating economic crisis, the government had to undertake massive stabilization and structural reform programs. The necessary prerequisite for this was provided by the peace agreement signed in June 1997. As a result, Tajikistan has made significant progress in macroeconomic adjustment. GDP actually increased by 1.7 percent in 1997, the first year of positive growth since independence. The upturn continued in 1998, with GDP growing by 4 percent. The recovery in 1998 was broadly based: estimates indicate that agricultural output grew by 3 percent because of an increase in cotton production, while industrial output increased by 5 percent. The service sector expanded as a result of the strong supply response of private traders and privatized small enterprises to the liberalization of prices and trade.

The official unemployment rate in 1998 was low at 2.8 percent of the labor force. Actual unemployment, however, is about 30 percent, because many unemployed people do not formally register as such. The repatriation of refugees from Afghanistan and the demobilization of soldiers since June 1997 have exacerbated the situation.

The government has made major efforts to improve fiscal management by raising revenues and rationalizing public expenditures. On the revenue side, major measures adopted included introducing a new tax code, extending the sales taxes to nine additional commodities, reducing value-added tax exemptions, unifying customs duties and excise taxes, raising the rates of import duties and land tax, and strengthening tax administration. On the expenditure side, the government took measures to restrain the growth of wages of public sector employees, reduce the number of civil servants, eliminate bread production subsidies, and introduce user charges for irrigation. As a result, the state budget deficit declined from about 11 percent of GDP in 1995 to 3.3 percent per year during 1997 and 1998. However, the government's fiscal position remains weak, as government revenues currently account for less than 15 percent of GDP. This is inadequate for the government to spend sufficient amounts on social services, protection for vulnerable groups, and capital investment.

In recent years, the authorities have taken steps to control the growth of credit and the money supply in an attempt to end the hyperinflation. In this they have been remarkably successful, with the rate of inflation falling from 159.8 percent in 1997 to 7 percent in 1998. Major measures undertaken included restricting the extension of credit to the government and state-owned enterprises, raising the refinancing rate, introducing Treasury bills and credit auctions, and strengthening bank regulations and supervision.

The balance of payments deteriorated in 1998. The current account deficit rose from 5.5 percent of GDP in 1997 to 7.2 percent in 1998 because of the worsening trade account. The value of total exports declined in 1998 as export earnings from cotton and aluminum, Tajikistan's two principal export commodities, fell. This was because of both the decline in world prices and the reduced demand from Russia and the other Central Asian republics.

Imports declined slightly in 1998, largely because of the lack of financing. The capital account registered a surplus in 1998 as increased disbursements from the international aid community offset a decline in foreign direct investment. The exchange rate was under considerable pressure as a large amount of Russian rubles flowed into Tajikistan for conversion (via Tajik rubles) into US dollars. The result was that the official exchange rate with the US dollar depreci-

Figure 2.4 GDP Growth and External Current Account, Tajikistan, 1992-1998

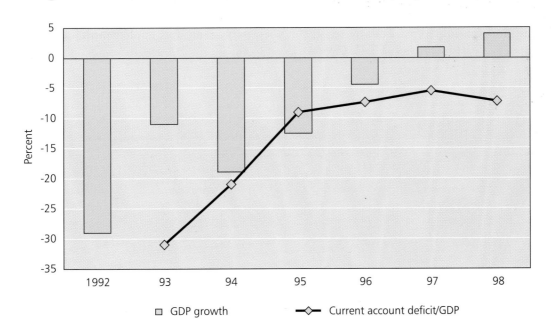

Sources: ADB (1998d); IMF (1998c).

ated by more than 10 percent in 1998. Although re-serves tripled from 1997 to 1998, they still covered less than two months worth of imports.

The Russian economic crisis and weak world commodity prices will dampen Tajikistan's economic growth prospects in the short term. Projections indicate that GDP will grow by 3 percent in 1999. Inflation is likely to rebound as depreciation of the currency results in an increase in the domestic prices of imported goods. The balance of payments is projected to remain weak because of uncertain export markets, the country's substantial import needs, and the lack of foreign direct investment. Unemployment and poverty will continue to be a major concern, as employment growth is insufficient to absorb the large number of refugees who will continue to return to the country from Afghanistan.

POLICY AND DEVELOPMENT ISSUES

Tajikistan's economic prospects depend heavily on peace. Without peace, sustained economic growth will not occur, just as lasting peace is unlikely in the absence of economic progress. Disruption of the peace process would discourage external aid and foreign direct investment, hamper domestic structural adjustment, delay the necessary reconstruction of the infrastructure, and worsen poverty. The government needs to work closely with the United Tajik Opposi-tion to accelerate implementation of the peace agreement. In particular, it needs to give high priority to introducing constitutional amendments, preparing for parliamentary elections, and demobilizing and integrating soldiers into civil society.

The process of macroeconomic stabilization needs to continue. The implementation of structural reforms aimed at developing a competitive market economy is also crucial for sustained growth. Tajikistan has favorable long-term growth prospects because of its abundance of natural resources, for example, hydroelectric power and gold, and a relatively well-educated but low-cost labor force. The government will need to pay special attention to privatizing and restructuring medium and large state-owned enterprises, implementing land reform and restructuring the farm subsector, and initiating banking reform.

Poverty is widespread in Tajikistan: some 80 percent of the population are unable to adequately meet their basic needs for food, clothing, shelter, education, and medical care. A major cause of this is the large numbers of unemployed. Fighting poverty must be a focal point of the government's development efforts. It is taking steps to address the poverty problem by promoting development, especially in rural and war-affected areas; raising the minimum wage; eliminating arrears of pension payments; improving the social security system; and implementing a microcredit program.

Uzbekistan

The weak world commodity markets, the Asian financial collapse, and the economic turmoil in Russia are adversely affecting Uzbekistan's economic recovery from its postindependence crisis. Strong stabilization and structural reform efforts are needed to minimize these adverse effects and maintain positive economic growth.

RECENT TRENDS AND PROSPECTS

After a strong recovery of output in 1997, the economy experienced slower growth in 1998. GDP grew by 2.8 percent in 1998 compared with a 5.2 percent increase in 1997. The slowdown resulted mainly from a disappointing cotton harvest and the adverse external environment: the weak world commodity markets, the Asian financial crisis, and the economic turmoil in Russia. The country depends heavily on agriculture, but in 1998 agricultural output grew by less than half the 1997 rate. This was due mainly to a fall in the production of cotton, the country's principal crop and export commodity, by 12 percent. Poor weather and the lack of effective incentives were both contributory factors. The growth of industrial output also slowed in 1998. This was primarily due to the fall in demand for Uzbekistan's major industrial exports, gold and gas, and the decline in their world prices. The service sector grew more slowly in 1998 than in 1997 as the government's policy of restricting imports of consumer goods stifled private trading activities.

The official unemployment rate was low at 0.4 percent of the labor force in 1998, but this figure masks considerable hidden unemployment in state-owned enterprises and in rural areas. State-owned enterprises and collective farms often retain surplus employees to avoid massive layoffs and potential social unrest. Furthermore, many unemployed people have not officially registered as such because of low unemployment benefits. The true figure may be well above 5 percent, and about 14 percent of the population is now living below the official poverty line.

To mitigate the social costs of transition to a market economy, the government has attempted to adjust the wages of public sector employees and improve the social safety net for vulnerable groups. A presidential decree issued on 1 July 1998 raised the wages of state sector employees by 50 percent and pensions by 60 percent. The state budget will finance these pension and wage increases, which will impose an additional fiscal burden on the government.

The government continued its efforts to mobilize revenues in 1998 by undertaking new tax measures. A new tax code and several tax policy changes designed to enhance government revenues became effective in January 1998. The major measures included raising the value-added tax from 18 to 20 percent; reducing the maximum profit tax from 36 to 35 percent; and increasing land, property, and mining taxes and water fees. Government revenues were equivalent to about 36 percent of GDP in 1998. The government's efforts on the expenditure side were, however, mixed. While it continued to reduce expenditures on state administration, subsidies on water and electricity, and capital investments, its spending on wages and pensions and defense rose. As a result, government expenditures as a share of GDP increased to around 38 percent in 1998, leading to an increase in the budget deficit. To reduce this, the government issued a decree in September 1998 requesting all ministries and agencies to cut their staff by a quarter, beginning in January 1999.

The authorities maintained tight monetary policy to contain inflation in 1998, with only moderate success. Inflation declined from 28 percent in 1997

to 22 percent in 1998. This small reduction also reflected a shift in the consumption basket toward price-controlled items, the increasing restrictions on cash withdrawals from bank accounts, and the accumulation of arrears on wage and benefits payments. The inflation rate deteriorated in the second half of 1998 because of wage increases granted to state employees and the fall in the US dollar exchange rate. The government responded by increasing interest rates from 36 to 40 percent in September.

The balance of payments came under pressure in 1998 after an improvement in 1997. The current account deficit for 1998 was lower than in 1997. This occurred because imports declined more than exports. The value of exports fell by 19.8 percent in 1998 as export earnings of cotton and gold declined. The crisis in Russia, Uzbekistan's main trading partner, also depressed exports. Imports contracted by 27.3 percent in 1998 because of the government's foreign trade and exchange restrictions, a reduction in grain imports as a result of the government's efforts to increase domestic grain production, and the substantial depreciation of the currency. The curb market exchange rate depreciated more rapidly than the official exchange rate so that the spread of the two rates increased from about 100 percent in 1997 to more than twice that in 1998. Official external debt increased to $2.8 billion in 1998, reflecting the persistent current account deficits. Foreign exchange reserves fell in 1998 to $0.9 billion, equivalent to just over three months worth of imports.

Economic prospects for 1999 are not bright because of the adverse effects of the weak world commodity markets, the Asian financial crisis, and the economic turmoil in Russia. Inflationary pressure is likely to increase as the depreciation of the currency is expected to continue. The fiscal situation is forecast to remain strained as the slowdown of economic growth reduces government tax revenues, while the government continues to try to maintain public expenditures on social services and protection for vulnerable groups. The balance of payments will remain under pressure as exports become sluggish and domestic demand for imports rises. Unemployment will remain a concern, because slower economic growth will reduce employment opportunities, which may lead to an increase in poverty.

Figure 2.5 GDP Growth and Inflation Rate, Uzbekistan, 1992-1998

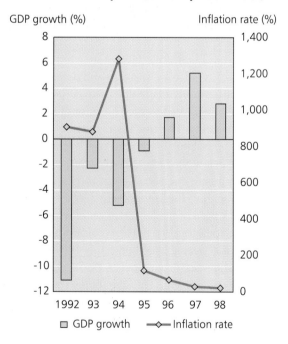

Sources: ADB (1997a); staff estimates.

POLICY AND DEVELOPMENT ISSUES

The government needs to make a concerted effort to create a more stable macroeconomic environment, especially in the face of the Russian economic crisis. First, it must further reduce inflation. To accomplish this, monetary policy should focus on restraining bank liquidity, restricting bank financing for the state budget deficit, and adjusting the central bank's refinancing rates in line with inflation to ensure positive real interest rates. Second, the government should pare its fiscal imbalance. It needs to pay special attention to reducing the scope of tax exemptions, strengthening tax collection and administration, restraining the growth of public sector wages, undertaking civil service reform to downsize the bureaucracy, and limiting transfers to loss-incurring state-owned enterprises.

Uzbekistan should accelerate the pace of structural reform to create competitive market conditions. Reform of the agriculture sector lies at the heart of structural reforms because agriculture plays a pivotal role in the overall economy, accounting for about 25 percent of GDP, 40 percent of employment, and 60 percent of exports. While the government has strengthened the rights of individuals working on collective farms, it still needs to complete a large reform agenda in this area. At present, the authorities continue to keep producer prices for cotton and wheat low, maintain the state order system for cotton and wheat, and retain tight control over production decisions and marketing arrangements. These defects should be remedied.

Another high priority is liberalizing the foreign trade system and the exchange markets; however, the authorities introduced foreign trade and exchange restrictions in late 1996 in response to mounting balance-of-payments pressures. These restrictions have resulted in the misallocation of resources between the traded and nontraded sectors, hampered private trading activities and investment, and offered substantial opportunities for rent seeking in the exchange market. While the government made some modest improvements to the situation in July 1998, the trade and exchange restrictions need to be abolished as soon as possible.

Finally, Uzbekistan remains too heavily dependent on Russia, both in terms of trade and of debt. The government should try to foster links and cooperation in areas such as energy, transport, and trade with other neighboring countries. In the short run this will mitigate the effects of the Russian economic crisis, and in the long run Uzbekistan will benefit from closer ties with, in particular, the Xinjiang Uygur Autonomous Region of the People's Republic of China.

Southeast Asia

Cambodia
Indonesia
Lao People's Democratic Republic
Malaysia
Myanmar
Philippines
Thailand
Viet Nam

Cambodia

The economic slowdown that began in mid-1997 with internal political disturbances and the regional financial crisis continued into 1998. Investment continued to decline because of the loss of external funds, both official and private. The political stalemate continued to depress tourism and private domestic consumption. The new government's stability and political will to implement reform will determine the growth prospects of the Cambodian economy.

RECENT TRENDS AND PROSPECTS

The economic expansion Cambodia enjoyed throughout the 1990s ground to a halt in 1998. The combined effects of uncertain political conditions surrounding the mid-year election, a prolonged regional economic downturn, and drought reduced the growth rate to zero. Agricultural growth was only modest because of drought conditions that limited the expansion of rice and livestock production and reduced fisheries production. A steep contraction in construction, caused by the loss of external funding, offset growth in manufacturing that occurred mainly in garments as a result of recent preferential access to the US market. As a consequence, there was no growth in industrial production. A fall in tourism and a loss of consumer confidence hit retail trade sharply, leading to a contraction of the service sector. Investment fell because of a drop in foreign aid brought about by the political stalemate, and because of a loss of foreign direct investment arising from the continued regional downturn.

Job creation continued in the garment sector, but urban service workers felt the economic slowdown, as did the rural population. Fewer seasonal employment opportunities in urban areas and rising rice prices squeezed real incomes. The most recently reported unemployment rate of 0.7 percent in 1997 is misleading, because underemployment and low incomes are significant problems, with 40 percent of the population living below the poverty line.

Preliminary estimates indicate that some deterioration occurred in the external sector. The current account deficit (excluding transfers) rose slightly as a percentage of GDP in 1998 relative to 1997. Exports grew by 12.8 percent, which was supported by growth in garments, while wood exports declined. Combined with a modest 3.4 percent increase in imports, this led to an improvement in the trade balance, which was offset by an increased deficit in services.

The 1998 capital account surplus fell because of a 20 percent drop in foreign direct investment from 1997 levels and a rise in the unexplained component of the balance of payments. Thus, the overall balance-of-payments surplus declined from $22 million in 1997 to $8 million in 1998. Gross official reserves increased from 2.2 months of imports in 1997 to 3.1 months in 1998 because of the release by the Bank for International Settlements of gold reserves frozen since the 1970s. About 63 percent of Cambodia's approximately $2.1 billion in external debt is debt incurred to the former Council for Mutual Economic Assistance, for which rescheduling is to be negotiated.

Turning to fiscal performance in 1998, revenues fell from 9.7 percent of GDP in 1997 to 8.5 percent of GDP, primarily because of shortfalls in nontax revenues such as forestry royalties. Expenditures were 12.5 percent of GDP, lower than in 1997. Although current expenditures were above the target set in the budget for 1998 (notably for wages and for defense and security), capital expenditures were cut back from a planned 5.1 to 3.6 percent of GDP. The overall budget deficit of 3.9 percent of GDP was smaller than in 1997. However, foreign financing was lower than expected. Thus the generally weak budget performance for 1998 included bank financing of about KR125 billion.

The increase in net credit to the government was, however, offset by a fall in foreign currency deposits caused by political uncertainty, so that the growth of total liquidity fell slightly from 16.6 percent in 1997 to 15.7 percent in 1998. The riel depreciated by more than 10 percent against the dollar, and also against regional currencies (nearly 30 percent against the Thai baht). This contributed to an increase in inflation from about 9 percent in 1997 to some 12 percent in 1998. These figures may overstate purchasing power erosion because of the widespread use of dollars in Cambodia, which negates the effects of depreciation on riel-denominated consumer prices.

The outlook for 1999 and 2000 is for the economy to improve, as the formation of the new government in late 1998 signaled at least a partial resolution of political differences. Thus services such as tourism and retail trade are expected to pick up. As aid flows increase, public investment will rise and construction should rebound. This will stimulate industrial growth. If the new government has the political will to tackle the reform agenda of improving forestry management, enhancing domestic resource mobilization, implementing civil service reform, and initiating

Table 2.7 Major Economic Indicators, Cambodia, 1996-2000
(percent)

Item	1996	1997	1998	1999	2000
GDP growth	7.0	2.0	0.0	4.0	6.0
Gross domestic investment/GDP	25.9	19.0	15.0	18.4	19.0
Gross national savings/GDP	10.6	10.6	5.9	7.6	8.1
Inflation rate (consumer price index)[a]	9.0	9.1	12.0	10.0	6.0
Money supply (M2) growth	40.4	16.6	15.7	30.0	25.0
Fiscal balance/GDP	-8.4	-4.2	-3.9	-2.1	-2.5
Merchandise exports growth[b]	22.1	63.1	12.8	17.7	15.0
Merchandise imports growth[b]	13.6	2.1	3.4	21.4	18.0
Current account balance/GDP[c]	-15.3	-8.4	-9.1	-10.8	-10.9
Debt service/exports[d]	5.1	2.3	2.6	2.3	3.1

a. Final quarter basis.
b. Excludes re-exports.
c. Excluding official transfers.
d. As percent of domestic exports of goods and services only; also in convertible currencies only.

Sources: Ministry of Economy and Finance; National Bank of Cambodia; National Institute of Statistics, Ministry of Planning; International Monetary Fund reports; staff estimates.

demobilization of the military, then Cambodia's long-term prospects are reasonably good.

ISSUES IN ECONOMIC MANAGEMENT

Immediately improving forestry management is critical. This issue affects nearly every facet of economic development in the country. Estimated long-run government revenues of $40 million to $80 million resulting from sustainable forestry are sizable relative to total 1998 revenues of about $245 million. In contrast, forestry revenues were about $6.1 million in 1998. In addition to hampering domestic resource mobilization, poor forestry management increases the potential for rapid environmental degradation. A loss of habitat is already affecting the fisheries sector. Crop production will also be threatened as soil erosion and water runoff increase. Finally, the rural population is heavily dependent on the forests for supplemental food and for cooking fuel.

Under international pressure because of the potential threat to economic development from inadequate forestry management, the government has made some progress in analyzing the problem with several studies sponsored by the international community and in enacting some of the recommended reforms. It is expected that the new government will make further progress in implementing reforms. These include improved regulation of forest exploitation arrangements, enhanced monitoring and control capabilities at the Department of Forests and Wildlife and the Ministry of Finance, and revised concession contracts that are equitable and are based on sound legal and forestry practice.

POLICY AND DEVELOPMENT ISSUES

One of the principal long-term constraints to economic development is the poor quality of human resources. Low productivity and low wages already characterize the private sector labor force. Moreover, the military and the civil service are overstaffed with low-skill, low-wage personnel that must now be integrated into the private sector labor force. One indicator of low productivity is the poor level of educational attainment. About 40 percent of the population never attended school, 32 percent are illiterate, and less than 1 percent has had any training beyond high school. Thus Cambodia lacks the skilled personnel to improve its administrative, legal, educational, and medical institutions. Furthermore, public expenditures on education are low, with the government share of educational expenditures as little as 25 percent.

Another indicator of low labor force productivity is poor health and nutrition. In 1995 life expectancy at birth was 53 years. In 1996 about 50 percent of children age five and under were malnourished. Infant mortality rates, maternal mortality rates, and total fertility rates are also extremely high. Leading causes of death include malaria, acute respiratory infections, tuberculosis, road accidents, and mines. An impending crisis is the HIV/AIDS epidemic, the worst in Asia, with 2.7 percent of the population infected, and the worst outside Africa. Public expenditures on health are also low, which has led to one of the lowest rates of health service utilization in the world. With the recent resolution of political conflict, expectations are that the government will be able to devote more resources to education and health.

Indonesia

Indonesia was the hardest hit of the Asian crisis-affected countries, with GDP falling by 13.7 percent in 1998. The economy suffered a severe contraction and was brought to the verge of total collapse, with soaring inflation, a sharply depreciating currency, and increasing interest rates. Violence broke out in many of the larger cities. The government needs to move rapidly on several fronts. It needs to ensure the adequate distribution of food supplies and to promote agricultural production. There must also be sufficient trade financing of exports, and the reform of the banking system should be continued. In the longer term, a plan to address the regional imbalances in the country is needed.

RECENT TRENDS AND PROSPECTS

Indonesia is battling its worst recession in 35 years. What started out as financial contagion developed into a full-blown economic crisis whose severity few could have foreseen. The crisis deepened from July 1997 until August 1998; however, by the end of the year economic indicators had begun to stabilize. The current crisis follows an extended period of high growth with low inflation and a sharp decline in poverty.

Recent GDP figures reflect the depth of the crisis. In the first quarter of 1998 GDP contracted by 4 percent compared with the same period the previous year, by 12.3 percent in the second quarter, by 18.4 percent in the third quarter, and by 19.5 percent in the fourth quarter. Overall GDP fell by 13.7 percent in 1998, a sharp contrast to the average annual growth rate of 8 percent attained in 1995 and 1996.

The social unrest in mid-May 1998 that culminated in the resignation of President Suharto brought the economy almost to a standstill. The violence that broke out in Jakarta and other provincial capitals un-dermined business confidence in the country. Massive capital flight and closures of business operations (especially those owned by the ethnic Chinese) ensued. The exchange rate weakened sharply, interest rates soared, and prices rose rapidly. The economy was plunged into a vicious cycle of rising inflation, falling exchange rates, and increasing interest rates.

The average inflation rate was 58 percent in 1998. While all prices rose, a major contributor to the overall rate was the price of foodstuffs, sparked by significantly lower rice production because of El Niño and inefficient management of the food distribution system.

The rupiah experienced great volatility in 1998. It plunged to its weakest level of Rp17,000 to the US dollar in February, before recovering to between Rp7,000 and Rp8,000 in October and remaining stable around this level during the last few months of 1998. In a bid to stabilize the rupiah and the inflation rate, the central bank tightened monetary policy. The domestic interest rate for one-month deposits peaked at 70.4 percent, but then declined to about 35 percent. To restore monetary stability, credit was squeezed, with

Table 2.8 Major Economic Indicators, Indonesia, 1996-2000
(percent)

Item	1996	1997	1998	1999	2000
GDP growth	7.8	4.9	-13.7	0.0	2.0
Gross domestic investment/GDP	30.7	31.3	18.0	17.5	20.0
Gross national savings/GDP	27.3	29.9	19.1	18.5	19.0
Inflation rate (consumer price index)	7.9	6.6	58.2	17.0	9.5
Money supply (M2) growth[a]	26.7	52.7	62.3	25.0	22.0
Fiscal balance/GDP	0.2	0.0	-4.7	-4.1	-2.5
Merchandise exports growth[a]	9.0	7.9	0.7	6.5	8.5
Merchandise imports growth[a]	10.4	-6.8	-11.3	9.0	13.0
Current account balance/GDP[a]	-3.4	-1.4	1.1	1.0	-1.0
Debt service/exports[a]	34.2	39.5	36.0	34.0	34.0

a. Fiscal year (1 April to 31 March).

Sources: Central Bureau of Statistics data; Indonesian Financial Statistics (various years); Government of Indonesia estimates; staff estimates.

bank lending at a virtual standstill. Foreign and domestic investment dropped by around 60 percent and 50 percent, respectively, in 1998, compared with 1997.

The worst hit sector was the construction industry, which contracted by some 39 percent. The manufacturing sector, which had been the main engine of Indonesia's development, growing by more than 10 percent per year during the last decade, declined by about 13 percent because of rising domestic prices of imported inputs and a collapse of domestic demand. The tourism and financial sectors also experienced massive downturns. The only sectors that still reported positive growth rates were the export-oriented oil and gas industry (3 percent), utilities (3.7 percent), and the agriculture sector (0.2 percent).

Trade performance was not encouraging. While the current account surplus was estimated at 1.1 percent of GDP, this was due mainly to the contraction in imports. The decline in imports was uniform across all categories, that is, consumer goods, raw materials, and capital goods. Despite the weak rupiah, a combination of falling world prices of commodity exports (including oil), sluggish global demand (particularly

from Japan), and export credit constraints combined to keep growth in export revenue flat. The crisis has also had a major negative effect on the textile industry, a key export sector. Because of the high costs of raw materials (virtually all cotton used is imported), the industry operated at only 60 percent of capacity in 1998.

To stimulate the economy, the government announced an expansionary fiscal policy in January 1998. However, the projections in the budget proved to be overoptimistic, and the government introduced a revised budget in July 1998. This assumed a GDP contraction of 12 percent, an inflation rate of 66 percent, and an exchange rate of Rp10,000 to the US dollar for FY1998/99.

Reflecting a major shift in fiscal stance, the revised budget showed a fiscal deficit of 8.5 percent of GDP. However, the deficit wound up substantially lower, at 4.7 percent of GDP, because of slow disbursement of development expenditures. The fiscal expansion was needed to mitigate the adverse social impact of the crisis, with subsidies alone accounting for 37 percent of current expenditures. The largest subsidies are on fuel, electricity, food, and interest rates on loans to the poor. For the first time, the budget showed public dissaving, with current expenditures exceeding current revenues. Thus external assistance was projected to finance not only all development expenditures, but also some current expenditures.

Given the magnitude of the crisis, Indonesia is not expected to grow until 2000. Projections indicate a bottoming out of the crisis in the first half of 1999 and the initiation of recovery toward the end of the year. This will depend critically on both macroeconomic and political stability in a year that will witness both the first democratic parliamentary election in the country's history and a presidential election.

ISSUES IN ECONOMIC MANAGEMENT

The severity of the crisis has confronted the country with many daunting tasks in the short run. Failure to address the social impact of the crisis in 1999 could easily spark another turbulent year. Preliminary estimates suggest that the incidence of poverty increased to 16 to 20 percent in 1998 from a precrisis (1996) level of 11 percent. Urban and suburban areas show the most visible effects of the crisis, with layoffs occurring mainly in the cities. All these events are placing immense social strains on the country, with outbreaks of violence and increased crime in the major cities.

As a consequence, a pressing need is to ensure adequate supplies of basic staples such as rice, sugar, flour, and other foodstuffs. The food shortage was created by distribution bottlenecks and falling per capita incomes. The government was able to maintain the stability of food prices until December 1997, but prices of foodstuffs increased sharply from February to August 1998. Keeping the prices of essential commodities stable in the short run remains the government's main priority if social unrest is to remain under control.

The government needs to address two key short-term structural concerns over the short term. First, export enterprises, especially small and medium enterprises, need access to financing. Without adequate access to trade finance these enterprises cannot boost their exports to markets where demand remains brisk. Second, agriculture still contributes nearly 20 percent of GDP, and can play a major role in the recovery process and act as a safety net sector. While the produc-

tion of estate crops, such as coffee, rubber, and spices, expanded greatly in 1998, the authorities must ensure an adequate supply of fertilizer and seeds throughout the country during the 1999 rice planting seasons. This is particularly important because in 1998 the government withdrew the fertilizer subsidy that farmers had previously enjoyed.

Maintaining the momentum of substantially improved macroeconomic performance toward the end of 1998 is also an important short-term challenge. While an easing of monetary policy is required, any attempt to lower the interest rate below the level to which it fell in the last quarter of 1998 to try to alleviate the burden of corporate debt and spark an early recovery would not, however, be prudent. A further interest rate reduction below the expectations of international markets may put further pressure on the exchange rate. It is imperative that the government implement a full range of structural reforms of the financial system.

On the fiscal side, the government should continue to maintain an expansionary stance, but achieving its stated aim of zero growth and 17 percent inflation may be difficult. The huge output contraction was caused by a collapse in investment. Because investment growth will depend critically on restoring investor confidence, the level of investment may take more than a year to show any substantial increase. Monetary targets may be exceeded in an election year. If this happens, some significant price increases may be apparent in 1999.

On the revenue side of the government's 1999/2000 budget, income tax is stipulated to provide more than half the revenue. This will be difficult to achieve given that the large increase in income tax revenues realized in 1998 was due to tax on interest incomes in a year of extremely high interest rates. The 1999 budget also forecasts large privatization proceeds, but the government's privatization program is well behind schedule. Even though the government is committed to speeding up the process, proceeds may fall short of the target. On the expenditure side, debt-service payments make up the highest proportion of total current expenditures at 25 percent. Subsidies have declined substantially as a proportion of current expenditures, but the subsidy on electricity remains high and needs to be reduced to sustainable levels. A large outlay of Rp18 trillion on bank recapitalization represents the fiscal cost of interest on bond issues to finance the recapitalization scheme. However, raising the needed financing through bond issues in the capital market may prove difficult in the present environment. Financing the fiscal burden of recapitalization, estimated at Rp100 trillion over three years, will be a major challenge for fiscal policy.

Restructuring the banking sector is another key priority, because economic recovery cannot begin without a resumption in bank lending. The banking system is technically insolvent, with a negative net worth estimated at a third of GDP. In 1998 nearly half of the more than 200 banks had a capital adequacy ratio below minus 25 percent, 56 had a capital adequacy ratio between minus 25 percent and plus 4 percent, and only 54 banks had a capital adequacy ratio above 4 percent. Conservative estimates of nonperforming loans were 60 percent for the state bank and 40 percent for the private banks.

In recent months the government has taken several steps to restructure the banking sector. The government's restructuring plan has four components: (a) resolution of banks under the control of the Indonesian Bank Restructuring Agency, (b) finalization of agreements with former owners concerning their repayment obligations to the government, (c) recapitalization of viable private banks, and (d) introduction of key laws and prudential regulations.

Restoring the normal operations of the corporate sector is another immediate priority. This requires full access to the international credit market, for which Indonesia must implement measures to address its mounting debt-service payments. Estimates indicate that total outstanding debt in 1998 was about $138 billion. The Frankfurt Agreement of June 1998 paved the way for restructuring of both the country's private and public external debts. The Indonesian Debt Restructuring Agency, which provides forward foreign exchange cover to domestic corporations, began to function in August 1998. To take advantage of the agency's scheme debtors and creditors must reach a negotiated debt settlement arrangement bilaterally. As this proved difficult without a proactive facilitator, the Jakarta initiative was launched on 9 September 1998 to play the role of facilitator for out-of-court settlements. A corporate restructuring task force was set up

in September to oversee the Jakarta initiative process. Although corporate debt restructuring made significant progress toward the end of 1998, the process has been painfully slow. Accelerating the process will be a priority concern of the government in 1999.

POLICY AND DEVELOPMENT ISSUES

Indonesia's success in reducing poverty before the crisis has been widely recognized; however, the crisis has undone some of these gains. Its impact goes beyond just unemployment and poverty. The lingering crisis has provoked despair in a country that was exuding a newfound confidence based on economic prosperity. Under these circumstances, keeping the development process on track over the long term to achieve sustained growth and poverty reduction is a major challenge for public policy.

The economic crisis has revealed the extensive governance problems in the country. A lack of transparency and accountability has characterized the development process in Indonesia. To return to its former growth rates, Indonesia must redress this situation in many sectors of the economy. The need to strengthen the system of both public and corporate governance is urgent.

The espousal of populist policies is not new to Indonesia, and some re-emergence of this has recently become apparent. The government has expressed a desire to establish a "people's economy." While it is crucial for the development process to be participatory in nature and essential for people to have a stake in the economy, it is also important to realize these policy goals efficiently and fairly. For example, in creating a level playing field for small and medium enterprises, policy must complement market principles. Competition, which ensures the efficiency of resource allocation, must remain the foundation of banking and corporate sector restructuring. The government faces a major long-term challenge in restructuring large monopolies and promoting competitive markets and firms.

The crisis highlights the need for a medium- to long-term economic strategy to address development imbalances between different regions of the country. In its latest budget, the government has shown its commitment to increase fiscal allocations to the

The economic outlook for 1999 and beyond depends foremost on the government's ability to reduce inflation and stabilize the exchange rate. This will require both fiscal and monetary discipline. Improving the implementation of Lao PDR's foreign investment laws will also be essential for sustained long-term development. If both the macroeconomic climate and the foreign investment environment can be improved significantly, then the country should be poised to take advantage of the regional recovery.

ISSUES IN ECONOMIC MANAGEMENT

The most vital task the government currently faces is restoring macroeconomic stability. The continued depreciation of the kip long after other regional currencies stabilized and began to recover and the high rate of inflation are both products of a weak financial sector. The monetary authority is crippled by limited policy tools, the widespread use of the Thai baht and US dollars as media of exchange and stores of value, and its lack of independence from the fiscal authority. To date, the monetary authority has been unable to halt the excessive credit expansion that is fueling in-

flation. The banking system is in disarray, as most state-owned banks appear to be insolvent and progress in reforming the system remains limited. To curb inflation the government is taking steps to halt credit expansion and reduce liquidity by reducing bank financing of the fiscal deficit and increasing the sale of central bank securities.

The government has also made some progress in increasing fiscal revenues, which would reduce the need to resort to inflationary deficit spending. For example, it raised excise taxes and the administered price of gasoline in November 1998 and increased turnover tax rates in January 1999. Another improvement in revenue collection was the change from using old exchange rates to using current exchange rates when converting dollar-denominated imports to kip for assessing import duties. In addition to continuing to improve revenue mobilization, the government should also prioritize public investment projects and resist the temptation to resort to bank financing to fund low-quality projects. With these measures in place and a regional recovery, both exchange rate depreciation and inflation should be reduced significantly in 1999.

Figure 2.6   Direction of Trade, Lao People's Democratic Republic, 1997

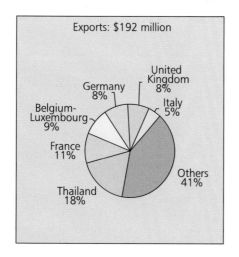
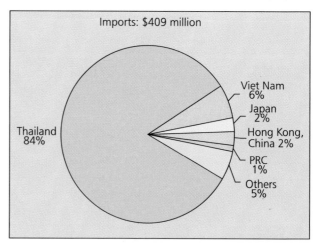

Source: IMF (1998d).

POLICY AND DEVELOPMENT ISSUES

International economic integration is a key component of the transformation to a market economy. Substantial recent progress for Lao PDR includes membership in the Association of Southeast Asian Nations and related regional agreements. The government is also working toward membership in the World Trade Organization. However, to realize the maximum benefits from this increased access to global markets, the government must now implement new trade and investment regimes that are consistent with a strategy of outward orientation. In particular, to take advantage of the opportunities for technology transfer and increased economic growth associated with foreign direct investment, the government must significantly improve the investment climate. This is especially critical given the current paucity of investment in the region and the increased selectivity with which potential investors are weighing investment opportunities.

The current foreign investment regime in the Lao PDR appears fairly liberal on paper, but in practice is highly restrictive, opaque, and susceptible to rent-seeking behavior. Combined with the current unfavorable macroeconomic conditions, the numerous price distortions that characterize the marketplace, and the generally weak system of legal and regulatory safeguards, the poor investment climate is likely to mean that Lao PDR attracts far less investment than its growth potential warrants. In the medium term the government must improve the investment process if it hopes to attract sufficient foreign investment to sustain its economic development strategy.

The following steps are essential for reforming the foreign investment system in the Lao PDR, and taken together will significantly improve the investment climate:

- The foreign investment law must be changed so that it clearly spells out which sectors are closed to foreign investment, which are open to joint ventures, and which are open to 100 percent foreign equity investments. The goal is to eliminate informal, ad hoc investment approval procedures that delay projects, often indefinitely.

- The many regulatory hurdles to investment, such as investment license renewals, import and export permits and licenses, business licenses, enterprise registration, worker termination measures, and building permits, must be streamlined or eliminated. This will reduce both public and private administrative costs.

- The existing laws pertaining to investment that are vague, contradictory, or not enforced must be reviewed and rationalized. This will reduce the opportunity for vested interests to subvert the intent of the foreign investment law.

- The various tax and duty incentives available to domestic and foreign investors must be harmonized. This will level the playing field and minimize the distortionary effects on investment decisions.

Figure 2.7 Private Sector Leverage Ratio, Malaysia, 1992-1997
(outstanding credit as a percentage of GDP)

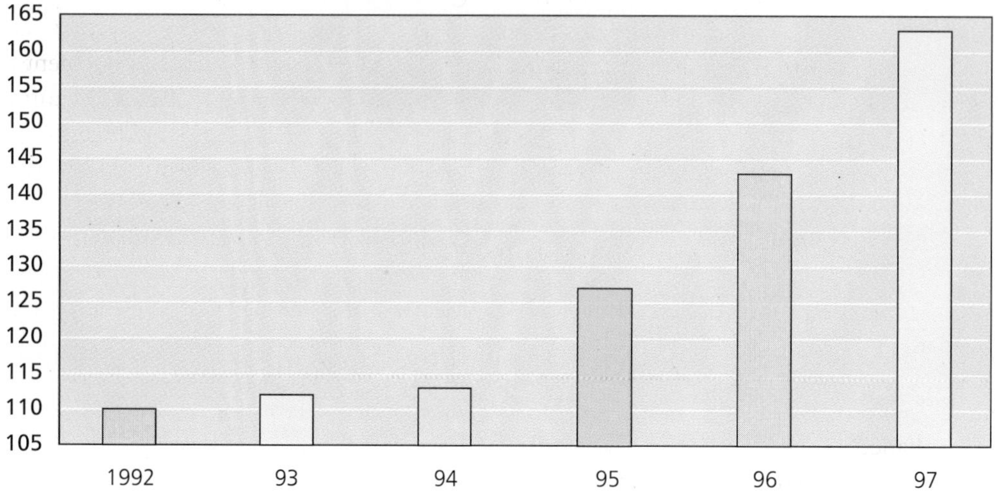

Source: Staff estimates.

serve requirement for banks was also reduced. In addition, the government relaxed prudential norms, provisioning requirements for substandard assets, and disclosure standards for banks that it had tightened in the wake of the crisis, because it believed that some of those measures had exacerbated the economic downturn, and if continued would push Malaysia into a deeper recession.

In September the government announced the introduction of exchange and capital control measures, because it felt that speculative activities in the open capital account were holding domestic monetary policy hostage. In particular, an active and growing offshore market for the ringgit was keeping the exchange rate volatile and constraining monetary policy options. Developments in Russia in August intensified the developing economies' fears of growing risks and their vulnerabilities. The government has stated that the exchange and capital control measures are short-term measures aimed at supporting economic recovery, protecting the domestic economy from instability caused by short-term capital flows and currency speculation, and helping the structural adjustment of the financial sector.

Growth projections for 1999 vary widely. Given current circumstances, economic forecasts are highly sensitive to assumptions made about the course of domestic economic management. They will also be influenced by the lingering uncertainties in the regional and global economic environment. Even if the exchange and capital control measures do arrest economic decline in 1999, the prospects for a robust economic recovery in the medium term depend on the government taking credible action to reform the financial sector. The revival of investor confidence, which is the key to sustainable growth, critically hinges on the speedy resolution of the banking system's nonperforming loan problem and of corporate debt issues in an objective and transparent manner.

Expansionary monetary and fiscal policies are expected to boost aggregate demand moderately in 1999. Forecasts suggest that private consumption will grow at 0.8 percent, while public consumption is likely to grow only marginally. The lower cost of financing and the relative stability of the exchange rate will induce new investment. Projections indicate that private investment will grow by 0.6 percent and public investment by 2.2 percent. Exports of goods will grow by 3.8 percent in 1999, because of the likely slow growth of the global economy. Given the slight overall growth in the domestic economy, imports are projected to rise by 6.6 percent. The current account will be in surplus. On the production side, the construction sector is expected to shrink further, with modest growth anticipated in other sectors. On balance, GDP should grow at 0.7 percent in 1999.

This forecast may be somewhat optimistic. It assumes the availability of adequate domestic and external funds for financing the public sector's borrowing requirements and covering the costs of bank restructuring. An unexpected increase in the level of banks' nonperforming loans would raise the funding requirements for bank restructuring. Export growth will depend on a pickup in the external environment, including recovery of the Japanese and other regional economies.

ISSUES IN ECONOMIC MANAGEMENT

The critical challenges for economic management in the short term include taking credible steps toward bank and corporate restructuring, mobilizing substantial domestic and external resources, and avoiding systemic macroeconomic risks.

The government has taken several major initiatives to deal with financial restructuring. It has set up an asset management company to deal with the nonperforming loans of banking institutions and established a special purpose vehicle for recapitalizing and restructuring banking institutions. It has also set up the Corporate Debt Restructuring Committee to orchestrate voluntary, coordinated debt workouts between financial institutions and borrowers to expedite debt restructuring and to prevent viable businesses from going into liquidation. The ability of banks and the corporate sector to foster economic recovery will depend on these agencies functioning in a transparent, objective, and efficient manner. Even though these agencies are set up as part of public policy and draw on public funds, independence and objectivity in their decisionmaking is essential for strengthening investor confidence. The authorities have stated that as the key agencies for bank and corporate restructuring, they will operate based on market-oriented principles in accordance with international best practices in corporate governance. They will also aim at equitable sharing of the burden among stakeholders.

The government faces the difficult challenge of raising sizable domestic and external resources to finance its 1999 budget and other requirements, including recapitalization of the banking system. As regards domestic sources, the Employees Provident Fund has been a major purchaser of sovereign debt. Economic contraction has, however, led to a decline in the number of net additional contributors to the fund, thereby reducing its revenues. Access to external commercial sources will depend on tangible improvement in the market outlook for Malaysian debt. Assistance from official multilateral and bilateral sources is expected to mitigate the resource constraints facing the government.

For economic recovery to be sustainable, Malaysia must avoid building risks that accentuated its vulnerability to the regional turmoil in the first place. Prudent limits on bank lending to the property sector and for share purchases must be adhered to. The banks' exposure to the property sector continues to be higher than that stipulated by the central bank. In addition, the corporate sector is highly leveraged with domestic loans. The financial shock emanating from the regional contagion has exposed the fragility and the underlying systemic risks of the overindebted corporate sector. Limits set on the amount of bank lending may delay much needed financial restructuring of the corporate sector. Such targets may dilute the quality of lending, and thus jeopardize the banks' asset quality.

The introduction of the exchange and capital control measures has brought with it a perception of the degree of risk to the domestic economy associated with changes in the external economy. These include the time lag involved in realigning the fixed exchange rate to reflect changing economic conditions, the adverse impact on the size of the inflow of external capital in the short and the medium term, and the possibility that the exchange and capital control measures may lead to arbitrary administrative actions. Capital that entered the country prior to 1 September 1998 is eligible for repatriation in September 1999 without attracting an exit tax, and this could lead to a bunching of capital outflows at that time. The likelihood of the

ISSUES IN ECONOMIC MANAGEMENT

If the government could reduce the budget deficit significantly and curb the increase in money supply, then it could reduce the inflation rate significantly. This is important, because if it succeeded in reducing the inflation rate to around 15 percent, it would not have to raise nominal interest rates to make real interest rates positive and thereby encourage saving. At present, the profit margins of most legitimate businesses and the rate of return from investments are relatively low. As a result, most private banks are finding it hard to make loans, even at the present nominal rate of interest. Therefore, raising the rate of nominal interest would further choke off investment and incur stagflation. The government also needs to move to market-based interest rates rather than rely on a regulated interest rate policy. This would be an important factor in leading to a sustainable and viable banking system.

POLICY AND DEVELOPMENT ISSUES

The adoption of a market-oriented economic policy has had some positive impact on the development of the economy in recent years. However, most observers agree that economic reforms have either been incomplete or short-lived—failing to achieve a fundamental transformation of the economic system—and that the economy is still beset with serious macroeconomic and structural problems. Thus there is a critical need to restore macroeconomic stability and strengthen economic reforms. Areas where reforms are urgently needed include foreign trade, taxation, industrial policies, exchange rate regulations, management of fiscal deficits, and divestment of public enterprises. The government must also not only take measures to support private sector development such as infrastructure building, but must assume greater responsibility in such areas as environmental protection.

While the government should raise certain taxes, such as those on the use of state-owned property, it should pay equal, if not more, attention to improving tax administration in light of widespread tax evasion.

On the expenditure side, the government need not curtail its current expenditures drastically if it could privatize the SOEs speedily and effectively (these enterprises are involved in processing, manufacturing, trade, and banking). Although the SOEs' contribution to the budget increased from 20 percent of total receipts in the early 1990s to just over 30 percent by 1996, they either barely covered or did not cover their operating losses in 1994, 1997, or 1998. In other words, the SOEs' net contributions to the budget are either negative or insignificant, and are well below their financing requirements. The difference between their net contributions and financing requirements in any one year indicates the burden they impose on the budget, and this burden can also be viewed as the cost to the government of not privatizing them.

This cost of not privatizing the SOEs works out to more than 40 percent of the overall budget deficit. For 1997 the figure was some 60 percent of the overall budget deficit. Hence speedy and significant privatization of the SOEs, along with other budgetary control measures, could effectively reduce budget deficits without a great deal of hardship. Thus privatization is the key to successful implementation of the government's comprehensive program of stabilization and reform.

Finally, setting a definite time frame for the reform and development of the banking and financial sector is extremely important. Otherwise, the sector may become like most SOEs, which have had the benefit of protection from competition for several decades without ever becoming competitive.

Philippines

With the combined effects of the Asian financial crisis and El Niño in 1998, the economy contracted slightly, led by a large shrinkage of agricultural output. Compared with its neighbors, however, the Philippines demonstrated greater resilience to the economic turmoil. Given its relatively robust banking and financial sector, in the short term monetary policy should shift to a focus on stimulating domestic credit for productive investment and reducing inflation. More serious attention should also be given to such longer-term issues as improving human resources and social services, curtailing population growth, and revitalizing agriculture.

RECENT TRENDS AND PROSPECTS

In 1998 the economy was severely buffeted by the Asian financial turmoil and the El Niño phenomenon. The latter caused a large contraction of agricultural output. Consequently, GDP shrank by 0.5 percent in 1998, compared with its growth of 5.2 percent in 1997. The economy has demonstrated more resilience than neighboring economies, which have experienced severe contractions in output and employment. Factors favoring the Philippines include greater attention paid to improving the banking and financial sector since the late 1980s, continued demand stimulus through exports and private consumption that helped offset the contraction in private investment, and adroit handling of the crisis by the monetary and fiscal authorities.

Interest rates were high at the beginning of 1998 as a result of the tight monetary policy following the floating of the peso. However, with reductions in key rates by the central bank and cuts in reserve requirements, interest rates have gradually declined. While this has helped the domestic banking system cope with the high debt-service costs, it could not revive private investment. The inflation rate rose steadily as a result of high import costs and crop failures, and resulted in a rate of 9.7 percent in 1998, compared with 6.0 percent in 1997.

Despite the severe curtailment of revenues as a result of the economic slowdown, the government attempted to maintain development and social safety net expenditures. Overall government consumption expenditures showed a slight positive growth in real terms in 1998 over the previous year. This was achieved at the cost of a significant budget deficit of 1.9 percent of GDP in 1998. However, a bigger fiscal impetus seems necessary to revive economic growth given prevailing weak demand, and also to strengthen safety nets. A budget deficit of 2.3 percent is planned for 1999.

The general economic slowdown, particularly the severe contraction in the agriculture sector, led to a sharp drop in employment growth, and consequently a rise in the unemployment rate in the fourth quarter of 1998 to 9.6 percent from 7.9 percent a year earlier. Together with high inflation and the economic slow-

Box 2.1 Population Policy and Economic Development in the Philippines

Demographic transition has been slow in the Philippines compared with that in neighboring countries. For instance, while Indonesia and Thailand have brought down their population growth rates to 1.5 and 0.9 percent, respectively, the Philippine population is still increasing at an annual rate of 2.3 percent. Ironically, in 1970 the Philippines was one of the first countries in Southeast Asia to launch a population program, which subsequently became a model for neighboring countries. However, its implementation in the Philippines has not been nearly as effective as elsewhere. In 1970 the population of the Philippines was 36 million, about the same as Thailand's. If it had maintained a population program with the same efficacy as in Thailand, its population would probably now be only about 60 million instead of the current 73 million.

High fertility has had adverse effects on development. The large dependency burden in the Philippines (see the following figure) has meant that savings and investment rates have been among the lowest in Southeast Asia. Growth in per capita income over the last two decades has been extremely low as compared with other countries in the region. While in the 1960s and 1970s the Philippines had among the best educated labor force in East Asia, this is no longer the case, because investment in education and health has had to cope with the increase in numbers at the expense of improving quality. Even though poverty incidence has been declining, it remains high and the number of poor people is not falling significantly. Moreover, one of the reasons for the persistence of income disparities is higher fertility among low-income groups. Rapid population growth has also contributed to accelerating urbanization and the blight and pollution that go with it, and has also had a negative impact on agricultural productivity,

conservation, and natural resource management.

The experience of the more successful developing economies in the region clearly suggests that governments need to have a strong population policy as an integral part of their overall development strategy. High population growth rates are the result of two factors. First are the incentives for couples to have many children. Second, even if couples do not wish to have large families, they often do not have the knowledge or the means to practice effective birth control.

Consequently, the population program needs to adopt a number of approaches. To begin with, it needs to change the incentives couples face to induce them to have fewer children. One way to do this is to reduce the high rates of infant and child mortality. Couples attempt to achieve the survival of a desired number of children to provide old-age security. When mortality rates are high, birth rates are also high as couples attempt to secure the desired number of

---

improved law and order conditions would also boost investor confidence.

Since the onset of the economic crisis, the government has embarked on a set of additional measures to improve the functioning of the financial sector, including adopting better provisioning and capital adequacy standards in the banking sector, imposing stricter controls on exposure to high-risk areas, and introducing regulations on contracting foreign debt. While these measures need to be implemented quickly, the problem of nonperforming loans of the banking system also needs to be addressed effectively to minimize systemic risks. Even though the magnitude of these nonperforming loans is still small enough for the private sector to handle and their level for the

banking sector as a whole appears to be stabilizing, the government nevertheless needs to keep a close eye on the situation. Further measures with greater public sector involvement could be necessary if recovery is delayed.

POLICY AND DEVELOPMENT ISSUES

The government must also pay more attention to such longer-term issues as human development, population control, environmental protection, agricultural development, and regional disparities in development. Despite difficulties in finding resources, efforts at furthering human development (because of its long-term implications) and redressing the vulnerabilities children. Consequently, measures to reduce these mortality rates will help bring down the birth rates.

In addition, raising the status of women by increasing their access to schooling and employment will increase the direct and indirect costs of raising children. Better educated mothers will lead to couples investing more in their children's education and health and in parental care, so the cost per child is higher. The population program must therefore be targeted at poorer households where opportunities for women are particularly limited. Other effective measures include encouraging girls to marry later than the current average age at marriage and to increase the spacing between births.

Another important facet of the approach to reduce fertility levels is for the government to provide a vigorous family planning program so that couples can actually achieve their desired family size. The 1998 National Demographic and Health Survey indicates that Filipino women would prefer smaller families (3.2 children compared with the current average of 4.0), and that one third of

all pregnancies are terminated by means of illegal abortions. The Asian Development Bank has provided financial assistance to develop a safe motherhood project based at the Department of Health.

The experience of the Philippines illustrates how a weak population policy can have serious adverse effects on economic

development and social welfare. If the country is to overcome its past economic lapses and move forward strongly, this will require, among other things, a strong population policy that is based on an appropriate mix of economic incentives and adequate family planning services, and, above all, sustained government commitment.

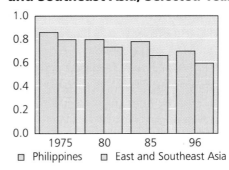

Dependency Ratio, Philippines and East and Southeast Asia, Selected Years

Notes: The dependency ratio is the ratio of dependents (population younger than 15 and older than 65) to the working-age population (15-64 years). East and Southeast Asia comprise Hong Kong, China; Indonesia; Korea; Malaysia; Singapore; Taipei,China; and Thailand.
Sources: World Bank (1998); ADB (1998); staff estimates.

of the agriculture sector (because of its implications for rural development and poverty alleviation) are particularly important at this time.

Human Development and Social Services

Despite the government's attempts to preserve expenditures on social services, it has made inadequate provisions, particularly for education and health, in its 1998 and 1999 budgets. With the continuing rapid growth of the population, basic education services are being stretched to the limit. Teacher-to-student ratios have been declining markedly, and teaching aids are inadequate. These problems have been reflected in increasing dropout rates in basic education and low

achievement scores. In poorer areas the quality of education is much lower. Regarding health, expenditure cuts could have negative implications for the control of communicable and other diseases. The devolution of health services to local governments whose finances during the crisis are in a worse situation than those of the national government makes the health situation even more critical. The program of population control has also suffered from a reduction in outlays, and this too has long-term implications for the economy (see box 2.1).

Urban and municipal services, especially in the critical areas of water supply and sanitation, and services directed at the urban poor also need to be maintained and improved. As in the case of health, these services have largely been devolved to local governments, and their financial capacity to handle such services needs to be assessed. The national government should also examine its own role carefully, reduce unproductive and overlapping expenditures, and provide support to local governments if necessary. The whole issue of local government finances requires study. Local governments have been unable to devote sufficient resources to development and have used most of their revenues for routine administrative expenditures. They need to augment their revenues, tap commercial sources of funds, and introduce greater efficiency in expenditure.

Development of Agriculture

The recent El Niño and La Niña phenomena have exposed the agriculture sector's vulnerabilities, and medium-term development strategies must therefore focus on its revitalization. Measures to reduce the impact of weather through irrigation and other infrastructure investments are as important as policy changes that would provide farmers with adequate price incentives. The market should have a greater impact on grain prices and poorer consumers should be protected through efficiently targeted interventions. In this context, the functioning of the National Food Authority should be improved and its regulatory functions separated from its operations. A tariff policy review is also essential for the rapid development of agriculture. For instance, high tariffs on corn and sugar have penalized the livestock and food processing industries and hurt consumers. The value-added tax structure for agroprocessing industries should also be reviewed, because they are effectively being taxed at higher rates than other manufacturing industries.

Agrarian reform is also critical for the development of the agriculture sector, yet the implementation of agrarian reform remains slow. This has distorted the rural land market and has prevented the use of land as collateral for investments in agriculture, thereby retarding the sector's development. Not only have land distribution targets not been met, but infrastructure development for land already distributed has been inadequate. The new government has attached high priority to the agrarian reform program and faster progress on this front should be expected.

Thailand

Even though the government's stabilization program helped restore macroeconomic stability, the economy experienced a severe recession in 1998. Export recovery has been weak, but a sharp decline in imports resulted in a substantial current account surplus in 1998. Immediate challenges facing the country are to initiate rapid economic recovery and financial sector restructuring.

RECENT TRENDS AND PROSPECTS

The impact of the 1997 financial crisis persisted in 1998, and the economic downturn deepened. GDP fell by 8 percent in 1998 after stagnating in 1997. Consequently, all macroeconomic indicators fell sharply. Private consumption fell by 14.2 percent in 1998, compared with an expansion of 0.2 percent in 1997. This was mainly because of a decline in household purchasing power caused by massive layoffs, a fall in asset prices, and a decline in consumer credit. Private investment dropped even further: by as much as 40 percent in 1998, compared with a fall of about 25 percent in 1997. Agriculture achieved a higher real growth rate of 2.1 percent in 1998 than the 1.4 percent achieved in 1997. Manufacturing production declined by 12.8 percent in 1998, after virtually stagnating in 1997. The manufacturing industries producing for the domestic market were the hardest hit, including those producing automobile and construction materials. Export-oriented industries fared somewhat better, because exports to Europe and North America expanded.

The recession resulted in a historically high unemployment rate of 5.3 percent of the total labor force. By August 1998 unemployment, including seasonally inactive labor, reached 1.8 million people. The figure would have been even higher had not the agriculture sector been able to absorb a significant portion of the workers laid off from the manufacturing sector. In anticipation of increased unemployment, the government postponed the annual minimum wage increase for 1997 from October 1997 to January 1998 and did not grant any further wage increase in 1998.

The depth of the recession was aggravated during the latter half of 1997 and early 1998 by fiscal contraction resulting from the government's stabilization policy. However, in the first quarter of 1998 the government started to relax its tight fiscal policy in an attempt to boost domestic demand. On the revenue side, because of the steep economic decline the government anticipated revenue shortfalls, especially in corporate income taxes and the earnings of state enterprises. The government increased its 1998 expenditure target, mainly to strengthen spending on the social safety net. Consequently, the overall public sector deficit for 1998 reached 3 percent of GDP, of which the central government accounted for 2.5 percent and state enterprises accounted for 0.5 percent. The expansionary fiscal stance has been maintained for 1999, with an overall public sector deficit target set at 5 percent of GDP, with 3 percent for the central government and 2 percent for state enterprises. In addition, of the interest costs of financial sector restructuring, estimated at 3 percent of GDP, the government will fiscalize an amount equivalent to 1.5 percent of GDP in 1999.

Reflecting the initial monetary policy response to the crisis, liquidity conditions in the money market remained tight in the first half of 1998; however, monetary policy became more expansionary in the second half of 1998. This brought the interbank rate down from 21.5 percent in January 1998 to 2.6 percent in December 1998, and the one-year fixed deposit rate from 10.00-11.50 to 6.0 percent during the same period. Meanwhile, the prime (minimum lending) rate declined at a much slower pace, from

15.25 percent in January 1998 to 11.50-12.00 percent in December 1998. The decline in interest rates indicates that the market now has sufficient liquidity. However, financial institutions are not lending to the real sector because they are concerned about nonperforming loans and loan loss provisioning requirements. The year-on-year growth of commercial bank credits, including Bangkok International Banking Facility lending (which enables licensed banks to borrow abroad and lend to domestic borrowers in foreign currencies), continuously decelerated from 25.9 percent in January to 12.7 in June, and further to 0.7 percent in September 1998. In the fourth quarter of 1998, bank credits started posting negative growth rates: minus 4.3 percent in October, minus 4.9 percent in November, and minus 9.7 percent in December. In January 1999, commercial bank credits decreased by minus 13 percent year-on-year.

Inflation averaged just under 10 percent during the first half of 1998, reflecting the depreciation of the baht, the increases in the value-added tax rate

Table 2.11   Major Economic Indicators, Thailand, 1996-2000
(percent)

Item	1996	1997	1998	1999	2000
GDP growth	5.5	-0.4	-8.0	0.0	2.5
Gross domestic investment/GDP	41.7	35.0	24.4	24.7	27.0
Gross savings/GDP	33.7	32.9	35.9	33.2	33.0
Inflation rate (consumer price index)	5.9	5.6	8.1	3.0	5.0
Money supply (M2) growth	12.6	16.4	9.6	11.0	13.0
Fiscal balance/GDP[a]	2.4	-0.9	-2.5	-3.0	—
Merchandise exports growth	-1.9	3.8	-6.6	5.1	8.5
Merchandise imports growth	0.6	-13.4	-32.3	12.6	14.5
Current account balance/GDP[b]	-7.9	-2.0	11.5	8.5	6.0
Debt service/exports	12.3	15.6	21.3	20.1	—

— Not available.

a. On a fiscal year basis. Covers central government budgetary and nonbudgetary accounts and social security funds, and excludes interest costs of financial sector restructuring.
b. Excluding official transfers.

Sources: Bank of Thailand; Ministry of Finance; National Economic and Social Development Board; Bureau of the Budget; Ministry of Commerce; International Monetary Fund; staff estimates.

and in excise taxes on luxury goods, and the higher food prices. However, after peaking in June 1998, inflation declined significantly in the second half of the year as the recession worsened and the baht stabilized. The rate for the whole year was 8.1 percent, compared with 5.6 percent in 1997.

Export earnings in dollar terms decreased by 6.6 percent, compared with a 3.8 percent increase in 1997, mainly because of lower export prices and constraints on export financing. Export volumes, however, grew steadily in 1998. The decline in imports was far more dramatic. The fall of 13.4 percent in 1997 turned into a decline of 32.3 percent in 1998, reflecting the severe contraction in domestic demand. As a result, the current account balance registered a surplus of $13.5 billion or 11.5 percent of GDP, showing a large turnaround from a deficit equivalent to 2.0 percent of GDP in 1997. This merely reflected the extent of the recession. The capital account posted a deficit of $11 billion, mainly because of external debt repayments and offshore swap settlements that offset inflows of foreign direct investment. At the end of December 1998 gross official reserves stood at $29.5 billion or 8.5 months of imports, compared with $27 billion or 5.3 months of imports a year before. The baht initially depreciated to around B50 to the US dollar in early 1998, but strengthened to about B36 to the dollar by the end of the year. The average exchange rate in 1998 was B41.3. Total external debt decreased from $93.4 billion at the end of 1997 to $85.4 billion at the end of 1998. The share of short-term debt declined from 37 to 28 percent during the same period.

Thus while Thailand has shown recent signs of moderate recovery in private consumption and manufacturing production, the decline in private investment has continued, and the performance of the external sector has remained weak. Agricultural production may also suffer because of serious water shortages caused by droughts in some areas.

The economy is expected to improve somewhat in the latter part of 1999, with a zero percent growth rate overall for the year, and to continue recovering in 2000 with an approximately 2.5 percent growth rate. Inflation is expected to continue to fall to about 3 percent in 1999 in the absence of inflationary pressures, but to increase slightly to 5 percent in 2000.

ISSUES IN ECONOMIC MANAGEMENT

The immediate challenge is to promote growth. The stabilization program, which the government adopted in consultation with the International Monetary Fund in August 1997, has been effective in eliminating the current account deficit and stabilizing the exchange rate, but at the cost of a severe recession. Furthermore, the unsettled conditions in the region have also reduced expected export demand and delayed the recovery in private capital flows. In response to the recession, the government has adjusted its macroeconomic policy stance appropriately since early 1998. It has relaxed its fiscal policy to allow larger public sector deficits, which should help stimulate the economy, and has also adjusted its monetary policy, reducing interest rates. Nevertheless, on their own these measures will not be sufficient to restore growth. Growth recovery relies largely on the success of financial sector restructuring and the progress made in recapitalizing financial institutions, restoring investor confidence, resuming liquidity flow to the real sector, and improving the external economic environment.

The government took initial steps to restructure the financial sector in the latter half of 1997. These included closing 56 insolvent finance companies and requiring the recapitalization of all remaining financial institutions. In the first half of 1998 the central bank took further steps, including changing the classification of nonperforming loans and related regulations in line with Bank for International Settlements standards to enforce prudential norms in the financial sector. The new definition of nonperforming loans, effective from July 1998, is three months or more of overdue payments instead of six months. Required provisioning for substandard loans that are up to six months overdue was raised from 15 to 20 percent for commercial banks. This tightening of loan classification and provisioning was essential for restructuring the financial sector.

Progress on the actual recapitalization of financial institutions in the latter half of 1997 and the first half of 1998 was limited. Adequate recapitalization is essential to provide enough liquidity to the real sector to revitalize economic activities. Therefore, to expedite financial sector restructuring the government announced a comprehensive financial sector restructuring package on 14 August 1998. The government decided to take over, dissolve, or merge troubled financial institutions, while allowing 9 banks and 24 finance companies to continue their operations. It will provide capital support through the Tier 1 Scheme and Tier 2 Scheme by issuing government bonds of B300 billion. The Tier 1 Scheme is to help solvent financial institutions recapitalize, and the Tier 2 Scheme is to provide capital support and incentives for corporate debt restructuring and new lending. The package also includes the imposition of strict terms and conditions for institutions drawing on government capital support to minimize moral hazard, permission to set up private asset management companies to deal with financial institutions' bad assets, improvements in the regulatory system to ensure prudent management of the financial sector, and changes in the related laws and regulations to implement the package.

The government has made progress in reorganizing the financial sector by nationalization, dissolution, and merger under the package. However, financial institutions' recapitalization has been slow and inadequate. Only two financial institutions have so far applied for the Tier 1 Scheme, because financial institutions wish to avoid central bank intervention in their management. Instead, they have been looking for strategic partners for recapitalization. The deadline for application for the Tier 1 Scheme is set for November 2000. However, all the financial institutions have to submit their recapitalization plans to the central bank every six months and complete their planned recapitalization by the end of each six-month period.

Regarding corporate debt restructuring, the Corporate Debt Restructuring Advisory Committee has been closely monitoring the first target group of 200 key debt restructuring cases, involving 353 companies and a total debt of B674 billion. Of these key cases, B82 billion for 47 companies had been restructured as of January 1999. In addition, six financial institutions have applied for the Tier 2 Scheme.

Relaxed monetary policy brought down interest rates substantially in the latter half of 1998. This reduction indicates that there is now sufficient liquidity in the market. However, the interest rate reduction alone has not helped increase credits to the real sector, as financial institutions have become extremely cautious about lending because of stricter provisioning requirements and increasing nonperforming loans. This has made otherwise viable companies become insolvent.

Another critical issue for economic recovery is legislation for economic reforms. The government has proposed 11 economic reform bills, of which 3 deal with foreign ownership and leasing of land and 5 cover changes in bankruptcy and foreclosure laws. These bills have been stalled in Parliament.

POLICY AND DEVELOPMENT ISSUES

In the longer term, the main policy and development issues are restoring competitiveness, achieving high growth, and improving the quality of life. The latter includes reducing disparities across income groups, regions, and genders; alleviating rural poverty; and improving environmental protection.

Restoration of competitiveness and high growth requires investments and policy and institutional reforms in agriculture, industry, human resource development, and infrastructure. One of the critical factors for long-term sustainable growth is agriculture. Given the country's economic and social structure and natural resource endowments, improved agricultural practices are critical for restoring export competitiveness, as well as for alleviating poverty and reducing regional disparities. Agricultural development will require substantial investments, including water resources management projects; institutional and policy reforms; and alternative income sources.

To improve industrial efficiency and competitiveness, the government has initiated legal and regulatory reforms and privatization of state enterprises. To this end, it has instituted three major legal changes as follows:

■ Introduction of the Bankruptcy Law to support the process of corporate reorganization (as opposed to liquidation), increase the scope for out-of-court settlements, and ensure fair treatment of both creditors and debtors. The latter is needed to allow creditors to extend credit to troubled firms without undermining creditors' rights to subsequent recovery of their loans.

■ Implementation of legislation governing foreclosure to expedite enforcement of creditors' security rights.

■ Introduction of the Alien Business Law to increase foreign participation and competition in key sectors of the economy.

Authorities recognize that privatizing state enterprises is necessary for economic recovery as a way to attract new local and foreign investment. In particular, the privatization strategy as laid out under the adjustment program emphasizes the establishment of the following: a central coordinating and monitoring agency within the Ministry of Finance, a master plan for state enterprise reforms and strategic action programs, a legal framework to enable the privatization of state enterprises, and a set of sectoral privatization plans.

To improve the quality of life, the government will continue to provide a social safety net to those particularly badly affected by the crisis. It will also introduce long-term investment in employment generation, public health care, education and vocational training, and rural development. For example, in the 1999 budget the government allocated 1.5 percent of GDP (approximately B75 billion) to social sector projects, including social safety net payments and related labor-intensive investments.

The government's strategy for immediate economic recovery and future sustainable growth is generally sound and balanced. Nevertheless, it needs to ensure that objectives such as balanced regional development, greater opportunities for women, improved environmental protection, and a more participatory approach to development are all an integral part of the mainstream development program and are not treated as side issues.

Viet Nam

Viet Nam is one of the few countries in Southeast Asia that continued to grow in the midst of the financial crisis. It was not, however, immune from the regional turmoil. Viet Nam needs to act convincingly on the structural reform front, particularly in the banking and state enterprise sector, to reinstate the momentum for growth.

RECENT TRENDS AND PROSPECTS

A slowdown in agriculture, construction, and services was principally responsible for the markedly lower GDP growth rate in 1998, which stood at an estimated 4 percent, down from just over 8 percent in 1997. Agricultural output grew by less than 3 percent, partly because of the adverse effects of natural disasters, in particular, Typhoon Linda at the end of 1997 and drought and floods in the central region in 1998. Nevertheless, rice output increased and rice exports reached 3.8 million tons, making Viet Nam the second largest world exporter of rice after Thailand. The construction sector was adversely affected by the sharp reduction in inflows of foreign direct investment (FDI) and by fiscal austerity measures. Services grew only marginally as tourism, air travel, hotels and restaurants, real estate, and financial services all experienced a sharp downturn. The industrial sector continued to expand, and manufacturing was its most dynamic component. Crude oil production also grew considerably in physical terms (nearly 26 percent), but its contribution to GDP and exports did not increase in value terms, because of the sharp decrease in the international price of oil by nearly 30 percent.

Despite a slowdown in the GDP growth rate, end of period consumer price inflation jumped to slightly over 9 percent in 1998, more than double the rate of the previous two years. The increase in food prices, particularly during May and June, which led to the adoption of temporary export bans on rice, was a significant contributory factor. The devaluation of the dong in February and September 1998 by a total of nearly 14 percent also contributed to the rise in prices.

In recent years FDI has accounted for nearly 30 percent of total investment in Viet Nam; however, new commitments were considerably lower in 1998 than in previous years, and disbursements were even further down. Two reasons account for this. The first was the crisis that affected the Asian countries, as these have been the source of more than two thirds of Viet Nam's FDI. Second, the foreign investment community became somewhat disenchanted with the pace of economic reforms and the potential for expansion in the domestic market.

To compensate for the low level of FDI, in 1998 the government implemented additional measures to stimulate domestic investment, of which the most important was the Domestic Investment Promotion Law, announced in April 1998. This provides incentives in a wide range of areas, including relaxing ownership restrictions; establishing support funds; and introducing preferential treatment for build-transfer and build-operate-transfer schemes, which permit private management and investment in power generation, water supply systems, sewage, urban bus services, and telephone services. These facilities are also extended to Vietnamese living overseas and foreigners with permanent residence in Viet Nam.

Viet Nam is an exceptionally open economy, with foreign trade (exports plus imports of goods and services) nearly equivalent to its total GDP. As a consequence, the country is quite vulnerable to external shocks. During 1998 exports to Japan and countries of the Association of Southeast Asian Nations declined by around 30 percent, while exports to the Republic of Korea fell by about 40 percent. A modest growth in overall exports was largely due to an increase in exports of rice and crude oil. Favorable rice and coffee prices helped offset the negative impact of the decline in world crude oil prices. A combination of the relative strength of the dong against neighboring currencies despite two devaluations and the weak demand from trading partners explain the modest performance of the export sector.

Nevertheless, the trade deficit fell by nearly half in 1998. The improvement was largely due to the contraction in imports, a result of the slower economic growth, the temporary import restrictions imposed on a number of goods, and the depreciation of the dong. The result was that Viet Nam's current account deficit fell from the record high of 11 percent of GDP in 1995 to a more manageable 4.1 percent in 1998. This contraction allowed Viet Nam to absorb the corresponding decline in FDI inflows without excessive pressure on its foreign exchange reserves.

Because of the economic slowdown, government revenues dropped below 20 percent of GDP in 1998. Fiscal revenues depend heavily on taxes from state and foreign enterprises and on trade taxes. These combined sources accounted for more than 80 percent of

Table 2.12 Major Economic Indicators, Viet Nam, 1996-2000
(percent)

Item	1996	1997	1998	1999	2000
GDP growth	9.3	8.2	4.0	3.7	4.5
Gross domestic investment/GDP	28.1	28.3	28.7	25.0	27.0
Gross savings/GDP	17.8	21.5	24.6	22.0	23.0
Inflation rate (consumer price index)[a]	4.5	3.6	9.2	8.0	7.0
Money supply (M2) growth[b]	22.7	26.1	22.0	19.0	20.0
Fiscal balance/GDP[c]	-1.3	-1.7	-1.5	-2.5	-2.0
Merchandise exports growth	41.0	22.2	3.9	5.0	6.0
Merchandise imports growth	38.9	-1.6	-2.3	4.0	6.5
Current account balance/GDP[d]	-10.3	-6.8	-4.1	-3.0	-4.0
Debt service/exports[e]	11.0	11.4	13.4	14.0	14.5

a. End of period.
b. Based on the expanded monetary survey that includes 24 nongovernment banks.
c. Excluding grants.
d. Excluding official transfers.
e. Based on debt service due.

Sources: General Statistical Office; State Bank of Viet Nam; Ministry of Finance; International Monetary Fund reports; staff estimates.

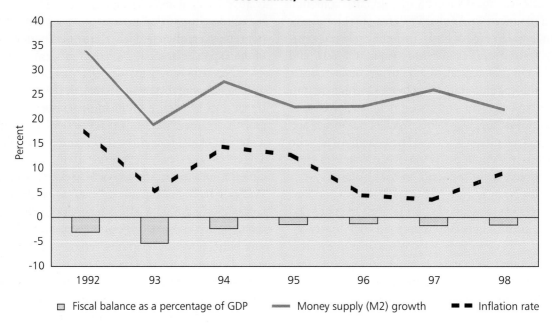

Figure 2.8 Fiscal Balance, Money Supply, and Inflation, Viet Nam, 1992-1998

□ Fiscal balance as a percentage of GDP   —— Money supply (M2) growth   ▪ ▪ Inflation rate

Sources: Ministry of Finance; State Bank of Viet Nam; General Statistical Office; staff estimates.

total current revenue in 1998. As GDP growth was considerably lower than the targeted 9 percent, revenues fell accordingly. The government reacted by freezing current expenditures in nominal terms, equivalent to an almost 10 percent drop in real terms. Capital spending was less severely affected, but many large projects were temporarily postponed. As a result of this fiscally prudent approach, the deficit was kept within bounds in 1998, evenly financed by domestic Treasury bills and external loans, without any significant recourse to monetization.

Projections indicate that the GDP growth rate is likely to be between 3.7 and 4.5 percent in 1999 and 2000, as the slow growth of exports and modest inflows of FDI persist. The government has indicated a commitment to prudent fiscal and monetary management. In 1999 it plans to introduce a value-added tax. In addition, adjustments to corporate and personal income tax rates and improvements in collection methods can be expected. It also plans to raise corporate and personal income tax rates, but these may be off-

set by exemptions and tax holidays for a number of firms. Along with teething problems with the introduction of the new value-added tax, some weakness may arise on the revenue side of the public budget. Inflation is expected to remain in single digits, probably in the 7 to 8 percent range.

The balance-of-payments outlook is for the current account deficit to remain close to its present share of GDP. If external demand recovers, this will allow for some easing of imports. The fall in FDI is expected to continue, as nearly a third of FDI disbursements during the 1990s has been in hotels and tourism in general, and in construction of apartments and office complexes, and there is general overcapacity in these areas.

ISSUES IN ECONOMIC MANAGEMENT

The Asian financial crisis has certainly played a significant role in Viet Nam's 1998 slowdown and accounts for the cautious outlook for 1999 and 2000. The problems, however, are exacerbated by structural weaknesses in Viet Nam's economy; its relatively high costs compared with those in regional markets, which experienced massive devaluations; uncertainty about foreign currency availability; and lack of transparency in regulations. Some of these fundamental problems can only be addressed by comprehensive reform measures.

Unless the regional and global macroeconomic situation improves rapidly, Viet Nam will have to continue exercising fiscal and monetary restraint if it is to counter the recession without recourse to significant macroeconomic imbalances. The government will have to pursue diversification of export markets and seek new sources of FDI inflows to reduce external vulnerability. In addition, to avoid pressures on foreign exchange reserves, it will need to monitor the exchange rate closely and, if necessary, make further adjustments to maintain its competitiveness in the face of domestic inflation and of possible realignments by some of Viet Nam's trade competitors.

The domestic investment climate needs to be improved to enhance the country's ability to compete for foreign capital. The Law on Foreign Investment was first amended in December 1987. Relatively few changes took place after that until 1998, when the government introduced incentive schemes, including tax incentives, export incentives, duty free imports, eased restrictions on ownership and domestic sales, and foreign currency assistance. On paper, the investment environment has been enhanced, but actual implementation will prove to be the true test of whether the business climate has really improved. Limitations on access to foreign exchange, restrictions on the hiring of labor, and other measures that artificially increase production costs all deter sustained high levels of FDI.

POLICY AND DEVELOPMENT ISSUES

State-owned enterprise (SOE) and financial sector reforms remain at the center of the overall reform agenda of the economy, and will have a major influence on medium-term macroeconomic stability and long-term growth rates. State-owned enterprises are exempt from collateral requirements and enjoy preferential access to bank financing. As a result of formal and informal preference in credit allocation, they continue to absorb more than half of total domestic credit. Because only some 40 percent of SOEs can be considered profitable, a large stock of potentially unserviceable debt has been building up over time, yet banks continue lending to them under the implicit assumption that ultimately the government will intervene to cover such obligations.

This situation has serious macroeconomic and microeconomic consequences. From a macroeconomic perspective, if the state had to intervene to cover borrowing by insolvent SOEs, the impact on the budget and/or the monetary aggregates would be substantial. From a microeconomic perspective, as banks do not screen potential borrowers as they do in market economies, the misallocation of scarce financial resources can be serious. This reduces both the productivity of the economy and its growth potential.

Reform and restructuring of the banking sector must be accompanied by SOE reform. To date, the privatization program has achieved only modest results: after an initial wave of mergers in the early 1980s, only a few dozen enterprises have been privatized. The government will have to adopt a combination of privatization, restructuring, divestiture, and liquidation as appropriate. Setting and meeting credible targets for such a program will be important. If the government were to undertake banking reform without parallel SOE reform, new unsound credit allocation would soon follow, recreating the same type of problems that the financial system is currently experiencing. The macroeconomic and microeconomic benefits that the country would reap from such reforms would be substantial, and could spur a second phase of accelerated growth, built on stronger and more lasting foundations.

South Asia

Bangladesh
Bhutan
India
Maldives
Nepal
Pakistan
Sri Lanka

Bangladesh

While economic performance in 1998 continued the growth trend of the past few years, the damage caused by recent floods will have a serious adverse effect on macroeconomic performance in 1999. Bangladesh needs to implement a number of reforms and raise levels of saving and investment to achieve the high growth rates that are essential for tackling the pervasive problem of poverty.

RECENT TRENDS AND PROSPECTS

Bangladesh's notable achievement in recent years has been the much improved GDP growth rate. Economic growth in the past three years broke the 4 percent barrier that persisted during the 1970s and 1980s. In 1998 GDP grew at a rate of 5.7 percent, slightly less than the 5.9 percent rate achieved in 1997. The grain output declined significantly compared with the bumper harvest of the previous year because of poor rains. By contrast, industrial growth had a strong recovery from its disappointing performance in 1997, partly because of the improving energy supply. The improvement in industrial growth was led mainly by the garments and textiles, cement, and sugar industries.

Devastating floods swept the country from July to September 1998. The continuous and heavy monsoon rains along with a tidal surge in the Bay of Bengal caused flooding in 51 of Bangladesh's 64 districts. The duration of the flooding surpassed all previous records. While the floods had some adverse consequences for

1998 refers to fiscal year 1997/98, ending 30 June.

the economy in 1998, their full impact will not be felt until 1999.

Since the early 1990s, improvements in saving and investment have been impressive. The savings rate as a percentage of GDP more than doubled from 1990 to 1997, and in 1998 remained the same as in 1997. However, because of a decline in foreign savings, particularly in foreign aid disbursement, the 1998 investment rate was about one percentage point of GDP lower than in 1997.

One of the most prominent fiscal developments in the early 1990s was the rise in the share of revenue as a proportion of GDP. Fiscal reforms broadened the coverage of the value-added tax and nontax revenue sources. Meanwhile, the government's current expenditure remained largely under control. As a result, it was able to increase the share of capital expenditure in its annual development program from nothing in 1990 to more than 45 percent in 1998. Despite improvements in the fiscal situation in the past few years, the budget deficit remained relatively high at 5.4 percent of GDP in 1998. The deterioration in the financial position of state-owned enterprises and recent stagnation in government revenue collection is cause for concern. The floods further strained the fiscal deficit and are expected to enlarge the already high budget deficits in 1999.

The rate of inflation more than doubled to reach 7 percent in 1998. Low yields of food crops, supply shortages caused by the floods, and salary increases granted to government employees all played important parts in this increase.

Trade liberalization and export promotion policies initiated in the early 1990s resulted in a sharp expansion of external trade. Export performance improved noticeably, with a growth rate of 16.8 percent in 1998, which was one of the highest in Asia. The garment and knitwear subsectors accounted for almost the entire increase in exports. By contrast, exports of jute, leather, and frozen foods fell. The growth rate of imports likewise increased in 1998. To date, the impact of the Asian crisis on Bangladesh's economy has been limited. Nonconvertibility of the capital account, the virtual absence of foreign portfolio investments, low current account deficits, and a moderate external debt burden have largely insulated the economy from external shocks originating from the world capital market. Foreign exchange reserves are now equivalent to just under three months of imports.

Although the pace of reform remained slow in 1998, the government made some progress in addressing the economy's structural problems. The authorities undertook several initiatives to tackle the difficulties of the banking system: the central bank used strong measures to deal with the problem of huge, outstanding, nonperforming loans; the Financial Loan Court Act was amended to empower loan courts to enforce debt recovery; and restrictions were imposed on the rescheduling of overdue loans. Furthermore, efforts were made to develop a fair, transparent, and efficient capital market; the Securities and Exchange Commission was strengthened; and automation of the stock exchange was achieved. To reduce the budget deficit, the government adjusted several administered prices, such as those for fertilizer, petroleum, and electricity. It also made some progress in opening up the infrastructure and energy sectors to private investment.

Were it not for the recent floods, the economy would be able to maintain the growth rate of 5 to 6 percent achieved in the past three years in 1999. However, the damage caused by the floods has adversely

Table 2.13 Major Economic Indicators, Bangladesh, 1996-2000
(percent)

Item	1996	1997	1998	1999	2000
GDP growth	5.4	5.9	5.7	3.6	5.5
Gross domestic investment/GDP	17.0	17.3	16.3	17.5	17.0
Gross national savings/GNP	14.3	14.8	14.8	14.5	15.0
Inflation rate (consumer price index)	6.6	2.6	7.0	8.0	6.0
Money supply (M2) growth	8.2	10.8	10.1	10.0	8.0
Fiscal balance/GDP	-5.9	-5.6	-5.4	-6.5	-5.5
Merchandise exports growth	11.8	14.0	16.8	8.0	12.0
Merchandise imports growth	19.1	3.1	5.3	10.0	8.0
Current account balance/GDP	-4.1	-1.7	-1.1	-3.0	-2.0
Debt service/exports	12.1	11.4	11.7	12.0	12.1

Sources: International Monetary Fund (various issues); Ministry of Planning; staff estimates.

affected economic prospects. Projections suggest that the GDP growth rate for 1999 will be only 3.6 percent, mainly because of serious setbacks in the agriculture sector. Increased government expenditure resulting from the floods will put pressure on both the budget and the balance of payments in 1999.

ISSUES IN ECONOMIC MANAGEMENT

In the short term, the government's main task is to speed up the pace of economic reform and institutional development. It needs to correct macroeconomic imbalances by keeping the fiscal deficit and inflation under control. Improvement in the fiscal position depends heavily on increasing the revenue-to-GDP ratio. Tax structure and coverage, administration, and compliance also need to be improved, and the annual development program has to be managed better to improve the efficiency with which concessional assistance is used. Given the possible declining trend in the availability of foreign aid, mobilizing more domestic resources to finance public expenditure is increasingly important. The balance of payments needs to be closely monitored in the coming months because of the low level of foreign exchange reserves. Finally, the government needs to pursue a more flexible exchange rate policy to restore the economy's competitiveness and to maintain macroeconomic stability.

One of the key challenges facing the country is how to mobilize more domestic resources for development. A major problem is that the financial system is characterized by inefficiency, poor quality of intermediation, and lack of accountability. A large proportion of the portfolio of commercial banks is classified as nonperforming. Supervision and regulation by the central bank is weak, as is enforcement of prudential norms. The high level of loan defaults has increased the costs of banking and has penalized private investors. Commercial banks have largely stopped long-term lending. As a result, private enterprises find the acquisition of long-term financing difficult. Development financing institutions, which tend to be government owned, are also facing serious financial problems, and for many years have virtually ceased making new loans. Without further deepening of the banking sector reforms, raising savings and investment rates will be difficult.

On a more positive note, the gas sector is poised to make a major contribution to economic growth. The possibility exists that gas reserves could be sufficiently exploited to eliminate the gap between energy demand and supply and to generate additional foreign exchange earnings. The industry may also offer a unique opportunity for attracting large-scale foreign direct investment. However, developing the gas industry may put a strain on the balance of payments, because a significant portion of profits may be repatriated to the investing countries once production comes on line, and because development of the industry will require extensive imports. The government needs to be aware of these problems and introduce a gas utilization policy, as well as ensuring that investors earn a sufficient rate of return on the project.

POLICY AND DEVELOPMENT ISSUES

Bangladesh's primary challenges will continue to be the progressive reduction of poverty and the improvement of living standards. Slow economic growth during the past two decades and rising income inequality are the primary reasons for the slow progress in poverty reduction. The government approved the Fifth Five-Year Plan (1997-2002) in March 1998, the first plan formulated by the current government since assuming office in June 1996. The plan has set the average annual growth target at 7 percent, a level necessary to make any significant impact on poverty. Achieving it will require significantly higher savings and investment levels than Bangladesh has managed to achieve so far.

The private sector has great potential to contribute to economic growth and poverty alleviation, and the government has been pursuing policies to strengthen the private sector's role in the country's development efforts. The success of this policy is reflected in the sharp increase in the share of private sector investment in the economy, which rose from just under 6 percent of GDP in 1991 to nearly 11 percent in 1997. The impressive development of the ready-made garment industry in the past decade showed that with appropriate policy support, the private sector could make a major contribution to the economy.

While the country has made a good start on private sector development, there is still much room for reducing the bias against the private sector and improving incentives for private sector participation. Currently, serious infrastructure weaknesses, particularly in port and power facilities, are having an adverse effect on the expansion of private sector activities. The private sector has also suffered considerably from the shortcomings of the banking system, the development finance institutions, and the capital market.

Bangladesh's long-term development prospects depend partly on the extent of foreign capital inflow, both official and private. Bangladesh has one of the most liberal trade and foreign payment regimes and provides the most favorable incentives to attract foreign investment in South Asia. Nevertheless, actual achievements have been limited to date. However, development of the gas industry could change all this.

How far the industry's potential can be realized will depend on the improvement of the overall investment climate. In addition, investments in the gas industry may not directly generate foreign exchange reserves. Unless the country can attract a large amount of foreign direct investment to support an export orientation by the industry, the medium-term outlook for the balance of payments could worsen rather than improve.

Bangladesh has a comparative advantage in its cost of labor, which is one of the lowest in Asia. Promoting private investment in labor-intensive industries is therefore vital for generating growth and employment and reducing poverty. In this regard, the development of several export processing zones, including those targeted for specific investors from the Republic of Korea and Japan, could bring in sizable foreign direct investment.

Bhutan

Bhutan's growth rate was above 5 percent in 1998, and the government is conscientiously implementing the Eighth Five-Year Plan. As a result, growth prospects are good. A major challenge facing policymakers in the medium term is generating employment opportunities for the rapidly growing labor force, which is better educated than in the past.

RECENT TRENDS AND PROSPECTS

Bhutan experienced strong growth in 1997, with GDP growth of 5.4 percent. Growth in 1998 was expected to remain above 5 percent, even without the major industrial projects that had previously led to double-digit growth in manufacturing and power generation. However, rapid population growth in excess of 3 percent per year continues to prevent a rapid increase in living standards. With a per capita income of $400 in 1997 (World Bank 1999), Bhutan is still one of the poorest countries in the world. While its standard of living surpasses that of Bangladesh and Nepal, it is similar to that of India.

The government continues to conduct a prudent fiscal policy, with current revenues exceeding current expenditures in 1998. The government receives most of its current revenues as profits from public enterprises and service fees from the ministries. While tax revenues are mostly from enterprise and goods taxes, the introduction of a personal income tax, due to begin generating revenue in 2000, should help broaden

1998 refers to fiscal year 1997/98, ending 30 June.

the tax base. Inflows of foreign grants in excess of development expenditures led to an overall budget surplus of 3.3 percent of GDP, compared with a 2.4 percent deficit the previous year. However, this apparent improvement in the country's fiscal stance was caused mainly by a decline in capital expenditures.

The dollar value of exports grew by 12 percent in 1998, much higher than the previous year's rate of 2 percent. In addition, slower import growth of 4 percent, down from the 18 percent in 1997, resulted in a decline in both the trade deficit (from 9 to 7 percent of GDP) and the current account deficit (from 16 to 12 percent of GDP). While Bhutan maintained a slight trade surplus with India, this was offset by the deficit in its trade in services.

Capital inflows, mostly in the form of aid for investment in infrastructure, exceeded the current account deficit. These boosted Bhutan's foreign exchange reserves, which now cover almost 19 months worth of imports. However, under the current fixed exchange rate system, the increase in reserves led to growth in the money supply of 42 percent, a large increase compared with the 31 percent growth experienced in 1997. This did not translate into high inflation, because of the increasing demand for money brought about by the progressive monetization of the economy. As a consequence, inflation only rose slightly from 7 percent in 1997 to 9 percent in 1998. However, the inflation rate is expected to increase slightly in 1999 following the rise in food prices in India.

External debt, owed mainly to multilateral development agencies, continues to be small. Debt service in 1998 was about 11 percent of merchandise export earnings. At the end of 1998, total public external debt was 34 percent of GDP. The composition of this debt has been changing, with a decline in nonconvertible and a rise in convertible currency debt. As more grace periods on the concessional debt that Bhutan acquired in the 1980s expire, the country's convertible currency inflows will come under increasing pressure.

The year 1998 was the first of Bhutan's ambitious Eighth Five-Year Plan. The government has made a satisfactory start in attaining its extensive goals, for instance, it has made progress in expanding the physical infrastructure, such as roads and power supply, as well as the social infrastructure, such as schools and health centers. This has often been accomplished with international donor support. Because of the government's commitment to the Eighth Plan, Bhutan should continue to experience output growth in excess of 5 percent in 1999.

ISSUES IN ECONOMIC MANAGEMENT

While the Eighth Plan will enhance Bhutan's growth prospects, overseeing the wide range of projects is straining the government's limited resources. Because of the broad range of skills involved, some ministries are experiencing difficulties in monitoring the progress of the numerous projects. To cope with this, the central government should devolve some project responsibilities to local governments and increase community involvement. This will have the additional benefit of increasing community ownership of the projects. In addition, greater private sector involvement will be required if the government is to maintain a compact civil service.

The capital investment program will have implications for the national budget. The schools and health centers will require staff and supplies, while the roads and power plants will require regular maintenance, all of which will put pressure on the budget. To relieve some of this pressure, the government needs to explore cost reduction measures, such as introducing community responsibility for school and clinic maintenance, as well as cost recovery measures, for example, introducing user fees for health services and price increases for electricity.

In addition to the pressure on the budget, many investments will also compete for scarce foreign currency. Foreign-made equipment will require foreign replacement parts to continue to function. Moreover, the country relies heavily on foreign technicians and workers for maintenance, and their repatriated earnings will put a further strain on foreign exchange reserves. A major objective is therefore to develop local capacity to undertake such maintenance. This will ensure that current investments continue to provide services in the future without causing balance-of-payments difficulties.

POLICY AND DEVELOPMENT ISSUES

One of Bhutan's major development issues arises from its demography. Bhutan has a relatively young population. In 1996 more than 40 percent of the population was younger than 15 years and the median age was less than 20. Both sexes in this cohort have better access to education than previous generations, and so the labor market will have increased access to better educated workers. In the case of women, the improvement in educational attainment will be complemented by greater family planning. A major challenge is to provide these workers with suitable employment. Development of the private sector can remove some of the burden of job creation from the government, but the latter needs to ensure the provision of the necessary legal framework and financial institutions for this to occur.

In the future, an excess supply of workers is likely, but the current position is the opposite, namely, an excess demand for labor. At present, Bhutan relies heavily on immigrants, particularly from India, to fill shortages in such white-collar professions as teaching and public administration. Consequently, in addition to creating new job opportunities, Bhutan must find ways to provide the next generation of Bhutanese workers with the specific skills to meet these needs. This requires the provision of formal education, particularly in management and the sciences, as well as vocational education. Expatriate workers are also concentrated in such low-skilled manual employment as road maintenance. Improving the working conditions for manual laborers will be necessary to induce Bhutanese workers to accept employment in this sector of the labor market.

To plan effectively for these developments in the labor market, the government requires reliable demographic statistics, which are currently lacking. A population census, together with labor force surveys, would help the government target programs and enable it to react quickly and flexibly to changing economic circumstances.

India

Although to date India has been relatively unaffected by the Asian economic crisis, uncertainties about the external environment and rising concern about the slowdown of economic growth will dominate economic policy in the short term. Infrastructure bottlenecks continue to impose constraints on economic development and need to be alleviated to enhance India's future growth prospects. Equally important, India must not neglect to develop its human resources.

RECENT TRENDS AND PROSPECTS

After three successive years of growth averaging above 7 percent per year during 1994 to 1996, growth slowed to about 5 percent in 1997. Growth was higher in 1998 largely because of a rebound in agricultural production, which had declined in 1997. The increase in agricultural production took place despite heavy rainfall and flooding in July and August 1998. Meanwhile, the performance of the industrial sector deteriorated still further in 1998 compared with 1997, and the growth rate of less than 5 percent was significantly lower than the spectacular rate of about 10 percent achieved in the mid-1990s. While capital goods industries recorded higher growth in 1998 than in 1997, the basic goods sector—which includes fertilizers, chemicals, cement, basic metals, electricity, and mining—and the consumer goods sector continued to be adversely affected by slow growth in consumer demand, subdued export demand, and infrastructure constraints.

1998 refers to fiscal year 1998/99, ending 31 March.

After significant weakening of the fiscal position in 1997, when the central government deficit was higher than the government's target, the 1998 budget was designed to rectify the process of fiscal consolidation. This was to be achieved through higher revenues from levying a special customs duty, divesting government shares in public sector enterprises, strengthening tax administration and widening the tax net, and curtailing expenditure.

However, the sluggish growth of tax revenues, which among other factors reflects the slowdown in industrial growth, the reduced level of imports, the lower than anticipated proceeds from divestment in public sector enterprises, and a sharp rise in expenditure, all put pressure on the central government's public finances. The end result was that the central government's overall deficit actually increased compared with that of the previous year. The government's financial position has been exacerbated by the deterioration of the state governments' consolidated finances. This was the result of a number of factors. First were the public sector salary increases in response to the recommendations of the Fifth Pay Commission in July 1997. Second, some slippage occurred in the reduction of nonplan expenditures. Third, the implementation of steps to strengthen the states' revenues by introducing realistic pricing and determination of user costs of electricity and irrigation encountered delays. The renewed deterioration of both central and state government deficits has reversed some of the recent gains in fiscal consolidation.

The conduct of monetary policy during 1998 was complicated by uncertainties in the external environment and pressure from the widening fiscal deficit. Following the easing of monetary conditions throughout most of 1997, in response to pressures in the foreign exchange market the Reserve Bank of India tightened monetary policy in January 1998 by raising the bank rate by 2 percentage points to 11 percent. It also increased banks' cash reserve requirements, which led to a sharp rise in the money market rate from less than 10 percent to about 30 percent. As stability in the foreign exchange market was restored, the Reserve Bank of India gradually eased monetary policy,

but this was short-lived. Faced with renewed international uncertainty in the emerging markets and increasing concern about India's poor export performance and widening trade deficit, the Reserve Bank of India was forced once again to tighten monetary conditions in August 1998.

Increasing central government recourse to central bank financing has led to an expansion in base money and a higher than envisaged increase in the money supply. This, together with higher domestic prices of imports caused by depreciation of the exchange rate, sharp increases in food prices, and emerging supply bottlenecks, led to a rise in the inflation rate. This stood at 14.4 percent in 1998, considerably higher than the 6.9 percent rate prevalent in 1997.

The banking system's performance seems to be improving. This conclusion is based on a number of indicators, namely, an increase in the commercial banks' net profits, an improvement in the average risk-weighted capital adequacy ratio of public sector banks, and a fall in the number of nonperforming loans.

Table 2.14 Major Economic Indicators, India, 1996-2000
(percent)

Item	1996	1997	1998	1999	2000
GDP growth[a]	7.8	5.0	5.8	5.9	6.0
Gross domestic investment/GDP	25.7	24.8	25.2[b]	25.2	25.3
Gross national savings/GNP	24.6	23.3	23.5[b]	23.7	24.0
Inflation rate (consumer price index)	9.4	6.9	14.4	7.5	7.0
Money supply (M3) growth	16.2	17.6	19.8	18.1	17.5
Fiscal balance/GDP[c]	-4.7	-5.5	-6.5	-5.8	-5.4
Merchandise exports growth	5.6	2.1	-5.1	1.5	4.5
Merchandise imports growth	12.1	4.4	0.9	4.5	7.7
Current account balance/GDP[d]	-1.2	-1.6	-1.8	-1.6	-1.4
Debt service/exports	33.7	32.5	31.8	31.0	28.5

Note: All figures are on a fiscal year basis.

a. Based on constant 1993/94 factor cost.
b. Staff estimates.
c. For consistency over time, the definition of fiscal deficit used by the MOF until 1999/2000 budget was maintained throughout the period.
d. Excluding official transfers.

Sources: Central Statistical Organization (1999); Ministry of Finance, Government of India (1999); Reserve Bank of India (1998).

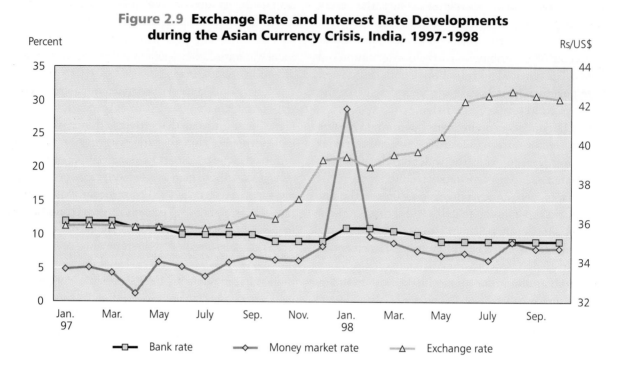

Figure 2.9 Exchange Rate and Interest Rate Developments during the Asian Currency Crisis, India, 1997-1998

Sources: IMF (various years); Reserve Bank of India (various years).

Nonetheless, substantial scope for further improvement in, and reform of, the banking system still exists. Prudential norms are not stringent enough and need to be tightened; some ambiguity concerning the proper classification of nonperforming loans persists; and the banking sector continues to be characterized by inefficiencies and high intermediation costs, which limit the scope for lowering interest rates. On a more positive note, in 1998 the Reserve Bank of India increased its supervision over nonbank finance companies by introducing a new regulatory framework for their operations.

As concerns the balance of payments, the deceleration in the growth of exports since 1996 continued during 1998, caused by a further slackening in world trade and a decline in India's terms of trade. Meanwhile, the growth of imports has been faster, as estimates indicate that non-oil imports increased by 15 percent due largely to a surge in gold. The trade

imbalance widened during the first six months of 1998 to $8.1 billion, compared with $7.3 billion a year before. The current account deficit almost doubled during April-September 1998 compared with the corresponding period in 1997.

A number of factors had an adverse effect on capital inflows during 1998, including heightened uncertainty associated with the Asian currency crisis, investors' concerns about the nuclear tests of May 1998 and the subsequent G7 sanctions on aid and multilateral lending, and loss of confidence in the region's stock markets. The exchange rate came under pressure in early 1998 and again in August 1998, because of renewed uncertainty about the emerging markets. Portfolio investment contracted sharply during the year for the same reason, largely reflecting net outflows of foreign institutional investors, and foreign direct investment inflows are unlikely to have exceeded the 1997 level of about $3.2 billion. As a result, in June

1998 the major international credit rating agencies downgraded India's sovereign rating from investment grade to speculative. The placement of the Resurgent India Bond, aimed at nonresident Indians and issued in August 1998, attracted about $4.2 billion, which has helped to alleviate some of the pressure on foreign exchange reserves.

Assuming gradual improvement in the external environment, policies that raise the profitability of exports, and renewed efforts to consolidate public finances both at the central government level and in the states, the economy is expected to grow by about 6 percent per year during 1999 and 2000. While improved fiscal performance could reduce some of the pressure on the balance of payments, in the short run external vulnerabilities will continue, stemming mainly from rising import levels. While the potential for a stronger recovery in 1999 and beyond exists, fostered by higher investment and a rise in export growth, infrastructure constraints are likely to increase. Thus the government needs to accelerate structural reforms to remove impediments and raise the growth potential, while maintaining prudent macroeconomic management.

ISSUES IN ECONOMIC MANAGEMENT

The most important challenges currently facing economic management are concerns about the widening balance-of-payments imbalances and existing fiscal pressures. Even though the likely tapering off of the emerging market crisis should reduce the volatility of international capital flows and lead to an improvement in the external environment, external account imbalances must be redressed so as not to undermine domestic policies that will help restore confidence in the economy.

In the short run, the external vulnerabilities are in the areas of trade and current account. Exchange rate management will need to support an improvement in the competitiveness of exports to narrow the trade imbalance and reduce pressure on international reserves. This should be accompanied by resumed trade reform to reduce the high level of protection of imports, which has increased the cost of scarce resources and raised the import price of inputs, thereby effectively taxing exports.

In the near future, macroeconomic management should also reduce the fiscal deficit. This would lower the demand for funds, reduce the pressure on interest rates, and create incentives for the crowding-in of private sector investment, and thus stimulate increased growth in the private sector. Alleviating the pressure on monetization of the public deficit would also reduce the risks of inflation.

Accelerating the pace of divestment and privatization of public sector enterprises could help reduce the public sector deficit by raising revenues, increasing the efficiency of resource use, and helping to realign government policy in a way that contributes to faster economic growth. Divestment proceeds could also assist in retiring domestic debt, thereby alleviating debt-service payments.

POLICY AND DEVELOPMENT ISSUES

Even though India has made considerable progress in implementing economic and structural reforms since the early 1990s, the reform process has slowed in the past few years, partly because of political uncertainty just before parliamentary elections, and partly because of the contagion of the Asian currency crisis. The government will need to resume and accelerate the pace of economic reform and widen its scope if it is to achieve higher, sustainable economic growth over the medium term. Among the many areas that need attention, public finance consolidation, infrastructure development, and financial sector and capital market reform are critical. However, as India continues to suffer from gross inequities in the delivery of basic education and health services, strengthening support for social infrastructure and human development is essential to ensure the sustainability of India's reform process.

Economic Reforms

As regards public sector reform, the emphasis to date has focused mainly on the central government's efforts to mobilize resources by broadening the tax base and revising the tax rate structure. The authorities need to take steps to strengthen nontax revenues, including implementing an appropriate pricing policy for utilities; rationalizing expenditures and curtailing subsidies, such as the food and fertilizer subsidies granted by the central government and the power subsidies granted by states; and restructuring and privatizing public sector enterprises. The sharp deterioration in the states' finances has also heightened the need for state governments to initiate broadly based fiscal reforms. Unless addressed, the trend toward replacing growth-inducing and socially productive investments by nonproductive expenditures will further weaken the states' capacity to deliver economic and social services, such as basic health and education services, and thereby hamper their social and economic development.

In key areas of the economy, particularly the power, road, and transportation sectors, investments have failed to keep pace with developments in the overall economy, and thus these sectors have emerged as major impediments to a higher, sustainable growth path. Given the enormous resource requirements for improving the infrastructure, the government will need to promote greater private sector participation. However, the commercialization of infrastructure faces several obstacles, including the absence of an appropriate regulatory framework, the lack of a policy incentive mechanism for private investment, the poor policy coordination among different government agencies in implementing large infrastructure projects, and a shortage of long-term funding. These critical issues need early resolution.

Given their long gestation periods, high costs, and irregular revenue flows, infrastructure investments rely heavily on long-term financing. However, India's debt markets are still not well developed and do not provide the range of financial instruments and the liquidity necessary for infrastructure funding. Although the recent government proposal to open up the insurance sector and allow the entry of foreign investors is a step in the right direction, more general reforms, including the implementation of an appropriate incentive framework and improved governance, are needed if the financial sector is to support economic growth effectively and provide resources to the private sector. To this end, the authorities convened several high-level committees—including the Narasimham Committee on Banking Sector Reform and the Khan Committee on Harmonizing the Role and Operations of Development Finance Institutions and Banks—that have recently presented their rec-

ommendations. These recommendations include moving toward universal banking, with progressive elimination of the boundary between banks and development finance institutions; strengthening prudential regulations by raising the capital adequacy ratio; tightening loan classification and provisioning standards; upgrading banks' risk management systems; and improving the legal framework for loan recovery. The authorities should implement these reforms in a timely manner to reduce systemic vulnerabilities of the financial sector, foster efficient resource mobilization, and deepen financial intermediation.

Education and Human Resource Development

While India must implement the foregoing reforms if its economy is to grow robustly, they will have to be complemented by a serious effort to improve literacy and education if that growth is to be broadly based and sustained over the longer term. Indeed, this is one of the critical lessons that emerges from an examination of such generally high-performing economies as the People's Republic of China, the Republic of Korea, and Thailand. While openness to trade and foreign direct investment and reliance on market forces have no doubt served these economies well, their literacy rates at the time when they initiated their market-oriented reforms were above those prevailing in India today: India's adult literacy rate is currently estimated at slightly higher than 50 percent, while in 1960 it was 71 percent in Korea and 68 percent in Thailand. What is perhaps most distressing is the high rates of illiteracy among Indian children, especially in rural areas where the bulk of the population lives.

Fortunately, the government is showing increasing awareness of the problems confronting the education sector in general, and primary education in particular. The Ninth Five-Year Plan (1997-2002) has called for increasing the share of GDP allocated to education from under 4 percent—which was among the lowest in the region—to 6 percent, with half of total outlays to be allocated to primary education. While the increase in resource allocation and the greater emphasis on primary education is welcome, this alone is clearly not enough. In particular, the incentive structures of public schools have serious problems, with teacher absenteeism and shirking endemic in certain parts of the country. While increasing the number of teachers may help in that studies suggest that this would improve teaching performance through peer monitoring effects, competition, and the greater scope for supervision, decentralization of education administration to local and village levels may be required. This would make teachers more accountable to local communities and, as the example of a few states where administration has been decentralized indicates, would significantly raise the attendance levels of primary school teachers. What will be critical is for such decentralization to be implemented in the remaining states.

The foregoing focus on primary education is not intended to suggest that the state of higher education is adequate. Although the number of institutes of higher education has expanded rapidly in recent years, at some 6 percent in the 18- to 23-year-old age group enrollment rates are low even in comparison with other developing countries. Moreover, with the exception of a few elite institutions, the quality of the education being imparted is problematic. Inadequate governance (teacher strikes are not uncommon) and outdated curricula with little relevance to private sector requirements are widespread. Insufficient financial resources are an important reason for this state of affairs, yet the fee structures in these institutions are basically unrelated to ability to pay. While the Ninth Five-Year Plan has identified the need to introduce a fee structure that reflects unit costs, course type, and ability to pay, whether India's policymakers will be able to implement these and other somewhat politically difficult measures remains to be seen.

Maldives

The Maldives' strong economic growth continued in 1998, led by growth in tourism and fisheries. Long-term growth requires encouraging these sectors by protecting the environment and ensuring that the exploitation of marine resources is sustainable. The government also needs to focus on developing the skill base and ensuring that growth is more equitable across the various atolls.

RECENT TRENDS AND PROSPECTS

To date, the Asian financial crisis had not had a significant effect on the Maldives' economy. After an estimated 6.2 percent growth rate in 1997, preliminary data indicate that GDP growth in 1998 was around 6.8 percent, sustained by increased tourist arrivals and higher international fish prices.

In 1998 the number of tourist arrivals increased by 9 percent over 1997 to nearly 400,000. The sharp increase in tourism has also stimulated economic activity in the construction, distribution, and transportation sectors. The fisheries industry is still a major sector in the economy, although its share as a percentage of GDP has declined in recent years. Nevertheless, it remains the principal source of livelihood for the majority of the population, providing direct employment to more than 22,000 people. Estimates indicate that the total fish catch grew by about 3 percent in 1998 to more than 110,000 tons.

According to the latest census, total employment stood at 67,500 workers in 1995. The labor force participation rate was 44.4 percent, about 64.0 percent for men and 24.0 percent for women. The number of expatriate workers has continued to increase, and is currently estimated at 21,000 people, or more than 20 percent of the total labor force. Most expatriate workers hold either the most skilled or the least skilled jobs, and this highlights two problems of the labor market. First, a skill shortage is constraining economic growth to the extent that workers from overseas cannot fill the gap. Second, Maldivians are unwilling to work at unskilled jobs.

In 1998 the overall budget deficit, including grants, stood at some 3 percent of GDP, compared with 5 percent in 1997. The government's continued prudent fiscal policy helped reduce the inflation rate from 7.6 percent in 1997 to an estimated negative 2.2 percent in 1998.

The aim of monetary policy has been to support macroeconomic stability and improve efficiency in financial intermediation. Specifically, the policy is intended to support low inflationary growth and to ensure that external reserve targets can be met without crowding out the private sector. The level of total domestic credit is mainly determined by the changes in net claims on the government and the extent to which banks are constrained by the quantitative credit limits set by the Maldives Monetary Authority. The authority periodically reviews quantitative credit limits for commercial banks and imposes new limits, the objective being to maintain the level of domestic credit expansion. The rate of domestic credit expansion fell from more than 50 percent in 1993 to 8.8 percent in 1997 because of a sharp drop in credit to the government and to public nonfinancial entities. Nevertheless, credit to the private sector grew by 18 percent between January and August 1998, facilitated by the repayment of some of the government's debt to the Maldives Monetary Authority.

The exchange rate of the rufiyaa against the US dollar has remained stable since 1994, at Rf11.77 to the dollar. In 1998 total merchandise imports were estimated at $317 million, about three and a half times the value of total merchandise exports. Despite a large deficit in the trade account, the current account deficit improved from 25 percent of GDP in 1993 to about 10 percent in 1998. The reason was the sharp increase in tourism receipts, estimated at $304 million in 1998, which accounted for 90 percent of total receipts.

The capital account has registered a high level of capital inflows since the early 1990s. This has been the result of three factors, namely: positive net aid disbursements; increasing private capital inflows associated with foreign direct investment; and private sector external borrowing for investment in tourism, construction, and transportation. The large capital account surplus has led to a balance-of-payments surplus and the buildup of foreign reserves. Gross official reserves increased from the equivalent of less than two months of imports in 1993 to more than four months in 1998. Available data indicate that the Maldives' total external debt was about $172 million at the end of 1997, with more than 94 percent being held as medium- and long-term public debt.

The economy remains vulnerable to external shocks because of its dependence on tourism and fisheries. While this could be a source of instability, these sectors have provided much of the impetus for the high growth rates achieved so far and will continue to

do so. The development outlook for the medium term remains bright, with GDP growth projected at around 6.4 percent for 1999 and 2000.

POLICY AND DEVELOPMENT ISSUES

The Maldives face three key policy and development issues: protecting the environment to ensure sustainable economic growth, fostering greater regional development so that growth on the different atolls becomes more equitable, and supporting human development to improve the skill base. The long-term future of tourism and fisheries, the mainstays of the economy, depends on protecting the coral reefs and ensuring the sustainable exploitation of marine resources. Significant efforts are required to improve the capacity for both monitoring and enforcing environmental rules and regulations. The government must also introduce appropriate measures for environmental protection.

While the country has achieved rapid economic growth in recent years, the inequitable distribution of growth has resulted in significant disparities in per capita income and access to social infrastructure between the central region and the outer atolls, where more than 74 percent of the country's total population reside. A recent vulnerability and poverty survey reported disparities in daily per capita incomes that ranged from Rf35 ($3) in Malé to Rf11-Rf28 ($0.9-$2.4) in the atolls. The provision of the necessary social and physical infrastructure in the outer islands is critical for promoting economic growth in these areas.

As concerns human resource development, policies should focus on enhancing the qualifications and productivity of Maldivian teachers by providing more multisubject training and introducing more multigrade teaching. In particular, the skills of primary school teachers must be enhanced, especially in the outer islands, which will raise the current relatively low level of student achievement. The provision of equal access to education for those residing in the outer islands is necessary for the decentralization of administrative responsibilities to the atolls and for ensuring more geographically balanced growth. Another major challenge relating to human resource development is to curtail the population growth rate, which is currently above 3 percent and one of the highest rates in South Asia.

Nepal

Economic performance has deteriorated, and Nepal's short-term prospects are unfavorable. Macro-economic management is poor and foreign aid dependency is increasing. Restoring political stability, improving revenue collection, and reinvigorating the structural reform process are vitally important for improved economic performance.

RECENT TRENDS AND PROSPECTS

Continuing the trend evident in recent years, overall economic performance deteriorated in 1998, registering a 1.9 percent increase, the lowest growth rate in more than a decade, half of that achieved in 1997. While most sectors experienced a slowdown, it was particularly evident in agriculture and industry. Growth in the agriculture sector was only about a quarter of that in 1997, mainly because of poor weather.

Industrial production stagnated in 1998, largely because of a continued decline in the growth of manufacturing and a contraction in the construction and utilities sectors. Manufacturing, which accounts for 10 percent of GDP, grew only about 2.4 percent in 1998. Problems in the carpet and garment industries that began in 1994 and are related to weak demand in export markets and child labor issues have continued to weaken the manufacturing and export base.

1998 refers to fiscal year 1997/98, ending 15 July.

Growth in the service sector was slightly higher in 1998 than in 1997, but was significantly lower than that achieved during 1991-1994. The economic slowdown hit the service sector particularly hard, especially trade, finance, transport, and communication services.

Estimates indicate that the official unemployment rate was 14 percent in 1997, with substantial variation across regions and sectors. Rural areas and the southern plains generally suffer from higher unemployment than other regions, but the statistics are misleading, as they conceal a great deal of disguised unemployment. Underemployment is widespread, and estimates suggest that about 50 percent of the working population work less than 40 hours a week. The result of the decreased growth in output and lowered productivity has been an increase in the number of people seeking work abroad. While precise figures are unavailable, there were indications that the scale of outmigration is significant, especially to India.

Government expenditure has outstripped growth in revenues, partly because revenue collection grew at less than half the target rate of 22 percent for

1998. Meanwhile expenditures grew by 14 percent, largely because of an adjustment of salaries for civil servants and an expansion in the number of public employees. Revenues are less than 10 percent of GDP, which is low compared with other countries at a similar level of development. In order to widen the tax base and improve the tax system, the government has introduced the value added tax in November 1997 despite opposition from the business community. The fiscal management of the economy has also not been helped by the frequent changes in the administration. The net result has been a widening of the fiscal deficit, a continuation of the trend apparent since 1995, when the International Monetary Fund programs prescribed some restraint. If the implementation of development projects had not slowed down because of political and administrative problems, the economic deterioration would have been even greater.

Nepal's dependence on foreign aid has increased in recent years, reversing the pattern of the late 1980s and the early 1990s. The share of foreign assistance in total development expenditures had declined from about 60 percent in the late 1980s to some 50 percent

in the early 1990s, but this had regained its previous high levels by 1998, and is expected to continue to rise in 1999 to more than 65 percent. This increasing dependence on foreign financing will continue until the government fully implements major reforms in tax rationalization and administration and in public expenditure management.

The rate of inflation is heavily influenced by that in India because of the open border trade between the two countries. Consumer price inflation has remained at about 8 percent per year in recent years, but improved in 1998 when the rate fell to about half that level. This reflected not only changes in India's inflation rate, but stable food and beverage prices. However, the depreciation of the Nepalese rupee by an average of almost 9 percent against the US dollar during 1998 increased pressure on the inflation rate.

Export growth continued to recover in 1998, increasing by 11.7 percent, compared with sluggish growth during 1994-1996. This was because of increased demand from India and a recovery in the garments subsector and in exports of primary products. The sharp decline in imports, which stands in marked

Table 2.15 Major Economic Indicators, Nepal, 1996-2000
(percent)

Item	1996	1997	1998	1999	2000
GDP growth	5.3	4.0	1.9	2.0	2.7
Gross domestic investment/GDP	27.3	25.1	25.5	25.0	25.5
Gross national savings/GNP	15.6	15.7	16.7	16.1	17.0
Inflation rate (consumer price index)	8.1	7.8	4.0	9.0	8.0
Money supply (M2) growth	14.4	11.9	16.9	16.0	15.0
Fiscal balance/GDP[a]	-5.7	-5.1	-6.4	-6.5	-7.0
Merchandise exports growth	1.9	10.2	11.7	9.0	9.0
Merchandise imports growth	5.8	21.6	-12.6	2.0	5.0
Current account balance/GDP	-11.7	-9.4	-8.8	-8.9	-8.5
Debt service/exports	5.4	7.3	9.0	8.7	8.7

Note: Data are on a fiscal year basis.

a. Includes grants.

Sources: Ministry of Finance, Government of Nepal (1998); Central Bureau of Statistics data; staff estimates.

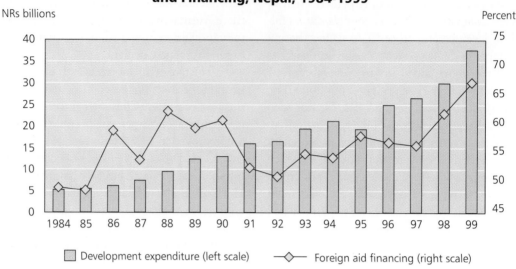

Figure 2.10 **Development Expenditure and Financing, Nepal, 1984-1999**

Sources: Ministry of Finance, Government of Nepal (1998); staff estimates.

contrast to the increase of more than 20 percent during 1997, further improved the balance of trade. Weak economic demand and delays in importers opening letters of credit because of uncertainties related to the implementation of the value-added tax contributed to the contraction of imports.

Much of Nepal's balance of trade depends crucially on its trade with India, which accounts for more than a quarter of Nepal's total trade, a proportion that has remained stable for the past decade. Exports to India consist mainly of agricultural products, such as vegetable oils, skins, leather, and cereals, and imports consist mostly of machinery, transport equipment, spices, cotton yarn, fabrics, miscellaneous processed goods, and fuel. A landlocked country, Nepal uses the closest sea port, which is in Calcutta, and shares a common border with India, which makes labor and product flows between the two countries relatively open. To fortify the traditional connection between their markets and strengthen economic cooperation, India and Nepal have signed a number of trade and transit treaties. With the renewal of the 1991 Trade Treaty in December 1996, India agreed to remove the 50 percent labor and local material content require-

ment for exports of Nepalese manufactured goods to India, which has since boosted Nepal's exports to India.

The current account improved in 1998, not only because of the improvement in the balance of trade, but also because of increased foreign exchange earnings from tourism, due partly to the "Visit Nepal Year" campaign; larger overseas remittances; and higher investment income. The level of foreign exchange reserves reached $712 million by mid-1998, equivalent to about six months of imports of goods and services. Total outstanding external debt increased to more than half the gross national product in 1998, while the debt-service ratio reached 9 percent of exports of goods and nonfactor services.

Nepal's short-term economic prospects are not encouraging, with overall GDP growth projected at 2 percent in 1999 and 2.7 percent in 2000. The untimely monsoons in the second half of 1998 will also have an adverse affect on agriculture in 1999. The structural weaknesses in the export and industrial base and in the financial sector will continue to constrain industrial growth. The service sector will experience moderate growth, mainly as a result of tourism. Fiscal and monetary discipline are likely to be further weakened because of slow revenue growth and an expansion in regular expenditures, which could be fueled further by the forthcoming election. While exports will continue to grow modestly, import growth will continue to be slow and the current account deficit will remain below 10 percent of GDP in the next few years. Inflation is expected to average 8 or 9 percent during the next two years.

POLICY AND DEVELOPMENT ISSUES

Nepal needs to safeguard its macroeconomic stability, particularly its fiscal and external positions, to protect its foreign exchange commitments and obligations. More important, the government needs to give high priority to tackling the roots of structural inefficiency, including separating politics and bureaucracy; developing a performance-based civil service; privatizing state-owned enterprises; enhancing accountability and ownership; and initiating institutional development, focusing on credibility and including the private sector and development administration. These elements need to be fully in place to ensure effective and efficient delivery of development and private sector activities.

To reduce overdependence on foreign assistance for the country's development requirements, the government needs to make continued efforts to mobilize domestic resources. This will require major tax reforms, including improving implementation of the value-added tax. The government also needs to focus on reforming and liberalizing the financial and industrial sectors, privatizing state-owned enterprises, developing the capital market further, and expediting the prioritization of development expenditures and preparation of a three-year rolling expenditure plan. The foreign trade regime also needs further liberalization and rationalization.

Agriculture is the predominant economic sector, but both physical and policy constraints have limited its development. The major factors contributing to slow growth in agricultural production are infertile land; exhausted soils; and rugged terrain, which implies high costs for building physical infrastructure. Slow adoption of improved technology and inefficient pricing and distribution policies for essential agricultural inputs and outputs are also crucial impediments that limit the potential of agricultural productivity. The Agriculture Perspective Plan, which the government introduced in mid-1995, details the strategy for agricultural development for the next 20 years. Successful implementation of the plan, including the necessary institutional and policy reforms, is critical for reversing the adverse trends recently observed in the agriculture sector.

Pakistan

Despite the improvement in Pakistan's growth rate in 1998, the economy is still beset by a number of serious problems, not least of which is the foreign exchange crisis, which necessitated assistance from the International Monetary Fund (IMF). The authorities need to focus on macroeconomic stabilization and export promotion policy, especially in relation to agricultural products. They must also take steps to increase economic efficiency, in particular, by financially restructuring the power utilities and improving the country's governance. Finally, the government also needs to introduce a policy of social protection for the poor.

RECENT TRENDS AND PROSPECTS

The growth of GDP in 1998 of 5.4 percent, the highest since 1993, was a considerable improvement over the 1.3 percent achieved in 1997. Nevertheless, Pakistan's economic performance has been handicapped in recent years largely by a lack of private sector dynamism, weak policy implementation, ineffective governance, persistent sectarian violence, and low labor productivity.

A major reason for this improvement was the rapid growth of the agriculture sector, which accounts for about a quarter of GDP. In 1998 this sector grew by slightly less than 6 percent, compared with zero growth in 1997. Although cotton production was below expectations, the sector achieved significant recovery in other major crops, including grain, sugarcane, and wheat, because of favorable weather conditions and increased support prices.

Industrial production increased by 6.2 percent in 1998. The manufacturing sector showed a strong recovery, growing by 7.0 percent in 1998, compared

1998 refers to fiscal year 1997/98, ending 30 June.

with just over 1 percent in 1997. The large-scale manufacturing sectors, such as sugar, air conditioning units, jute goods, and tractors, exhibited strong growth. By comparison, the performance of the construction sector was disappointing at 1.7 percent growth, largely because of the low level of investment in the economy.

The low rates of saving and investment continue to be one of the major impediments to economic development. However, the gap between investment and saving, which has ranged from 4 to 7 percent of gross national product during the last five years, fell significantly to about 2 percent in 1998. This was caused by a sharp rise in saving, while investment remained static. In May 1998 the G7 imposed economic sanctions on Pakistan in response to its nuclear tests. The sanctions virtually blocked inflows of bilateral and multilateral assistance and foreign investment flows to Pakistan. These sanctions are bound to have an adverse effect on the volume of savings in 1999, especially deposits in foreign currency. They are also certain to affect the level of foreign investment.

In 1998 the budget deficit fell to 5.4 percent of GDP, an improvement compared with the previous year. Total revenue as a percentage of GDP increased slightly in 1998 over 1997, largely because of the introduction of tax reforms. The most notable of these reforms was the agricultural income taxation legislation introduced in all four provinces, and intended to meet the dual objectives of promoting equitable sharing of the tax burden and widening the tax base. Total expenditure as a percentage of GDP remained roughly the same as in 1997.

Government borrowing from the banking sector declined considerably during 1998, mainly because of tight fiscal policy. Controlling inflation was another of the IMF's requirements, and inflation fell to 7.8 percent in 1998, down four percentage points from 1997. Although the IMF package was approved in October 1997, it was suspended in May 1998 following the economic sanctions imposed by the G7, and then resumed in January 1999.

Both the trade balance and the current account improved in 1998, because of a modest growth in exports of 4.0 percent and a dramatic decline in imports of 8.2 percent. The growth of exports was curtailed by a decline in cotton yarn exports, the result of the economic recession in Hong Kong, China and Japan. The Asian financial crisis also had an adverse effect on Pakistan's exports. The decline in imports was due mainly to a 27.7 percent fall in the machinery subsector that occurred because of the completion of several power plants, and a 30.3 percent drop in the petroleum subsector because of a steep decline in international oil prices. The overall result was that the current account deficit improved from 5.8 percent of GDP in 1997 to 3.0 percent in 1998.

Following the nuclear tests in late May 1998, the G7 countries imposed economic sanctions. The IMF also suspended its $1.5 billion Enhanced Structural Adjustment Facility/Extended Fund Facility package, which had been agreed with the government in October 1997. The sanctions magnified Pakistan's socioeconomic difficulties. Because of the erosion of investor confidence, the virtual cessation of private capital flows, and the suspension of new official development assistance, the incidence of poverty worsened. Although the government adopted short-term policies to conserve foreign exchange, the measures were insufficient to prevent a decline in foreign currency reserves, which fell below $300 million in early December 1998. The likelihood of default was high, especially following policy reversals in the energy sector, which further undermined the support of the donor community.

The United States announced a partial waiver of its economic sanctions in early December 1998 and supported the resumption of lending assistance from international financial institutions, including the Asian

Table 2.16 Major Economic Indicators, Pakistan, 1996-2000
(percent)

Item	1996	1997	1998	1999	2000
GDP growth	5.2	1.3	5.4	3.4	4.6
Gross domestic investment/GNP	18.7	17.5	17.4	14.8	16.2
Gross national savings/GNP	11.6	11.3	15.1	12.2	13.0
Inflation rate (consumer price index)	10.8	11.8	7.8	8.0	9.0
Money supply (M2) growth	14.9	12.2	14.2	9.0	12.0
Fiscal balance/GDP	-6.3	-6.2	-5.4	-4.3	-3.3
Merchandise exports growth	7.1	-2.6	4.0	-10.1	10.2
Merchandise imports growth	16.7	-6.4	-8.2	-16.9	10.0
Current account balance/GDP	-6.7	-5.8	-3.0	-2.5	-1.9
Debt service/exports	33.9	38.0	40.0	20.0	22.0

Sources: International Monetary Fund (various issues); Government of Pakistan (1998); staff estimates.

Development Bank (ADB). The IMF consequently revived the Enhanced Structural Adjustment Facility/Extended Fund Facility package on 14 January 1999. In addition, the World Bank approved a $350 million structural adjustment loan on 22 January 1999. The Paris Club Meeting, held during 28-30 January 1999, reached an agreement between the government and bilateral creditors to reschedule official debt of $3.3 billion, and the London Club is anticipated to meet soon to reschedule commercial debt.

Despite a partial waiver of the US economic sanctions and the resumption of the IMF assistance, economic growth in1999 is expected to be 3.4 percent, which is less than in 1998. This is largely due to import constraints, which limit crucial foreign intermediate inputs, and the industrial recession accompanied by low levels of private investment. Both total investment and savings are expected to decline as a proportion of GDP. The agriculture, industry, and service sectors are all likely to be sluggish in 1999 compared with 1998. Foreign remittances are expected to shrink further in 1999 because of the uncertainty related to the foreign exchange regime.

The current account deficit is expected to narrow to $1.6 billion in 1999, compared with $1.8 billion in 1998, because of a considerable reduction in the trade deficit, although net private transfers into the country will also contract significantly.

ISSUES IN ECONOMIC MANAGEMENT

Pakistan is unlikely to solve its underlying economic problems rapidly, despite the IMF financial package. This is mainly because the problems are structural bottlenecks rather than temporary constraints.

The most critical issues are debt servicing and a shortage of foreign reserves. Pakistan's total external debt is estimated at $31 billion as of the end of December 1998, equivalent to about half of its GDP. In addition, foreign exchange reserves still remain at a low level. Another important issue is the fiscal imbalance caused by both a sharp increase in debt servicing and continued high defense spending. Rapid deterioration of the financial position of power utilities has also posed serious budgetary problems.

POLICY AND DEVELOPMENT ISSUES

Major issues concern the need to achieve macroeconomic stabilization and promote exports, increase economic efficiency, and ensure that social protection is available for the poorest members of society.

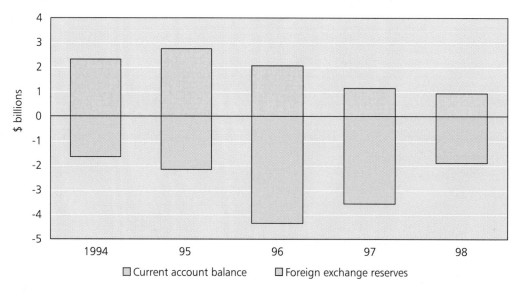

Figure 2.11 Current Account and Foreign Reserves, Pakistan, 1994-1998

□ Current account balance   □ Foreign exchange reserves

Sources: Ministry of Finance and Economic Affairs (1998); State Bank of Pakistan (1998).

Macroeconomic Stabilization and Export Promotion

Attaining fiscal stability remains one of the government's most important goals. To reduce the budget deficit the government needs to broaden the tax base, reduce tax exemptions, and improve tax administration. Export promotion is crucial, given the severe shortages of foreign exchange and the likely large cost of servicing the external debt. However, the growth rates of exports have declined steadily, and in recent years exports have increasingly become concentrated on a few items. To expand exports the government must revitalize small and medium enterprises; address the general problems prevalent in industry; and help modernize the equipment of export industries for increasing exports of nontraditional goods such as textiles, sports equipment, and light manufactured products.

Because of its size the agriculture sector has a crucial role to play in the expansion of exports. In addition to contributing a quarter of total output, it employs nearly two thirds of rural households and is the basis of more than 60 percent of Pakistan's exports. The sector plays a critical role in the balance of payments. The foreign exchange crisis has hit agriculture because it has prevented sufficient imports of phosphate fertilizers, which has depressed major crop yields, including those of cotton, a major export. Thus proper sectoral policies and timely availability of inputs are critical for agriculture sector development.

Economic Efficiency

Improving economic efficiency includes such issues as restructuring the power sector, reforming the governance of the economy, and introducing financial sector reform.

The power sector, which includes two utilities, the Water and Power Development Authority and the Karachi Electric Supply Corporation, has been under intense financial stress since the end of 1996. This has resulted from a combination of factors: energy losses during transmission, low cost recovery and theft, inadequate tariff increases, large increases in fuel costs, and purchases of power from independent power producers at a cost that was higher than the average tariff level. The financial crisis in the power sector has,

in turn, seriously affected the government's handling of the economy by increasing the fiscal deficit. Consequently, financial restructuring of the two utilities is urgently needed.

A necessary precondition for successful implementation of any policy is effective and efficient governance. Weak governance, which in Pakistan is largely associated with corruption, weak law enforcement, and sectarian violence, has been one of the leading causes behind the country's poor economic performance. Although good governance has become a high priority of the incumbent government, policies to implement this are still at an early stage and it is critical that the government continue to make strong efforts.

Finally, financial sector reform is essential to enhance the efficiency of the economy. The government is implementing a capital market development program and banking sector reform with assistance from the ADB and the World Bank.

Social Protection

The poverty profile has worsened in recent years. The number of people living below the poverty line grew from 25.2 percent in 1990 to 34.0 percent in 1994. In addition, both rural and urban Gini coefficients for the 1990s show that the distribution of income has been worsening. Similarly, urban and rural wage rates have also decreased. An increasingly vulnerable group consists of those who are educated, but unemployed. Unemployment of educated workers has risen because of the combined effects of the liberalization of the economy under structural adjustment programs, the privatization of public enterprises, and the recession that has affected the private sector. To mitigate the effects of this increase in poverty, the government is planning to establish a national poverty line for Pakistan by 2000. The government has also established the Pakistan Poverty Alleviation Fund Company, and such efforts by the government will also be supported at the policy level through the Ninth Five-Year Plan.

The ADB has supported the government's efforts to alleviate poverty by actively participating in its Social Action Program since 1994. The Bank will support policies and reforms that facilitate investment in industry and infrastructure, and through its lending program will also support microfinance.

Sri Lanka

Despite the adverse impact of the regional financial crisis on investment and the increased expenditure on national security because of the ongoing civil conflict, Sri Lanka's economy grew at about the same rate as the annual average for the last four years. Continued fiscal consolidation is critical for sustainable growth and macroeconomic stability.

RECENT TRENDS AND PROSPECTS

Despite the Asian crisis and the ongoing civil conflict, Sri Lanka's economy grew by 5.3 percent in 1998, a decrease from the 6.4 percent growth achieved in 1997. Manufacturing and construction each grew by about 7 percent, and the service sector grew even faster. However, the production and export performance of such products as rubber, coconut, ceramics, plastics, gems, and jewelry was disappointing. These were affected by reduced demand and by increased competition from the crisis countries of Southeast Asia. Agriculture grew by 3.5 percent in 1998, benefiting from good weather and the privatized management of the plantation sector.

In 1998 investment increased slightly compared with 1997, and the savings-investment gap remained at about 7 percent of GDP. Despite a modest increase in private investment in infrastructure projects and the flow of private capital from continued privatization, the regional instability following international sanctions on India and Pakistan for conducting nuclear tests adversely affected the confidence of private sector investors. This lack of confidence was reflected in a marked change in the performance of the Colombo stock exchange. Estimates indicate that the net outflow of foreign investor funds from the stock exchange in 1998 amounted to $25 million, a stark contrast from the $13 million inflow recorded in 1997.

The unemployment rate declined from 10.4 percent in 1997 to 9.5 percent in 1998, the result of the high growth rate and of emigration to work abroad; however, the unemployment rate remains extremely high among educated youth. Overall, unemployment remains a serious problem and is one of the major causes of poverty: about 22 percent of the population live below the official poverty line. Alongside the persistently high unemployment, labor shortages are apparent in some sectors, such as computers, information technology, and financial services.

The fiscal deficit, which in 1998 stood at 7.7 percent of GDP, remained roughly the same as in 1997. Privatization revenues were lower than expected because of depressed conditions of capital markets in all the developing countries. The new goods and services tax reduced revenue collection because of the relatively low rate of 12.5 percent at which it was being introduced. Total expenditures exceeded the budget target somewhat, largely because of an overrun of defense expenditures.

The government relaxed its monetary policy in early 1997 to reduce interest rates, thereby boosting credit to the private sector. However, it later tightened the policy to cope with the higher than expected inflation and some uncertainties experienced in the foreign exchange market because of the Asian currency crisis. The overall tightening of monetary policy resulted in a lower 1998 inflation rate of 9.4 percent.

Imports grew slightly more than 7 percent in 1998, much slower than exports. Good performance by industrial products such as textiles, garments, and leather goods led export growth. Tea was the mainstay of the growth in agriculture exports. Imports grew mainly as a result of the importation of investment goods, particularly those associated with infrastructure projects. The overall result was a deterioration in the current account that was, however, offset by larger capital inflows that mainly reflected foreign borrowing by the government and the private sector. A consequence was an increase in reserves to about

four months of import cover. While the debt service ratio is estimated at some 12 percent of exports, external debt remained at around the 1997 level of 56 percent of GDP.

In the absence of any large internal or external shocks, the economy should grow at 5 to 6 percent in 1999 and 2000. The fiscal deficit will be reduced by an average of one percentage point each year, assuming that defense expenditures remain at their current levels. With the implementation of restrictive money and credit policies facilitated by fiscal consolidation, inflation will fall slightly to about 8 percent by 2000. The balance of payments is expected to change little and continue to record a small surplus.

ISSUES IN ECONOMIC MANAGEMENT

The principal issues the government faces are continued consolidation of the fiscal situation, reform of public administration, reform of the financial sector, and removal of obstacles to private sector development.

Table 2.17 Major Economic Indicators, Sri Lanka, 1996-2000
(percent)

Item	1996	1997	1998	1999	2000
GDP growth[a]	3.8	6.4	5.3	5.0	6.2
Gross domestic investment/GDP	24.2	24.4	26.6	28.6	30.0
Gross domestic savings/GDP	15.5	21.4	19.3	20.8	22.1
Inflation rate (consumer price index)	15.9	9.6	9.4	9.0	8.0
Money supply (M2) growth	10.8	13.8	13.0	13.4	11.5
Fiscal balance/GDP[b]	-9.4	-7.9	-7.7	-6.0	-5.0
Merchandise exports growth	7.6	13.3	6.7	6.0	7.0
Merchandise imports growth	2.4	7.6	7.1	6.2	5.6
Current account balance/GDP[c]	-5.3	-2.9	-3.1	-5.2	-5.2
Debt service/exports	13.4	13.4	12.1	12.1	10.8

a. At constant 1982 factor cost.
b. Excluding grants and privatization proceeds.
c. Excluding official transfers.

Sources: International Monetary Fund (various issues); Central Bank of Sri Lanka (1998); Ministry of Finance and Planning; staff estimates.

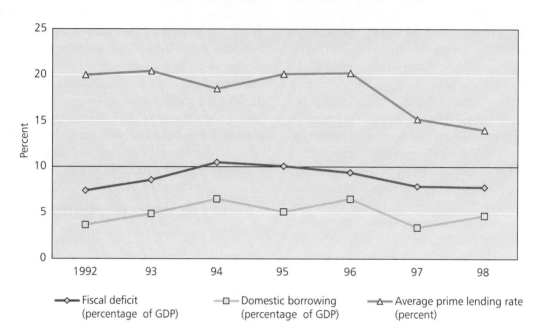

Figure 2.12 Fiscal Deficit, Domestic Borrowing, and Interest Rates, Sri Lanka, 1992-1998

Sources: Central Bank of Sri Lanka (1997); International Monetary Fund data.

A major requirement is the need to reduce the fiscal deficit to prevent the crowding out of private investment, but this must not be done at the expense of essential social spending and development of much needed infrastructure facilities. Sri Lanka's expenditure on health and education is well below that of other countries at a similar level of development. In comparison, the country has relatively high expenditure on interest payments, defense, and civil servant pensions. This structure of public expenditure is not conducive to future growth, as more needs to be spent on developing human resources. However, there is little scope for cutting spending or for raising substantially more revenues. Consequently, the additional necessary resources must come from higher efficiency and savings from public sector restructuring and public administration reforms. These reforms should focus both on improving the management of public services and restructuring government departments and statutory boards. The generous civil service pen-

sions need to be reformed not only because they contribute to the fiscal deficit, but also because they make employment in the public sector overly attractive compared with employment in the private sector. Such reform will require strong commitment from the government if it is to be implemented successfully.

Reform of public employee pensions will complement financial sector reforms, where the government has made substantial progress in recent years. The most prominent achievement in 1998 includes the development of a long-term debt market by increasing Treasury bond issues and mobilizing resources in the international debt market. In this regard, the Development Finance Corporation of Ceylon, one of Sri Lanka's two development finance organizations (which are largely private sector institutions), issued a $65 million ten-year floating rate note at LIBOR plus 2 percent. Other key accomplishments include the signing of a memorandum of understanding between the two state banks and the Treasury to facilitate management contracts, the initiation of a scripless secondary market for government securities, and the introduction of screen-based automated trading on the Colombo stock exchange.

POLICY AND DEVELOPMENT ISSUES

In the medium term, to support high rates of economic growth and to reduce unemployment, Sri Lanka needs to reorient its productive structure toward high-technology sectors and to increase productivity. In the industrial sector, the diversification from the relatively low-technology products such as textiles and garments to high-technology electronics and other engineering products is seen to be the real engine for future growth. Diversification of the industrial production structure will require developing higher levels of technical skills, increasing capital investment, and providing government support to create a policy environment that will encourage both domestic and foreign investments and exports.

In the agriculture sector, a major challenge is to improve agricultural productivity to offset the escalation of costs, and thereby maintain the international competitiveness of the country's agricultural exports.

Policy support and concerted efforts are required to promote research and extension services, develop an active land market for intensive land use and improved productivity, and provide support to encourage the private sector to engage in processing and marketing agricultural products. Preservation of the natural resource base, with a special focus on soil conservation and comprehensive water resource management, remains another important policy issue for sustainable agricultural growth.

As the achievement of higher productivity and growth will depend on the performance and dynamism of the private sector, the government should gradually remove the remaining obstacles to the development of private sector initiatives in the areas of trade, financial services, and tax and labor legislation. The role of the private sector in providing health services and training for skills improvement will also become increasingly important in the future. This will complement public services, as it will have substantial implications for the reduction of the government's budget for health and education. In this respect, increased private sector participation in economic activities requires the development of a competitive market environment.

The Pacific

Fiji
Papua New Guinea
Cook Islands
Kiribati
Marshall Islands
Federated States of Micronesia
Nauru
Samoa
Solomon Islands
Tonga
Tuvalu
Vanuatu

Fiji

The economy was in recession for the second year in succession in 1998, with output falling by nearly 4 percent, largely because of the effects of a drought on sugar production and reduced gold production. Growth will resume in 1999, provided that tourism picks up and investment increases. A coherent, credible, and predictable economic policy framework is needed, particularly with respect to sugar land leases.

RECENT TRENDS AND PROSPECTS

Fiji's GDP fell by 3.9 percent in 1998, even more than in 1997. Sugar production was down again, as the effects of a prolonged drought followed those of the cyclones and industrial disputes of the previous year.

As in 1997, uncertainty about the renewal of sugar land leases expiring in 1999-2000 hampered production. The combined output of sugarcane and raw sugar was just 42 percent of the peak 1994 level. A further decline in gold prices caused the temporary closure of one of the two operating gold mines and the indefinite postponement of plans for a third mine. Mining sector output consequently fell by a fifth compared with its 1997 level. Activity in the construction, finance, and especially the wholesale and retail trade sectors also declined.

Expansion in the tourism sector, which accounts for about one sixth of GDP, prevented an even deeper recession. The 20 percent currency devaluation in January 1998 helped maintain the attractiveness of Fiji as a tourist destination, and visitor arrivals rose 4 percent above their record 1997 level. The garment industry also made a positive contribution. In general,

however, business confidence and investment were down on the low levels of the previous year. Emigration of skilled Indo-Fijians continued, even though the new, less ethnically biased constitution came into force in July 1998.

The average annual inflation rate increased to 5.7 percent, up from 3.4 percent in 1997. Wage pressures built up during the year, following the April withdrawal of wage settlement guidelines. Public service wages increased by around 3 percent. Despite a relaxed monetary policy designed to expand domestic demand and aid the expansionary effect of the devaluation, the money supply contracted by about a fifth in the first eight months of 1998 compared with the same period in 1997. Nominal interest rates remained low. The overall budget balance improved from a deficit of 6.5 percent of GDP in 1997 to 3.4 percent in 1998. However, if adjustments are made for one-off expenditures in 1997 arising from the rehabilitation of the National Bank of Fiji and for 1998 privatization receipts, the underlying budget balance may have actually deteriorated.

Foreign exchange reserves showed a small net increase in 1998, because of a turnaround in the capital account. This outweighed the current account deterioration, which went from a small surplus to a substantial deficit. The foreign reserves cover of imports therefore rose slightly from its 1997 level to 5.5 months. The external debt-service ratio rose from 1.4 percent in 1997 to 2.2 percent in 1998, and the ratio of external debt to GDP rose from 6.6 to 8.8 percent. At the end of 1998, the real effective exchange rate was 13 percent below its predevaluation level.

Forecasts indicate that GDP will grow by 2.7 percent in 1999. This prediction of an economic recovery is based on the assumptions of a 5 percent increase in visitor arrivals, a 5 percent expansion in the construction sector from hotel investments and public infrastructure projects, a 10 percent growth in garment production, and a 25 percent growth in mining output.

ISSUES IN ECONOMIC MANAGEMENT

In the short term, the government faces two major tasks. One is to ensure that the stimulus to the traded goods sector from the currency devaluation is not further eroded by wage and price rises. With the inflation rate running at 10 percent at the end of 1998, a tightening of monetary policy may be required in 1999. The second task is to reverse the deterioration of the fiscal position that occurred in 1996-1998. The objective of the 1999 budget is to move to underlying fiscal balance by 2001; however, this may not be easy to achieve. Projections indicate that the underlying budget deficit will increase to 5.6 percent of GDP in 1999, and even inclusive of asset sales, the deficit is expected to rise. Moreover, the historic surplus of operating revenues over operating expenditures is expected to continue to fall. These projected balances rest on substantial growth in customs and excise tax revenues, which in turn assumes achievement of the GDP growth target and of greater tax compliance through the new Fiji Revenue and Customs Authority.

On the expenditure side, current expenditures are projected to grow by 7.1 percent and capital expenditures by 27.1 percent. The government is pursuing a strategy of raising public investment spending

Figure 2.13 Growth of Real GDP, Fiji, 1993-1998

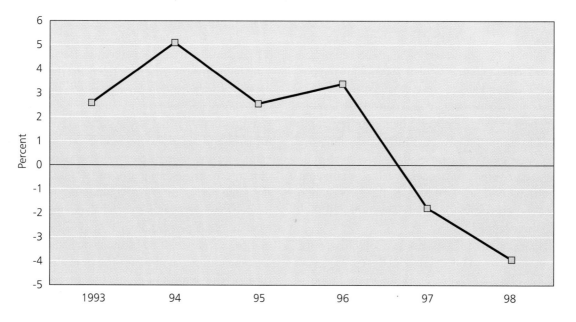

Source: Bureau of Statistics (1998).

on health, education, and infrastructure, both to provide a short-run demand stimulus to the economy and to lay the foundations for future growth. The government needs to accomplish this through a reallocation of spending, rather than an increase in spending, if it is to reduce debt levels and realize its medium-term objective of fiscal balance. Such a reallocation would involve reducing the administrative costs of about 50 ministries and the relatively heavy expenditure on the military. It also needs to contain wage growth in the civil service.

POLICY AND DEVELOPMENT ISSUES

If Fiji is to achieve economic growth at a reasonable and sustainable rate, restoring investor confidence is essential. This, in turn, requires political stability and a government that delivers a coherent, credible, and predictable policy framework. The government has successfully dealt with the National Bank of Fiji crisis and begun the process of privatizing public enterprises. However, with elections due in early 1999, the political environment remains uncertain, and the government continues to send somewhat mixed signals on

its policy direction. In particular, the sugar industry will effectively be undermined during 1999-2001 if Fijian landowners do not renew Indo-Fijian farmers' expiring land leases. This will occur precisely at the time when the sugar industry must face the prospect of losing its preferential access to European markets. The outcome of the deliberations by the Joint Parliamentary Committee on Land Issues is therefore crucial to the future of the sugar industry.

Clear and enforceable property rights are also a basic necessity to encourage foreign investment in the tourism sector, which has experienced some insecurity because of landowners unlawfully demanding that hotels pay for land and water use. Burdensome regulations and restrictions on the repatriation of profits discourage foreign direct investment. The one-stop Fiji Trade and Investment Board reportedly has yet to reduce transaction costs, and the new Foreign Investment Act that proffered an appropriate legislative framework has not been passed, though it will be resubmitted to Parliament in 1999. A growing law and order problem is also discouraging foreign investors. The government needs to address all these issues speedily if Fiji's economic growth is to be revitalized.

Papua New Guinea

The economy grew by 2.5 percent in 1998. Balance-of-payments pressure resulted in depreciation of the currency and a substantial tightening of monetary policy, while the budget deficit exceeded original projections. The economic growth rate is forecast to be 2.9 percent in 1999. Maintaining a stable macroeconomic environment and implementing planned economic reforms will continue to be the government's major challenges.

RECENT TRENDS AND PROSPECTS

Following the 1997 recession, the economy recovered in 1998 to record a GDP growth rate of 2.5 percent. The positive growth was due entirely to a 60 percent increase in output from the mining sector and strong growth in the petroleum sector, as nonmining GDP fell by 3.7 percent. Output in the agriculture, forestry, and fisheries sector fell by 6.4 percent, largely because of severe drought, but also suffered from a fall in commodity prices. Although it only accounts for 30 percent of GDP, the agriculture, forestry, and fisheries sector is important, because it provides a living for 80 percent of the population. Output also fell in the community and social services, commerce, and manufacturing sectors. Investment recovered partially from its decline in 1997, to reach 24 percent of GDP.

The currency came under severe pressure early in the year as export revenues from primary products fell while import expenditures remained steady. In addition, perceptions of political instability fueled currency speculation. The central bank intervened in the foreign exchange market and tightened monetary

policy in an attempt to defend the kina. Measures included a sharp rise in interest rates and the requirement that commercial banks place 10 percent of their deposits in noninterest bearing accounts with the central bank. The defense of the currency was also aided by a A$59 million advance aid payment from the Australian government. Nevertheless, the end result was a 20 percent depreciation.

In 1998 the current account deficit was about 1 percent of GDP. By the end of the year external reserves amounted to 3.3 months of import cover, slightly less than in 1997. External public debt was equivalent to 35 percent of GDP, and the servicing costs of external public debt were 6 percent of receipts on the current account. The inflation rate jumped from 3.9 percent in 1997 to 10 percent in 1998, partly because of the depreciation of the currency, and partly because of a 14.4 percent increase in the money supply largely attributable to lending by the state-owned commercial bank.

The 1998 budget presented to Parliament in April turned out to be overoptimistic because of an unanticipated shortfall in revenues from taxes on mining companies and log export duties, and substantial unappropriated expenditures. The overall budget deficit was 1.6 percent of GDP. Most of the growth in expenditure was attributable to transfer payments to provinces, districts, and statutory institutions; increased development expenditures at the national level; and debt servicing. The costs of a relief operation for the victims of a tidal wave were an added, unexpected burden. The stock of public debt at the end of 1998 approached 70 percent of GDP, and imposed a servicing burden that was projected to absorb 17 percent of total revenue and grants in 1999.

GDP is expected to grow by 2.9 percent in 1999. Estimates indicate that the agriculture, forestry, and fisheries sector will expand by almost 5 percent, mining by 6 percent, and petroleum by 13 percent, while the community and social services sector will continue to contract. Inflation is forecast to drop to 8 percent.

ISSUES IN ECONOMIC MANAGEMENT

The critical issue in the short term is whether the 1999 budget will be implemented effectively. As presented to Parliament in November 1998, it estimated a slight reduction in the overall deficit and an increase in total revenue and grants by 6.3 percent and in total expenditure by 5.0 percent. The budget also reaffirmed a commitment to the stalled medium-term structural reform program begun in 1994 with International Monetary Fund and World Bank assistance. A value-added tax and tariff reform will become effective on 1 July 1999, while a public sector restructuring and contraction will be the primary source of a 19 percent drop in noninterest recurrent spending. This, in turn, will permit a 50 percent expansion in development expenditure.

In addition to the risk of unfavorable commodity price movements, the government's commitment

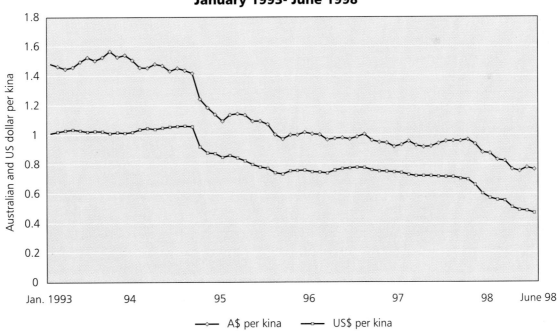

Figure 2.14 **Monthly Exchange Rates, Papua New Guinea, January 1993- June 1998**

Source: Bank of Papua New Guinea (1998).

to macroeconomic discipline may be undermined by a combination of the recent easing of short-term macroeconomic pressures and a political backlash against the proposed public sector reforms. Any large increase in the budget deficit will exert pressure on the currency, and thus on monetary policy. A failure to bring interest rates down from their currently high level would have potentially serious consequences for private sector investment.

POLICY AND DEVELOPMENT ISSUES

The fundamental development problem is that social development has not kept pace with economic growth. Expansion of the formal economy has generated only about one sixth of the jobs required to keep up with the growth of the workforce. Open unemployment in urban areas and in some rural towns has increased, and with it has come the seemingly intractable problem of lawlessness. The bulk of the population lives in rural areas fragmented by rugged terrain and inadequate physical infrastructure, and relies heavily on subsistence and smallholder agriculture. The medium-term development strategy for 1997-2002

recognizes this problem, which is addressed in the 1999 budget.

The issue is now one of effective implementation. Unfortunately, this is hampered by weak governance that has been complicated by government decentralization under the Organic Law of 1995. The objective of increasing participation in decisionmaking and of raising the accountability of provincial and local government is laudable. However, delays in fund transfers; confusion about the respective roles of departments at the district, provincial, and national levels; and severe human resource constraints continue to be basic problems. The 1999 budget initiative requiring provincial and local governments to review progress and to develop more effective implementation plans is unlikely to bear much fruit. In addition, how the direct allocation of rural development funds to the 89 districts will assist the reform process is unclear, given the lack of effective administrative and financial support systems. In this regard, the recently established National Economic and Fiscal Commission could play a crucial role by assessing and coordinating requests for development funding from provincial and local governments.

Cook Islands, Kiribati, Marshall Islands, Federated States of Micronesia, Nauru, Samoa, Solomon Islands, Tonga, Tuvalu, and Vanuatu

The poor economic performance of the Pacific countries in 1997 continued in 1998. Eight of the ten Pacific countries registered absolute declines in their GDP, and in the case of Nauru and Solomon Islands, the fall was as large as 10 percent. A legacy of poor economic management has exacerbated the problem for some of the countries. The Asian crisis was not a major factor in explaining the poor growth rates of most of the Pacific countries, as their direct exposure to the rest of Asia is generally limited. Their growth prospects are modest at best.

The ten Pacific countries are small by any of the conventional criteria of land area, population, and GDP, although some have large exclusive economic zones. All have populations of less than 1 million people. In addition, land areas are often fragmented, dispersed, and both geographically and economically distant from world markets. However, a broad distinction must be drawn between those countries made up largely or entirely of volcanic or continental islands and those that are either made up entirely of atolls or of a mix of atolls and volcanic islands. Fiji, Samoa, Solomon Islands, Tonga, and Vanuatu are in the first group. Cook Islands, Kiribati, Marshall Islands,

Federated States of Micronesia, Nauru, and Tuvalu belong to the second group, which is characterized by the extreme smallness of the states, their relatively high dispersion and isolation, and their limited natural resource endowments. For this last group, growth has historically occurred through the exploitation of mineral deposits (Kiribati and Nauru) or through the expansion of a public sector heavily financed by aid donors (the rest). The economic growth potential of the first group is greater because of their larger and richer natural resource endowments. Agriculture, forestry, mining, fishing, and tourism—in varying combinations—have been, and remain, engines of growth.

1998 refers to fiscal year 1997/98 for Cook Islands, Nauru, Samoa, and Tonga, where the fiscal year ends on 30 June; and for the Marshall Islands and the Federated States of Micronesia the fiscal year ends on 30 September. All other references are to the calendar year.

Population growth rates are high, especially in Solomon Islands and Vanuatu, so that economic expansion must be rapid if average incomes are to rise and employment is to be generated for new entrants to the workforce. On the whole this has not happened in the 1990s.

In 1998 GDP fell in eight of the ten Pacific countries. In six cases it was the second year of recession. Solomon Islands was the hardest hit by the Asian economic crisis because of its heavy dependence on forestry and the collapse of log export markets in Japan and the Republic of Korea. Nauru and Vanuatu also experienced significant adverse impacts. Solomon Islands devalued its currency, while Vanuatu averted a balance-of-payments crisis through monetary tightening and imposition of capital controls. Tonga also relied on monetary tightening to maintain external balance in the face of declining commodity exports. Samoa's current account balance improved as a result

of growth in remittance flows. Fiscal policy was the only instrument available to countries with no national currency. Kiribati, Nauru, and Tuvalu use the Australian dollar; the Cook Islands use the New Zealand dollar; and the Marshall Islands and the Federated States of Micronesia use the US dollar. All these countries have tightened their fiscal policy.

COOK ISLANDS

During 1995-1998 the Cook Islands economy was in recession because of contractions in tourism and the public sector. GDP fell by 4.4 percent in 1995, 0.2 percent in 1996, 0.5 percent in 1997, and 1.0 percent in 1998. The number of visitors in 1997 was 13 percent down on the peak 1994 level, and in the first three quarters of 1998 the number had fallen 8 percent compared with the same period in 1997, although visitor days did not fall to the same extent.

Table 2.18 **GDP Growth Rates and Inflation Rates, The Pacific, 1997-1998**
(percent)

DMC	GDP		Inflation	
	1997	1998	1997	1998
Cook Islands[a]	-0.5	-1.0	-0.4	1.0
Fiji[b]	-1.8	-3.9	3.4	5.7
Kiribati[a]	1.5	1.5	2.2	2.0
Marshall Islands[a]	-5.3	-5.0	4.8	4.0
Federated States of Micronesia	-4.0	-3.1	3.0	3.0
Nauru	(...)	(...)	6.1	4.0
Papua New Guinea	-4.6	2.5	3.9	10.0
Samoa[c]	0.8	-0.4	6.8	6.0
Solomon Islands[a,b]	-0.5	-10.0	8.1	12.3
Tonga[b]	-6.6	-0.3	2.1	3.0
Tuvalu[a,b]	2.5	2.0	1.4	0.8
Vanuatu[a]	1.7	-2.0	2.8	3.9

(...) Estimated to be negative.

a. Refers to the inflation rate in the capital city.
b. Refers to GDP growth at factor cost.
c. 1998 GDP growth refers to first half of the year.

Sources: Country sources; staff estimates.

At the same time that tourism went into decline, a crisis in government finances emerged as a result of years of unsustainable fiscal expansion involving a growing wage bill, an expanding welfare system, and a surge in capital expenditure largely funded by external borrowing. The government formulated an Economic Reform Program based on the New Zealand model, which led to a substantial reduction in public sector employment. Between 1996 and late 1998, the number of civil servants was reduced from about 3,350 to 1,340 and the number of ministries was cut from 52 to 22. The resident population dropped from 19,100 to 16,600, as Cook Islanders took advantage of their New Zealand citizenship to work in Australia and New Zealand and to benefit from these countries' health, education, and social security systems.

The inflation rate edged up to 1 percent in 1998, following a decline in prices in 1997. Given the use of the New Zealand dollar as the domestic currency and the heavy reliance on imports, 75 percent of which come from New Zealand, the inflation rate is largely determined by price changes in New Zealand. After declining in 1994-1996, imports grew by 14.9 percent in 1997, primarily because of a rise in the machinery and transport equipment category. In the first three quarters of 1998 they dropped by 1 percent on the comparable period in 1997. Exports, which consist principally of pearls, fell each year during 1994-1997, but in the first three quarters of 1998 were up 6.7 percent on the comparable period in 1997. Even though the trade deficit declined, it remained substantial at NZ$46.7 million in the first nine months of 1998. In the past, private remittances and official transfers have kept the current account in surplus.

The official economic outlook is gloomy. Forecasts indicate that GDP will fall by up to 1 percent in 1999 before gradually recovering to reach growth of 3 percent per year by 2003. Underlying this forecast is an assumption of sustained growth in the tourism, agriculture, and marine resources sectors, following a short-term adverse impact of the Asian economic crisis. Given that tourists from Asia accounted for only 1 percent of total visitor arrivals in 1997, the direct impact of the crisis on tourism is negligible. However, the indirect effect is potentially more serious. Currency devaluations in Asia and lower prices in competing tourist destinations in the Pacific, especially Fiji, have

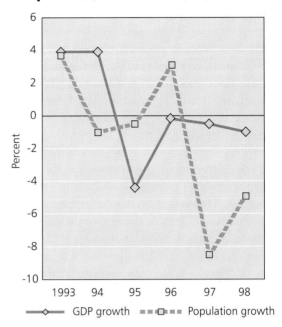

Figure 2.15 Growth of Real GDP and Population, Cook Islands, 1993-1998

Sources: Cook Islands Statistics Office (1998); staff estimates.

made the Cook Islands relatively more expensive, even after allowing for the 9 percent depreciation of the New Zealand dollar in 1998.

In the first nine months of 1998, a drop of nearly 3,000 in visitor numbers on the same period in 1997 was largely the result of a fall in tourists from Australia, the United States, and Europe, while the number of visiting New Zealanders increased slightly. Even though many variables affect the number of tourists to the Cook Islands, particularly the frequency and scheduling of international air services, the decline in tourist numbers is worrying.

In addition, the Japanese recession may have an adverse effect on the pearl industry, not only because Japan is the Cook Islands' main market, but also because it is the world's major buyer of cultured pearls, and this may cause a general fall in pearl prices.

The principal policy issue for the Cook Islands was the completion of the Economic Reform Program and the consolidation of its achievements, particularly in improving fiscal governance and creating an environment conducive to private sector growth. There was cause for concern about the effectiveness and durability of some of the changes. Despite attempts to balance the operating budget in 1997 and 1998, deficits were recorded, and the government was unable to service fully an external debt of NZ$143.9 million, equivalent to nearly the whole of GDP. In September 1998 debt renegotiations brokered by the Asian Development Bank led to major concessions from the chief creditor, Italy, and from Nauru and New Zealand. Nonetheless, the fiscal situation remained fragile, with tight restrictions on cash effectively undermining the output budgeting system.

The 1999 budget was not in compliance with the requirement that the operating budget be balanced, and relied on asset sales to fund current expenditure. One major asset sale has not been fully transparent, and the privatization of the government-owned telecommunications monopoly paid insufficient attention to regulatory arrangements. Effective efforts to realize fiscal surpluses are needed and will have to include a planned completion of public service reform. The number of ministries and civil servants is still far too high for such a small population. The failure to reduce the size and cost of a Parliament of 25 members and concerns about the commitment to improved governance also need to be addressed. The fate of the recommendations of the 1998 Political Reform Commission, which include one to reduce the size of Parliament, will be a key test for the government. The devolution to local government of basic service provision that was implemented under the Economic Reform Program is attractive as a way to increase participation in the reform process, but care will be needed to ensure that it does not increase the public expenditure burden by creating new layers of bureaucracy. Finally, the high and distortionary tariff system needs reform.

KIRIBATI

After growing at an average annual rate of 4.3 percent during 1990-1995 and at 6.3 percent in 1996, GDP growth fell to an estimated 1.5 percent in 1997 and 1998. The 1997 and 1998 rates were barely sufficient to keep pace with the population growth rate in the 1990s of 1.4 percent. The small population of 80,000 remains the poorest among Pacific countries, with a

per capita GDP of $670 at the end of 1997. That same year per capita gross national product (GNP) was higher at $890 because of revenues from fishing license fees; remittances from overseas workers; and, most important, investment income from the assets of the Revenue Equalization Reserve Fund, a trust fund originally built up from phosphate mining royalties. The fund consists of equities and bonds invested in several different international capital markets and is valued at about eight times the level of GDP.

The public sector dominates the economy. Government services accounted for 44 percent of GDP at the end of 1995, and public enterprises accounted for a further 32 percent. Including island councils, the public sector employs three quarters of the formal workforce.

The government has maintained a relatively expansionary fiscal policy stance since 1995. Recurrent spending in 1997 was up by more than half on its 1994 level. A public sector wage rise of just over 30 percent was phased in during this period. Expenditure

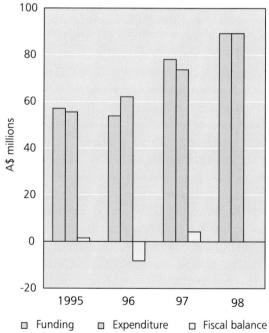

Figure 2.16 Fiscal Balance, Kiribati, 1995-1998

Source: Ministry of Finance and Economic Planning (1997).

on social services, transport, and communication rose substantially. Subsidies to ailing public enterprises were increased, and transfer payments went up. Domestic revenues fluctuated widely because of variations in fishing license fees, and even though revenues averaged nearly 60 percent of GDP during 1995-1997, they fell well short of recurrent expenditure levels. Drawdowns from the Revenue Equalization Reserve Fund increased, and covered just over a fifth of recurrent expenditures in 1995-1997, compared with just under a tenth in 1990-1994. External agencies continued to fund the bulk of capital expenditure, and in 1997 amounted to more than three times the historically low 1994 level. The overall budget balance moved into deficit in 1996, but moved back into surplus in 1997, when recurrent expenditure above the budgeted level was more than outweighed by an unexpected rise in fishing license fees. At the end of 1996 public debt stood at A$12.6 million, or 18 percent of GDP.

The 1998 budget focuses on 1998-2001. As the government moves to a more cautious fiscal policy stance and attempts to balance the budget, the emerging fiscal position during this period is as follows. It envisages an 11 percent decline in recurrent revenue, inclusive of another A$12.6 million drawdown from the Revenue Equalization Reserve Fund and the carrying forward of the A$3.5 million 1997 surplus. Recurrent expenditure is estimated to fall by almost 4 percent, so that a recurrent balanced budget will be achieved. Capital expenditure during this period is expected to increase by 85 percent on the 1997 level as a result of planned sanitation and port development projects.

The external position deteriorated in 1996, improved in 1997, and remained sound in 1998. The 1996 deterioration in the current account from a surplus to a deficit was due to a fall in fishing license fees by two thirds and in copra exports by a quarter, while imports remained steady. However, the shift of the balance of payments into a small deficit does not pose any policy problems, because gross official reserves are sufficient to cover almost nine years of imports. Moreover, total external debt was less than 15 percent of GDP, and external debt service was less than 1 percent of exports of goods and nonfactor services. In 1997 a more than threefold increase in fishing license fees, growth in copra exports, and

increased remittances from seamen collectively far exceeded a decline in interest income from the Revenue Equalization Reserve Fund, while imports (net of aid-funded equipment imports) fell. The consequence was that the level of external reserves rose. The Asian economic crisis had little impact on merchandise exports in 1998, other than an indirect effect through a fall in world prices for seaweed and copra following devaluations by the major producers, Indonesia and the Philippines.

The use of the Australian dollar as legal tender closely links Kiribati's inflation rate, international competitiveness, and small financial system to economic conditions in Australia. The retail price index for urban Tarawa actually fell 1.5 percent in 1996, and then rose by an estimated 2.2 percent in 1997. International competitiveness declined with the 1996 appreciation of the Australian dollar, but increased with the 1997 depreciation. Inflation remained subdued in 1998 and competitiveness improved slightly. Domestic credit dropped by 11 percent in 1996, as claims on public enterprises fell and credit to the small private sector remained static. Only A$4 million out of A$35 million in deposits with the sole commercial bank (Bank of Kiribati) was lent domestically. Little changed in 1997. The interest rate spread increased slightly in 1996-1998 as deposit rates tracked Australian rates downward and lending rates remained unchanged. Long-term lending by the Development Bank of Kiribati increased by 12 percent in 1996.

The medium-term strategy the government adopted in late 1997 identifies three key macroeconomic issues: the lack of almost any growth in per capita GDP since independence in 1979, the need to find employment for the 60 percent increase in the workforce that will occur in the next 15 years, and the government's ability to sustain the growth in public services. Strategies to address these issues include reducing the size of the central government; reforming public enterprises; and facilitating private sector development, including encouraging foreign investment. A number of Pacific countries have adopted this strategic framework, but in the past Kiribati authorities have been slow to follow their example. It is important for the government to translate the stated policy commitments into effective policy implementation.

MARSHALL ISLANDS

The economy of the Marshall Islands is in deep trouble. GDP declined for the third successive year in 1998, falling by an estimated 5 percent. With the population continuing to grow at 3.5 percent per year, GDP per capita dropped from $1,893 in 1995 to $1,567 in 1998. Declines in output occurred in all sectors of the economy, caused by cuts in government expenditure and employment made under the Policy Reform Program, which began in 1996, and by the poor performance of agriculture and fishing. Public administration contracted by approximately a quarter during 1996-1998. Agriculture and fishing output contracted by a fifth in 1996-1997, and is expected to have fallen again in 1998, partly because of poor weather conditions. Low producer prices, interisland transport problems, and an aging tree stock continued to have an adverse impact on copra production. Food and livestock production also fell. The inflation rate fell from almost

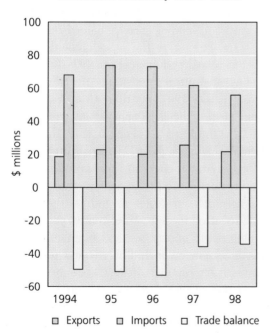

Figure 2.17 Merchandise Trade, Marshall Islands, 1994-1998

Source: ADB data.

10 percent in 1996 to 5 percent in 1997, and fell further to 4 percent in 1998.

The main aim of the Policy Reform Program is to restore stability to public finances after years of heavy spending that involved substantial borrowing secured against future receipts of grant money under the Compact of Free Association with the United States. The program has made progress: the number of government employees fell by 27 percent between late 1995 and March 1998, though this reduction was still below target; a wage freeze has remained in place since 1995; the rationalization of several ministries has occurred; the tariff schedule has been simplified and a basic duty of 12 percent imposed; the subsidies to state-owned enterprises have been reduced or eliminated; and efforts to strengthen tax and customs administration are under way. These measures combined with a substantial drop in capital expenditure helped to move the overall budget balance into surplus in 1996 and 1997. The budget for the fiscal year ending 30 September 1998 aimed at achieving a surplus of 11 percent of GDP through a 17 percent cut in expenditure. However, in March 1998 a supplementary budget provided for a 13 percent increase in estimated expenditures and revenue receipts were running below original expectations. Projections indicated that at best a fiscal surplus of 4 percent of GDP would be realized.

Estimates indicate that merchandise imports fell by a quarter during 1995-1998, while exports dropped by almost 6 percent. The trade deficit therefore declined, and the current account surplus (inclusive of declining official transfers) rose sharply from 1.5 percent of GDP in 1995 to more than 20.0 percent in 1998. The capital account remained in deficit following the cessation of government borrowing in 1995 and the repayment of loans in 1996-1998. Overall, the balance of payments was in deficit throughout this period. Government holdings of US dollar reserves fell dramatically from $40.4 million in 1994 to less than $4.0 million in 1998, which is equivalent to just three weeks of merchandise import cover. External debt stood at $125 million at the end of 1997, which was down 16 percent on the 1995 level, but still too high at 122 percent of GDP. External debt service was equivalent to 41 percent of exports of goods and services.

The money supply grew by 7 percent in 1996, and then contracted by 1 percent in 1997. Both these movements largely reflected balance-of-payments effects on foreign assets stocks. Domestic credit grew by only 1.4 percent in 1996, but expanded by 7.0 percent in 1997 because of an increase in consumer loans to the private sector for travel, construction, and education. These loans were at 18 percent interest, compared with 11 percent on commercial loans, average rates of 2.8 percent on savings, and average rates of 4.3 percent on three-month deposits. The difficulties of using land as collateral and limited investment opportunities continued to constrain growth in long-term lending. Lending by the Marshall Islands Development Bank has been stagnant since 1995.

The government has sought to strengthen the economy by reforming the public sector and improving the environment for private sector development. Parliament approved legislation on investment approval and business licensing procedures in 1998, which now awaits implementation. The Private Sector Unit has been set up in the Office of the President to promote the establishment of a competitive environment, the privatization of public enterprises, and the contracting out of government services. Improving the functioning of the labor market, introducing bankruptcy legislation, and facilitating the leasing of land and its use as collateral are on the agenda. In the absence of independent monetary and exchange rate policies (because the US dollar is used as the currency), increased international competitiveness depends on productivity improvements taking place in a stable, low-inflation economy. The government has therefore emphasized the importance of vocational and skills training. The effects of all these measures, however, will only be realized in the medium to long term.

The private sector has contracted as public sector expenditure has been reduced, and international competitiveness has been eroded as the US dollar has appreciated against other currencies. One positive development in late 1998 was the growth in revenue from fishing license fees and the prospect of some related trans-shipment business. However, the El Niño weather conditions that had pushed tuna schools east into Marshall Island waters, and thus attracted foreign purse seiners, are not a permanent change.

The key current issue is how effectively the government will implement the measures that are still needed to put the country on the path to fiscal and external balance. Public service employment has yet to be reduced to its targeted level, and action is required on a number of revenue raising measures. A further commitment to reforming public enterprises and creating an environment for private sector development is also needed. This may not be implemented to the necessary degree if the government believes that external funding will be maintained beyond the scheduled end of the Compact Association agreement in 2001. This may occur because of the continued strategic value the United States Defense Department places on the Kwajalein atoll, and because of the country's geopolitical significance to Taipei,China.

FEDERATED STATES OF MICRONESIA

The 111,000 people of the Federated States of Micronesia have experienced declining living standards in the 1990s. GDP fell by an estimated 3.1 percent in 1998, following a 4.0 percent fall in 1997. The main reason for this was the contraction in public administration, which accounted for 42 percent of GDP in 1996. This sector is being reduced in size under a public sector reform program aimed at medium-term restructuring of the economy. This has lowered economic activity. The reduced public sector activity had a negative effect on the wholesale and retail trade sector, which accounted for more than one fifth of GDP. The decline in GDP was also exacerbated by a drought, which had an adverse effect on agricultural output. This is an important sector and accounts for 17 percent of GDP. GNP exceeded GDP because of private remittances and fishing license fees.

As the US dollar is the currency used and more than 70 percent of imports come from the United States, the inflation rate closely tracks the US rate. In 1998 it remained at 3 percent. Lending by the commercial banks contracted for the third year in succession, as borrowing by civil servants for consumption purposes and public enterprise commercial borrowing fell. Also reflecting the economic recession, imports continued the decline that began in 1995, but exports remained stagnant. Consequently, the current account deficit improved slightly as a result of the small improvement in the trade balance and some growth in private remittances. The current account deficit, exclusive of official transfers, was in deficit of 16.7 percent of GDP, a slight improvement on 1997. Nevertheless, large official transfers turned this deficit into a current account surplus equivalent to 31.4 percent of GDP. The capital account was in deficit, primarily because of short-term capital outflows arising from overseas investment by the social security administration and public enterprises. An overall balance-of-payments surplus of 8 percent of GDP was recorded, compared with 3.5 percent in 1997. The financial holdings of the state and national governments, which serve as a measure of external reserves, increased to cover almost nine months of imports at the greatly reduced 1998 level. The external debt level at the end of 1997 was $111.4 million, or 52.3 percent of GDP, and servicing this debt absorbed 25.8 percent of the revenue from the exports of goods and nonfactor services. This high level of debt and the dependence on official transfers underscore the economy's vulnerability to external shocks and demonstrates the need for major structural adjustment to overcome this problem.

The economic outlook in the short to medium term is gloomy. Reductions in external grants made under the Compact of Free Association with the United States will require further fiscal adjustments that will relatively quickly further reduce living standards. Meanwhile, the private sector development needed to generate employment and income will be slow in coming, and may not be adequate. In these circumstances, many more Micronesians may choose to emigrate, while at home the government negotiates for donor support.

The focus of the reform program begun in 1996 was on managing the transition to a post-Compact economy in which US grants would be much lower, or even terminated. With the support of an $18 million Asian Development Bank loan in 1997-1998, the reform program has involved the following:

■ Reducing the size and cost of the public service while mitigating the social impact of redundancies

■ Generating more domestic revenue

■ Restructuring the government and removing it from direct involvement in the agriculture, fisheries, and tourism sectors

■ Facilitating private sector development.

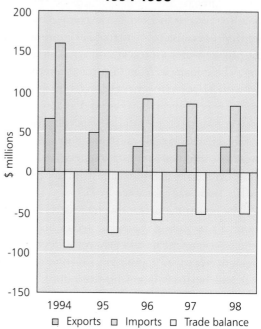

Figure 2.18 Merchandise Trade, Federated States of Micronesia, 1994-1998

$ millions

□ Exports   □ Imports   □ Trade balance

Source: ADB data.

The implementation of government policy has met with some success. The government had planned to reduce the workforce by 1,732 people, or one quarter, by mid-1999. By the end of 1998, at both the national and state level, the authorities had managed to reduce public service wages and travel expenses in three of the four states, followed by a general wage freeze; to merge government departments and ministries; and to contract out some services.

Revenue raising measures implemented include shifting import duty calculations from a free-on-board to a cost-insurance-freight basis, reducing tax exemptions, and strengthening tax administration. Planned measures scheduled for implementation by the end of 1999 include raising state taxes, creating a single federal tax department, and increasing user charges.

Projections of the consolidated general government accounts for 1998 showed a substantial increase in the current budget surplus to 11.3 percent of GDP, and an overall budget surplus of 0.3 percent. This was achieved as a result of public sector reform. Excluding separation payments funded by the Asian Development Bank, the overall surplus rose to 9 percent of GDP. This represents an important first step toward greater fiscal self-reliance, but further adjustments will be required. In 1998 domestic revenue of $69 million still only accounted for 62 percent of current expenditure. Moreover, the consolidated accounts do not show the variation between the national and state governments: while the national and three state governments ran current and overall budget surpluses, the remaining state, Pohnpei, ran deficits because of delays in raising taxes and relatively slow reduction of its wage bill, and confronted a potential liquidity crisis. Like Chuuk, it also had an outstanding stock of domestic arrears.

Progress in restructuring and privatizing public enterprises has been slow, although the move to pricing public utility services on a full cost recovery basis has succeeded in three states. The government's commitment to implementing a privatization policy, cutting the number of public service employees, reducing wages, and contracting out government services has facilitated private sector development. A new foreign investment law is aimed at reducing transaction costs incurred by potential investors, though two states have yet to ratify it. Legislative changes that will provide secure access to land through leasehold arrangements and permit the use of land as collateral are on the agenda, but are still to be enacted. Similarly, the legislative framework for enforcing commercial contracts and bankruptcy procedures remains to be established. Once implemented, these measures should encourage private investment in the targeted areas of agriculture, fishing, and tourism.

Although dominated by subsistence farming and by declining copra production, the agriculture sector has diversified into production of betel nuts, bananas, black pepper, and citrus fruits. As concerns fisheries, foreign fleets may make greater use of Federated States of Micronesia ports and onshore facilities for transshipment and for processing tuna for the lower-grade canning market and the high-quality sashimi market in Japan. Niche marketing of the country as an ecotourist and diving destination and the development of small-scale resorts could stimulate the economy and increase the number of tourists from their present level of about 15,000 per year.

NAURU

Since 1906 phosphate mining has dominated Nauru's small economy. With the imminent exhaustion of this natural resource, the economy in fiscal crisis, and the financial system in a state of near collapse, the population faces a difficult future. The problem is that the funds of the Nauru Phosphate Royalties Trust (NPRT), which were built up from phosphate royalties to generate income once mining ceased, are much reduced as a result of poor management. Indeed, it is unclear what the unencumbered asset base of the NPRT is, and therefore what future level of consumption it can sustain.

Phosphate exports dropped by a third from an annual average of 1.58 million tons in the 1980s to 0.51 million tons in 1990-1997. This was primarily because of the collapse of the major Australian market due to unacceptably high cadmium levels in the Nauru product. Consequently, average annual export values were just 60 percent of the 1980s' average of A$86.4 million. In 1998 the volume of phosphate exports fell further by almost 18 percent on the previous year's levels, because the Asian crisis reduced sales to Indonesia and the Republic of Korea.

As a result of this export slump, the level of economic activity has declined. GDP is roughly estimated to have fallen by about 14 percent between 1992 and 1996, and by a further 20 percent in the subsequent two years, while the population has increased at the rate of 1.5 percent per year, from 9,919 to 10,850 people. In 1998 GDP per capita in current prices was about A$4,600, and the inflation rate was 4 percent.

The export slump had a direct and major impact on government finances, because historically the dividend from the government-owned Nauru Phosphate Corporation provided between 60 and 75 percent of its revenues (exclusive of loan proceeds). The corporation's dividends have fallen dramatically, and with them so have government revenues. No corresponding fall took place in government expenditure until after 1996. The reduction since then, moreover, has been artificial, to the extent that the government did not pay A$10 million in interest on public debt and accumulated several million dollars in arrears to suppliers. The financial system is consequently in disarray, largely as a result of government borrowing to finance the budget deficits. As recorded in official accounts, these have averaged A$44 million per year in the 1990s. In addition, government-owned entities have engaged in substantial off-budget expenditure. The problem is that successive governments have financed the deficits in a largely ad hoc way. These include borrowing directly from the NPRT, and employing the government-owned Republic of Nauru Finance Corporation as an agency that borrowed from the NPRT and used NPRT assets as collateral for external commercial borrowing. The government has borrowed from the only domestic bank (the government-owned Bank of Nauru), accessed the two government-owned pension funds, sold assets, and introduced legislation to allow direct funds transfer from the NPRT.

In an attempt to rectify the position, the 1999 budget provides for cuts in expenditure on wages and salaries, travel and entertainment, and overseas medical services and for increased taxes on imports. An overall budget surplus is projected, but another deficit seems likely.

The financing of the budget deficits and debt servicing created a liquidity crisis in 1996 that has continued and intensified in subsequent years. As liquid funds in the NPRT and in government corporations such as the Nauru Phosphate Corporation have been depleted, the government has relied on extending its overdraft with the Bank of Nauru. The issuing of Bank of Nauru checks has drained the bank of its reserve holdings of Australian dollars, leaving it unable to effect international transfers or meet depositors' withdrawal demands. The bank has been insolvent for two years, financial intermediation has broken down, and confidence in the payments system has disappeared. Thus after many years of unplanned excessive spending and borrowing, the public and private sectors are operating on a hand-to-mouth cash basis, and the NPRT assets that were to secure sustainable consumption levels for an almost totally import-dependent society have been substantially run down. The book value of these assets dropped from A$1,255.1 million in June 1991 to A$707.6 million in June 1997. Provisions appear inadequate, most of the properties that dominate the portfolio are mortgaged, and market valuations are needed to arrive at a true value for the assets.

The government needs to address two immediate issues. First, the banking sector must be revived, either by restructuring and recapitalizing the Bank of Nauru or by facilitating the establishment of a foreign bank, perhaps in a joint venture arrangement. Second, as part of a medium-term move toward improved fiscal planning and a balanced budget, the government must reduce its expenditures and increase its revenues. This applies not only to government operations proper, but also to government corporations that have part of their expenditure financed by the government budget and that contribute to revenues. The need to reduce the number of public sector employees, reduce wages by cutting back on working hours, and institute a nominal wage freeze will seriously reduce living standards. The government directly provides 56 percent of employment for Nauruans and other government entities provide a further 41 percent. The private sector is miniscule, and a subsistence sector that accounts for just 1 percent of GDP does not offer the safety net available to other Pacific populations. Nonetheless, a

Figure 2.19 **Fiscal Balance, Nauru, 1993-1997**

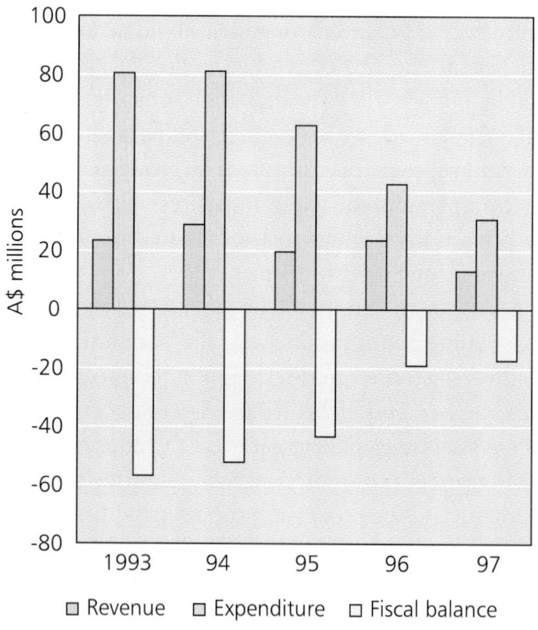

Source: Republic of Nauru annual accounts.

drop in average income is inevitable if the remaining NPRT assets, which will be the major source of income when phosphate deposits run out in three or four years, are to be protected.

SAMOA

Samoa's economic growth has slowed down in the last two years following its recovery from several natural disasters in the early 1990s. New national accounts estimates show GDP growth of 6.5 percent in 1995, 6.9 percent in 1996, but only 0.8 percent in 1997. Estimates for the first half of 1998 reveal that GDP was 0.4 percent lower than during the same period in 1997.

The tertiary sector, which grew at an average annual rate of 8.1 percent, led growth during 1994-1997. An expansion in tourism has stimulated commerce, hotels and restaurants, transport and communication, and personal services, while public administration and finance and business services have grown fairly rapidly, at 6.3 and 13.1 percent, respectively. The other sectors have performed less impressively. Manufacturing overall has declined at an average annual rate of 0.3 percent. The primary sector has grown at the rate of 1.9 percent, with agriculture growing at 1.5 percent and fisheries at 3.3 percent.

The balance of payments remained in overall surplus in the first half of 1998. Commodity export growth, a fall in imports, increased tourism receipts, and a substantial rise in remittances contributed to improved current account performance, but the capital account surplus fell substantially. The external position remained sound, with net foreign assets at the end of the second quarter reaching about $56 million. In the first half of 1998 the tala appreciated against the yen and the New Zealand, Australian, and Fijian dollars and depreciated against the US dollar and the deutsche mark. The nominal effective exchange rate depreciated by about 4 percent. Given that the inflation rate of 6 percent was above that of Samoa's trading partners, the real effective exchange rate appreciated, continuing the trend of real appreciation of about 3 percent per year that emerged during 1991-1997. The implied loss of international competitiveness requires monitoring, given the possible adverse implications for the balance of payments.

The budgetary situation has improved since 1995. The overall balance moved into surplus in 1996 and remained in surplus in 1997. While a small deficit was budgeted for 1998, the outcome was a surplus of just under 2 percent of GDP. This primarily reflected lower than expected development expenditure. Official external debt was equivalent to 72 percent of GDP, down from its peak of 91 percent in 1993. The debt-to-GDP ratio is still high, but debt servicing costs of around $5.6 million in 1998 were manageable in terms of their call on revenues from exports of goods and nonfactor services and from private remittances. The government is budgeting for an overall surplus of 1.1 percent of GDP in 1999.

Credit to the private sector expanded significantly, by 17.4 percent, and reached 25 percent of GDP in 1998. During the year, the composition of commercial banks' loan portfolios with the private sector and public institutions shifted away from personal loans toward loans to the primary and secondary sectors. The creation of a stable macroeconomic environment

Figure 2.20 Growth of Real GDP and Major Sectors, Samoa, 1995-1997

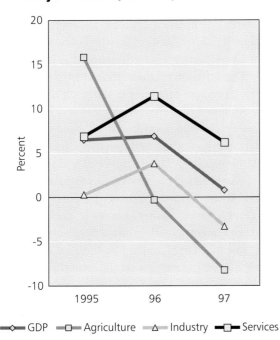

Source: Ministry of Finance, Statistics Office.

and progress in implementing the financial sector liberalization program clearly have contributed to the
achievement of private sector-led growth. The implementation of plans for further commercialization,
corporatization, and privatization of public enterprises
will also play an important role in introducing a new
dynamism into the economy.

The government has reaffirmed its commitment
to economic reform through its revised economic
strategy for 1998-1999 and its 1999 budget. The rate
of investment is a crucial determinant of the actual
growth rate, and in this regard Samoa needs to
enhance its attractiveness to foreign investors. Political and economic stability, tax and tariff reform,
improved transport and communications infrastructure, and development of the offshore financial
services industry are all positive features. The relative
strength of the tala may have a deterrent effect, but
the current complexities and delays in the investment
approval process are more important. It is therefore
encouraging that the simple and transparent Foreign
Investment Act is in the pipeline. Together with
arrangements for secure access to land, this will
provide a legislative framework conducive to greater
foreign investment flows. The latter would provide
not only capital, but also management skills, technology, and training that would increase the productivity of the workforce. In the case of tourism, a
potential additional benefit is that the related investment and job creation could be in rural areas, thereby
helping to stem urban drift and its attendant social
problems.

Provided the economy is not subject to severe
external shocks and the government is committed
to effective, continuing economic reform within a
stable macroeconomic environment, Samoa can
achieve economic growth at a modest, sustainable rate
of around 3 percent per year. This will permit an
increase in average income of around 2 percent
annually, and will generate jobs for the 500 new entrants to the labor force each year. Such a growth outcome will require durable improvements in the
performance of the agriculture sector, continued expansion in fisheries, and realization of the potential
for further manufacturing and tourism development.
The official forecast for 1999 is for real GDP growth
of 3 to 4 percent.

SOLOMON ISLANDS

Solomon Islands was in economic crisis in 1998. After
a drop in GDP of 0.5 percent in 1997, it fell an estimated 10 percent in 1998 as the collapse of log export
markets in Asia compounded the adjustments forced
by years of economic mismanagement. Government
finances and the balance-of-payments position were
weak, the financial system remained under pressure,
inflation remained in double digits, and unsustainable
harvesting of forest resources continued. Business confidence remained low. The government that took office in August 1997 was preoccupied with restoring
macroeconomic stability within the context of the
Policy and Structural Reform Program.

The central bank tightened monetary policy,
which raised deposit rates somewhat, but they remained negative in real terms. Commercial banks also
continued to earn negative real returns on their substantial holdings of Treasury bills, because even with
the government's effective commitment to servicing
its debt for the first time in two years, the 6 percent
rate on bills was half the inflation rate. The banks
maintained wide intermediation margins of 10 percent. A rise in Treasury bill rates was precluded by the
accompanying implications for the budget. Clearly any
restoration of investor confidence depends on a revival of the financial sector, which must be under-
pinned by a domestic debt restructuring program.

The inflation rate accelerated from 8.1 percent
in 1997 to 12.3 percent in 1998 as a result of the 20 percent devaluation of December 1997 and increases in
indirect taxes. The government will need to maintain
its stance on ending the traditional indexation of public
service wages to prices to consolidate the remaining
real devaluation. The balance of payments was in a
precarious position throughout the year, with external reserves ranging between two weeks and two
months of import cover. External debt arrears fell, but
were still high at $7 million at the end of the year.
The value of log exports in the first three quarters
was about 60 percent below the comparable 1997 level,
but production was more than a third higher than the
estimated sustainable level of harvesting. Fish became
the major export earner, and palm oil and palm ker-
nel exports grew because of price and production increases. These positive developments ameliorated the

Figure 2.21 Growth of Real GDP, Solomon Islands, 1993-1998

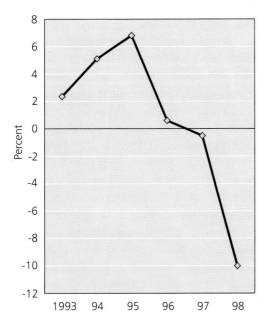

Sources: ADB (1997c); ADB data.

impact of depressed log markets, resulting in a small trade surplus.

Prior to presenting its budget in April 1998, the government took a number of initiatives to increase revenues and contain expenditures. As concerns revenues, among other measures it cancelled tax exemptions and remissions that did not involve legally binding agreements, effective immediately; completed and introduced a simplified tariff system; and revised income taxes to broaden the tax base and improve equity. On the expenditure side, the government instituted a public service wage freeze, restricted payments of allowances, and froze all recruitment in anticipation of further actions to reduce and streamline the civil service. It also began a limited clearance of domestic and external arrears. The 1998 budget projected a current surplus of $3.3 million and a near zero overall balance. A reduction in domestic and external arrears was planned on the assumption that the necessary funds could be raised through privatization, some borrowing from the National Provident Fund, and external borrowing.

In the event, domestic revenues fell well short of budget expectations, and the situation was so serious that day-to-day cash availability dictated expenditure levels. Given a delay in efforts to reduce the number of public service employees, an increase in the wage bill by 6 percent on the 1997 level, and the priority assigned to debt servicing, the enforced cuts largely fell on the operations expenditure of departments. This exacerbated the acknowledged problems of the poor quality of public services and deteriorating infrastructure. Debt and nondebt arrears were reduced by a total of $18 million, primarily through external concessional borrowing from the Asian Development Bank and securitization of arrears to the National Provident Fund. As a result, the overall level of public debt decreased slightly from $198 million at the end of 1997 to $195 million at the end of 1998. Domestic debt totaled $83 million, external debt $105 million, and trade creditor and other arrears $7 million. The 1999 budget aims at a current surplus of SI$17.9 million, and an overall deficit of SI$26.7 million to be financed from external borrowing. Additional Policy and Structural Reform Program expenditure on arrears settlements totals SI$92.2 million, funded by asset sales of SI$29.2 million and further external concessional borrowing of SI$63 million.

Economic performance in 1999 will depend on the international economic environment, and on the extent to which the government can successfully tackle the inherited fiscal crisis and implement its program of economic reform. The outlook for commodity prices in general, and log prices in particular, is not encouraging. On the positive side, the Gold Ridge gold mine will be in full production in 1999, and the Asian crisis has led to lower prices of intermediate inputs. The government has made progress in restoring macroeconomic stability by servicing its domestic debt and paying arrears, which it plans to clear entirely by the end of 1999.

While the process of public service reform has encountered delays, the government now plans to reduce the number of employees by 550 and has been appointing new departmental secretaries on the basis of merit. In addition, it will introduce a performance orientation and intends to reform the provincial government system. It does, however, need to accelerate progress on privatization, and has identified impediments to private sector development that it needs to address, including the difficulties in accessing (buying, selling, and leasing) land, the poor infrastructure, the burdensome investment approval processes, and the lack of professional skills. Most important, the policy framework and management regime essential for ensuring the sustainable and equitable development of natural forest resources are yet to be put in place.

TONGA

In 1998 Tonga underwent its third successive year of recession. GDP declined by 1.5 percent in 1996, 6.6 percent in 1997, and 0.3 percent in 1998. The inflation rate was 3.0 percent in 1998, up from 2.1 percent in 1997. The economic downturn largely reflected the performance of the agriculture sector, which has contracted in each of the last three years as squash production has declined because of drought, disease, and lower world market prices. In addition, commerce

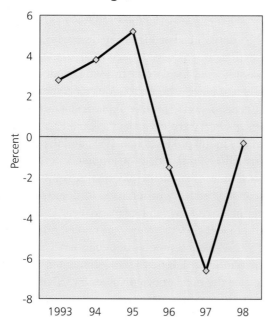

Figure 2.22 **Growth of Real GDP, Tonga, 1993-1998**

Source: ADB data.

and the hotel and restaurant sector contracted in 1997, partly reflecting falling tourist numbers. Activity in the construction sector dropped dramatically in 1997 as aid-funded projects were completed. While the manufacturing sector was stagnant, government services, which constitute about 15 percent of GDP, expanded at about 3 percent.

In 1998 the merchandise trade deficit worsened as a result of declining squash exports and a resurgence of imports that was fueled by a strong credit expansion. In the 12 months from April 1997 through March 1998 total domestic credit grew by 20 percent. Private sector credit rose 40 percent, while the government changed from becoming a net lender to a net borrower as its budgetary position deteriorated. While private remittances held up, the balance of payments was placed under considerable pressure. The current account deficit grew to 7.3 percent of GDP, and gross foreign reserves fell to an equivalent of two months of merchandise imports, compared with five months in 1997. In response, the central bank raised the reserve requirement for banks from 10 to 15 percent and sought to reduce liquidity by tendering short-term securities, though the weakness of its profit base constrained action in this regard. While currency devaluation was neither contemplated nor forced, the level of foreign exchange reserves remained fragile. Continued restraint of domestic demand was needed to allow foreign exchange reserves to build up to a level that instilled confidence in the economy.

Fiscal policy was not supportive of the tight monetary policy, however. The historic practice of balancing the recurrent budget ceased in 1997 and continued in 1998, when the wage and salaries share of recurrent expenditure reached 53 percent. The projected overall budget deficit in 1998 was approximately 4 percent of GDP. The public debt at the end of the year was 43.3 percent of GDP, with 80 percent of it external. Debt servicing costs were manageable at 28.3 percent of merchandise exports. The 1999 budget envisages a return to a small recurrent budget surplus and an 18 percent rise in development expenditure, but these outcomes will only be realized if extrabudgetary appropriations and development spending in excess of that planned for are avoided.

The short-term economic outlook is gloomy, and medium-term prospects are that economic recovery will be uncertain, and at best modest. Squash production is expected to increase in 1999, assuming that major shocks from disease or cyclones do not occur and that the Japanese market remains strong. Competition from other suppliers, whose entry into the market was responsible for the falling prices during the last two years, will continue. Fish and root crop exports are expected to hold up, but vanilla producers currently holding unsold stock are likely to continue to confront low prices as a result of greater international competition. Tonga is trying to develop markets for papaya in Australasia and Japan and for potatoes and watermelons in Fiji, but how successful they will be is uncertain. In addition, some indirect fallout from the Asian crisis could be a problem. Adverse effects on the economies of Australia, New Zealand, and the United States could reduce tourist earnings and lower private remittance flows to Tonga.

The fundamental development challenge remains generating jobs and exports through private sector development. Tonga has met this challenge successfully in the past, when copra and banana export markets were lost and replaced with squash. The government, aware of the economy's structural deficiencies, will need to rationalize the public sector to allow the private sector to grow. The government needs to reduce the civil service wage bill. It could also achieve major fiscal savings by converting the noncontributory pension scheme for public servants to a pension system that depends on contributions. Legislation to introduce such a pension scheme in mid-1999 was enacted in late 1998. Major reforms to enhance the efficiency of Tonga's large and diverse public enterprise sector will also be necessary. While most state-owned enterprises are not a drain on the budget, they do not generate taxes or dividends of any consequence.

To stimulate private sector growth and provide a more reliable revenue flow, the government needs to remove distortions in the current tax and tariff structures. The Industrial Development Incentives Act remains in effect, providing tax incentives, tax holidays, large discretionary duty exemptions, special depreciation provisions to approved enterprises that are classified as "developmental," and exemptions to the entire public sector. The country's dependence on

taxation levied on trade needs to be lowered by reducing import tariffs, eliminating the port and services tax, and introducing a tax system that is based on sales. Experts have recommended the adoption of a harmonized system of tariff classification in line with the standards set by the World Trade Organization as a way to clarify tariff codes and reduce the scope for evasion of import duties. The government also needs to reform the cumbersome system of granting business, trade, and development licenses and to introduce a simple company registration system. The establishment of a neutral, transparent, and nondiscriminatory policy toward foreign direct investment would also improve the country's access to urgently needed capital, technology, and management skills. The tourism and fisheries sectors would be the major beneficiaries of increased foreign investment flows, and could generate much of the 4 percent annual growth in employment that is required if new entrants are to be absorbed into the formal private sector.

TUVALU

Tuvalu is the smallest Pacific country by any of the conventional criteria of land area; population; and GNP, which totals around $12 million and is approximately $1,300 per capita. Just over half of the population of approximately 10,000 is concentrated on Funafuti, the only urban center and the seat of government, which accounts for 27 percent of GDP. The other 49 percent lives in the outer islands, where subsistence production is especially evident. Subsistence economic activities account for approximately one third of GDP, and are supplemented by income from copra exports and, most important, remittances from Tuvaluan seamen. These remittances are among the key, long-established links with the global economy, along with overseas investments.

GDP grew at an average annual rate of 2.9 percent in 1990-1995, with the marketed component growing at a higher rate of 3.7 percent. The engine of growth, and the primary source of fluctuations in marketed output, was the public sector. Aid-funded projects were central to this sometimes erratic economic expansion. Since 1995 GDP has grown at 2 to 3 percent per year, with public administration and public enterprises again leading the way and stimulating the growth of a small private sector made up mostly of service businesses. The GDP growth rate in 1998 was 2 percent.

Government and private consumption are not constrained by domestic output alone, because of significant workers' remittances and because of income from the Tuvalu Trust Fund. The latter was established in 1987 to underpin Tuvalu's financial viability by supporting recurrent government expenditure. Estimates indicate that GNP can be between a third and a half higher than GDP because of these cash flows from abroad. In addition, remittances in kind may add a further 10 to 15 percent to GDP.

In recent years inflation has dropped to as low as less than 1 percent. This reflects the fall in Australia's inflation rate, because Tuvalu uses the Australian dollar as its currency and because about half of merchandise imports come from Australia. A further 20 percent of imports are from Fiji, so that further downward pressure on prices came from the January 1998 devaluation of the Fijian dollar. Remittances, investment income, fishing license fees, and official transfers financed the substantial trade deficit. Virtually all the capital expenditure undertaken by the public sector is funded by aid grants, while the government has generally run recurrent budget surpluses. Drawdowns from the Tuvalu Trust Fund have provided approximately 20 percent of recurrent revenues, with import taxes and fisheries and telecommunications license fees as the other main contributors. In 1998 there was a recurrent budget surplus in excess of original projections, equivalent to more than 20 percent of GDP. This reflected an increase in fishing license fees from an expected A$1.5 million to A$5.0 million and a rise in telecommunications license fees.

The signing of a contract leasing out Tuvalu's Internet domain address (".tv") to a foreign company had a potentially significant effect on government finances and on Tuvalu's economic situation in general. Under the contract, the company committed to an up-front payment to the government of $50 million by 31 December 1998, which was recoverable against the government's 65 percent share of future earnings. Using current exchange rates, this amount represented A$85 million, which is 25 percent more than the total asset base of the Tuvalu Trust Fund. Investment of the amount on the same basis as the

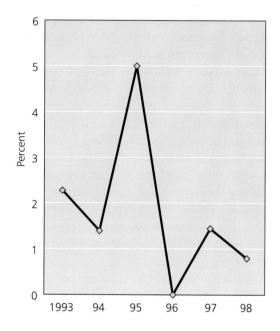

Figure 2.23 Inflation Rates, Tuvalu, 1993-1998

Source: ADB data.

fund's investments would generate an income equivalent to 25 percent of recurrent expenditures, but the government had already made some commitments for expenditure in 1999 against expected ".tv" revenue. Unfortunately, at the end of 1998 it seemed increasingly unlikely that the $50 million would be forthcoming, as renegotiation of the original deal began.

The government's medium- to long-term development strategy focuses on improved governance, greater and more effective expenditure on health and education, and greater equality of income distribution between Funafuti and the outer islands. The government also plans to facilitate private sector development of export-oriented activities, and to this end has created a new legislative framework for foreign direct investment. While the government is making progress on the interisland distribution issue through the planned creation of an outer island development fund, progress on public sector reform has been slow, and some policy analysts are concerned about a lack of transparency and accountability in some government decisionmaking.

Access to land in Funafuti and difficulties in using it as collateral continue to constrain private sector development. Perhaps the most binding constraint on economic development, however, is the lack of reliable and frequent domestic and international transport services. A single aged vessel serves the outer islands and constitutes a substantial drain on the budget. International air services have deteriorated to the point where cancelled flights and enforced stays in Tuvalu are the norm. An improvement in domestic transport services would increase both domestic and international trade in agricultural and marine produce, and simultaneously improve essential health- and education-related passenger services. Better international air services are vital if Tuvalu is to attract investors and tourists. Any employment generation through the creation and expansion of viable businesses is to be welcomed, given the rate at which the excess supply of unskilled labor is growing. Nevertheless, overseas employment opportunities will remain crucial simply because the small private sector could not grow rapidly enough (at about 20 percent per year in employment terms) to absorb new labor force entrants. This makes the training of seamen at the Tuvalu Maritime School a key investment in Tuvalu's economic future.

VANUATU

Vanuatu's economic performance deteriorated during 1996-1998, some fiscal fragility became evident, and political instability contributed somewhat to disarray in macroeconomic policy. The GDP growth rate slowed from 3.5 percent in 1996, to 1.7 percent in 1997, and to an estimated minus 2.0 percent in 1998. The growth slowdown is the result of declining activity in the manufacturing, electricity, and construction sectors, compounded in 1998 by a substantial drop in primary sector production and sluggishness in tourism.

The traditional exports of copra, beef, timber, and cocoa fell because of the direct and indirect impacts of the Asian crisis and currency devaluations in Fiji, Papua New Guinea, and Solomon Islands. The declaration of a state of emergency during the January 1998 Port Vila riots, which occurred after the publication of an ombudsman's report questioning the sound-

ness of investment decisionmaking at the Vanuatu National Provident Fund, affected tourism. Following the riots, the government allowed unconditional withdrawal of retirement savings from the fund. As the fund could provide less than half the required funds, the government, as guarantor, had to make up the shortfall, leaving it with a projected overall budget deficit of 14 percent of GDP. Given the implications of the payouts for the balance of payments and the recent devaluations in Fiji and Solomon Islands, it was not surprising that a run on the currency began. Capital outflow combined with reduced exports of goods and services and higher import spending caused a drop in foreign exchange reserves from almost 6 months of import cover at the end of 1997 to 3.5 months at the beginning of April 1998. On 27 March the governor of the central bank, on the last day of his term of office, unilaterally announced a 20 percent devaluation, but the minister of finance reversed this decision the same day.

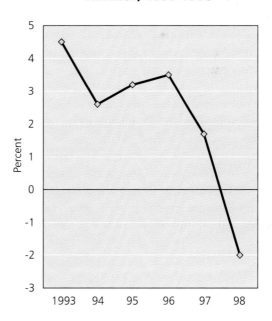

Figure 2.24 Growth of Real GDP, Vanuatu, 1993-1998

Sources: ADB (1997d); ADB data.

The new government that took office on 30 March sought to restore credibility to macroeconomic policy and to revive investor confidence. It appointed a new central bank governor and endorsed the previous government's reversal of the devaluation decision. It tightened monetary policy by replacing the 10 percent statutory reserve deposit requirement with a 16 percent prescribed asset ratio, and a substantial rise in the central bank base lending rate. Foreign exchange controls were effectively imposed on capital transactions. Although the devaluation reversal and the maintenance of capital controls initially intensified speculative pressure, the monetary tightening persuaded the public of the government's determination to defend the vatu and, together with concessional external borrowing, facilitated a recovery in the foreign reserves position.

Approximately 87 percent of the projected 1998 budget deficit was a one-off expenditure arising from compensation payments to public servants dismissed following the 1994 strike, the Vanuatu National Provident Fund payout, and payments related to the Comprehensive Reform Program funded by the Asian Development Bank. As a result of these higher expenditures the fiscal deficit rose to more than 10 percent in 1998. The budget policy statement for 1999 suggests a fiscal improvement. However, a significant improvement will be hard to realize. In particular, how a 6.3 percent rise in domestic revenues will be achieved in the context of a forecast 4.5 percent growth in nominal GDP is unclear. In addition, pressures for wage increases may threaten the anticipated 10.5 percent reduction in domestically financed expenditure. No official forecast is offered for inflation in 1999, but assuming it will be in the range of 3 to 4 percent, GDP growth is expected to be slow, at 0.5 to 1.5 percent.

Achievements under the Comprehensive Reform Program have been substantial and include the following:

- A convergence of local ownership around the key theme of improved governance, along with strong public participation
- A reduction in the number of ministries from 34 to 9 and a 7 percent cut in civil service employment
- An improvement in public servants' autonomy and efficiency
- The establishment of a legislative framework for improved governance
- The beginning of a process to prepare a public investment program that includes aid-financed projects
- The introduction of a value-added tax and the simplification and reduction of import duties and business license fees
- The restructuring of the National Bank and the Development Bank and the amendment of the Vanuatu National Provident Fund Act to achieve progress in financial reform.

However, some problems and concerns remain. The rapid passage of a large volume of legislation left little time for parliamentary scrutiny. The new Foreign Investment Act included schedules that are contrary to the letter and spirit of the Comprehensive Reform Program, and by reserving a wide range of areas for the indigenous population, the act will discourage foreign investors. A planned government review of the schedules needs to be completed quickly. Weaknesses in law enforcement continue to impose high transaction costs on business and the community as a whole. Reform of the public sector is incomplete and will need to be consolidated. The severity of Vanuatu's human resource constraint and the heavy reliance on external technical assistance also raises questions about the durability of some reforms. Finally, the coalition government continues to experience difficulties in maintaining political consensus. Despite these difficulties, commitment to implementation of the Comprehensive Reform Program, which began in August 1997, has been strong.

Part 3
Economic Openness:
Growth and Recovery in Asia

Economic Openness:
Growth and Recovery in Asia

The historical record indicates that countries that have espoused a policy of economic openness have been well served by it. The experience of outward-oriented Asian economies is a case in point. The recent financial crisis in Asia, which has besieged many of these open economies, has raised a number of serious questions regarding the role of openness in promoting sustainable growth. This part of the Outlook examines these questions. While the case for openness with regard to trade, labor movement, and direct investment remains strong, developing Asia faces the challenge of ensuring that the global trading system continues to evolve fairly and takes into account the interests of developing countries. To meet this challenge, developing Asia will have to play a more proactive role in future multilateral trade negotiations. As for openness to financial flows, the case is compelling, yet nuanced. It depends on the strength of domestic financial systems; however, rather than providing a reason to postpone financial integration, this means that reform of domestic financial systems is an imperative.

Openness matters. By offering countries opportunities to trade with the outside world, openness stimulates growth through easier access to new technologies and skills and to investable resources in international capital markets, and through the promotion of market discipline. Empirical studies show a strong link between economic openness and growth. A recent Asian Development Bank study (ADB 1997b) reveals that between 1965 and 1990, annual economic growth was, on average, 2 percent higher in those Asian economies that maintained outward-oriented policies than in those that had adopted inward-looking policies.

However, the Asian financial crisis, which began in 1997, has raised serious questions about the role of economic openness in a long-term development strategy. Does economic openness mean greater economic vulnerability and volatility? How quickly, and in what order, should a developing country open itself up to different types of capital flows? Should

countries aim at complete liberalization of capital flows? Given the central role that financial flows may have played in the Asian financial crisis, should developing economies take a more cautious stance toward openness to financial transactions in the future? What approach should Asia take in multilateral trade negotiations? These are some of the issues this part of the *Outlook* addresses.

Among developing regions, Asia has taken the lead in adopting outward-oriented development policies. Following a period of moderate import substitution during the 1950s and early 1960s, the newly industrialized economies (NIEs)—Hong Kong, China; Republic of Korea (henceforth referred to as Korea); Singapore; and Taipei,China—and a group of Southeast Asian economies made a decisive switch to an outward-oriented strategy. These countries actively encouraged exports, reduced import tariffs, and removed quantitative restrictions. Over time, they dismantled barriers to capital inflows and outflows.

Learning from the success of the NIEs and Southeast Asia, the People's Republic of China (PRC) and India—two of Asia's potential economic giants—have turned toward liberal trade strategies in recent years. After pursuing virtually autarkic trade policies for several decades, the PRC began to open its economy to international trade at the end of the 1970s. Before the launch of its trade liberalization program, external trade accounted for less than 10 percent of the PRC's gross domestic product (GDP), and trade and foreign investment were centrally planned and centrally controlled. Today the PRC's economy has achieved a large measure of openness in both trade and foreign direct investment (FDI), and its share in global trade has risen dramatically. Trade now accounts for about 40 percent of the PRC's GDP.

India began trade and investment liberalization almost a decade after the PRC. Starting in 1991, the government introduced a number of liberalizing measures, including reducing tariffs significantly, abolishing all quantitative restrictions on nonconsumer goods, unifying the exchange rate, introducing current account convertibility, and adopting a liberal set of rules for FDI. These reforms substantially improved export performance and resulted in sizable FDI inflows. The share of trade in GDP has increased by about 50 percent since the inception of trade reforms, and now accounts for more than a quarter of India's GDP.

Other developing economies in Asia, including the former socialist economies of Indo-China and Central Asia, have also embarked on programs aimed at opening their economies. While many of these countries face formidable challenges in gaining access to international markets some, such as the Kyrgyz Republic and Viet Nam, have achieved notable successes.

The economies of East and Southeast Asia with a record of sustained openness have undergone a remarkable transformation from widespread poverty to visible prosperity. In one generation, these economies achieved progress that in many Western economies took several generations. The World Bank (1998c) ranks Hong Kong, China; Korea; and Singapore among high-income economies and Malaysia among the upper middle-income economies. It ranks other Southeast Asian countries, such as Indonesia, the

Philippines, and Thailand, among lower-middle-income countries. The World Bank does not include Taipei,China in its rankings, but it too is a high-income economy. The success of these economies has not been limited to economic growth. They have achieved equally impressive results in social development. In many of these economies the scourges of poverty, low life expectancy, malnutrition, and illiteracy are a thing of the past.

However, the Asian financial crisis has interrupted—and to some extent reversed—this "miracle" of economic and social development in East and Southeast Asia. The flood of short-term capital, seen as a sign of Asian success when it flowed into these economies in abundance, has been reversed. The herd has stampeded in the other direction, and the massive outflow of capital has caused an economic crisis bigger than any previous setback in East and Southeast Asian development since World War II. It has undermined economic growth, and threatens to wipe out much of the progress made in recent years. This has already happened in Indonesia, where per capita income in dollar terms has plummeted to pre-1980 levels.

While capital flows can be an important source of economic dynamism in that they provide resources for investment in countries that lack them, they can also cause excessive economic volatility in countries with weak domestic financial systems, poor regulatory frameworks, and pervasive policy distortions. Capital flight can wreak havoc, and revolutionary changes in information technology mean that capital can exit at lightning speed. Countries that allow unfettered movement of capital have suffered during the current crisis, while those that permit only limited mobility have generally escaped a similar fate. The PRC and the economies of South Asia, which are relatively closed to financial capital flows, have remained essentially unscathed by the crisis.

The *Outlook* distinguishes between openness to trade, labor movements, and FDI and openness to financial flows of all kinds. While openness to all types of trade can be beneficial, the benefits of financial capital movement can sometimes be tempered with the costs of volatility. This does not, of course, dilute the case for openness to international financial markets, but rather, it highlights the need for a careful, orderly, well-sequenced approach.

The lesson from recent experience in Asia is not that countries should hastily retreat from their commitment to openness toward international financial markets. In countries where free mobility of capital already exists, in addition to orthodox stabilization measures, economic recovery and sustained growth require comprehensive reform of weak financial systems. Capital control, which is permissible under Article VI of the International Monetary Fund's Articles of Agreement, should be invoked only under exceptional circumstances. In countries where free mobility already exists, the effectiveness of imposing controls in the middle of a crisis is doubtful. While they may provide some breathing space for short-term policy manipulation, they will not encourage capital that has been withdrawn to return, and may induce capital that would have otherwise remained in the country to seek a way out.

Countries that do not currently have open capital markets should wait until they have undertaken the necessary banking and financial sector reforms before opening up. For example, in India many state-owned banks are poorly managed and have high proportions of unrecoverable loans. Until the authorities take the measures needed to close down the worst banks and recapitalize the others so that they can be privatized, and until foreign banks have entered the country on a significant scale, the costs of unfettered mobility of financial capital could be significant, and could even outweigh the benefits.

Nevertheless, in all countries openness to trade and FDI remain essential ingredients for achieving faster growth. To maximize the benefits of openness, Asian developing countries must accelerate the pace of privatization and reduce restrictive business practices. In addition, human capital development is crucial, and countries must invest in better quality education. This is a particularly pressing need in South Asian countries, which lag behind East and Southeast Asia. However, as the *Asian Development Outlook 1998* showed, even the higher-income East and Southeast Asian economies suffer from conspicuous failures in higher education, which has significant and adverse implications for their international competitiveness.

Internationally, the Asian developing countries should use their joint bargaining power to ensure that the global trading system continues to develop in such a way that it preserves and advances developing countries' interests. To this end, they should push for a new, comprehensive round of multilateral trade negotiations.

OPENNESS IN DEVELOPING ASIA

Openness has major implications for economic growth, income distribution, and welfare. Developing countries that have been open to trade and investment have benefited from globalization, enjoying faster growth and generally more equitable distribution of income than those developing countries that have remained closed. Individual Asian developing economies (ADEs) have adopted different degrees of economic openness, and different country groups are characterized by different degrees of openness in trade, investment, and other factor flows. However, while describing the various dimensions of openness is easy, quantifying them, let alone aggregating them to produce an index for openness, is more difficult. Box 3.1 describes a number of ways to measure economic openness.

The Asian Development Bank publication *Emerging Asia* (ADB 1997b) calculates trade openness indexes based on four important aspects of trade policy: the average tariff rate, nontariff barriers (NTBs), the black market premium on foreign exchange, and the extent of export taxes. A fully closed economy scores zero and a fully open economy scores one. On this set of indexes East Asia scores 0.97, Southeast Asia scores 0.73, and South Asia scores 0.06. The average for all countries in the sample was 0.43. Irrespective of the particular indicators of openness employed, the ranking of country groups remains surprisingly unchanged. Reflecting their openness to trade, the economic performance of the East and Southeast Asian countries has been particularly strong (see figure 3.1).

The relative rankings of country groups in terms of openness to FDI follow the same pattern as openness to trade, although ADEs have generally been less open with respect to investment than trade (a later section provides more detailed discussion of the foreign investment regimes in the ADEs). In terms of openness to financial flows, while the PRC and South Asian economies have maintained relatively closed capital

Box 3.1 **Indexes of Openness**

Openness can refer to transactions relating to trade in goods and services, movements of capital and labor, and movement of financial assets. A number of measures of openness to trade and capital flows are available, but no single, generally accepted index to describe the overall level of openness for all economies exists.

Openness to Trade

Leamer's openness index is commonly used in empirical studies as a measure of openness. Using statistical analysis, the level of net exports for a chosen good is predicted for the country based on endowments, transport costs, and the country's overall trade balance. The index for the country is measured by the difference between the predicted level of net exports and the actual level. A higher level of divergence between predicted and actual levels of net exports implies a higher level of distortions in the economy. Economies that are more open are associated with a lower level

of distortions. Thus a higher Leamer's openness index indicates greater distortion, and so a lower degree of openness. An attractive feature of this index is that it reflects all types of trade restrictions, independent of whether they are export promoting or import substituting. The index is consistent across countries, and so permits cross-country comparisons, although as predicted net exports are estimated by using a particular trade model, the accuracy of the index depends on the specifications of the model employed. However, to date Leamer's openness index has only been computed for 1982, therefore examining the evolution of trade restrictions for countries over time is not possible.

Average tariff rates provide the most extensive measure of trade restrictions, either as data on tariff rates on imports for each country for a particular year or as a weighted average computed for the country that reflects relative export volumes. However, this measure does not take nontariff barriers (NTBs), which can

be highly restrictive in developing countries, into account.

Nontariff barriers, such as the extent of quotas and licensing, can be measured using the percentage of goods, weighted for import levels, facing trade restrictions as a proxy for NTBs. However, this sort of index does not capture the intensity of NTBs.

The black market exchange rate premium, which is the difference between the exchange rate that clears the currency market and the official exchange rate, gives some indication of the intensity of NTBs. A large premium is evidence of rationing of foreign exchange, which may prevent the free flow of goods and capital.

The index of price distortions provides another measure of openness. The basic notion behind the index is that those countries with more trade restrictions in place will have greater price distortions in relation to the international price level than those that do not. To arrive at this index of price distortions, purchasing power parity exchange rates are computed

---

accounts, many East and Southeast Asian economies have adopted a policy of capital account liberalization. Indeed, Hong Kong, China; Indonesia; and Malaysia moved to more open capital accounts as early as 1973, and Singapore in 1978.

Foreign Trade Policy in Asian Developing Economies

During the 1980s the NIEs and the Southeast Asian countries, particularly Indonesia, Malaysia, Philippines, and Thailand, maintained more open economies than other developing countries, and consequently enjoyed more robust import growth, which benefited both consumers and import-dependent producers. The PRC has also reaped these benefits of openness: while the country protected its large, state-

owned industrial sector, it allowed its nonstate sector to operate under much greater openness. The openness also contributed to these countries' overall export and growth performance by promoting efficient allocation of resources and attracting FDI, which resulted in additional beneficial effects on domestic production and exports.

Trade in Goods. As table 3.1 shows, the average growth of trade in goods in the PRC, the NIEs, and Southeast Asia outpaced that in South Asian countries, and even that in the world as a whole. A similar pattern of growth in trade is also apparent for primary products and manufactures.

Table 3.2 compares the evolution of protection in ADEs and in other groups of developing countries using data on tariffs and NTBs. While tariffs refer to for each country. The purchasing power parity exchange rate is the exchange rate that equalizes price levels for the same consumption basket across countries. The ratio of the purchasing power parity exchange rate and the official exchange rates—a ratio that is indeed equivalent to the ratio of price levels between countries (the United States is usually taken as the "numeraire" country, that is, a country that reflects the international price level with its open trade policies)—offers an indicator of openness. The larger the price ratio, the greater the level of price distortion. Given the presence of nontradables in the consumption basket and the lower price of nontradables in poorer countries, the price ratio is sometimes adjusted by the GDP level to take this into account. This adjusted price ratio provides a better indicator of openness.

The share of the export sector in domestic output is used as a measure of trade openness in many empirical studies. Although this is a convenient measure, many factors in addition to trade policy determine the share of exports in GDP, and so this can be a poor measure of openness.

Openness to Capital Movements

Restrictions on capital flows are documented in the International Monetary Fund's annual report *Exchange Arrangements and Exchange Restrictions*. Empirical studies of capital controls use these data to construct an index for openness. They usually include three types of restrictions: restrictions on payments for capital transactions for domestically owned funds, separate exchange rates for different types of capital transactions, and restrictions on payment for trade in goods and services. Restrictions on payment for trade in goods and services is included since these transactions can be used to avoid restrictions on capital transactions through the overinvoicing of imports and underinvoicing of exports. The limitation of using this kind of index to measure restrictions on international capital flows is that it does not provide a measure of the intensity of controls. Attempts to construct indexes of the extent of controls are generally not comparable across countries and across time. Moreover, the imposition and removal of capital transaction restrictions is typically undertaken together with other macroeconomic and structural reforms. This makes isolating the impact of capital controls more difficult.

Interest rate parity reflects the degree of integration across countries in international capital markets. Where deposits in all currencies offer the same expected rate of return, there is interest rate parity. Deviations from interest rate parity can be used as a measure of the intensity of capital controls, with data available on a daily or monthly basis. To the extent that deviations from interest rate parity are independent of exchange rate risk, they indicate the presence of capital and exchange controls, differential tax treatment for capital from abroad, or fears of the imposition of capital controls and other regulations in the future.

Source: Pritchett (1996).

taxes on imported goods, NTBs cover various other forms of import restrictions that do not include taxes or subsidies, such as quantitative restrictions on imported goods and import licensing.

As table 3.2 shows, the NIEs and the Southeast Asian countries maintained much lower average rates of protection than South Asia and other non-Asian developing economies in the 1980s. In South Asia average tariffs were roughly 60 percent, and the average percentage of goods affected by NTBs was around 48 percent. In the NIEs average applied tariffs were less than 10 percent during the same period. Tariff rates and NTB incidence were lower in developing countries outside Asia than in South Asia, but appreciably higher—especially for NTBs—than in the NIEs.

In the 1990s many developing countries—including the PRC and most South Asian countries—have attempted to emulate the trade and growth performance of the NIEs and Southeast Asian countries by gradually adopting economic policy reforms, of which the most important is trade liberalization. Many developing countries have moved decisively toward integrating their economies into the global economy. The Uruguay Round of multilateral trade negotiations under the General Agreement on Tariffs and Trade (GATT) included the participation of a dramatically larger number of developing countries than previous trade rounds.

Table 3.2 presents the results not only of concerted trade liberalization under the Uruguay Round of trade negotiations, but also of unilateral trade liberalization in developing countries. In nearly all cases, developing countries succeeded in substantially reducing their levels of tariff protection,

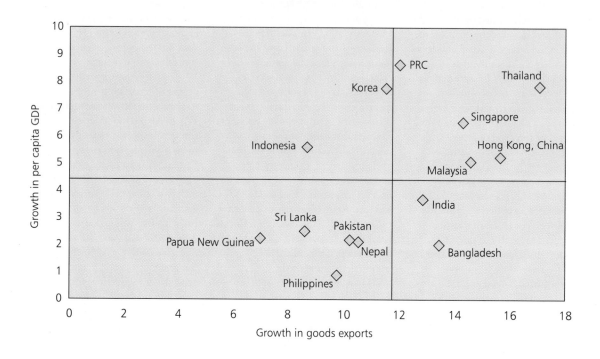

Figure 3.1 Annual Growth of Goods Exports and Per Capita GDP
Selected Asian Countries, 1985-1995
(percent)

Note: The vertical line represents the average real growth of goods exports of the 14 sample countries. The horizontal line indicates the average real growth of per capita GDP of the same set of sample countries.
Source: World Bank (1998b).

especially NTB protection, during the last decade. By 1997 a number of developing countries both within and outside Asia had already reduced their tariffs on imports to below Uruguay Round levels.

Thus the leadership of the East Asian countries in maintaining more open trading regimes than other developing countries has been eroded in recent years, particularly when judged against non-Asian developing economies. Looking beyond the current financial crisis in Asia, this means that a rebalancing of international trade and investment flows may take place during the next decade in response to the liberalization of trade regimes in developing countries worldwide.

Figure 3.2 illustrates the recent evolution of patterns of commodity protection in ADEs and other developing countries. The figure demonstrates radial patterns of protection in nine categories of traded primary products and manufactures for 1984-1987 and 1994-1997. In each subfigure the radial axes indicate levels of tariff and NTB protection by commodity or manufacturing category. The further from the center of the subfigure the level of tariffs or NTBs, the greater the protection in the traded goods category. Where rates of protection across traded goods categories are uniform, the radial pattern of protection will be nearly circular. A skewed pattern represents different rates of protection across different categories of traded goods.

Table 3.1 Annual Growth in Trade, Selected Country Groups, 1985-1995

(percent)

Country group and economy	Goods		Services		Trade/GDP 1995
	Exports (1985-1995)	Imports (1985-1995)	Exports (1985-1995)	Imports (1985-1995)	
East Asia	17.95	17.78	18.89	21.25	95.42
PRC[a]	17.66	15.85	20.14	25.88	40.35
Newly industrialized economies	17.42	17.85	18.50	19.29	151.76
Hong Kong, China	19.18	20.61	—	—	302.88
Korea	15.01	15.58	16.71	21.15	67.18
Singapore	17.87	16.81	20.36	16.75	355.59
Southeast Asia	15.42	19.07	19.28	16.41	90.79
Indonesia	9.33	14.76	21.01	10.13	51.67
Malaysia	16.78	19.63	19.27	13.91	194.41
Philippines	13.98	18.00	15.38	23.10	80.52
Thailand	23.08	22.50	21.95	26.34	89.57
South Asia	12.98	8.43	9.24	12.05	31.33
Bangladesh[b]	11.73	9.99	11.16	12.62	36.67
India	13.46	8.31	8.31	13.51	27.67
Nepal	8.34	3.13	17.03	10.83	58.84
Pakistan	11.62	6.95	9.05	9.54	35.81
Sri Lanka[b]	11.43	9.86	12.81	10.12	81.64
World	10.96	10.52	11.72	11.14	42.52

— Not available.

a. Average growth rate is for 1984-1995.
b. Average growth rate Is for 1985-1996.

Source: World Bank (1998b).

The figure shows the developing countries' move toward greatly reduced reliance on NTBs, although this is less so in the case of the PRC. Levels of protection are lowest in the NIEs, although residual protection remains in place for food growers and food processors in these countries, as exists in Japan, the United States, and the European Union (EU). Levels of tariff protection remain highest in South Asia, with tariff levels averaging 40 to 50 percent for all commodities and manufactures. Among East and Southeast Asian economies, recent trade liberalization has been the greatest in the Southeast Asian countries; however, average tariff rates remain relatively high in these countries (20 to 30 percent) for two goods cat-

egories: food and miscellaneous other manufactures. This observation is curious given that the Southeast Asian countries have abundant natural resources and are internationally competitive in labor-intensive manufactures, which largely make up the category of other manufactured products in the figure, and agriculture. In the case of the PRC, trade liberalization has been more pronounced in terms of tariff reductions, although curiously, the tariff reductions on food and other manufactures have not been as significant as might have been expected on the basis of comparative advantage. NTB protection has declined in some industries, but increased in others, particularly in iron and steel production. This suggests a

Table 3.2 Indicators of Protection by Major Product Categories, Developing Country Groups, 1984-1987 and 1994-1997
(percent)

Product and country or country group	Average applied tariff				NTB incidence		
	1984-1987	1994-1997	Change	Post-Uruguay Round	1984-1987	1994-1997	Change
All goods							
East Asia	23.3	12.7	-45.7	9.3	19.5	2.8	-85.4
PRC	39.5	16.6	-58.0	—	10.6	7.3	-31.1
NIEs	7.7	5.3	-31.5	3.0	9.0	0.1	-98.9
Southeast Asia	22.8	16.1	-29.2	15.6	38.9	1.1	-97.1
South Asia	61.7	43.6	-29.4	29.8	47.6	11.0	-76.9
Non-Asian developing economies	30.4	14.7	-51.7	13.3	40.6	4.2	-89.6
Primary products							
East Asia	20.0	15.7	-21.5	—	24.4	2.9	-88.2
PRC	33.1	17.6	-46.8	—	17.8	6.2	-65.2
NIEs	7.3	11.1	51.7	—	13.3	0.2	-98.3
Southeast Asia	19.6	18.4	-5.9	—	42.1	2.2	-94.8
South Asia	50.7	41.8	-17.4	—	49.4	11.6	-76.4
Non-Asian developing economies	28.2	14.2	-49.8	—	36.8	2.8	-92.3
Manufactures							
East Asia	24.6	11.8	-52.2	9.5	17.6	2.9	-83.7
PRC	41.9	16.3	-61.1	—	7.9	7.7	-2.5
NIEs	7.9	3.6	-54.3	2.7	7.2	0.1	-99.0
Southeast Asia	24.0	15.4	-35.9	16.4	37.6	0.8	-97.8
South Asia	65.9	44.0	-33.2	28.1	46.6	10.8	-76.8
Non-Asian developing economies	31.2	14.8	-52.7	13.1	41.9	4.6	-89.0

— Not available.

Sources: Finger, Ingco, and Reincke (1996); UNCTAD (1994, 1998a).

desire to shelter domestic iron and steel producers from international competition, and possibly from greater participation by multinational corporations in developing the PRC's iron and steel industry through FDI. In South Asia, alongside high levels of tariff protection, NTB protection is targeted principally at food and the category of other manufactured products, for which incidence is roughly 20 percent. In part, this reflects a hangover from state trading in food commodities. However, domestic vested interests have also played a part in maintaining protection in inefficient subsectors of both agriculture and labor-intensive manufacturing.

Where countries maintain protection, it is widely accepted that tariffs are preferable to NTBs. Uniform tariffs can be seen as more desirable than nonuniform tariffs, because they do not create distortions in the relative prices of goods and services, thereby minimizing misallocation of resources. In addition, uniform tariffs make protection more transparent and are more straightforward to enforce. A credible commitment to a uniform regime of tariffs tends to reduce rent-

Figure 3.2 *Ad Valorem* **Tariffs and Incidence of NTBs,
Selected Country Groups and the PRC,1984-1987 and 1994-1997**
(percent)

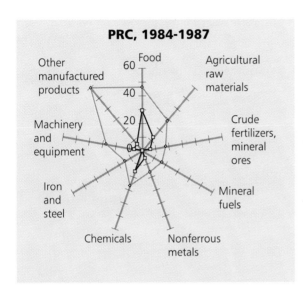

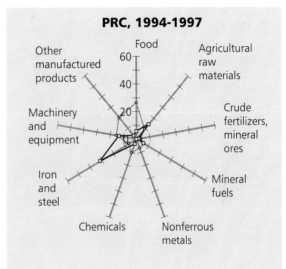

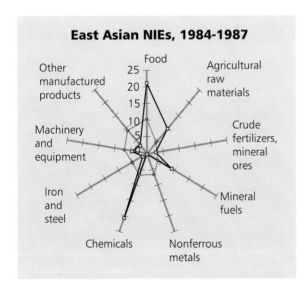

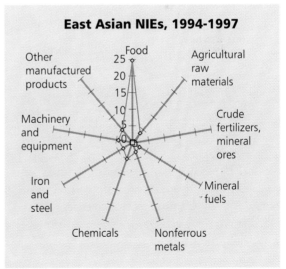

◇— Tariffs   □— NTBs

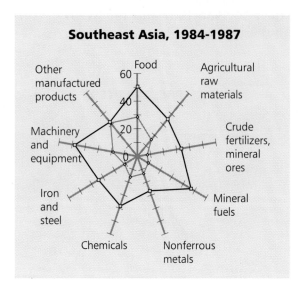

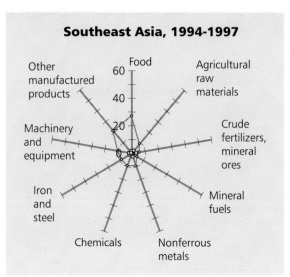

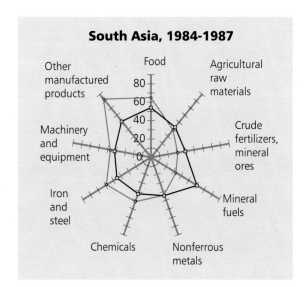

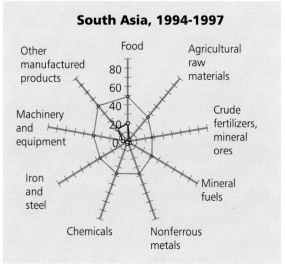

—◇— Tariffs   —□— NTBs

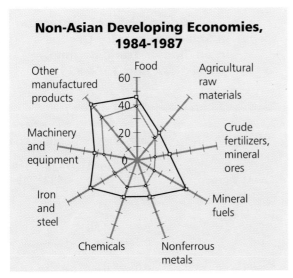

Non-Asian Developing Economies, 1984-1987

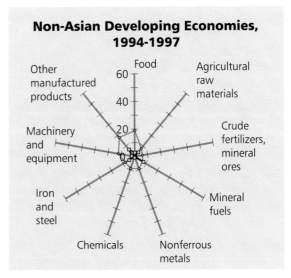

Non-Asian Developing Economies, 1994-1997

—◇— Tariffs   —□— NTBs

Sources: UNCTAD (1994, 1998).

seeking and lobbying activities for protection because it requires all tariffs to be increased simultaneously. However, such a tariff escalation across the board is difficult for any pressure group to engineer successfully.

While the NIEs and Southeast Asian countries have generally reduced their average levels of tariff protection, the dispersion of their tariff rates has increased in comparison to South Asian and non-Asian developing economies in recent years. Table 3.3, which compares the actual protection regimes shown in figure 3.2 with an "ideal" trade regime (see the table for a definition), demonstrates this. The comparison of actual and ideal trade regimes is formalized using the cosine measure of similarity, which ranges between -1 and +1. Positive values approaching unity indicate the near identity of commodity patterns of protection between two trade regimes.

By far the sharpest increase in variance in tariff rates across goods categories has taken place among the East Asian NIEs. This reflects the increase and concentration of tariff measures to protect domestic food growers and food processors, as noted earlier. In the case of the PRC and the Southeast Asian countries, the increased dispersion of tariff rates reflects the increased concentration of tariff measures to protect labor-intensive manufactures as well as food producers. Thus even though East and Southeast Asian

countries have successfully continued to reduce their levels of tariff protection in recent years, the similarity analysis suggests that at the same time they have increased the variability of their tariff protection (as compared to an ideal trade regime), potentially ceding a measure of international competitiveness to South Asian countries, and especially to competing developing countries outside Asia.

The results of the similarity calculations for NTB protection show that the ADEs and developing countries outside Asia have widely increased the dispersion of enforced NTBs in recent years. This development should be regarded more favorably than in the case of tariff protection. As developing countries reduce their reliance on highly trade-distorting NTBs, it is natural that the similarity measure for NTB protection should show a decline in value. This is desirable so long as more selective use of NTBs does not generate greater rent-seeking and special demands for protection by domestic producers. Thus the widespread increase in variability of NTB protection revealed by the similarity analysis may have less important ramifications for competitiveness than a similar measure for tariffs. It may even be beneficial to the extent that it reflects declining reliance and more selective use by Asian and other developing countries of highly trade-distorting quantitative restrictions.

Trade in Services. Increasing trade in services in ADEs reflects a global trend, as table 3.1 reveals. Transport, travel, and insurance have long been associated with the growth of goods trade and tourism in Asia. The growth of FDI in Asia, including FDI by Asian multinational corporations, has also been an important contributor to the recent growth of the service trade in ADEs, boosting demand for legal and other professional services, computer programming and data services, and telecommunications. However, accurately measuring the growth of demand for services caused by FDI is difficult, because in many cases international flows of services are on an intrafirm basis.

Table 3.1 shows that between 1985 and 1995, service exports grew at an average annual rate of 19 to 20 percent in East and Southeast Asia and around 9 percent in South Asia, compared with around 12 percent in the world as a whole. During the same period, service imports grew at an average annual rate of between 16 and 21 percent in East and Southeast Asia and around 12 percent in South Asia, compared with 11 percent in the world as a whole.

Widespread restrictions remain on international trade in services, and services were subject to separate negotiations during the Uruguay Round. This produced the first set of multilateral rules covering trade in services, the General Agreement on Trade in Services (GATS). Like the agreements for goods (GATT), the general principles on which the GATS is based include Most Favored Nation treatment, whereby all trading partners should be treated equally without discrimination; and national treatment, whereby foreigners and nationals are treated equally. The other requirements for GATS include transparency of national laws and regulations governing services and country-specific commitments to liberalize domestic markets for services. GATS also provides for exemptions whereby signatory countries can elect— temporarily, but for a number of years—to withhold Most Favored Nation or national treatment in specific areas of trade in services.

Several ADEs are signatories to GATS, and are thus bound to schedules for specific commitments to liberalize their domestic markets for traded services. Yet many of these ADEs also hold temporary exclusions under GATS; however, these exclusions cannot remain in force for more than ten years. Future rounds

Table 3.3 Comparison of Protection in Selected Country Groups in an "Ideal" Trade Regime, 1984-1987 and 1994-1997
(cosine)

Country group	Tariff protection		NTB protection	
	1984-1987	1994-1997	1984-1987	1994-1997
East Asia				
PRC	0.89	0.86	0.73	0.69
NIEs	0.94	0.66	0.73	0.64
Southeast Asia	0.91	0.86	0.98	0.85
South Asia	0.95	0.98	0.99	0.63
Non-Asian developing economies	0.93	0.92	0.97	0.80

Note: The unit is the cosine of the angle formed by average levels of tariff and NTB protection across nine broad categories of traded goods in the indicated groups of sample countries and an ideal trade regime, using the data underlying Figure 3.2 and assuming that the hypothetical trade regime enforces tariffs at a uniform, *ad valorem* rate of 2.5 percent, and imposes NTBs with a uniform frequency of 0.1 percent.

Source: Figure 3.2.

of multilateral negotiations under GATS, which will begin as early as 2000, will speed the elimination of these exclusions.

Policies toward Capital Flows: Real and Financial

Trade in capital, both real and financial assets, is not a new phenomenon. Capital has long flowed between countries, with the direction of flow generally running from the rich to poorer countries. What has changed in recent years is the composition and size of this trade in capital. Whereas official and private flows of capital to developing Asia were roughly equal in magnitude in the mid-1980s, a surge in private capital flows, especially to East and Southeast Asia, since then has resulted in their making up a much larger fraction of total capital flows to the region. As table 3.4 indicates, while net private capital flows to the PRC and Southeast Asian countries were less than 2 percent of

their GDP in 1985, they had grown to more than 5 percent of GDP by 1995. Given the rapid growth of GDP in these economies, the magnitude of the flows involved is impressive. Compared with flows to these economies, the size of capital flows to South Asia was modest. This indicates that East and Southeast Asian economies have made greater strides toward liberalizing capital flows than South Asia.

A distinct change has also occurred in the composition of private capital flows in recent years. In particular, while the majority of private capital flows to the ADEs consisted of bank and trade-related lending in the early 1980s, the last decade has seen a sharp increase in FDI and portfolio bond and equity flows.

Foreign Direct Investment. FDI is among the major forces propelling the globalization of the world economy and is integral to the growth prospects of developing countries in the modern global economy. Globalization entails increasing specialization of production and trade through international networks of production and distribution, pioneered and operated by multinational corporations. FDI involves the acquisition of existing businesses or development of new business enterprises in a foreign country with the intent of managing these businesses. It is this management dimension that distinguishes FDI from portfolio investment in bonds and equities (where the management responsibility is invested with the issuing host companies or governments). FDI flows also include equity investment by multinational corporations, reinvested earnings in foreign subsidiaries, and short-term and long-term lending of funds from multinational corporations to their affiliates in foreign countries.

Figure 3.3 shows that during 1985-1995, FDI in East and Southeast Asia represented a growing share of total FDI in developing countries. In 1995 East and Southeast Asia accounted for half of total FDI flow worth $101 billion to developing countries. The PRC received the lion's share of this FDI, $36 billion, while Indonesia and Malaysia each attracted $4 billion. During the same year FDI in South Asia was negligible in comparison, amounting to just $3 billion.

The main source of FDI in East and Southeast Asia has been the region itself. The four NIEs were the largest single source of FDI for the PRC, Indonesia,

Table 3.4 Private Capital Flows to Selected Developing Country Groups, Selected Years
(percentage of GDP)

Country group and types of flows	1985	1990	1995
East Asia			
PRC			
Net private capital	1.33	1.89	5.21
FDI	0.49	0.81	4.28
Portfolio bond	0.29	-0.01	0.04
Portfolio equity	0.00	0.00	0.34
Bank and trade lending	0.56	1.09	0.56
NIEs[a]			
Net private capital	—	—	—
FDI	1.14	2.19	1.84
Portfolio bond	—	—	—
Portfolio equity	—	—	—
Bank and trade lending	—	—	—
Southeast Asia			
Net private capital	1.71	3.18	6.85
FDI	0.63	2.23	2.27
Portfolio bond	1.22	-0.31	1.49
Portfolio equity	0.02	0.37	2.13
Bank and trade lending	-0.16	0.90	0.95
South Asia			
Net private capital	0.90	0.58	1.53
FDI	0.10	0.12	0.67
Portfolio bond	0.12	0.04	0.07
Portfolio equity	0.00	0.03	0.54
Bank and trade lending	0.68	0.39	0.26
Latin America[b]			
Net private capital	1.19	1.12	3.95
FDI	0.69	0.67	1.68
Portfolio bond	-0.15	-0.01	0.81
Portfolio equity	0.00	0.09	0.49
Bank and trade lending	0.65	0.37	0.96

— Not available.

a. Includes Korea and Singapore only.
b. Includes Argentina, Brazil, Chile, Colombia, Mexico, and Peru.

Source: World Bank (1998b).

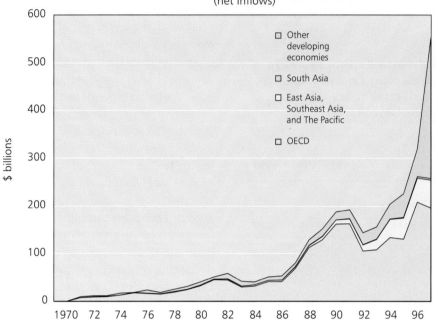

Figure 3.3 Foreign Direct Investment, Selected Country Groups, 1970-1996
(net inflows)

Source: World Bank (1998b).

and Malaysia between 1986 and 1992. In the case of Thailand, the NIEs were a close second to Japan during the same period. The NIEs have played a smaller role in the Philippines, for which the United States has been the main source of FDI; however, even in the Philippines the NIEs accounted for about 18 percent of total FDI.

What accounts for this pattern of intraregional FDI? Broadly speaking, FDI takes place to exploit an abundance of natural resources, use a relatively low-wage economy as a base for exports of labor-intensive products, and circumvent trade barriers that limit the direct importation of products. Indonesia and Malaysia have traditionally attracted FDI because of their abundant natural resources. FDI in the PRC from parent companies in Japan, Europe, and the United States has resulted from multinational corporations circumventing tariffs to exploit the vast potential of the Chinese market. However, in the case of each of these economies, the most rapidly increasing type of FDI has been of the form that seeks to use abundant labor

resources as a platform for exports. This is especially the case for the FDI emanating from within the region as rising real wages have led to reduced international competitiveness in the production of labor-intensive products in the four NIEs and Japan. At the same time, the less developed economies of East and Southeast Asia were taking significant steps to liberalize trade. This allowed the export sector to import capital goods and other inputs required to produce internationally competitive products. These events set the stage for a mutually beneficial flow of capital from the more developed to the less developed economies of East and Southeast Asia.

In recent years, FDI flows to developing countries outside Asia have begun to match those to the ADEs. In 1996 FDI in the ADEs outpaced FDI in non-Asian developing economies by less than $2 billion, compared to more than $3 billion in 1994 and more than $12 billion in 1993. An important question for development in Asia is whether the declining dominance of developing Asian countries in FDI flows observed during the early to mid-1990s represents a permanent shift.

Describing and classifying foreign investment regimes is extremely difficult. Restrictions and performance requirements on FDI are often intertwined with various tax reduction and fiscal incentives and with other subsidies in special packages designed to attract more FDI. Broadly speaking, foreign investment regimes in developing countries during the early to mid-1980s put greater emphasis on import substitution as a means of achieving industrialization and economic transformation and on more extensive systems of FDI incentives and performance requirements than they do today.

A recent study (Naya and Iboshi 1998) reviews foreign investment policies in the ADEs, including specific policies that place restraints or performance requirements—that is, a certain quantity of production must be exported—on FDI in key sectors. The study focuses on the PRC and the other major East and Southeast Asian countries. For South Asian countries it includes only India and Pakistan. Among the East and Southeast Asian countries, restrictions on foreign investment are heaviest in Korea, Malaysia, and Philippines and lightest in Hong Kong, China and Singapore. The restrictions arise principally from general policies governing FDI, such as limitations on foreign majority ownership of public companies and from provisions that restrict FDI in specific sectors. Particularly prominent are restrictions on land ownership and employment by foreign multinational corporations in Malaysia and the Philippines, requirements for meeting export performance standards in India and Thailand, and requirements for meeting local content standards in Korea, Malaysia, and Thailand.

The 1998 *Index of Economic Freedom* (Johnson, Holmes, and Kirkpatrick 1998) documents the climate for FDI in developing countries. It assigns scores for individual countries based on the restrictiveness of foreign investment codes, the regulations governing foreign ownership of businesses and property, the restrictions or bans on foreign investment in specific industries, the extent of performance requirements for foreign investment projects, and the ability of foreign investors to repatriate their earnings.

Figure 3.4 presents scores from the *Index of Economic Freedom* for a group of ADEs alongside scores

derived by Naya and Iboshi (1998). These two sets of data accord reasonably for the East Asian NIEs and Southeast Asian countries; however, the *Index of Economic Freedom* scores indicate that foreign investment regimes in the PRC and South Asia are more restrictive than the Naya and Iboshi study suggests. FDI regimes are most restrictive in the PRC and South Asia, which have an aggregate score of 3.0 according to the *Index of Economic Freedom*, compared with aggregate scores of 1.8 for the East Asian NIEs, 2.3 for the developing countries, 2.5 for the Southeast Asian countries, and less than 2.5 for the other non-Asian developing economies.

With the exception of East Asian NIEs, foreign investment regimes in developing Asia are not substantially more liberal than in other developing regions. The 1998 *Index of Economic Freedom* shows that foreign investment regimes in PRC; Malaysia; Philippines; and Taipei,China are all substantially more restrictive than in the non-Asian developing economies. In South Asia only Pakistan, with a score of 2, has a relatively liberal foreign investment regime.

These findings on foreign investment, especially for East and Southeast Asian countries, stand in contrast to the findings on foreign trade policies discussed earlier. While maintaining relatively open trade regimes, many ADEs have relatively restrictive FDI regimes compared with other developing regions. However, this may be changing, at least for the Asian economies affected by the financial crisis. These affected economies are loosening rules on a number of fronts, including relaxing export performance requirements and foreign equity ceilings, to re-attract foreign capital. Whether this further liberalization of policies toward FDI will be extensive enough to strengthen the international competitiveness of developing Asia, bolster export performance, and rekindle high and sustained levels of economic growth remains to be seen.

Financial Flows. The rapid growth of private capital flows, and portfolio flows in particular, to developing Asia in the last decade or so reflects the increasing financial integration of the ADEs internationally. This growth has been propelled and facilitated by technological progress, which has reduced the transaction costs of buying and selling financial assets. However,

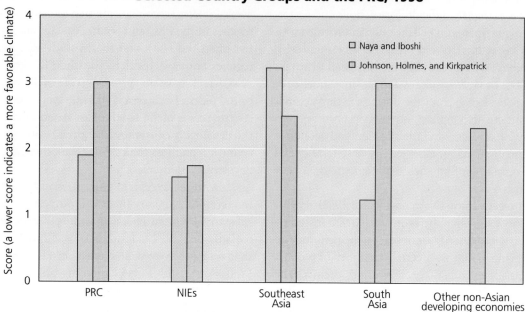

Figure 3.4 Foreign Investment Climate, Selected Country Groups and the PRC, 1998

Note: Naya and Iboshi data are unavailable for other non-Asian developing economies.

Sources: Johnson, Holmes, and Kirkpatrick (1998); Naya and Iboshi (1998).

the liberalization of policies on international capital flows in both industrial and developing countries has also been critically important.

The key policy variable in this context is the extent of capital account convertibility. Complete capital account convertibility involves removing all controls and prohibitions on movement of capital. These barriers usually take the form of quantitative restrictions on capital movements and exchange controls and dual or multiple exchange rates.

Assessing the policy stance of the ADEs regarding capital account convertibility is not easy, and providing a quantitative measure that facilitates comparison is even more difficult. For example, an economy could have generally liberal policies relating to direct investment by foreigners, yet it may severely constrain the activities of foreigners in the purchase and sale of financial assets. Moreover, the extent to which restrictions within the same category of capital account transactions apply can also vary.

Quinn's (1997) study permits a comparison of capital accounts across economies. By examining the restrictions on capital account transactions of 64 economies in place until 1988, Quinn constructs an index of openness of the capital account. Among the ADEs, Hong Kong, China and Singapore had the most liberal capital accounts; Indonesia, Korea, and Malaysia appear to have had fairly open capital accounts, while Thailand maintained a somewhat less open capital account; and the South Asian countries and the Philippines were the least open.

Because Quinn's study does not extend beyond 1988 and does not include the PRC, it is useful to examine the results of another study (World Bank 1997a) which, while not providing a direct comparison of the openness of capital accounts across nations, provides a comparison of a sufficiently related variable: the degree to which an economy is financially integrated internationally. Table 3.5 presents an overall index of financial integration across two periods: 1985-1987 and 1992-1994. The index takes into account a country's access to international financial markets, its ability to attract private capital from abroad, and its level of diversification of financing.

Table 3.5 Changes in the Extent of Global Financial Integration, Selected Countries, 1985-1987 to 1992-1994

Country	1985-1987	Country	1992-1994
Korea	High	Thailand	High
Malaysia	High	Korea	High
		Indonesia	High
Thailand	Medium +	Malaysia	High
India	Medium	Pakistan	High
Indonesia	Medium	Philippines	High
Sri Lanka	Medium -		
Philippines	Medium -	India	Medium +
Pakistan	Medium -	PRC	Medium +
		Sri Lanka	Medium -
Myanmar	Low		
PRC	Low	Myanmar	Low
Bangladesh	Low	Bangladesh	Low

Note: The changes in the extent of global financial integration are based on an overall index of integration, which takes into account a country's access to international financial markets, ratio of private capital to GDP, and diversification of financing based on the composition of flows.

Source: World Bank (1997a).

While the comparison does not include Hong Kong, China and Singapore, this is not much of a loss: these two economies are now ranked among the most open in the world. For example, the only restrictions that exist on capital account transactions in Hong Kong, China are for prudential reasons. As table 3.5 shows, Indonesia, Philippines, Thailand, and even Pakistan had joined Korea and Malaysia as economies with a high degree of financial integration by the early 1990s. Given the less than medium extent of financial integration in Pakistan and the Philippines in the mid-1980s, the process of opening up to financial flows accelerated sharply in these economies. This also seems to be the case for the PRC, which started from a low degree of financial integration in the 1980s, but had caught up with India by the early 1990s.

While the PRC's relatively lower ranking may seem odd given the size of private capital flows to that economy—not just in absolute terms, but relative to its GDP—as table 3.4 shows, direct investments are the dominant form of private capital flows to that country. The method of constructing the index reported in table 3.5 explains the PRC's ranking: the index is based on the reasonable assumption that larger flows of portfolio capital and commercial bank lending relative to FDI reflect greater integration of financial markets, other things being the same. Indeed, the activities of nonresidents in the PRC are severely constrained when it comes to capital account transactions that relate to trade in financial assets, including capital market securities, money market instruments, and financial derivatives. Restrictions on capital account transactions relating to financial assets have been fewer in Southeast Asia, and the large share of portfolio flows in total private capital flows among the Southeast Asian economies (as shown in table 3.4) reflects that the sum of portfolio bond and equity flows to these economies amounted to about 3.6 percent of their GDP in 1995. This figure was substantially larger than the contribution of portfolio flows to total private capital flows in the PRC, South Asia, and even emerging markets in Latin America.

Different types of capital flows are subject to different degrees of volatility. Because capital flows involving direct investment typically entail large sunk costs of entry and are, therefore, made with a longer time horizon in mind, these flows display less volatility. Moreover, while advances in communication and information technology have made transactions in financial assets much more fluid, detecting and controlling direct investments remain much easier. For these reasons capital flows involving financial assets such as portfolio capital and short-term debt are considered to be volatile. Volatile flows thus defined made up nearly three quarters of the net private capital flows to Korea between 1990 and 1996, the period when Korea saw large surges in capital flows into the country. A large component of the capital flows into Indonesia, the Philippines, and Thailand was also composed of volatile flows, at least 50 percent in each case. By contrast, volatile flows made up only 16.6 percent of net private capital flows to the PRC during 1987-1996, the period when it saw large surges in capital flows. Thus while the PRC's greater restrictions on its capital account transactions relating to financial assets may have somewhat reduced the total flow of capital to the PRC, the restrictions have also protected its economy from the adverse effects of the sudden and large outflows of capital that have destabilized other more open economies in the region. The same can be said for South Asia.

THE GAINS FROM TRADE: THEORY

Trade between countries not only involves the flow of goods and services across countries, but also of factors of production, labor, and capital. Thus trade, which facilitates an efficient allocation of resources across countries, generally leads to greater specialization of outputs as well as to accelerated economic growth. Trade also enables countries to achieve higher returns on their financial assets and diversify risks. In short, trade offers countries a potentially powerful mechanism to achieve a higher, stable, and steadily increasing standard of living than would otherwise be feasible by allowing them to exploit economic opportunities beyond their own geographic boundaries.

Trade in Goods and Services

Free trade in goods can lead to significant efficiency gains in resource allocation in trading countries. Moreover, it can lead to large dynamic gains by increasing incentives to innovate, thereby enhancing growth and welfare in the global economy.

The fundamental idea of trade theory—the theory of comparative advantage—is both simple and compelling. Countries trade so as to benefit from their differences in factor endowments. Countries will specialize in producing those goods and services that best suit their natural resources and physical and human capital endowments. They will trade the goods and services produced at home for goods and services produced abroad. Countries differ in their endowments of resources: some are rich in natural resources, others lack natural resources; some are rich in human skills, others have few educated people; some have abundant physical capital, others have few capital resources. According to theory, free trade, with trade flows determined by comparative advantage, will yield the most efficient allocation of the world's resources, and thereby maximize global welfare, while restrictions on trade will reduce efficiency, and therefore welfare. Box 3.2 illustrates this concept graphically.

The traditional theory of comparative advantage is based on the assumption that there are no increasing returns to scale. However, many industries do exhibit economies of scale. Greater scale leads to greater returns and more efficient production. This means that the size of the market can constrain both the variety of goods the country can produce and the scale of its production. When trade becomes free and countries form an integrated world market that is larger than any individual national market, nations are no longer bound by the limited size and resources of their domestic economies. Each country can specialize in producing a narrower range of products than it would in the absence of trade. At the same time, each country can buy a wider variety of goods than it produces. This means that free trade can result in mutual gains from trade, even if the countries do not differ in terms of their resource endowments or the state of their technology.

This idea of gains from trade based on the notion of economies of scale is similar to the concept of traditional comparative advantage. However, the essential distinction is that according to the traditional comparative argument, it is comparative advantage that leads to specialization. When economies of scale are introduced, specialization can lead to comparative advantage. As trade restrictions are removed and countries specialize in a narrower range of products, they benefit from efficiencies in production arising from economies of scale, and the international economy benefits from a more efficient allocation of world resources.

Moreover, in addition to these static efficiency effects that deal with improved allocation of existing resources, trade can have a dynamic effect on the economic growth of trading countries through the exchange of goods, technology, and ideas. Recent advances in economic growth theory describe a number of mechanisms through which free trade can contribute to higher growth by creating incentives to innovate and generate technology.

A country that is integrated into the world economy will enjoy access to a larger technical knowledge base than a country living in isolation. Trade helps the process of technological acquisition and dissemination. Exposure to international competition can also reduce international duplication in industrial research.

Box 3.2 The Geometry of Gains from Free Trade

The gains from trade can be illustrated using a simple diagram. Country A, represented in the following figure, is open to trade, but has some trade restrictions. The diagram shows the benefits of unilaterally moving to free trade. This simple model assumes that there are no nontrade distortions in the goods market and that factor markets are competitive.

The diagram shows the market for a single product, for example, radios, imported by the small country A. $D_A D_A$ and $S_A S_A$ represent the domestic demand and supply of radios. P^* is the world price for radios. The world supply of radios is represented by $P^* P^*$.

Country A levies a tariff on all imported radios. The price of radios including the tariff is P. The tariff is equal to $P \text{-} P^*$, the difference between the world price and the domestic price.

Removing the tariff increases consumer welfare. This increase in consumers' surplus is shown by areas $1 + 2 + 3 + 4$. There is a transfer from domestic producers to domestic consumers, shown by area 1; the loss of tax revenue is shown by area 3; the net gain to country A is equal to areas $2 + 4$. These two triangles represent the so-called deadweight loss that arises because a tariff creates distortions in incentives for consumers and producers that cause the market to allocate efficiently. This gain, which represents an improved allocation of resources in the economy, arises purely from country A's unilateral liberalization. It reaps the gain regardless of whether other countries reduce their tariffs or not.

However, for equal tariff reductions, the gain to a small country from liberalization by partner countries is far larger than that from its own liberalization. Thus if the rest of the world were to lower its tariff, t, by the same amount as country A, $t = P \text{-} P^*$, the gain to country A would not be limited to the small triangles 2 and 4, but would include a rectangle (in addition to two triangles similar to 2 and 4) whose base equaled the entire initial quantity of imports and whose height represented the tariff reduction. Trade liberalization by the rest of the world improves country A's terms of trade by the full amount of the tariff. The improvement in the terms of trade, in turn, generates a large redistributive rectangle in favor of country A rather than small efficiency triangles generated by the country's own liberalization. This partially explains why even the governments of small countries often focus on increased market access—trade negotiator's jargon for partner country's liberalization—rather than unilateral liberalization.

The gain for country A from the rest of the world liberalizing depends critically on the extent of its own openness. If a country imposes prohibitive trade restrictions, it will fail to benefit from liberalization by its partner countries. For example, during the period of trade liberalization 1960-1990, India failed to take full advantage because of its restrictive trade regime. However, economies with liberal trade regimes such as Hong Kong, China; Korea; and Singapore benefited greatly.

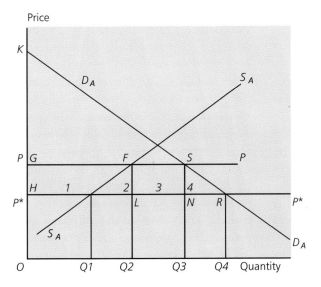

Gains from Free Trade

If a company is competing only in a protected market, it only needs to stay ahead of the local competition. If a company is competing in the international market, it needs to compete and innovate on a global scale. Furthermore, international market integration expands the size of the potential consumer base, and so bolsters incentives for industrial innovation.

The pattern of innovation in the industrial countries and imitation in the developing countries gives rise to product cycles in international trade. Companies in the industrial world produce and export many goods early in their technological lives. Manufacturing then shifts to the developing world as production methods become more widely known. New advances in growth theory suggest that the effect of product-cycle trade on incentives to innovate is positive. With trade, the innovations of the industrial world are copied in developing countries. Production migrates abroad and the production resources in industrial countries are released for new products and innovation. Recent literature on growth theory illustrates how, by easing manufacturers' demand in industrial countries, product-cycle trade actually increases innovation and growth in the world economy.

Trade in Factors: Foreign Direct Investment and Labor

FDI brings benefits through four main channels as follows:

■ For the host country, FDI is an additional source of capital. By adding to domestic savings, it can help increase the rate of growth of output.

■ If the return to capital is higher in the host country than in the source country, FDI will improve the international allocation of capital.

■ FDI can serve as a vehicle for technology transfer. Multinationals often bring in new production technologies, which generate benefits for both host and source countries.

■ In the area of services, such as banking, insurance, and telecommunications, FDI is the main instrument for promoting trade.

Trade barriers undermine the benefits of FDI. Then, in effect, at least some of FDI may represent tariff-jumping rather than efficient investment decisions, particularly if the import-competing sector already has excess capacity because of protection. Moreover, the size of the domestic market in a closed economy is likely to limit any benefits arising from the importation of superior technology.

The benefits of international labor mobility parallel those of FDI. In the host country it can alleviate labor shortages. It also permits efficient allocation of world resources. Another benefit of labor mobility is that it can help facilitate the flow of new technology through knowledge embodied in skilled workers. A temporary inflow of foreign skilled workers can help train local workers in the use of new technology; a temporary outflow of local workers can allow local workers to develop new skills abroad. In certain service industries the movement of skilled personnel is essential, for example, to run banking and insurance operations smoothly, foreign firms often need personnel from their home country in place in the host country. In other cases, such as computer programming services, labor mobility may be an important complement to trade through electronic media. The World Trade Organization (WTO) has recognized this, and under the GATS considers the movement of people as one of the four modes of international trade in services.

To achieve an efficient allocation of world resources, capital and labor flows are often seen as substitutes for each other. However, in the absence of perfect factor mobility, which equalizes returns between the source and host countries, capital and labor mobility have different distributional implications. If one factor, say labor, is mobile and the other, say capital, is fixed, the factor that is permitted to move, namely, labor, will capture the benefits of equalizing differences in returns between two regions. The return to capital is higher in the developing than in the industrial world. When capital is allowed to move, capital owners—mainly in the industrial world—capture the lion's share of the difference in returns. In contrast, because wages are higher in the industrial world, when workers are allowed to move they capture the lion's share of the differential.

Trade in Factors: Financial Capital

The case for international financial capital mobility is based on four simple arguments as follows:

■ As capital-scarce countries have a higher marginal product of capital, capital mobility will increase income in both capital-rich and capital-scarce economies. In a world of capital mobility, a lack of domestic savings need not constrain countries with profitable investment opportunities.

■ Capital mobility allows households and firms to hold an internationally diversified portfolio of assets. This reduces the vulnerability of income streams and wealth to real and financial shocks that hit the domestic economy.

■ Liberalization of capital flows can lead to efficiency gains because of increasing returns to scale. The production of many wholesale financial services is subject to increasing returns to scale (brought about by economies of scale and scope) that may be exploited through specialization. Economies that do not produce such services or produce them inefficiently will find it more beneficial to import these services and to pay for them by exporting goods or other services in which they have a comparative advantage. Moreover, capital mobility can also lead to greater dynamic efficiency as the domestic financial sector is forced to become more efficient and innovative in response to import competition from foreign capital.

■ As the domestic capital market becomes integrated with the international capital market, domestic policymakers become subject to scrutiny by global investors. The discipline that this scrutiny brings helps to discourage the pursuit of excessive monetary and fiscal expansion (which can quickly lead to reserve outflows and currency depreciation). Thus, capital market integration is a powerful disciplining device for policymakers to pursue policies that are conducive to macroeconomic stability and ensure growth.

The foregoing points all seem to support a favorable view of international financial integration. However, experience during the 1920s and 1930s and the recent Asian financial crisis indicates that private capital flows, particularly those relating to short-term debt, can be unreliable and excessively volatile. If the financial sector is underdeveloped and the government has limited regulatory capacity, then volatility in financial flows can translate into a full-fledged currency and financial crisis. Thus depending on an economy's stage of financial sector development, for many developing countries the cost of financial integration may exceed its benefits. (See box 3.3 for a more detailed explanation of why international financial integration can occasionally be harmful rather than helpful and needs to be handled with care.)

While full capital market integration should be the long-run objective of countries, the crucial question is whether the weaknesses in the domestic capital market as discussed before justify the imposition of limits to capital mobility. Chapter 2 of Part I of the *Outlook* discusses the issue at length. While one may make a case for capital control as a prudential measure for countries with weak financial institutions that have yet to open up their financial markets or as an emergency measure for countries that are severely seized by a financial crisis, capital control should be adopted as a last resort. Weaknesses in the domestic financial markets that lie at the root of the market failure should first be addressed before taking recourse to capital control. For example, in the case of domestic distortions that are policy induced, a more appropriate response would be simply to eliminate the distorting policies. Problems of asymmetric information apply to both goods and financial markets although they are more severe in the latter. Before imposing wholesale restrictions on capital mobility, the first challenge for policymakers is to minimize these problems through better policy. Adherence to world-class standards for accounting, auditing, and information disclosure will go some way toward alleviating information asymmetries. Strict supervisory regulation of domestic financial markets is vital to ensure that risk is managed prudently in the financial sector.

THE GAINS FROM TRADE: EMPIRICAL EVIDENCE

A large body of research has attempted to quantify the impact of trade on economic efficiency and growth. The literature has followed a few broad approaches. The first approach, which most of the studies reported here have employed, is cross-country regression analysis. The second approach, which has become increasingly popular in many other areas of economic analysis, is computable general equilibrium analysis. This refers to a fully articulated quantitative model that is used for numerical simulation. Other approaches

Box 3.3 When International Financial Integration can be Detrimental

Perhaps the most important insight of modern economic theory is that the market is the best mechanism for allocating resources. While this insight applies to financial markets as well as to goods markets, market failures tend to occur in financial markets more frequently than in goods markets. The major cause is an information problem: market participants are not equally well informed. In particular, participants on one side of the market have more information than participants on the other side. This asymmetric information can lead to two specific types of market failures: adverse selection and moral hazard.

Adverse selection refers to a precontractual problem, that is, before agreement on a contract is reached, when the uninformed party to the contract has an adverse selection of informed parties to deal with. In financial markets, adverse selection can occur when, because of a lack of information, creditors cannot easily distinguish between good and bad potential borrowers, that is, between those likely to repay

their loans and those unlikely to do so. Offering to lend at an interest rate that reflects the average quality of loan applicants might seem like a sensible approach; however, such an interest rate would lead to an adverse sorting of credit risks, that is, it would deter good credit risks while attracting bad credit risks. Lenders that anticipate this are likely to react by withdrawing their funds from the financial market. The result is the coexistence of investable funds and profitable investment opportunities, but with little or no lending actually taking place.

Moral hazard refers to a postcontractual problem, where the informed party to a transaction engages in activities detrimental to the uninformed party. In financial markets, once a loan has been made, borrowers have an incentive to alter their projects in a manner that increases their riskiness. If a favorable outcome results, the borrower gains. If the outcome is bad, the project fails, and the borrower cannot repay the loan, the lender bears the burden. Information asymmetries mean that

borrowers can alter the riskiness of their projects without lenders knowing. As with adverse selection, lenders may recognize the moral hazard imposed by information asymmetries and react by withdrawing from the market.

Another problem the financial system, especially the banking system, is subject to is the risk of a bank run. That is, a bank's depositors might suddenly—with or without good reason—lose confidence in the bank and withdraw their funds. If many depositors do this, even strong banks can fail, and the failure of one bank causes runs on others. Most governments therefore provide a system of safety nets, such as deposit insurance to discourage bank runs and lender of last resort facilities to provide banks with ample resources to draw on during emergencies.

Unfortunately, deposit insurance exacerbates the moral hazard problem. If depositors know that they will not lose their money if a bank fails, they may not withdraw their deposits when they suspect that the bank is taking on too much risk.

include microeconometric studies and those based on empirical survey methods and case studies.

Trade in Goods

During the last three decades, virtually all developing countries that grew rapidly on a sustained basis also exhibited rapid growth in exports. A review of GDP growth rates and export growth rates for all the developing economies that grew at average rates of at least 5 percent per year during 1965-1990 reveals that of the 12 economies that achieved this high growth rate, 8 are Asian. Not unexpectedly, these countries include the PRC; the NIEs; and the dynamic South-

east Asian economies such as Indonesia, Malaysia, and Thailand. No Latin American countries are included in this group. In most cases, an increase in the GDP growth rate is accompanied by an increase in the growth rate of exports. Figure 3.5 presents further evidence of this link between trade and growth. It shows the average annual percentage change in world trade in goods and output during 1950-1995. During 1950-1990, rising output and trade moved together. Only during the first half of the 1990s was increasing trade accompanied by falling output growth, and this may prove to be only a short-term anomaly.

The gains from trade can be measured using two broad approaches: assessing static gains from trade and

Thus the government guarantee replaces creditor discipline. In addition, banks with deposit insurance can incur greater risks than would otherwise be possible. Similarly, because insured depositors have little reason to impose discipline on a bank, risk-loving entrepreneurs will be attracted to the banking industry, and the problem of adverse selection will arise. When the financial system is underdeveloped and lacks prudential risk management and a well-developed regulatory framework, such circumstances can begin to set the stage for a financial crisis.

International financial liberalization increases the risk of a financial crisis. It gives weak financial institutions, which are already in financial distress, a greater opportunity to engage in more risky activities for financial redemption. At the same time, however, it makes it more difficult to raise funds during emergencies, because the central bank has limited capacity to undertake a lender of last resort function given that the liabilities of the banks and other borrowers are denominated in foreign currencies.

Moreover, the problem of asymmetric information becomes worse when financial transactions are conducted internationally (as opposed to domestically), because acquiring and processing information becomes more difficult with increased geographical and cultural distances between financial markets.

Information asymmetries can also lead to herding behavior. Lenders with incomplete information may infer information about underlying conditions from the actions of other lenders, and therefore act like them. Similarly, because investors cannot distinguish perfectly between low- and high-quality money managers, low-quality money managers have an incentive to blindly follow high-quality money managers to avoid detection. At the very least, this behavior is likely to cause volatility in asset prices. Herding behavior can also result in situations where the payoffs to investors who emulate the actions of other investors increase with the number of other investors taking that action. For example, an investor's profits from buying stock in a particular company depend on how many others have bought stock in the

same company. Herding can result in large, sudden, and destabilizing capital movements across geographic borders.

Finally, in countries characterized by microeconomic distortions, capital flows can be misused, even if they are directed to the private sector. A developing economy with abundant labor may artificially raise returns to capital by protecting capital-intensive industries. Extreme examples of this include several developing countries' "national" automobile and "national" aircraft projects. If protection is maintained while capital flows are liberalized, capital may flow to capital-intensive sectors at the expense of labor-intensive sectors.

Overall, domestic distortions and asymmetries of information leading to market failure in financial markets weaken the case for capital mobility. Financial integration may fail to produce an efficient allocation of world financial resources. Moreover, it can be highly destabilizing for capital-importing countries with weak financial institutions.

dynamic gains from trade. Static gains from trade refer to efficiency gains that reduce distortions in the economy and improve the efficiency of resource allocation. These gains cannot be measured directly. One way to measure the static gains from trade is to estimate demand and supply schedules for an economy with trade restrictions, and then calculate the efficiency gains of trade liberalization. Another approach is to use a computable general equilibrium model of the economy and to simulate the gains from trade liberalization. However, with both these methods, the gains from liberalization are guaranteed by assumption. The next stage is to calculate the magnitude of the gains from trade. This depends on the extent of

the distortions in the protected economy. Standard estimates in the international trade literature suggest that in most cases, static gains from trade are equal to 1 to 2 percent of GDP in most cases, but in highly distorted economies these gains can be as much as 5 to 6 percent of GDP.

These gains are far from insignificant. However, the performance of economies over time clearly shows that the largest impacts of openness are dynamic in nature. Rather than merely improving the allocation of existing resources, trade leads to higher growth. A large body of empirical literature seeks to quantify the link between growth and openness systematically through cross-country regression analysis. Regression

Figure 3.5 **World Goods Trade and Output by Major Product Group, 1950-1995**

(average annual percentage change in volume)

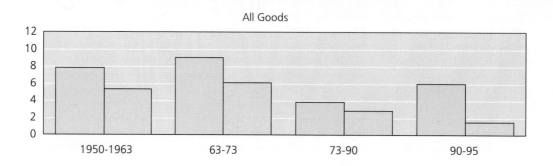

All Goods

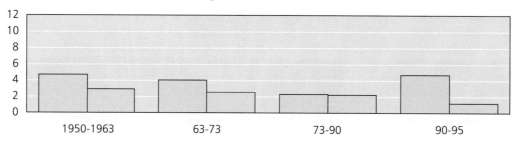

Agricultural Production

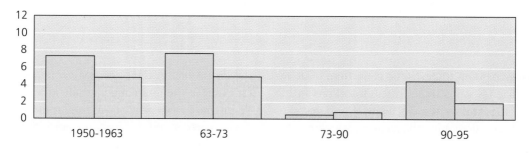

Mining Products (including petroleum)

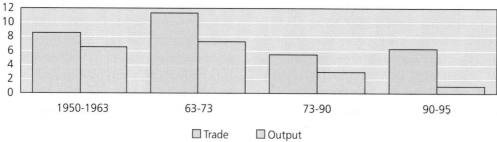

Manufactures

☐ Trade   ☐ Output

Source: WTO (1996).

analysis allows economists to control for other sources of growth, and therefore isolate the dynamic effect of trade on growth. Typically, regression analysis controls for factors such as initial levels of income and literacy in the economy, government policy, macroeconomic variables relating to saving, inflation and exchange rate management, and demographic and structural factors.

Table 3.6 shows the results of a range of empirical studies. These studies vary in terms of the measures of openness employed, which are discussed in box 3.1. Overall, this body of evidence establishes a strong link between openness and economic performance, measured by economic growth or total factor productivity growth. As always, this empirical work is open to criticism. Some economists have queried the measures of openness employed, while others have queried the direction of causation, saying that the association between openness and growth could reflect growth leading to greater openness. However, given that a large number of studies using a variety of approaches finds openness to be a critical factor in the economic success of more outward-oriented economies, this strongly suggests that the findings are robust.

One of the most comprehensive and ambitious investigations in this area is a recent study by Edwards (1997). This uses comparative data for 93 countries to analyze the relationship between openness and total factor productivity growth (see box 3.4 for an explanation). The analysis focuses on three possible determinants of growth: the initial GDP per capita, the initial level of human capital, and the extent of openness. It shows a strong relationship between total factor productivity growth and the level of openness in an economy, a positive relationship between total factor productivity growth and human capital, and a negative relationship between total factor productivity growth and initial GDP levels, implying convergence in growth rates. Edwards tests his results by using nine different indexes of openness, various statistical techniques, and a number of time periods, and in all cases finds a robust link between openness and growth.

Trade in Technology

A clear benefit of economic openness is that it gives a country access to technology developed elsewhere in the world. New technology can be embodied in the capital goods used in actual production. A recent study (Lee 1995) uses cross-country data from 89 countries to investigate the impact of capital goods imports on per capita growth between 1960 and 1985. Lee shows that countries with a higher ratio of capital goods imports to investment grow faster in terms of GDP per capita, even when the overall ratios of investment to GDP and total imports to GDP are taken into account. The implication is clear. Economies that have erected barriers to the importation of capital goods have done so at a significant cost to their economic growth.

Foreign technology may also be imported in disembodied form through arm's length licensing agreements between domestic and foreign firms. Again, barriers to the importation of such technology can be costly. Empirical studies of Indian firms (for example, Basant and Fikkert 1996; Hasan 1998), show that Indian policies restricting technology licensing agreements and the importation of disembodied technology have been costly, denying Indian firms an important source of productivity growth. While the policy may have succeeded in spurring Indian firms to conduct their own research and development (R&D) as intended, estimates of the rate of return from a dollar's purchase of foreign technology have been as much as triple the equivalent expenditure on in-house R&D (Hasan 1998).

Trade in Factors: Foreign Direct Investment

One means of technology transfer is through FDI and the resulting operations of foreign firms, especially multinational corporations, in developing countries. Multinationals account for a considerable portion of world R&D, and as a result often control highly valuable production, management, and marketing skills and technologies. By investing in and operating production facilities in developing countries, multinationals transfer this knowledge and technology to their local affiliates. To the extent that a transfer of technology takes place, the gains from FDI will be more than just the equivalent accumulation of capital raised from domestic sources.

A recent empirical study (Borensztein, de Gregorio, and Lee 1998) investigates whether FDI has

Table 3.6 Evidence on Openness and Growth

Openness measure	Number of countries	Period	Impact	Source
Measures based on trade shares			*Coefficient on openness*	
Deviation from predicted trade	45	1973-78	Significant, >0	Balassa (1985)
Deviation from predicted trade (Leamer 1988)		1982	Significant, >0	Edwards (1992)
Changes in trade shares	19	1960-85	Significant, >0	Helliwell and Chung (1991)
Trade shares	81 developing countries	1960-85	Weakly significant, >0	Quah and Rauch (1990)
Price-based and administrative measures				
Bhalla and Lau (1992), using the relative price of tradables to international prices	60	1960-87	Raises GDP growth	Bhalla and Lau (1992)
Relative domestic price of investment goods to International prices	98	1960-65	Raises GDP growth per capita	Barro (1991)
Relative price of traded goods	95	1960-85	Raises GDP growth per capita	Dollar (1991)
Effective rate of protection in manufacturing	47	1950-80	Lower protection rate raises GDP growth	Heitger (1986)
Trade liberalization index from Thomas et al. (1991)	35	1975-85	Export incentives positively affect GDP per capita growth, insignificant impact of import restrictiveness	Lopez (1990)
Trade liberalization index from Thomas et al. (1991)		1978-88	Trade reform positively affects GDP growth	Thomas and Nash (1992)
Micro and productivity studies				
Deviation from predicted export share	108	1960-82	Positive	Syrquin and Chenery (1989)
Export growth	4	1955-78	Positive	Nishimizu and Robinson (1984)
Export growth	17	1950-80	Positive	Nishimizu and Page (1990)
Export growth	4	1976-88	Positive	Tybout (1992)
Import penetration	17	1950-73 1973-85	Ambiguous Negative	Nishimizu and Page (1990)
Import substitution (1-import penetration)	4	1955-78	IS negatively affects TFP	Nishimizu and Robinson (1984)
Import substitution	4	1976-88	IS positively affects TFP	Tybo (1992)
Effective rates of protection and domestic resource costs	Turkey	1963-76	Ambiguous	Krueger and Tuncer (1982)
Change in import shares	United Kingdom	1976-79	Ambiguous	Geroski (1989)
Tariffs and import penetration	Côte d' Ivoire	1975-87	Positive	Harrison (1994)

IS Import substitution.

TFP Total factor productivity.

Source: Adapted from Harrison (1996, table 1).

promoted growth in developing countries, and if so, the necessary conditions under which it has done so. The study looks at 69 developing countries using a cross-country regression framework. The key finding is that the higher the stock of human capital in an economy (proxied by education levels), the greater the impact of FDI on economic growth. The relationship holds even when controlling for total investment, indicating that the benefits of FDI are over and above those stemming from the accumulation of capital in

economies that have reached a minimum threshold for investment in human capital. In other words, the benefits of a dollar of FDI have exceeded those of a dollar of domestic investment for the average developing country.

A number of surveys of companies in Southeast and East Asia (for instance, Fry 1993; Kawaguchi 1994; Sung 1994) have found that in terms of positive growth effects, the diffusion of knowledge through FDI is more important than its general contribution to

---

Box 3.4 **What Is Total Factor Productivity?**

Economists explain the relationship between the factors of production, such as capital and labor, and the quantities of goods and services produced using production functions. The relationship between input and output in a production function depends not only on the amount of inputs used, but also on the technology available in the economy. Technological progress is measured by total factor productivity.

With technological progress, an economy can produce more output with the same inputs. Output grows not only because of increases in

capital and labor, but also because of increases in total factor productivity. While this is not directly observable, statistics are available on growth in output, capital, and labor. Total factor productivity is calculated as a residual in the production function, the addition to output that results from technological progress, rather than as an increase in the factors of production. This residual is often called the Solow residual, after the Nobel Laureate economist Robert Solow of the Massachusetts Institute of Technology, who first showed how to calculate total factor productivity.

Given the spectacular economic performance of the Asian NIEs, one expects a similar spectacular performance in total factor productivity growth. However, somewhat surprisingly, many researchers have concluded that total factor productivity growth accounts for a relatively modest share of the overall economic growth in these economies. The table below shows estimates of total factor productivity growth for selected ADEs. It has been modest, but is increasing. The accumulation of physical and human capital has been more important.

Estimates of Total Factor Productivity Growth, Selected Periods
(percent)

Economy	Young (1995) 1966-1990	Bosworth and Collins (1996) 1960-1994	Bosworth and Collins (1996) 1984-1994	Sarel (1995) 1975-1990	Sarel (1996) 1979-1996
Hong Kong, China	2.3	—	—	3.8	—
Korea	1.7	1.5	2.1	3.1	—
Singapore	0.2	1.5	3.1	1.9	2.5
Taipei,China	2.6	2.0	2.8	3.5	—
Indonesia	—	0.8	0.9	—	0.9
Malaysia	—	0.9	1.4	—	2.0
Philippines	—	0.4	-0.9	—	-0.9
Thailand	—	1.8	3.3	—	2.0

— Not available.

Source: IMF (1997).

raising investment levels. This transfer of knowledge relates to marketing know-how, as well as to technological issues, especially in the international arena. A recent survey of 122 Taipei,China firms operating in Malaysia revealed that a large part of the invested capital was raised domestically (Ariff and Tho 1994). Nevertheless, FDI benefited the local economy by generating commercial links between the home and host country firms, which facilitated the transfer of considerable manufacturing, managerial, and marketing knowledge (see box 3.5 on FDI in Asia).

It is not only the individual developing country firm that benefits from importing technology or hosting FDI. Spillovers and demonstration effects mean that other domestic firms may also benefit by observing foreign technologies and management practices at work, or by hiring employees who have worked with the domestic affiliate and are familiar with its manner of operations. Domestic firms may also learn about better marketing practices and new markets by observing the strategies multinationals employ. For example, the entry of one Korean garment exporter into Bangladesh prompted the establishment of virtually hundreds of locally owned garment exporters. While such spillover benefits and demonstration effects have traditionally been thought to apply to manufacturing firms, it is increasingly clear that they apply equally in the service sector, particularly in financial services.

Trade in Factors: Financial Flows

While the benefits of international mobility of financial capital are widely acknowledged, surprisingly, rigorous quantitative estimates of these benefits are lacking. However, historical evidence suggests that a number of European countries benefited substantially from foreign financial flows. For example, Norway borrowed the equivalent of about 14 percent of its GDP in the 1970s and Portugal borrowed an amount equivalent to some 17 percent of its GDP in the 1980s. While both these economies have benefited considerably from foreign financial capital, the exact magnitude of these benefits is unknown.

Two recent studies have attempted to investigate the impact of capital account convertibility on an economy's macroeconomic performance. Rodrik

(1998) investigates this issue using data on almost 100 industrial and developing countries between 1975 and 1989. The countries include high achievers, but also many underperformers. Most of these economies have had a long stretch of openness, such as Bolivia (1987-1996), Ecuador (1973-1993), Liberia (1973-1984), and Mexico (1973-1982), while Hong Kong, China; Indonesia; Malaysia; and Panama maintained openness continuously since the early 1970s. However, Rodrik finds no conclusive evidence that countries without capital controls have grown faster, invested more, or experienced lower inflation.

In contrast, Quinn's (1997) more detailed study finds a strong, positive correlation between capital account liberalization and economic growth. Quinn uses an index of capital account openness—described earlier in the section on financial flows—for a set of 64 industrial and developing countries to determine whether changes in the index are systematically related to economic growth. His results appear to be robust to changes in the specification of the model.

Thus Quinn's results cast some doubt on Rodrik's. However, both suffer from a number of methodological problems that limit the reliability of their results. While the absence of rigorous quantitative evidence does not mean that financial capital flows do not have a positive impact on countries, it demonstrates the urgent need for more rigorous empirical studies in this area.

Trade in Factors: Labor Mobility

Three decades ago, Johnson (1967, p. 107), the noted Chicago economist, wrote that "immigration policies of developed countries, which discriminate severely against immigrants from less developed countries, especially the poorly trained and educated, may be said to lie at the core of the development problem." If wages reflect the value of the last unit of output of workers, that is, the marginal product of workers, observed large differences in wages internationally suggest that restrictions on labor mobility constitute by far the most important source of inefficiency. However, few econometric studies estimate the beneficial effects of international labor mobility on growth.

Hamilton and Whalley (1984) use a simulation study to estimate the beneficial impact of international

Box 3.5 "Flying Geese" and Foreign Direct Investment in Asia

FDI has played an important role in the economic development of Southeast and East Asia. The "flying geese" theory of FDI gives a simple and picturesque explanation of the pattern of FDI across Asia. According to this theory, FDI leads to a gradual transfer of production of labor-intensive products and their export from source countries to lower-wage host countries. Thus the pattern of FDI resembles the pattern formed by flying geese.

Low wages and openness are the essential dynamic factors in the flying geese theory of FDI. Beginning in the 1970s, low wages and openness in the East Asian NIEs—principally Hong Kong, China and Singapore—attracted a large amount of FDI in labor-intensive industries. Transfers of technology from countries of the Organisation for Economic Co-operation and Development (OECD), especially Japan, were substantial. Subsequently, however, increasing levels of labor skills and higher wages in the NIEs resulted in flows of FDI in labor-intensive industries to Southeast Asia, and to the PRC still later, as that economy opened up, as illustrated by the figure below, which shows how FDI flows from the OECD to eight East and Southeast Asian economies varied over time. After peaking at 80 percent in 1986, the importance of the NIEs (Hong Kong, China; Singapore; and Taipei,China) as a destination of FDI outflows from the OECD declined steadily in favor of Indonesia, Malaysia, Philippines, and Thailand. However, the importance of the latter countries as a destination for OECD FDI diminished as the PRC, with its abundance of labor, moved toward greater economic openness.

In recent years the NIEs have been able to transform themselves into major sources of FDI for the region, with their outflows of FDI also displaying the flying geese pattern. This is especially true for FDI flows originating from Taipei,China, which became a net outward investor starting in 1988. The first country to see a boom in investments from Taipei,China was Thailand because of its relatively open policies relating to FDI. Thailand saw 50 instances of FDI from Taipei,China in 1986, and this peaked to around 300 in 1988. After this time, however, FDI from Taipei,China to Thailand declined sharply, but increased to Malaysia, the Philippines, and Indonesia in that order. By the 1990s, the number of cases of FDI from Taipei,China to these Southeast Asian economies had stabilized at lower levels, with many of the new cases of FDI going to the PRC, and more recently to Viet Nam.

Given the emphasis on differences in wage levels between Asian countries and the creation of overseas export platforms by multinational firms, the flying geese theory of FDI helps explain the remarkable performance of East and Southeast Asian exports. However, the theory also highlights the challenge higher-income countries face from lower-income countries in being a recipient of FDI as the latter open up to investment flows from abroad. The challenge for the higher-income economies is to develop new comparative advantages in more products that use physical and human capital and technology more intensively.

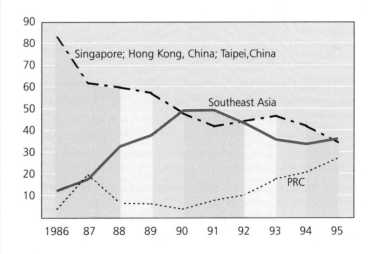

OECD Outflows to Eight Major Asian Destinations
(percentage of total OECD outflows to these countries)

Source: OECD (1998).

migration in the world economy. They obtain dramatic results that appear to confirm Johnson's statement. The simulation attempts to calculate the worldwide efficiency gains of removing controls on labor mobility. It divides the world into seven regions: four industrial country regions, one oil exporting region, one newly industrialized country region, and one developing country region. The simulation shows that removing global immigration controls and allowing labor to move from poor to rich countries could double world output. The calculations show that the efficiency gains from a marginal increase in labor mobility are likely to outweigh the corresponding efficiency gains from either trade or investment liberalization. Thus relaxation of controls on labor mobility is one of the most important policy issues facing the global economy.

Most of these efficiency gains result from labor migration between rich and poor regions, not between particular countries. The impact of restrictions on labor mobility is thus clearly an issue between high-income countries as a bloc and low-income countries as a bloc rather than between individual countries. For political reasons, the chance of big increases in labor movements from developing to industrial countries in the foreseeable future is minimal. However, Hamilton and Whalley's simulations suggest that even minor increases in labor mobility could confer substantial gains.

In addition to efficiency gains, recent empirical studies suggest the possibility that the migration of workers accelerates GDP growth. Barro and Sala-i-Martin (1992) investigate the effect of migrations between regions in Japan and the United States on regional per capita income. The study shows that migration led to convergence in incomes between regions and that a positive relationship existed between growth and migration. The extension of this empirical study for a number of industrial economies corroborates this result (Barro and Sala-i-Martin 1995). Drawing robust conclusions about the relationship between migration and growth from just one or two studies is impossible. Nevertheless, these results certainly suggest the possible existence of a close association between economic growth and labor movement—either directly affecting growth or through the convergence effect—that needs to be confirmed by further studies.

THE LESSONS OF THE EAST ASIAN EXPERIENCE

Starting in the early 1960s, a number of East Asian economies achieved extremely high rates of growth on a sustained basis. Within three decades the NIEs transformed themselves from low- or middle-income countries to high-income countries. Starting slightly later, PRC, Indonesia, Malaysia, and Thailand also achieved extremely high growth rates. While recent events have added a new twist to the story of the Asian miracle, explaining Asia's growth and development performance before the recent financial crisis remains a central question in economics and a source of lively debate.

The "orthodox" view—associated with such economists as Bhagwati, Krueger, Balassa, Srinivasan, and Little—of Asia's growth performance contends that outward orientation and an export promotion strategy were the most important reasons for the region's miraculous growth performance. This approach downplays the role of interventionist policies, and argues that price distortions were minimal. The World Bank's highly publicized study, *The East Asian Miracle* (1993), essentially expounds this orthodox view, pointing to the importance of "export-push" development as one of the central lessons emerging for other developing countries from the East Asian experience.

The "revisionist" view—associated with such economists as Wade, Amsden, and Rodrik—of Asia's economic success assigns the central role to industrial policy and downplays the importance of outward orientation. Revisionists assign much of the credit for the rapid growth of Korea and Taipei,China to the respective governments' success in addressing an investment coordination failure. They note that market forces alone could not reach the optimal mix of investment projects that would best spur economic development, and that the government used policy to overcome this coordination failure. Revisionists assign outward orientation only a residual role, arguing that it was the outcome of, rather than the cause of, high growth.

The "eclectic" view, which is associated with such economists as Westphal and Pack, attempts to draw together the insights of both the orthodox and revisionist camps in explaining the Asian economic miracle. This eclectic approach recognizes the importance of outward orientation, but nonetheless assigns a substantial role to industrial policy in helping to spur technological change in selected industries. Economists in this middle camp draw heavily on Korea's experience, arguing that outward orientation, industrial policy to encourage technological change, and the interaction between the two holds the key to Korea's spectacular growth performance.

Korea's strategy was to promote exports while protecting infant industries. Exporters were permitted to import all inputs necessary for production and to export their products at world prices. Imports were subject to restrictions that were applied uniformly across all products. Additional protection for infant industries in the domestic market supplemented these measures. Targeted infant industries were granted absolute protection via import controls, giving them a guaranteed domestic market. At the same time, using export targets that were closely monitored, the government demanded that protected infant industries export a rapidly growing proportion of their output at world prices. Unlike sales in the protected domestic market, exports were not subsidized, forcing firms to achieve the productivity levels needed to compete at world prices. Thus rather than an import-substitution bias, Korea had an export-promoting bias. Thus the eclectic view assigns a critical role to export orientation even for the purpose of infant industry promotion.

In the 1960s, during a brief import substitution phase, Singapore pursued a slightly modified version of this approach to infant industry protection. Rather than requiring firms to export an increasing proportion of their output, Singapore automatically removed protection from infant industries that failed to grow within a short, prespecified period. When industries were able to function without further protection from the government, quotas were immediately removed.

Revisionists argue that outward orientation was much less important in Korea and the government's role much wider in promoting investment. According to this view, as exports accounted for only 5 percent of Korea's GDP in 1960, they could hardly serve as an engine of growth. Moreover because the relative prices

of Korean exports showed no positive trend according to the available empirical evidence, the incentive to export was not important for export growth. Thus the revisionists argue that, on the contrary, export expansion itself was the result of an investment boom that the Korean government was able to engineer by solving the coordination problem. The investment boom generated the demand for imports of machines, which in turn required exports of other goods. However, this argument is not convincing. Even though at 5 percent the initial ratio of exports to GDP was small, at the margin it could still have contributed a larger proportion of the extra demand for investment. There is no reason for the marginal contribution to be constrained by the initial average contribution. Government commitment to a free trade regime for exporters made investment in the export sector an attractive proposition, especially because world markets provided far greater opportunities for expansion than the domestic market. Moreover, even if the revisionist argument was correct, the policy lesson on trade openness from the Korean experience remains unchanged. If Korea, like India, had chosen an import substitution strategy, the expansion of investment demand would have either failed to translate into actual investment, or would have led to an expansion of sectors with low productivity, as happened in India. Either way, the role of trade openness in leading to or facilitating Korea's growth should not be underestimated. When pushed, even the revisionist view appears to admit to the importance of a liberal trade regime.

The second contentious issue is whether infant industry protection contributed significantly to Korea's growth. Both the revisionist and eclectic schools regard the contribution of infant industry promotion to have been significant, even critical. The orthodox school disputes this, arguing that the costs of intervention have, in all probability, outweighed its benefits. For example, in the case of Korea's promotion of heavy and chemicals industries during 1973-1979, the government incurred significant direct costs from subsidizing these industries by directing bank loans to them at subsidized rates and offering tax exemptions. Indeed, estimates indicate that the real effective value of subsidies to these industries was as high as 3 percent of gross national product (World Bank 1993). However, while the ending of direct subsidies to the heavy and chemicals industries after 1979 led to the elimination of direct costs, other indirect costs began to develop as certain groups of these industries performed much more poorly than expected. The rapid accumulation of nonperforming loans in commercial banks that had lent to these industries was a particularly troubling problem, because it had a serious negative effect on the banks. On a more general note, the orthodox school has claimed that the amount of information required for governments to be able to identify the precise set of industries that deserve nurturing over any meaningful time horizon is simply too great. Moreover, the possibility that interest groups might capture government policy on intervention makes infant industry protection a dangerous policy. Finally, the orthodox school argues that as the less interventionist economies of Hong Kong, China and Taipei,China grew faster than Korea, the case for industrial policy loses much of its strength. Thus the proponents of this view agree that while industrial policy played a role in Korea, they question the claim that its contribution was strictly positive.

LESSONS FOR NATIONAL POLICIES

An uncontested lesson from the Asian growth experience is that openness to trade is highly desirable. Irrespective of whether exports led to investment demand or investment demand led to exports, both were essential for growth in the NIEs. Without openness to trade the cutting-edge technology that is often embodied in capital goods would not have been available, nor would the NIEs have been able to obtain disembodied technology through licensing. This is supported by experience in India, where the reliance on domestic equipment for investment as well as restrictions on imports of disembodied technology led to much slower growth than in the NIEs.

The contribution of industrial policy in the most closely studied case, that of Korea, is controversial. Some argue that under a different policy regime that excluded infant industry protection Korea would have done better. The experience of interventions in South Asia, notably in India, has been unequivocally negative. The inefficiency of the Indian automotive industry, supported by both the infant industry and economies of scale arguments, stands out in this respect. The experience of South Asia suggests that developing countries should err on the side of caution and steer clear of infant industry protection.

Governments have better prospects for contributing positively at the initial stage of industrialization. India's industrial policy was a success story in its early years. However, as development proceeds, the competing demands for education, infrastructure, legal services, regulation, and macroeconomic stability are likely to limit the government's ability to act in the interests of its infant industries. Moreover, once the economy has grown large and diversified, organizational diseconomies of scale diminish the government's ability to manage the economy, as demonstrated in India, and more dramatically in the former Soviet Union. Even Korea, which by many accounts had a successful record in the 1960s, found itself handicapped in the promotion of new infant industries in the 1970s.

If a developing country does promote infant industries, the Asian experience suggests the following four rules:

■ The country should target only a small number of industries. Targeting too many industries will spread government managerial resources and private entrepreneurial talent too thinly. Moreover, the willingness to provide such protection with relative ease invites an ever increasing number of industries to seek infant industry protection.

■ The criterion for picking industries should be their ability to increase rapidly the share of exports in total sales to some benchmark level. Such a strategy ensures that those industries already on the verge of achieving comparative advantage are the ones targeted. By contrast, an import substitution approach to infant industry protection is likely to pick industries that are at the bottom end of the country's comparative advantage ladder.

■ The industries targeted should be warned that the protection is strictly temporary. Credibility should be established by withdrawing protection from any industry that fails to achieve benchmark levels of exports at various stages.

■ The countries must be able to adapt quickly to new technologies to make their infant industries competitive. This requires high skill levels and high levels of investment in human capital.

Box 3.6 contrasts infant industry protection in the hydraulic excavator industries in India and Korea.

POLICIES FOR ECONOMIC RECOVERY IN EAST AND SOUTHEAST ASIA

East and Southeast Asia's impressive growth performance over the last 30 years has been attributed to economic openness. However, the Asian financial crisis has sparked a fierce debate on whether economic openness contributed to the recent crisis and whether it can continue to be the engine of growth for the region. Strategies for economic recovery have been far from uniform. While all countries affected by the crisis have adopted, implicitly or explicitly, a recovery strategy based on export-led growth, they differ in their strategies with respect to capital market liberalization. For example, Malaysia, one of the affected countries, is experimenting with a more closed strategy of exchange controls. This section of the *Outlook* concentrates on economic recovery for Asia and the role of economic openness. Part I of the *Outlook* deals with issues of economic recovery in Asia more broadly.

Commitment to an Open Trading Regime

Exports have been one of the main engines of Asian growth for 30 years; however, since 1996 exports from the region have exhibited a sharp slowdown. This has sparked fears about whether the external sector can continue to fuel Asian economic growth. Export deceleration in the crisis-affected countries began with a collapse of the electronics industry, which accounts for 50 percent of total Asian exports, caused by overcapacity in world markets and the subsequent deterioration of intraregional trade. Box 3.7 provides more details about this deceleration of exports.

While Asian exports are showing some signs of recovery, the question remains whether export accel-

---

Box 3.6 Industrial Promotion and Openness: Hydraulic Excavator Production in India and Korea

India and Korea both started producing hydraulic excavators, or equipment used to remove soil and stones, in the 1970s. Both countries protected these infant industries by restricting imports of finished hydraulic excavators. Technology was imported through licenses. Protection was supplemented by requirements for local component inputs, which became more stringent over time. Despite these initial similarities, the development of the hydraulic excavator industry has differed substantially in the two countries, and the way India and Korea promoted their infant industries contrasts sharply.

By the late 1980s the two Korean excavator manufacturers, Samsung and Daewoo, were producing more than ten times the annual production of Larsen and Toubro, the largest Indian excavator manufacturers.

Moreover, the Korean manufacturers had designed and developed their own excavators, which were competitive enough to be exported starting in 1987. By contrast, neither of the Indian manufacturers had introduced an excavator based on their own design and neither was in any position to export.

Two aspects of government policy in the countries are crucial in explaining this difference in industry performance. First, although both governments guided private investment decisions in the industry, the Korean government recognized the importance of economies of scale. It limited the Korean industry to two firms and allowed them to expand production capacity and exploit production economies. The Indian government, by contrast, encouraged a large number of firms to enter the industry and limited their individual production capacities in the belief that this would foster competition in an otherwise protected market. Second, the Korean government managed to instill a sense of competition and dynamism in its two producers by announcing a credible program of time-bound protection. Indian protection was not time-bound. This impending liberalization of the industry was the main factor driving the Korean firms to formulate a clear strategy for developing an internationally competitive design for excavators and an export marketing plan. Thus the cases of India and Korea reinforce the critical role that greater openness after a limited period of protection plays in developing competitive infant industries.

Source: Jacobsson and Alam (1994).

Box 3.7 The Slowdown in Asian Exports

Exports have been one of the main engines of Asian growth. A number of successful Asian economies have pursued a development strategy of export-led growth, using policy to shift their industrial structures toward exports and to exploit economies of scale. However, starting in 1996, in most of Asia a deceleration in export growth interrupted some 30 years of export-led growth.

After growing by 20 percent in 1994 and by 22 percent in 1995, Asian exports grew by only 4.3 percent in 1996. This deceleration in export growth affected economic performance across the region. Quarterly growth rates show that this deceleration in exports began in the second quarter of 1995. This initially went unnoticed, because the average annual growth rate of exports remained high in 1995. Between 1995 and 1996 export growth fell 23 percent to 6 percent in Indonesia, Malaysia, Philippines and Thailand; from 22 percent to 2 percent in the PRC; and from 23 percent to 7 percent in India.

Along with the rise in the real effective exchange rate in some economies, the depreciation of the yen beginning in 1995, and a significant decline in the prices of major export products of some large exporting economies in the region, structural factors are also important in explaining the export slowdown. A striking aspect of Asia's changing export structure was increased specialization and fast growth in the electronics industry in 1990-1995.

In 1995 electronics exports made up more than 50 percent of total exports in Malaysia, more than 45 percent in the Philippines, 40 percent in Korea, and more than 30 percent in Thailand. In the PRC and Indonesia electronics exports were a smaller, but rapidly rising, share of total exports. Asian economies were aggressive in expanding capacity and capturing significant market share, but in the process they also became more vulnerable to a fall in trade demand, price fluctuations, and overcapacity problems. This new export structure exposed them to the risk of export instability and to contagion. Since mid-1995 Korea has experienced the largest declines in the unit prices for its exports, followed by Thailand and the Philippines.

The financial crisis that erupted in Asia in 1997 provided a stimulus to exports through depreciating exchange rates. However, despite large depreciations in Asian currencies (83 percent in Indonesia, 57 percent in Korea, 55 percent in Malaysia, 46 percent in the Philippines, and 40 percent in Thailand), Asian export growth continued to be slow. Part of the explanation for continued sluggishness in exports lies in the structure of intraregional trade. As Asian economies compete with and export from one another, the currency depreciations did not have a strong immediate impact. Until mid-1998 only Korean export volumes grew rapidly. Export recovery was particularly disappointing in Malaysia and Thailand. This is largely explained by intraregional links. Malaysia and Thailand depend heavily on Singapore as an export market,

whereas Korea competes with Japan in several markets and is less dependent on regional markets.

More than half of total Asian exports are intraregional, and thus the collapse in growth in the region has caused a significant reduction in export volumes. Import demand fell by 25 percent in affected Asian economies. The credit crunch and loss of trade credits associated with the financial crisis has also adversely affected the supply response in the crisis countries. Total intraregional export volumes have contracted by about 5 percent.

Asian exports are unlikely to recover in the short term because of the low growth in world trade, the recession in Japan, and the weakening of intraregional trade. However, over the medium term, as the regional economy pulls out of the crisis and world trade picks up, Asian exports should start to recover. Japan has announced a large fiscal stimulus package, which may boost growth and imports, in the process underpinning Asian export performance.

An immediate priority in Asia is the expansion of trade financing. Not only would this help to establish an export-led recovery, it would also bolster intra-Asian demand. Encouraging FDI in the affected countries, especially in the tradable sectors, should also spur exports. Most important, the resolution of Asia's financial and banking sector problems would help ensure access to loans by creditworthy firms in exporting sectors.

Source: World Bank (1998c).

eration can reverse the harm done by export deceleration and fuel a sustained recovery. Currency depreciations following the crisis, which lowered export prices in US dollar terms, have improved the competitiveness of Asian exports. However, the pickup in export volumes has been less than predicted by standard economic models.

Two reasons account for a lower than expected impact of currency depreciation on export growth in the crisis countries. First, many Asian economies are heavily dependent on electronics for their exports. The buildup of capacity in the electronics industry, which led to a collapse in world prices for electronics, led to a slowdown in economic growth in the region and a drop in intraregional trade. This helped to spread the contagion, because intraregional trade accounts for 50 percent of total exports. The second constraining factor is the credit crunch that emerged because of the collapse of financial markets and institutions in the region. Foreign capital inflows should be encouraged to aid financial restructuring and to provide trade finance.

For export-led recovery in Asia to succeed, demand in the industrial countries must rise to absorb the exports. Substantial uncertainty surrounds the prospects for a recovery in Japan. Japan had an average annual growth rate of 1 percent between 1992 and 1997. If growth does not pick up, then Japan cannot be the engine of growth for the rest of Asia. However, Japan is not the major importer of goods from the ADEs. Recent figures from Morgan Stanley Dean Witter (Roach 1998) show that Japan's share of Asian exports (12 percent) is now below that of the United States (21 percent) and Europe (15 percent). Moreover, Japanese FDI as a share of the region's GDP was declining even before the crisis hit Asia.

In 1998 the United States experienced the largest current account deficit in its history. Moreover, industrial production indicators point toward a weaker US economy in the next few years. This suggests that growth in demand for Asian exports in the United States may be limited. Economic growth in Europe is also slowing, and as a consequence, increasing demand for Asian goods in Europe seems unlikely. Given sluggish growth in world trade (according to available estimates, trade growth has declined by more than half), the recession in Japan, weakening intraregional trade,

and low growth prospects in the industrial economies, Asian exports are unlikely to recover speedily.

However, as the regional economy pulls out of the crisis and world trade picks up, Asian exports should start to pick up and provide the impetus for recovery in Asia. Despite the regional slowdown, no reversal in open trade policies has occurred to date. Indeed, the NIEs such as Hong Kong, China and Singapore have not deviated from their traditional open trade policies. Southeast Asian economies have not used—or at least not extensively—the leeway afforded by the gap between bound (agreed upon) and applied tariff rates to raise the latter. Indeed, members of the Association of Southeast Asian Nations (ASEAN) have decided to accelerate tariff reduction and to further reduce restrictions on FDI. The PRC's trade policy has exhibited no discernible backtracking. The same positive pattern with respect to open trade policies has prevailed in South Asia, where India has reduced duties on a number of essential agricultural commodities. All this points to a strong commitment to trade liberalization in most ADEs. However, notwithstanding the financial crisis, any future backsliding on trade liberalization should be strongly discouraged. In this way, growth in the region and the diversity and intensity of interregional and intraregional trade and global integration of trade in goods and services will be promoted.

Commitment to International Financial Integration

Despite the economic turbulence in the crisis-affected countries in Asia, remarkably, they have not suspended their capital account convertibility and have adhered to the principle of openness. They have experimented with orthodox stabilization approaches of tight monetary policies and high interest rates with varying degrees of success. Where these policies have been ineffective in stabilizing the economy and containing the economic downturn, the question of whether suspending capital account convertibility and imposing restrictions on capital flows should form part of the ADEs' recovery strategy has arisen. Malaysia imposed exchange controls in September 1998, but no other ADE followed suit (see box 3.8 for a discussion of Malaysia's exchange control policy).

Box 3.8 Exchange Controls in Malaysia

In September 1998 Malaysia imposed exchange controls to allow its central bank to cut interest rates and promote growth without prompting an overwhelming outflow of capital. These new measures included the establishment of a fixed exchange rate system. This combination of foreign exchange controls and a fixed exchange rate is expected to stabilize the domestic currency. The government hopes that by limiting exposure to global capital market volatility, it can promote faster economic recovery.

Whether exchange controls prove effective will take time to determine. Industrial production was down 11.5 percent year-on-year in November 1998, little changed from the 11.6 percent year-on-year decline in August. Growth in M3, the broadest measure of money supply, was 3.3 percent year-on-year in November 1998, down from 4.3 percent in August. Loans grew by 0.5 percent at an annual rate in November 1998, compared with 2.2 percent in October. This all suggests that the imposition of exchange controls and expansionary policies have not had a strong initial impact.

In February 1999 the government announced a relaxation of some of the exchange controls. Portfolio investment made before 15 February 1999 will be allowed to be repatriated subject to a levy based on the duration of the investment. Capital repatriated within seven months of the investment will be subject to a 30 percent levy that gradually falls to zero after a year. Funds brought in as of 15 February will be subject to a 30 percent levy on profits if repatriated within a year and a 10 percent levy after a year. This relaxation of capital control measures is a step in the right direction.

The Malaysian government should use the temporary respite offered by exchange controls to address, rather than paper over, macroeconomic and structural weaknesses in the economy. In particular, the government should address major problems in the banking sector and the underdevelopment of the securities market. Corporate sector debt, which accounts for more than 70 percent of domestic debt, is overwhelmingly short term, and the banking sector is overexposed in the property sector. The government should also sort out

its large explicit and implicit exposure in private infrastructure projects.

The government seems to have backtracked in financial sector reforms, in particular, reduced the prudential standards for banks. However, this will jeopardize prospects for generating sustained economic growth in the medium and long term. A fixed exchange rate system and capital controls may be useful in providing protection for the Malaysian economy from external shocks, but only as a short-term measure. Over the longer term the best chance for sustained recovery in Malaysia lies in restoring macroeconomic stability and economic reform, strengthening financial institutions, and liberalizing the economy. This includes dismantling exchange controls and adopting a more market-based exchange rate system to allow fuller integration with the global trading and financial system. This lesson applies not only to Malaysia, but also to other countries in Asia.

Sources: ADB (1998a); Bank Negara Malaysia (Web page).

Exchange controls are regulations designed to preserve a country's international reserves by imposing limits on the convertibility of the national currency or its movement across national frontiers. Exchange controls therefore represent an intermediate regime between total convertibility of the national currency and a total ban on exchange. Exchange controls may include restrictions on import financing; restrictions on terms of payments, such as fixed payment delays for imports and exports; limitations on travel spending; and restrictions on capital flows. As most countries are now committed to current account convertibility, exchange controls are used mostly to restrict capital flows. The recent exchange control measures adopted by Malaysia are no exception. The currency is still convertible on the current account as before, but not on the capital account.

While exchange controls are unlikely to restore confidence among international investors, they do enable a country to delink its exchange rate from domestic interest rates and pursue monetary policy. With exchange controls in conjunction with a fixed exchange rate policy, a country can reassert some form of monetary sovereignty and pursue an independent monetary policy to stabilize the economy and pursue growth.

Exchange controls are undesirable from a global perspective, because they create market fragmentation, thereby frustrating the integration of the global trading and financial systems. They are also undesirable from an individual country perspective because they create new distortions in the economic system, which may reduce growth. When exchange controls are misaligned with the economy's macroeconomic fundamentals, they can lead to widespread arbitrage, rent-seeking, and control evasion.

Evidence from Latin America and developing Asia suggests that exchange controls have been largely ineffective. Many international financial transactions are difficult for governments to monitor, and hence to enforce controls. Evasion of exchange controls has been widespread through underinvoicing and overinvoicing of exports and imports. Widespread illegal activities, such as laundering funds, increases as the gap between domestic and foreign returns widens. This suggests that exchange controls are neither desirable nor effective long-term instruments for macroeconomic stability and economic growth, although they may have some use as a short-term measure for economic stabilization. To the extent that exchange controls act as a brake on expenditure on imports and prevent capital flight and herd behavior, they help prevent an impending balance-of-payments crisis.

In conclusion, notwithstanding the ongoing economic crisis, the ADEs must not flinch from their commitment to openness. Trade liberalization in Asia must be maintained to facilitate export growth. This is essential as much for short-term recovery as for long-term economic growth. Similarly, those economies that have already adopted an open capital account should not hastily retreat from it. However, if orthodox economic remedies prove ineffective and the economy is faced with the dire prospect of a meltdown, at first view a case can be made for exchange control as a short-term measure to help economic stability. However, this should not be seen as an easy alternative to difficult financial sector and structural reforms, the absence of which were at the root of the crisis. Reforms must continue, regardless of whether exchange controls are imposed. As reforms are successfully implemented, the ADEs should aim for the orderly liberalization of their capital accounts.

Greater integration with the world economy has been the main engine of growth for developing Asia. Despite the recent setback, this remains the course for short-term recovery and long-term growth.

OPENNESS, THE WORLD TRADE ORGANIZATION, AND DEVELOPING COUNTRIES' INTERESTS

International trade and open world markets are vital for the growth of Asian economies. However, for the most part, the ADEs have played a reactive rather than a proactive part in multilateral trade negotiations (this section develops themes explored in a recent Asian Development Bank study [ADB 1998b]). The WTO Information Technology Agreement was presented to East and Southeast Asian ADEs for the first time at the Manila Asia-Pacific Economic Cooperation summit in 1996 and signed soon after at the first WTO Ministerial Conference—the highest decisionmaking body of the WTO—in Singapore. The agreement was signed without any examination of its implications. South Asian countries were not included in the agreement. Some industrial countries are pushing for a link between trade policies and labor and environmental standards and for the accommodation of competition policy in the WTO. Negotiations on the Multilateral Agreement on Investment within the Organisation for Economic Co-operation and Development (OECD) have not included developing countries. It is time for ADEs to take a proactive stance.

A Comprehensive Round of Trade Liberalization

The GATT, now administered by the WTO, was designed to liberalize cross-border trade restrictions such as tariffs and quotas. It is in this area that multilateral trade agreements have been the most successful and the least controversial. The most important aspect of a more proactive ADE approach to multilateral negotiations must be to keep the process of trade liberalization moving forward. This could be accomplished through a comprehensive, multilateral round of trade negotiations.

The Uruguay Round of trade negotiations, which concluded in 1994, includes in its agenda the establishment of a new round of negotiations on agriculture and services starting in January 2000. However, there is no reason why trade in goods should be excluded from the new trade round. This should be an integral part of developing Asia's strategy for the millennium negotiations.

Beginning with the agreements on Trade-Related Intellectual Property Rights and Trade-Related Investment Measures (and despite the prefix Trade-Related), the industrial countries have increasingly focused the WTO on what is essentially a nontrade agenda. The most extreme example of this approach is the attempt by some industrial countries to bring labor standards into the WTO agenda. Thanks to a concerted effort on the part of developing countries and support from some key industrial countries, this issue has now been delegated to the International Labour Organisation. However, continuing pressure for nontrade issues, which often involves virtually one-way concessions by developing countries, to form part of the WTO agenda will persist. The ADEs should resist this pressure and seek to refocus the agenda on conventional border trade measures where liberalization brings gains for all parties concerned.

Even though average tariffs in industrial countries are coming down to levels of 3 or 4 percent following the Uruguay Round, there is still a long way to go before free world trade in goods is achieved. Despite an end to the Multifibre Arrangement—scheduled to be completed by January 2005—tariffs in Japan, the United States, and the EU on textiles and clothing will remain high. According to the United Nations, average tariff rates on products in this category are 15 percent in the United States, 9 percent in the EU, and 8 percent in Japan. Many products within this category attract much higher rates. In the United States tariff rates on more than half of all textile and clothing imports are in the 15 to 35 percent range. Despite the Uruguay Round, average tariffs on leather, rubber, and footwear remain at 8 percent in Japan, 7 percent in the United States, and 5 percent in the EU.

Even though the ADEs have made great strides toward liberalization in recent years, they continue to have sufficiently high tariffs to give them the bargaining power to engage the industrial countries in a new round of multilateral trade negotiations. Tariffs in

South Asia remain extremely high. Tariffs in East and Southeast Asia are lower, but still remain high by industrial country standards. Even though trade barriers in the ADEs are higher than in the industrial countries, trade liberalization does not mean that the ADEs will have to give more in concessions than they receive in return, resulting in an uneven bargain. Industrial country markets are much larger than developing country markets, and so a 1 percent tariff reduction in industrial countries is worth more than a similar reduction in developing countries.

Some may argue that a comprehensive round of trade talks is not necessary on the grounds that the Information Technology Agreement and agreements on telecommunications and financial services have been successfully concluded, and that negotiations can therefore proceed on an ad hoc basis. However, not only is this an inefficient way to conduct negotiations, but it serves the interests of developing countries poorly. The recent Information Technology Agreement was to a large extent forced upon developing countries. To the extent that the industrial countries set the liberalization agenda, sectors of interest to industrial countries will be liberalized first. This means that the sectors of interest to developing countries, such as textiles and clothing, will be pushed to the back of the liberalization queue. A comprehensive round of negotiation offers much greater scope for striking bargains than sectoral negotiations. During the Uruguay Round, developing countries agreed to accept the Trade-Related Intellectual Property Rights Agreement in return for the Agreement on Textiles and Clothing. In isolation, neither of these agreements would have been made.

In terms of economic efficiency, simultaneous liberalization in several sectors is superior to sector-by-sector liberalization. The former offers opportunities for resource allocation across sectors, while the latter limits this to the single sector involved. Liberalization that is limited to a few sectors that already have low tariffs will lead to a diversion of trade flows from sectors with high protection. This could lead to a less efficient allocation of world resources and to new distortions rather than the efficiency gains that liberalization is supposed to achieve. The Uruguay Round took ten years to complete, and the Uruguay Round Agenda is still under implementation. It is time to begin preparations for a new, comprehensive round of multilateral trade negotiations.

Multilateral Agreements on Investment and on Labor Mobility

The establishment of relatively open goods markets in the products that industrial countries export means that they have shifted their attention from liberalizing goods markets to liberalizing service and factor markets. The phenomenal expansion of FDI has created a powerful lobby in industrial countries for introducing an international regime to smooth the flow of FDI. Multinational firms face different investment regimes in different countries and operate under a host of bilateral investment treaties. They therefore have strong incentives to establish an international and uniform set of rules for FDI, sanctioned by the WTO and protected by its dispute settlement body. Demands for a multilateral agreement on investment are at the top of the industrial country agenda.

Some industrial countries exerted pressure to bring investment into the multilateral framework of the Uruguay Round Agenda; however, in return for including capital mobility, developing countries demanded that labor mobility be included in the negotiations. The industrial countries did not want to deal with the sensitive issue of labor mobility. At the Montreal Mid-Term Ministerial Meeting in 1988 the negotiators reached a compromise to bring capital and factor mobility into negotiations by defining trade in services to include "commercial presence" and labor mobility. Commercial presence implies foreign companies setting up subsidiaries or branches to provide services in other countries. Labor mobility, which is officially referred to as "movement of natural persons," covers individuals who reside in a foreign country temporarily to provide a service. It does not include people seeking permanent employment or citizenship. However, to date virtually all the commitments to liberalize service trade have been made in the commercial presence category.

Two factors combined to bring investment on to the agenda for the Singapore Ministerial Meeting in December 1996: first, the provision in the Trade-Related Investment Measures Agreement for possible negotiations on investment and competition policies

within five years of the Uruguay Round coming into force; and second, negotiations already under way within the OECD on the Multilateral Agreement on Investment, with pressure from some industrial countries for a similar agreement within the WTO. In the Singapore Ministerial Declaration, WTO members agreed to set up one working group to examine the relationship between trade and investment, and another working group to examine trade and competition policy. The OECD adopted a report at the ministerial level (OECD 1995) that set out the future agenda for multilateral negotiations. However, negotiations for the Multilateral Agreement on Investment have now broken down, as noted in a recent editorial in the *Financial Times* (20 October 1998), in large part because of the belated realization among industrial countries that under WTO rules, they would not be allowed to grant each other's investors preferential access.

The following four priorities should guide the ADEs in any future discussion of multilateral investment agreements:

- The ADEs should ensure that any agreement is strictly limited to FDI. Trade and FDI are indisputably beneficial for developing countries, while the benefits of other capital flows differ across countries. Indeed, in the absence of well-developed financial systems and prudential regulatory mechanisms, such flows provided the necessary ingredients for the financial crisis that still afflicts Asia. These capital flows should be a matter of discretion for individual countries, rather than subject to a WTO-sanctioned multilateral agreement.

- The ADEs should not take part in negotiations on investment that do not include the PRC, which is the world's second largest recipient of FDI and among developing countries is by far the largest recipient. The ADEs limit their bargaining power in negotiating on FDI without the PRC, and negotiations on a multilateral agreement on investment will be largely ineffective until the PRC is brought into the WTO.

- The ADEs should insist that any agreement contain provisions to end subsidies for FDI. In this regard, the proposed OECD multilateral agreement on investment is a poor model, in that it is driven by the interests of multinational firms. This means that it does not refer to the undesirability of FDI subsidies, which distort FDI in the same way that export subsidies distort trade. Trade subsidies are prohibited under the GATT. They should be prohibited by any agreement on investment.

■ The ADEs should agree to an investment agreement only in return for one on labor mobility. Labor mobility is also the area in which market access has, for obvious political reasons, been most restricted. International labor mobility offers the largest single source of efficiency gains for the world economy. The efficiency gains accrue from the equalization of the disparity in labor productivity across countries. The productivity of essentially similar workers varies vastly across countries, as demonstrated by differences in wages across countries. Gains from factor mobility liberalization are often asymmetrically distributed between the source and the host country. When mobility is unbalanced so that it does not fully equalize international factor prices, most of the benefits accrue to the source country. As industrial countries are likely to be the source country for investment, they will reap the much larger share of benefits from the mobility of capital. In contrast, because developing countries are likely to be the source country for labor movements, they will capture the greater share of the benefits of labor mobility.

The OECD countries have placed the issue of multilateral investment rules at the center of the agenda. Giving equal consideration to labor mobility is only fair. Even though labor mobility is included in the GATS, political economic constraints in OECD countries may preclude them from making labor mobility a key issue in the WTO agenda. In recent years the wages of unskilled workers in the United States have declined and unemployment in the EU has increased. However, the problems unskilled labor faces in the industrial countries are not a result of labor mobility. Trade liberalization has had a much bigger impact than labor mobility, and as box 3.9 explains, skill-biased technological change has been a more important factor than trade. Moreover, the pressures in the United States and the EU are largely concentrated in the market for unskilled labor, and the increased mobility of skilled workers provides the potential for substantial gains, given that for many professional services, shortages exist. Progress on increased labor mobility has been extremely limited to date, but would yield mutual benefits. As with goods

liberalization, negotiations on market access with respect to labor services will lead to agreements that come into practice ten years or more from now. In addition, there is no reason to believe that current pressures in OECD labor markets will persist that long. The United States already appears to show some reversal of the trend, with the wages of unskilled workers beginning to make gains in recent years.

Making labor mobility a central item in the WTO agenda requires progress at three levels: first, identifying specific areas where both industrial and developing countries stand to make mutual gains; second, calculating the benefits of increased labor mobility and mobilizing public opinion to bring negotiations to a conclusion; and third, and most important, having the developing countries agree on a mutual position to serve as the basis for negotiations with industrial countries. Without a general agreement among the OECD countries, the matter of investment policy is unlikely to be included in the WTO agenda. Without agreement among developing countries, labor mobility will not be included.

Competition Policy

Competition policy is concerned with restrictive business practices (RBPs). A consensus has emerged between industrial and developing countries in favor of initiating the work on possible inclusion of competition policy into the WTO. In the Singapore Ministerial Declaration, WTO members agreed to establish a working group on trade and competition policy; however, given the complexity of the issues involved and members' diverse interests, developing a multilateral code on competition policy will be a difficult and drawn out process.

All practices that allow firms to exert market power can be described as RBPs, but a distinction is usually made between horizontal and vertical RBPs. Under horizontal RBPs, suppliers, manufacturers, distributors, or retailers collude to increase prices and extract economic rents by restricting supply. This kind of collusion can affect trade flows, for example, collusion among distributors can result in an import cartel that restricts imports to drive the price up. Governments may give the import licenses to mandate an import cartel. Even in the absence of tariffs,

Box 3.9 Does Trade Hurt Workers?

Increasing world trade has led to a radical shift in the international division of labor. In the 1960s developing countries exported mainly primary commodities. In the 1980s and 1990s exports of labor-intensive manufactures have predominated. At the same time, the demand for unskilled workers has fallen in industrial economies. In the United States this trend became apparent in falling real wages for less educated workers, although the number of hours these workers worked also declined. In Europe the less skilled faced increasing unemployment. During the same period, manufacturing imports from developing countries to the OECD increased greatly. These events have spurred a debate about the economic impact of trade on less skilled workers in the industrial world, and some calls for trade restrictions and a return to protectionism.

Opponents of free trade concerned with the falling economic fortunes of workers can find some support in modern trade theory. According to the theory of factor price equalization, in an integrated world economy, wages in one country should not remain above those of comparable workers in countries that are their trading partners. Countries tend to produce and export goods that make intensive use of their more abundant factors of production. This suggests that wages or employment of the less skilled in industrial countries

will be driven down because of competition from low-wage workers overseas.

Competition from imports brings about changes in product prices, and therefore changes in the profitability of different industries. Firms will respond by shifting resources toward industries in which profitability is rising and away from those in which profitability is falling. Trade flows thus give rise to shifts in the demand for labor, as more workers are needed in newly profitable sectors and fewer in unprofitable sectors. This lowers the demand for low-skilled labor in industrial countries and results in unemployment or lower wages.

However, determining whether changes in relative product prices are a result of trade or of other influences is important. A great deal of research has been conducted in this area. Overall, studies tend to show that prices in less skill-intensive sectors have fallen by 8 to 9 percent relative to most skill-intensive sectors in industrial countries. This appears consistent with the argument that increasing world trade means lower living standards for the unskilled in industrial countries.

Several studies have investigated the impact of trade on the relative employment of less skilled workers in industrial countries. Most of them conclude that trade has only a modest, if any, impact. A recent study calculates that during the past two decades the demand for unskilled

workers in industrial nations has fallen by 3 million to 9 million. This might seem to be large in absolute terms, but amounts to only about 1 to 3 percent of total unemployment.

Thus there does not appear to be any strong evidence that trade hurts unskilled workers in industrial countries. The effect of trade also seems modest when compared with other changes in labor markets. In the United States alone, for example, employment in services grew by more than 6 million workers in a labor force of 150 million during 1970-1990.

Rising wage inequality within skill groups and increases in the ratio of skilled to unskilled employment, along with the trend of falling wages of the less skilled, suggest that other forces are at play. Technology has been increasingly labor saving, and has led to widening wage differentials between the skilled workers who can use technology and the unskilled workers who cannot.

Overall, most economists agree that technology has had a much bigger impact on unskilled workers in industrial countries than trade. According to a recent study (Cline 1997), the contribution of technology has been more than three times as important as the contribution of trade and migration combined in widening the wage differentials.

Sources: Cline (1997); Freeman (1995); Wood (1995).

the domestic price will exceed the world price. Similarly, export cartels can raise prices in the importing country above the level in the exporting country even in the absence of tariffs or export taxes. International cartels can also influence trade flows and prices worldwide. The most famous example is the oil shocks of

the 1970s brought about by the establishment of the Organization of Petroleum Exporting Countries. Vertical RBPs relate to the exercise of market power by an agent at one stage of production over an agent at another stage. For instance, a manufacturer may fix the price at which the distributor sells its product, confer exclusive rights to sell the product to a single distributor, or bundle one product with other products the distributor is obliged to take. Such practices may ensure high-quality after-sales service. They may also be instruments of monopoly power.

Foreign Direct Investment and Competition Policy.
FDI by multinationals makes competition policy both more important and more difficult. When the size of a national market is small, large multinationals can exert market power and engage in RBPs. A common fear among Asian developing countries is that because of their superior technology, brand name, financial strength, size, and global orientation, multinationals may acquire dominant market positions in certain products and engage in RBPs. For example, this has been a long-standing fear in India with respect to the entry of Coca-Cola and Pepsi Company in the soft drinks industry. In the context of privatization, because of their deep pockets, multinationals may also acquire a dominant position in the provision of infrastructure. When privatizing telecommunications or power sectors, finding local buyers may be difficult, thereby leaving multinationals as the only credible buyers. Because these sectors have a large element of natural monopoly, host countries fear that private owners will engage in RBPs.

National firms could engage in many of the RBPs multinationals employ; however, multinationals have some additional instruments available to them: they can fix prices internationally; they can use predatory pricing to cut prices below the cost of production so as to drive out competition and deter future entry; and they can use transfer pricing (that is, the prices a multinational uses for transactions between divisions and between subsidiaries and profit centers) as a powerful tool against national firms competing with its subsidiary. Enforcing competition laws can be more difficult in the presence of multinationals, because the parent firm is located overseas and the assets of the local subsidiary are too small to induce ready compliance. When RBPs are suspected, the evidence may be located overseas. In addition, proceedings against a multinational may also be hampered by the threat of relocation.

These kinds of problems mean that national competition authorities need to exchange information,

consult, and cooperate. Several bilateral and regional agreements on competition regulation and multinationals are in effect. A cooperation agreement between the United States and the EU means that the EU can request the United States to take action against an RBP that falls under US jurisdiction that affects the EU's interests and vice versa. A similar agreement exists between Canada and the United States. Instruments of this kind should be incorporated into any future WTO competition policy agreement.

Nevertheless, despite the possibility of international RBPs, whether the WTO needs a competition policy mechanism is debatable. A mechanism to regulate goods exports from developing countries is unlikely to be needed, as most developing countries are too small to have much market power in world markets. Therefore, as long as the distribution system is competitive, free trade can largely substitute for a competition policy, as demonstrated by Singapore, which has no competition policy.

Japanese and EU Proposals. Before the Singapore Ministerial Meeting set up a working group on trade and competition policy, Japan and the EU had already put proposals on RBPs before the WTO. The EU proposal focused exclusively on the traditional RBPs companies employ. The intent was that WTO members would adopt a competition policy containing rules for investigating RBPs, an administrative procedure, enforcement rules, and as a last resort, a judicial procedure. The proposal also includes provisions for cooperation in handling global RBPs. The WTO dispute settlement procedure would be applied where countries failed to deliver on their commitments. The Japanese proposal deals not only with RBPs employed by private companies, but also with practices employed by governments to restrict trade, such as antidumping rules, subsidies and countervailing duties, and voluntary export restraints, that can be used to limit competition. The EU proposal pays greater attention to producers' interests by focusing on RBPs that restrict market access, while the Japanese proposal puts consumers' interests more firmly onto the agenda.

The EU proposal appears to be more concerned with suspected unfair business practices in Japan, while the Japanese proposal is aimed more at anticompetitive government practices prevalent in the United States and the EU. The agenda for the working group proposed by the Singapore Ministerial Declaration includes anticompetitive practices as well as RBPs. Therefore, at least in the initial work, the WTO working group will consider anticompetition policies employed by governments as included in the Japanese proposals for possible incorporation into the WTO-administered competition policy.

For the ADEs, if competition policy is eventually to be included in the WTO, two considerations are particularly important. First, the working group on competition policy should pay equal attention to the interests of all members of the WTO, to developing country members as well as industrial country members. The momentum for including competition policy in the WTO system on the part of the United States and the EU has emerged out of frustration with *keiretsu* and retail distribution systems in Japan that impede market access. Thus the US and EU proposals will likely focus excessively on RBPs prevailing in Japan. However, asymmetries in developing the WTO code on competition policy should be avoided at all costs. This can be accomplished to some extent by including practices to restrict competition on the part of governments as well as RBPs in the private sector.

Second, many developing countries are simply not equipped to implement a comprehensive competition policy. Therefore, the WTO competition policy should either be limited in scope—focusing on the most egregious RBPs and competition-restricting practices—or developing countries should be permitted exemptions until they have adequate enforcement machinery in place. The danger otherwise is that countries with lagging competition policies become vulnerable to trade sanctions in retaliation for failure to deliver on competition policy commitments. This would mean that in a complete reversal of its stated objective, competition policy would be in danger of becoming an instrument of protection.

Antidumping

With the hands of WTO members increasingly tied with respect to conventional instruments of protection such as tariffs and quotas, the use of safeguard measures, especially antidumping measures, has intensified. Safeguard measures refer to actions by countries to protect domestic industries from unfair foreign competition. WTO rules allow countries to act unilaterally to restrict imports by imposing antidumping duties if imports are priced below "normal value" as determined by comparing export prices and producers' domestic market prices.

The number of antidumping cases initiated worldwide increased from less than 150 during the early 1990s to 300 in 1998. Until the early 1990s, outside the EU only a few other countries regularly used antidumping measures, including Australia, Canada, New Zealand, and the United States.

The Antidumping Measures Code of the Uruguay Round introduced several provisions to prevent antidumping from becoming a protectionist tool, although in several cases additional provisions weakened these measures. For example, to prevent open-ended antidumping measures, the Antidumping Code introduced a "sunset" clause under which antidumping duties are generally terminated after five years. However, this clause was watered down by the provision that if national authorities determine that expiration will lead to further dumping and material injury, they can extend antidumping measures beyond five years, and apparently indefinitely.

More positively, the Antidumping Code now has more detailed rules for calculating the amount of dumping. The methods the United States and the EU had used for years to calculate dumping were to some extent biased toward determining the existence of dumping. As a result of the Antidumping Code, the United States has, in general, adopted the new methodology to determine antidumping cases.

From the perspective of the ADEs, however, many concerns remain. First, the incidence of antidumping measures against ADEs is rising. From July 1994 to July 1995, of 153 antidumping and countervailing investigations initiated or measures imposed, as reported to the WTO, nearly half were targeted at the ADEs. The Asian WTO members that have been subject to antidumping include Bangladesh; PRC; Hong Kong, China; India; Indonesia; Korea; Malaysia; Singapore; Taipei,China; and Thailand. Of these, the PRC and Korea have been most subject to recurrent actions. As the Multifibre Arrangement is phased out, a danger for ADEs is that industrial countries will attempt to replace Multifibre Arrangement restrictions with antidumping measures. This has already happened in the case of the EU's antidumping case against a textile import from India (woven wool shirts and blouses) that is still subject to a Multifibre Arrangement quota. Common sense might suggest that a product subject to an effective and binding quota could not be dumped; however, this does not rule out dumping under the technical definition in the GATT. Thus the scheduled expiration of the Multifibre Arrangement could be largely nullified by more intensive and extensive antidumping actions by industrial countries.

Second, industrial countries may use the sunset clause in the Antidumping Code to legitimize antidumping duties for five years, even though the industry concerned may have recovered far more quickly from the injury that led to the duties. The five-year rule could be misused to make five years the standard regardless of the injury.

Third, the ADEs are concerned that the prohibition by the Uruguay Round against using voluntary export restraints could lead to increased antidumping actions that might be more damaging than voluntary export restraints and might fall disproportionately on developing countries. Note that little about voluntary export restraints is really "voluntary," and they are, in essence, a form of import quota. A well-known example of a voluntary export restraint is the pressure the US government has often brought on Japanese automakers to reduce their car exports to the United States.

Fourth, small and medium firms in ADEs have difficulties defending their interests because of the complexities of the system and the cost of compliance with antidumping investigation proceedings. ADE governments can provide at best limited assistance to these firms. This helps to explain why a larger share of cases result in prosecution for ADE firms than for industrial country firms.

Fifth, and a matter for particular concern for the ADEs, are anticircumvention measures. Circumvention occurs when firms subject to antidumping duties bring components rather than the final product into the importing country and assemble the final product there, thereby circumventing antidumping duties. Alternatively, the same firms may take the components to a third country, assemble them there, and then export to the country where they face antidumping duties on direct exports from their home countries. The major industrial countries raised this issue and discussed it at length during the Uruguay Round negotiations, but no agreement could be reached, so the Antidumping Measures Code left the issue effectively unresolved. At Marrakesh in April 1994, the Ministerial Declaration concluding the Uruguay Round recognized that the matter had not been successfully addressed and relegated it to the Committee on Antidumping Practices.

Because the domestic laws of some countries, including the United States; the EU; and some developing countries such as Argentina, Malaysia, Mexico, Thailand, and Venezuela allow anticircumvention measures, some countries have already begun to implement such measures. For example, in October 1995 the EU decided in favor of the possibility that the PRC; Japan; and Taipei,China were circumventing antidumping duties on their exports of microdisks to the EU by using Canada; Hong Kong, China; India; Indonesia; Macao; Malaysia; Singapore; and Thailand as a base for re-exporting microdisks to the EU.

Anticircumvention measures could become a highly potent instrument of protection. Given the high degree of global integration and multinationals operating simultaneously in many countries, determining the origin of a good is often difficult. Frequently the final product is produced by assembling components made in a number of countries. Thus the potential reach of anticircumvention measures is broad, and the WTO should address this issue. This kind of unilateral action should be subject to WTO discipline, with appropriate surveillance by the WTO's dispute settlement system. Moreover, the WTO should consider the proliferation of antidumping measures through anticircumvention and attempt to minimize their protectionist impact.

One possible response for ADEs to antidumping measures is to retaliate to prevent industrial countries from taking recourse to antidumping. Antidumping actions are costly to the countries imposing such measures. Therefore, the ADEs should consider a strategic approach, mimicking the restrictive elements of US, EU, and other countries' laws. This course has two potential benefits. First, if challenged in the WTO as inconsistent with the Antidumping Measures Code, the same challenge would apply to other countries' similar antidumping laws. Litigation by a single country would effectively liberalize the laws of many countries. Second, even if restrictive antidumping measures are not challenged, or are upheld as permissible under the code, the symmetry of restrictive antidumping measures across countries would set the stage for negotiated liberalization. Indeed, Korea's use of antidumping measures had an important impact on the Antidumping Code negotiated in the Uruguay Round Agreement. The first case under Korea's amended antidumping law, which involved polyacetal resin from Japan and the United States, led to a GATT complaint by the United States regarding procedural and substantive deficiencies of Korea's decision. Partly in response to the United States' concerns, industrial countries agreed to more stringent procedural rules in the Uruguay Round Antidumping Code.

Trade Policy and the Environment

WTO members differ enormously on the question of whether trade policy should be used to pursue environmental objectives. Some industrial countries advocate trade sanctions against trading partners that fail to enforce minimal environmental standards, but developing countries largely oppose such measures. To investigate the validity of linking environmental standards and trade policy, a distinction is needed between national and international environmental pollution. When pollution affects primarily the population of the country of origin, such as the contamination of drinking water by a country's own industries or people or air pollution in big cities caused by auto emissions, the pollution is national in nature. There is no legitimate case for trade sanctions to combat national pollution problems. International pollution originates in one country, but affects people in one or more other countries, for instance, acid rain that carries pollutants from the United States into Canada is an example of "bilateral" international pollution. Global warming and depletion of the ozone layer are examples of "multilateral" international pollution. In contrast to national pollution, it is possible to make a case for international action, including trade measures, to combat international environmental problems.

Ideally, international pollution requires a cooperative solution at the international level. The natural vehicle for achieving this cooperation is a multilateral environmental agreement. The best known examples of multilateral environmental agreements containing trade provisions are the 1987 Montreal Protocol on Substances that Deplete the Ozone Layer, the Basel Convention on Transboundary Movements of Hazardous Waste, and the Convention on International Trade in Endangered Species. However, a central problem multilateral environmental agreements face is free-riding. The benefits of environmental agreements accrue to the countries that sign up and abide by the rules, but also to countries that choose not to sign them or to break the rules. This is a public good problem. The benefits are nonexcludable and nonrivalrous, and so countries can free-ride. To ensure participation and compliance, sanctions are needed. Trade sanctions are one way to encourage countries to sign environmental agreements and to play by the rules.

However, a country may refuse to sign an international environmental treaty not simply to free-ride, but because its government sees the agreement as illegitimate, inefficient, or inequitable. For example, rich and politically powerful countries may devise treaties that place too much of the burden on poor, politically weak countries, and then use the treaty, possibly sanctioned by the WTO or another multilateral body, to impose trade sanctions if the poor countries quite reasonably refuse to shoulder the unfair burden. These matters are under discussion at the WTO Committee on Trade and Environment, established in 1995 to decide whether existing provisions in the WTO permit the use of trade sanctions to meet environmental objectives.

The most important item on the committee's agenda is the question of whether WTO rules can be modified to pursue environmental objectives and impose trade sanctions to force compliance with the multilateral environmental agreements (MEAs). GATT Article XX allows members to break GATT rules if this meets a necessity test; that is, it is needed to protect human, animal, or plant life; to protect health; or to conserve exhaustible natural resources. In addition, trade policy measures meeting the necessity test must be undertaken in conjunction with restrictions on domestic production or consumption. The GATS includes identical provisions with respect to services.

The key question under discussion in the Committee on Trade and Environment is whether GATT Article XX should be revised specifically to accommodate trade policy measures in conjunction with an MEA, and whether the necessity test for them should be weakened. Some members have proposed a lower level of scrutiny for these measures relative to those taken outside the terms of an MEA. The EU has proposed amending GATT Article XX to waive the necessity test for all measures involving MEAs. Instead, panels would presume that such measures are necessary provided certain procedural criteria are satisfied. In a closely related proposal Switzerland has suggested that the necessity test be waived for specific trade measures provided for by an approved list of MEAs. Meanwhile Korea has proposed that the necessity test be waived only for specific trade measures applied between parties to an MEA. Nonspecific trade measures among parties would remain subject to the test, specific trade measures against nonparties would require a waiver, and nonspecific trade measures against nonparties would be ruled out.

Another important item on the committee's agenda is ecolabeling, the formal labeling of traded goods and services to reflect their environmental impact and national environmental standards and regulations. The objective of ecolabeling programs is to provide consumers with information about products' environmental attributes. Product regulations relate to the control of externalities resulting from consumption. WTO rules under the Agreement on Technical Barriers to Trade permit countries to subject imports to the same product regulations as domestically produced goods. Labeling imports that fail to comply with these regulations is justified.

Process regulations control externalities caused by production. In the absence of cross-border externalities, production methods do not affect the environment of an importing country. Thus, unless cross-border externalities exist, process standards should be set entirely by the exporting country. Requirements that impose process standards for traded goods that meet the importing country's process standards are unjustified.

Trade measures relating to process and production methods raise issues of extraterritoriality. The Rio Declaration on Environment and Development cautions against unilateral actions taken to deal with environmental challenges outside the territory of the importing country. The GATT/WTO has taken the same position, reflected in the ruling of a special trade dispute settlement panel: the US embargo on Mexican tuna captured by fishing nets that harmed dolphins violated GATT rules. The WTO does not allow discrimination between domestically produced and identical imported products simply because they are produced using different process and production methods.

There is no reason why the Committee on Trade and Environment should change trade rules to accommodate domestic environmental policies; however, the issue of process and production methods has nevertheless entered through the back door by means of the ecolabeling issue. If ecolabeling relates to product characteristics, this does not violate WTO rules, but whether ecolabeling referring to information on process and production methods that is not product related is consistent with WTO rules is highly questionable. The accommodation of MEAs, as well as process and production methods ecolabeling, in GATT and GATS—signed by only a subset of WTO members—would be harmful for ADEs, because it would carry the risk of proliferation of arbitrary trade restrictions against the goods these countries export. Ecolabels are already being developed rapidly in sectors such as textiles and footwear that are the major exports of many developing countries. Labeling criteria extend even beyond process and production methods not only of the final product, but also of inputs such as cotton and leather. This is a matter of serious concern.

Regionalism

In the early 1980s, in the face of EU reluctance to engage in a new round of multilateral trade negotiations, the United States turned to regionalism as a vehicle for trade liberalization. This switch in US policy has launched a new wave of regional agreements around the world. Of the 153 arrangements registered with the WTO, almost half were entered into in the 1990s, with more than 40 concluded since 1995, when the Uruguay Round Agreement was signed.

Economists tend to be skeptical about the benefits of regional trade agreements for three main reasons. First, regional arrangements are discriminatory. They liberalize trade between member countries, but maintain trade barriers against nonmembers. As a result, they lead to trade diversion. Imports from less efficient partner countries may replace imports from more efficient suppliers outside the regional bloc. The resulting inefficiency reduces welfare both inside the regional bloc and for nonmembers. While the effects of trade creation within the regional bloc may partially or wholly offset the loss of welfare for member countries, there is no such offsetting effect for nonmember countries.

Empirical studies confirm that regional trade arrangements, such as the Common Market of the South (MERCOSUR), EU, and North American Free Trade Agreement (NAFTA), have substantial trade diversion effects. According to Hufbauer and Schott (1993), NAFTA will divert about $300 million of US manufactured imports per year that previously came from Korea and Taipei,China, with machinery and transport equipment being the largest component. Annual trade diversion from South Asia and East Asia, excluding Korea and Taipei,China, will reach $350 million of manufactures and $100 million of primary products per year. Hardest hit sectors will be machinery, transport equipment, and clothing and other consumer goods. Effects of EU integration on developing Asia's exports are estimated to be larger than the trade effects of NAFTA. According to some recent studies (Davenport and Page 1991; Page 1992), the net effects as a percentage of the region's existing exports to the EU will be -0.3 for ASEAN, -6.1 for the East Asian NIEs, and -0.3 for the PRC. While such estimates are imprecise and vary from study to study, they all suggest a substantial and adverse effect on ADEs' exports.

A major concern in Asia is NAFTA's impact on FDI. Recent empirical studies, including Kreinen (1992) and McCleery (1993), predict that FDI will be diverted from ASEAN countries to Mexico in the food, chemicals, textiles, metals, electronics, and transport sectors. McCleery estimates that Indonesia will lose 4 to 5 percent of FDI annually, Malaysia will lose 5 to 7 percent, and Singapore will lose 2 to 3 percent.

A second reason for skepticism about regional trade arrangements is the proliferation of overlapping and confusing tariff regimes across the world. When countries are signing overlapping regional trade agreements with different trading partners, each arrangement has its own period for phasing out tariffs, typically 10 to 15 years. This is sometimes referred to as a "spaghetti bowl" of tariffs. During the transition, tariff rates for the same good vary according to the country from which it is imported. Each regional trade agreement also has different rules for origin and tariff preference. Tariff preference is granted only if a prespecified proportion of the value added comes from within the union. This percentage can differ across products as well as across different trade blocs.

A third source of skepticism is that regional trade arrangements distract and detract from multilateral liberalization, a superior route to international trade liberalization. Regional trade arrangements reduce a country's incentive to liberalize trade on a nondiscriminatory basis. For example, NAFTA undermined the momentum built up for unilateral liberalization in Latin America. Following NAFTA, Latin American countries immersed themselves in negotiations about their own regional arrangements. The average level of tariff protection in Latin America dropped from 40 percent in 1986 to below 20 percent in 1991, but since that time virtually no progress has been made in reducing tariffs further. Indeed, in many cases, after the conclusion of regional trade arrangements members have gone on to raise their external tariffs. In the wake of Brazil's recent fiscal crisis, MERCOSUR raised its common external tariff by 3 percent. Internal trade liberalization in the EU has been accompanied by more vigorous antidumping against outside countries. Now that Eastern and Central European countries are implementing tariff preferences under association agreements with the EU, they too are raising tariffs on imports from nonmembers to make up for shortfalls in tariff revenues. The Central African Customs and Economic Union has introduced across-the-board increases in tariffs on nonmembers to support trade preferences among member countries.

Regional Arrangements in Asia. Regional trade arrangements in Asia are limited. Only three WTO members do not participate in any regional schemes and they are all Asian: Hong Kong, China; Japan; and Korea. The most important regional institution in

Asia, the Asia-Pacific Economic Cooperation Forum, has a strict principle of nondiscrimination in trade policy, even though the United States, a prominent member, has often advocated reciprocity in trade liberalization.

The two institutions in Asia that appear in the WTO register of regional trade agreements are the ASEAN Free Trade Area and the South Asian Preferential Trade Area; however, to date neither of these institutions has promoted significant preferential trade policy. Members of the ASEAN Free Trade Area have generally opted for liberalizing trade on a multilateral basis, so that any tariff reductions they undertake as a part of their obligations are extended to nonmembers as well. The South Asian Preferential Trade Area, which came into operation in 1995, has so far had little impact on trade policies in South Asia.

Open Regionalism. Advocates of the current wave of regional trade arrangements sometimes defend it on the grounds of it being open regionalism, in contrast to the closed, import-substituting regionalism of the 1950s and 1960s. Liberalization undertaken by members of Asian regional groups has been largely open in the sense of being nondiscriminatory, in contrast to regional arrangements in Latin America, North America, and Western Europe. However, considerable confusion remains about the implications of open regionalism, and indeed, about whether it is a useful concept at all. Critics of open regionalism point out that the notion is inherently contradictory. If arrangements are open, they cannot be regional.

The second annual report of the Asia-Pacific Economic Cooperation Forum (APEC 1994) represents one of the first attempts at establishing criteria for open regionalism. It suggests three requirements: freedom for member countries to liberalize further unilaterally or with nonmembers on a reciprocal basis; consistency with GATT Article XXIV, which prohibits an increase in average external barriers; and open membership with positive encouragement to nonmembers to join.

The requirement that members be free to pursue unilateral or bilateral trade liberalization makes customs unions incompatible with open regionalism, even though they are perfectly compatible with GATT Article XXIV. In a customs union, individual members are not free to lower their tariffs, the common external tariff can only be lowered by common consent, members are not permitted to arrange preferential trade arrangements with outside countries on their own, and the entry of new members into the customs union has to be a joint decision. This means that NAFTA can pursue open regionalism while the EU cannot, even though the EU has signed more new preferential trade arrangements than NAFTA.

The second criterion, compatibility with Article XXIV, serves as a necessary, but insufficient, condition for openness. If two countries start out with prohibitive tariffs and then form a preferential trade arrangement while maintaining their prohibitive tariffs on outside countries, they may satisfy the requirements of Article XXIV, but such arrangements can hardly be characterized as open regionalism. This second criterion is of no help in explaining why the regionalism of the 1950s and 1960s was more closed while the regionalism being pursued today is open.

The remaining criterion, open membership, is the most important. It is what gives the term open regionalism meaning. On this criterion, if outsiders see membership of the open regional arrangement as attractive and seek membership, then the preferential trade agreement has the potential eventually to encompass the entire world, and so lead to multilateral free trade. However, despite this theoretical possibility, the open membership criterion has three important limitations that give critics reason to remain skeptical of open regionalism. To begin with, discrimination against nonmembers is still possible. The admission price to the trading club might involve items that are essentially unrelated to trade, such as accepting a stronger intellectual property rights regime, investment rules, and higher labor and environmental standards. Moreover, open membership does not necessarily mean speedy membership: the EU took more than 40 years to grow from 6 to 15 members. The Canada-US Free Trade Agreement, concluded almost ten years ago, has only been widened to one extra member through NAFTA, and Chile's attempts to join have met with serious resistance. While open membership of regional trade arrangements can in principle lead to global free trade, it will lead to fragmentation during extended periods of transition, and quite possibly to two or three large trade blocs rather than to free world trade. In contrast, if all countries stuck to the Most Favored Nation principle, the cornerstone of the GATT and the WTO, the result would be free international trade.

CONCLUSIONS

The Asian developing countries' best route for ensuring economic growth and prosperity is through economic openness and liberal economic policies. They should continue to strive to maintain their leadership among developing countries worldwide in liberalizing their foreign trade and investment regimes. This will allow the ADEs to maintain their international competitiveness in markets for traded goods and services and their attractiveness for FDI.

The recent financial crisis in East and Southeast Asia was not caused by the outward-oriented trade policies the affected countries pursued. Economic theory and empirical evidence clearly demonstrate that outward-oriented trade policies should be a central part of development strategies in poor countries. The financial crisis does not change this; however, it does raise questions about the desirability of completely free capital movement and full capital account convertibility. The financial crisis did not engulf countries such as the PRC and India, which had greater restrictions on capital account convertibility, especially pertaining to trade in financial assets, than the economies worst hit by the financial crisis. The PRC and India must reform their banking and financial sectors before liberalizing capital movements.

Countries that do have a high degree of convertibility should not hastily retreat to close their capital account in the face of a crisis. To reduce economic volatility they may wish to consider introducing some friction in financial flows, but using strictly price-based measures, such as taxes on short-term capital, to avoid wholesale distortions to beneficial capital account transactions, including those related to FDI flows. In the middle of a financial crisis, however, the introduction of capital controls to slow down speculative capital flows is unlikely to be effective. While they may provide some breathing space for short-term policy manipulation, they will not redress the fundamental weaknesses in the economy that created the crisis in the first place.

ADEs should take a proactive rather than a reactive approach to multilateral trade negotiations. To maximize the benefits of economic openness as East and Southeast Asia emerge from the financial crisis, the ADEs should push collectively for a comprehensive round of multilateral trade negotiations and develop a common negotiating strategy to promote Asian interests. Many of the products that the ADEs export remain subject to high tariffs. This new comprehensive trade round should include not only agricultural goods and services—as required by the built-in agenda of the Uruguay Round Agreement—but also international trade in goods. If the industrial countries continue to demand a multilateral agreement on investment, developing Asian countries should ensure that it is limited to FDI, and the PRC must be included in any agreement on FDI. The choice of policy regime for other forms of investments should remain in the hands of national governments. In return for a multilateral agreement on investment, developing countries should insist on a multilateral agreement on labor mobility.

Empirical studies suggest that the EU and NAFTA have a large and increasing effect on trade diversion at the expense of the ADEs. If the trend toward regionalism continues, with the EU and NAFTA expanding to include more countries, the ADEs stand to suffer a considerable loss of market access and export demand. Therefore, it is in Asia's interest to push for a sunset clause on regional arrangements in the next round of multilateral trade negotiations. Such a clause would require that preferences granted within a preferential trading area be extended to all WTO members within a specified period of less than ten years. It would thus discourage the formation of trade blocs that intend to stay closed forever, and would ensure that future trade blocs are opened fully to the rest of the world within the specified time period.

Finally, as the world nears the start of the new millennium, the global economy faces a number of issues: the ADEs, the traditional high performers in the global context, are still in the throes of an ongoing economic turmoil; the EU, which launched its single currency, the euro, this year, seems to be facing prospects of diminished growth and high unemployment; and the US economy, which appears robust and as yet largely unscathed by the ongoing global economic turmoil, is likely to slow down (yet despite its robust growth, US industries have resorted to frequent antidumping suits against imports).

In view of recent economic developments and the prospects of a global slowdown, the director general of the WTO, in his 9 December 1998 annual review of development in multilateral trading systems, noted the growth of protectionist tendencies in advanced economies and the weakening support for trade liberalization and openness, a development that will further exacerbate the frailties of the global economy. Ironically, while the ADEs, in the face of tremendous economic difficulties, have remained resolute in their commitment to trade liberalization and openness, the industrial countries vacillate and engage in restrictive trade practices. While the industrial countries ask developing countries to undertake painful liberalization measures that entail the loss of jobs and

industries, the industrial countries take recourse to antidumping and safeguard measures to protect their jobs and industries. While the industrial countries succumb to political pressures as they adopt protectionist policies, they blithely ignore the enormous political problems developing countries face as they liberalize their trade. These negative protectionist tendencies in the industrial countries must be checked. If global markets are kept open, the impending slowdown in the global economy will be short-lived, but if these negative tendencies triumph and markets are closed, the global slowdown is likely to be long, arduous, and painful. Indeed, the path to continued global prosperity—and recovery from the ongoing economic crisis—lies in an open global environment and not in a move away from it. This is an important lesson the global economic leadership would be well advised to heed.

Selected Bibliography

Selected Bibliography

ADB (Asian Development Bank). 1997a. "Country Economic Review on Uzbekistan." Manila.

———. 1997b. *Emerging Asia: Changes and Challenges.* Manila.

———. 1997c. "Solomon Islands 1997 Economic Report." Manila.

———. 1997d. "Vanuatu 1997 Economic Report." Manila.

———. 1998a. "Exchange Controls: The Path to Economic Recovery in Asia?" EDRC Briefing Notes no. 4. Manila.

———. 1998b. *The Global Trading System and Developing Asia.* Manila.

———. 1998c. *Key Indicators of Developing Asian and Pacific Countries.* Manila.

———. 1998d. "Economic Report and Interim Operational Strategy for Tajikistan." Manila.

Akerloff, G. 1970. "The Market for Lemons." *Quarterly Journal of Economics* 84(3): 488-500.

Amsden, Alice. 1989. *Asia's Next Giant: South Korea and Late Industrialization.* New York: Oxford University Press.

APEC (Asia-Pacific Economic Cooperation). 1994. *Annual Report to Ministers.* Committee on Trade and Investment. Singapore.

Ariff, M., and N. S. Tho. 1994. "Taiwanese Investment in Malaysia: Profile and Performance." Chung-Hua Institution for Economic Research, Taipei,China.

Bagehot, W. 1866. "One Banking Reserve or Many?" *The Economist* 24(September 1): 1025-26.

———. 1873. *Lombard Street: A Description of the Money Market.* London: William Clowes and Sons.

Balassa, Bela. 1982. "Development Strategies and Economic Performance: A Comparative Analysis of Eleven Semi-Industrialized Economies." In Bela Balassa, ed., *Development Strategies in Semi-Industrialized Economies.* Baltimore, Maryland: The Johns Hopkins University Press.

Bank for International Settlements. 1998. *Statistics on External Indebtedness.* New Series no. 20. Paris. (Online). Available: http://www.bis.org.

Bank of Mongolia. 1998. *Monthly Bulletin* (December). Ulaanbaatar.

Bank of Papua New Guinea. 1998. *Quarterly Economic Bulletin* XXVI(2), June. Port Moresby.

Barro, R. J., and X. Sala-i-Martin. 1992. "Regional Growth and Migration: A Japan-United States Comparison." *Journal of the Japanese and International Economy* 6(4): 312-46.

———. 1995. *Economic Growth.* New York: McGraw Hill.

Basant, R., and R. Fikkert. 1996. "The Effect of R&D, Foreign Technology Purchase, and International and Domestic Spillovers on Productivity in Indian Firms." *The Review of Economics and Statistics* 78(2): 187-99.

Bhagwati, Jagdish. 1971. "The Generalized Theory of Distortions and Welfare." In *Trade, Balance of Payments, and Growth: Papers in International Economics in Honor of Charles P. Kindleberger.* Amsterdam: North-Holland.

———. 1978. *Anatomy and Consequences of Exchange Control Regimes.* Lexington, Massachusetts: Ballinger Press.

———. 1998. "The Capital Myth: The Difference

between Trade in Widgets and Dollars." *Foreign Affairs* 77(May/June): 7-12.

Borensztein, E., J. de Gregorio, and J.-W. Lee. 1998. "How Does Foreign Direct Investment Affect Economic Growth?" *Journal of International Economics* 45(1/2): 115-35.

Borjas, George. 1995. "The Economic Benefits from Immigration." *Journal of Economic Perspectives* 9(2): 3-22.

Borjas, George, Richard Freeman, and Lawrence Katz. 1992. "On the Labor Market Effects of Immigration and Trade." In George Borjas and Richard Freeman, eds., *Immigration and the Workforce.* Chicago: University of Chicago.

Buiter, W., and A. Siebert. 1998. "UNDROP or You Drop: A Small Contribution to the New International Financial Architecture." Unpublished manuscript. Department of Economics, Yale University, New Haven, Connecticut.

Buiter W., G. Corsetti, and P. Pesenti. 1998. *Financial Markets and European Monetary Cooperation, The Lesson from the 1992-93 ERM Crisis.* Cambridge, UK: Cambridge University Press.

Calomiris, C. 1998a. "Blueprints for a New Global Financial Architecture." Unpublished manuscript. Columbia University, New York.

_____. 1998b. "The IMF's Imprudent Role as Lender of Last Resort." *Cato Journal* 17(3): 275-95.

Calomiris, C., and A. Meltzer. 1998. "Reforming the IMF." Unpublished manuscript. Columbia Business School, New York.

Central Bank of Sri Lanka. 1998. *Annual Report 1997.* Colombo.

Central Statistical Organization. 1999. *National Income: Consumption Expenditure, Saving, and Capital Formation 1997-1998.* New Delhi.

Chang R., and A. Velasco. 1998. "Financial Crises in Emerging Markets: A Canonical Model." Working Paper no. 6606. National Bureau of Economic Research, Cambridge, Massachusetts.

Claessens S., S. Djankov, and L. Lang. 1998. "East Asian Corporates: Growth, Financing, and Risks over the Last Decades." Unpublished manuscript. World Bank, Washington, D.C.

Cline, W. 1997. *Trade and Income Distribution.* Washington, D.C.: Institute of International Economics.

Cook Islands Statistics Office. 1998. *Cook Islands Annual Statistical Bulletin* (June). Rarotonga.

Cordella, T. 1998. "Can Short-Term Capital Controls Promote Capital Inflows?" Working Paper WP/98/131. International Monetary Fund, Washington, D.C.

Corsetti G., P. Pesenti, and N. Roubini. 1998a. "Paper Tigers, a Model of the Asian Crisis." Working Paper no. 6783. National Bureau of Economic Research, Cambridge, Massachusetts.

_____. 1998b. "What Caused the Asian Financial and Currency Crisis?" Working Paper no. 6833-6834. National Bureau of Economic Research, Cambridge, Massachusetts.

Crockett, A. 1997. *The Theory and Practice of Financial Stability.* Princeton, New Jersey: Princeton University, Department of Economics, International Finance Section.

Davenport, M., with S. Page. 1991. *Europe: 1992 and the Developing World.* Boulder, Colorado: Westview Press.

Deutsche Bank Research. Various issues. *Global Emerging Markets. London.*

deVries, M. G. 1987. *Balance of Payments Adjustment, 1945 to 1986: The IMF Experience.* Washington, D.C.: International Monetary Fund.

Díaz-Alejandro, C. F. 1985. "Good-Bye Financial Repression, Hello Financial Crash." *Journal of Development Economics* 19(1/2): 1-24. Reprinted in A. Velasco, ed., 1988. *Trade, Development and the World Economy, Selected Essays of Carlos Díaz-Alejandro.* Oxford, UK: Blackwell.

Dornbusch, R. 1998. "After Asia: New Directions for the International Financial System." Unpublished manuscript. Massachusetts Institute of Technology, Boston.

Edwards, Sebastian. 1997. "Trade Policy, Growth, and Income Distribution." *American Economic Review* 87(2): 205-210.

Edwards, S., and M. Savastano. 1998. "Exchange Rates in Emerging Economies: What Do We Know? What Do We Need to Know?" Paper presented at the Conference on Economic Policy Reform: What We Know and What We Need to Know, 17-19 September, Stanford University, Palo Alto, California.

Eichengreen, B. 1999. "Toward a New International Financial Architecture: A Practical Post-Asia Agenda." Unpublished manuscript. Institute for International Economics, Washington, D.C.

Feldstein, M. 1998. "Refocusing the IMF." *Foreign Affairs* 77(2): 20-33.

Finger, Michael J., Merlina D. Ingco, and Ulrich Reincke. 1996. *The Uruguay Round: Statistics on Tariff Concessions Given and Received.* Washington, D.C.: World Bank.

Fischer, S. 1998. "The IMF and the Asian Crisis." Paper presented at the Forum Funds Lecture, 20 March, University of California at Los Angeles.

_____. 1999. "On the Need for an International Lender of Last Resort." Paper presented at the annual meetings of the American Economic Association and the American Finance Association, 3 January, New York.

Fleming, J. M. 1972. "Towards a New Regime for International Payments." *Journal of International Economics* 2(4): 345-74.

Freeman, R. 1995. "Are Your Wages Being Set in Beijing?" *Journal of Economic Perspectives* 9(3): 15-32.

Fry, M. J. 1993. *Foreign Direct Investment in Southeast Asia: Differential Impacts.* Current Economic Affairs Series. Singapore: Institute of Southeast Asian Studies, Association of Southeast Asian Nations Economic Research Unit.

Furnam J., and S. Joseph. 1998. "Economic Crises: Evidence and Insights from East Asia." Unpublished manuscript. Prepared for the Brookings Panel on Economic Activity, Washington, D.C.

G22 (Group of 22). 1998a. "Report of the Working Group on International Financial Crises." Washington, D.C., International Monetary Fund.

_____. 1998b. "Report of the Working Group on Strengthening Financial Systems." Washington, D.C., International Monetary Fund.

_____. 1998c. "Report of the Working Group on Transparency and Accountability." Washington, D.C., International Monetary Fund.

Goldstein, M. 1998. *The Asian Financial Crisis: Causes, Cures, and Systemic Implications.* Washington, D.C.: Institute for International Economics.

Hamilton, Robert, and John Whalley. 1984. "Efficiency and Distributional Implications of Global Restrictions on Labor Mobility: Calculations and Policy Implications." *Journal of Development Economics* 14(1): 61-75.

Hasan, Rana. 1998. "The Impact of Imported and Domestic Technologies on the Productivity of Firms: Panel Data Evidence from Indian Manufacturing Firms." Economics and Development Resource Center, Asian Development Bank, Manila.

Harrison, Anne. 1996. "Openness and Growth: A Time-Series, Cross-Country Analysis for Developing Countries." *Journal of Developing Economies* 48(2): 419-47.

Hufbauer, G., and J. Schott. 1993. "Regionalism in North America." In K. Ohno, eds., *Regional Integration and its Impact on Developing Countries.* Tokyo: Institute of Developing Economies.

IMF (International Monetary Fund). 1997. *World Economic Outlook 1997.* Washington, D.C.

_____. 1998a, 1999a, various years. *International Financial Statistics.* Washington, D.C.

_____. 1998b. *International Capital Markets, Interim Assessment.* Washington, D.C.

_____. 1998c. *Article IV Consultation* (Online). Available: http://www.imf.org/external/pubind.htm.

_____. 1998d. *Direction of Trade Statistics Yearbook.* Washington, D.C.

_____. 1998e. *World Economic Outlook 1998.* Washington, D.C.

_____. 1999. *The IMF's Response to the Asian Crisis.* Washington, D.C.

Jackson, J. 1989. *The World Trading System.* Cambridge, Massachusetts: MIT Press.

Jacobsson, Staffan, and Ghayur Alam. 1994. *Liberalisation and Industrial Development in the Third World: A Comparison of the Indian and South Korean Engineering Industries.* New Delhi: Sage Publications.

Johnson, Harry. 1967. *Economic Analysis Toward Less Developed Countries.* New York: Praeger.

Johnson, B. T., K. R. Holmes, and M. Kirkpatrick. 1998. *Heritage Foundation/Wall Street Journal 1998 Index of Economic Freedom.* Washington, D.C. and New York: The Heritage Foundation and Dow Jones & Company.

Kawaguchi, O. 1994. *Foreign Direct Investment in East Asia: Trends, Determinants, and Policy Implications.* Report no. IDP-139. Washington, D.C.: World Bank.

Kreuger, Anne O. 1978. *Foreign Trade Regimes and Economic Development: Liberalization Attempts and Consequences.* Lexington, Massachusetts: Ballinger Press.

Kreinen, M. 1992. "Multinationalism, Regionalism,

and Their Implications for Asia." Paper presented at the Conference on Global Interdependence and Asia-Pacific Cooperation, 8-10 June, Hong Kong, China.

Krugman, Paul. 1979. "A Model of Balance of Payments Crises." *Journal of Money, Credit, and Banking* 11(3): 311-25.

———. 1998. *The Eternal Triangle* (Online) Available: http://www.web.mit.edu/krugman/www/triangle.html.

Lee, Jong-Wha. 1995. "Capital Goods Imports and Long-Run Growth." *Journal of Development Economics* 48(1): 91-110.

Litan, R. 1998. "Does the IMF Have a Future? What Should it Be?" Remarks made at the IMF/Federal Reserve Bank of Chicago Conference on the IMF, October.

Little, I. M. D. 1996. "Picking Winners: The East Asian Experience." Occasional Paper. Social Market Foundation, London.

Mason, E., and R. Asher. 1973. *The World Bank since Bretton Woods.* Washington: D.C.: The Brookings Institution.

McCleery, R. 1993. "Modelling NAFTA: Macroeconomic Effects." In K. Ohno, ed., *Regional Integration and Its Impact on Developing Countries.* Tokyo: Institute of Developing Economies.

McKinnon, R. J. 1998. "Exchange Rate Coordination for Surmounting the East Asian Currency Crises." Paper presented at the conference on Financial Crises: Facts, Theories, and Policies; Panel on Crisis Management." 18 November, International Monetary Fund, Washington, D.C.

Meltzer, A. 1998. "Asian Problems and the IMF." Testimony prepared for the Joint Economic Committee, US Congress, 24 February.

Ministry of Finance, Government of Fiji. 1998. *Economic and Fiscal Supplement to the 1999 Budget Address.* Suva: Bureau of Statistics.

Ministry of Finance, Government of India. 1999. *Economic Survey 1998/99.* New Delhi.

Ministry of Finance, Government of Malaysia. 1998. *Economic Report 1998/99.* Kuala Lumpur.

Ministry of Finance, Government of Nepal. 1998. *Economic Survey, 1997-98.* Kathmandu.

Ministry of Finance and Economic Affairs, Government of Pakistan. 1998. *Economic Survey 1997/98.* Islamabad.

Ministry of Finance and Economic Planning, Government of Kiribati. 1997. *Medium-Term Strategy: An Action Programme for the National Development Strategy through to the Year 2000.* Kiribati.

Ministry of Trade and Industry, Government of Singapore. 1996. *Economic Survey of Singapore.* Singapore.

Morris, S., and H. S. Shin. 1998. "Unique Equilibrium in a Model of Self-Fulfilling Currency Attacks." *The American Economic Review* 88(3): 587-97.

National Statistics Office. 1998. *Monthly Statistics of Korea.* Seoul.

Naya, S. F., and P. I. Iboshi. 1998. "Trade and Investment Policy Matrix and Liberalization Agenda for Asia and the Pacific." Paper prepared for the United Nations Economic and Social Committee for Asia and the Pacific. Bangkok, Thailand.

Obstfeld, Maurice. 1994. "The Logic of Currency Crises." *Cahiers Economiques et Monetaires* 43: 189-213.

———. 1996. "Models of Currency Crises with Self-Fulfilling Features." *European Economic Review* 40(April): 1037-47.

———. 1998. "The Global Capital Market: Benefactor or Menace?" Working Paper no. 6559. National Bureau of Economic Research, Cambridge, Massachusetts.

Obstfeld, Maurice, and Alan M. Taylor. 1998. "The Great Depression as a Watershed: International Capital Mobility over the Long Run." In Michael D. Bordo, Claudia D. Goldin, and Eugene N. White, eds., *The Defining Moment: The Great Depression and the American Economy in the Twentieth Century.* Chicago: University of Chicago Press.

OECD (Organisation for Economic Co-operation and Development). 1995. "The Multilateral Agreement on Investment: The Original Mandate." (Online) Available: http://www.oecd.org.

———. 1998. *Recent Trends in Foreign Direct Investment.* Paris.

Pack, H., and L. E. Westphal. 1986. "Industrial Strategy and Technological Change: Theory versus Reality." *Journal of Development Economics* 22(1/2): 87-128.

Page, S. 1992. "Some Implications of Europe 1992 for Developing Countries." Technical Paper no. 60. OECD Development Center, Paris.

Pernia, Ernesto M., and James C. Knowles. 1998. "Assessing the Social Impact of the Financial Crisis in Asia." EDRC Briefing Note no. 6. Asian Development Bank, Manila.

Pritchett, Lant. 1996. "Measuring Outward Orientation in LDCs: Can it Be Done?" *Journal of Development Economics* 49(1-2): 307-335.

Quibria, M. G. 1997. "Labour Migration and Labour Market Integration in Asia." *The World Economy* 20(1): 21-42.

Quinn, Dennis. 1997. "The Correlates of Change in International Financial Regulation." *American Political Science Review* 91(3): 531-42.

Rana, Pradumna B. 1998. "Surges and Volatility of Private Capital Flows to Asian Developing Countries: Implications for Multilateral Development Banks." Occasional Paper no. 19. Manila: Asian Development Bank.

Reserve Bank of India. 1998. *Annual Report 1997/98.* Mumbai.

_____. Various issues. *Reserve Bank of India Bulletin.* Mumbai.

Roach, Stephen. 1998. "Global: Asia Bottoming." *Global Economic Forum.* A Feature Publication of the Morgan Stanley Dean Witter Economists. 22 October. (Online) Available: http://www.ms. com/main/link9.html.

Rodrik, D. 1998. "Who Needs Capital Account Liberalization?" In Peter B. Kenen, ed., *Should the IMF Pursue Capital Account Convertibility? Essays in International Finance no. 207.* Princeton, New Jersey: Princeton University, Department of Economics, International Finance Section.

Sachs, Jeffrey D. 1998. "Creditor Panics: Causes and Remedies." Paper prepared for the Cato Institute's 16th Annual Monetary Conference cosponsored with *The Economist,* 22 October, Washington, D.C.

Sachs, Jeffrey D., and S. Radelet. 1998. "The East Asian Financial Crisis: Diagnosis, Remedies, Prospects." *Brookings Papers on Economic Activity* 1: 1-74.

Sachs, Jeffrey D., and Howard J. Shatz. 1994. "Trade and Jobs in US Manufacturing." *Brookings Papers on Economic Activity* 1: 1-69.

Schott, Jeffrey, ed. 1989. *Free Trade and US Trade Policy.* Washington, D.C.: Institute of International Economics.

Singapore Department of Statistics. 1998. *Monthly Digest of Statistics.* Singapore.

Snape, Richard. 1993. "Discrimination, Regionalism, and the GATT." In Takatoshi Ito and Anne Kreuger, eds., *Trade and Protectionism.* Chicago: University of Chicago Press.

Soros, G. 1999. "To Avert the Crisis." *Financial Times* 4 January, p. 18.

Srinivasan, T. N. 1998. *Developing Countries and the Multilateral Trading System: From the GATT (1947) to the Uruguay Round and the Future Beyond.* Boulder, Colorado: Westview Press.

State Bank of Pakistan. 1997. *Annual Report 1997/1998.* Karachi.

State Statistical Bureau. 1998. *Statistical Yearbook 1998.* Beijing.

Summers, Lawrence. 1999. "Reflections on Managing Global Integration." Lecture delivered at the Annual Meeting of the Association of Government Economists, 4 January, New York.

Sung, Y. W. 1994. "Subregional economic integration: Hong Kong, Taiwan, South China, and beyond." In Edward K.Y. Chen and Peter Drysdale, eds., *Corporate Links and Foreign Direct Investment in Asia and the Pacific.* Canberra: Harper Educational Publishers in association with The Pacific Trade and Development Conference Secretariat; The Australian National University; and Centre of Asian Studies, The University of Hong Kong.

Svensson, L. E. O. 1994. "Fixed Exchange Rates as a Means to Price Stability: What Have We Learnt?" *European Economic Review* 38(3/4): 447-68.

Tobin, J. 1978. "A Proposal for International Monetary Reform." *Eastern Economic Journal* 4: 153-59.

UNCTAD (United Nations Conference on Trade and Development). 1994. *Directory of Import Regimes,* Part I. Geneva.

_____. 1998a. Trade Analysis and Information System.

_____. 1998b. *World Investment Report 1998: Trends and Determinants.* New York.

Valdes-Prieto, S., and M. Soto. 1997. "The Effectiveness of Capital Controls: Theory and Evidence from Chile." Unpublished manuscript. Universidad Catholica de Chile, Santiago.

Wade, R. 1990. *Governing the Market: Economic Theory and the Role of Government in East Asian Industrialization.* Princeton, New Jersey: Princeton University Press.

Warr, Peter G. 1998. "Growth, Crisis, and Poverty Incidence in Southeast Asia. Unpublished manuscript. Australian National University, Canberra.

Westphal, Larry. 1990. "Industrial Policy in an Export-Propelled Economy: Lessons from South Korea's Experience." *Journal of Economic Perspectives* 4(summer): 41-59.

Westphal, Larry, and K. Kim. 1982. "Korea." In Bela Balassa, ed., *Development Strategies in Semi-Industrialized Economies.* Baltimore, Maryland: The Johns Hopkins University Press.

Wood, Adrian. 1995. "How Trade Hurt Unskilled Workers." *Journal of Economic Perspectives* 9(3): 57-80.

World Bank. 1992. *World Development Report 1992.* New York: Oxford University Press.

_____. 1993. *The East Asian Miracle: Economic Growth and Public Policy.* Policy Research Report Series. New York: Oxford University Press.

_____. 1997a. *Private Capital Flows to Developing Countries: The Road to Financial Integration.* Policy Research Report Series. New York: Oxford University Press.

_____. 1997b. *World Development Report 1997.* New York: Oxford University Press.

_____. 1998a. *East Asia: The Road to Recovery.* Washington, D.C.

_____. 1998b. *World Development Indicators.* Washington, D.C.

_____. 1998c. *World Development Report 1998.* New York: Oxford University Press.

_____. 1998d. *Global Economic Prospects 1998/99.* Washington, D.C.

_____. 1999. *World Development Report 1999.* New York: Oxford University Press.

WTO (World Trade Organization). 1996. *Annual Report,* vol. II. Geneva.

Wu, Chung-Shu. 1998. "Recent Developments and Near Future Outlook for Taipei,China." Paper prepared for the Asian Development Bank. Institute of Economics, Academia Sinica, Taipei,China.

Statistical Appendix

Statistical Notes

The Statistical Appendix presents selected economic indicators for the 37 developing member countries (DMCs) of the Asian Development Bank (ADB). A total of 23 tables embodies these selected indicators, which are presented by account as follows: sectoral components of national income accounts, consumer price index, money supply, components of the balance of payments, external debt outstanding and debt service ratio, exchange rate, and the budget accounts of the central government. These tables encompass the time series from 1993 to 1998. Except for the exchange rate and the financial account of the central government, which are considered as policy variables, the tables give projections for 1999 and 2000. The table on foreign direct investment shows figures from 1992 to 1997 only because of the unavailability of data for 1998. The following sections describe the source, scope, and conceptual definition of the data in each table.

Historical data are derived mostly from updated statistical publications of official local sources; other publications; and working papers and other internal documents of the ADB, the World Bank, the International Monetary Fund (IMF), and the United Nations. Some of the preliminary data for 1998 are ADB staff estimates calculated from quarterly and/or monthly data available for the year. Projections for 1999 and 2000 are purely staff estimates.

Despite limitations occasioned by differences in statistical methodology, definitions, coverage, and practice, efforts were made to standardize the data, not only to allow comparability of these data over time and across the DMCs, but also to ensure consistency across accounts. In cases where irregularities and peculiarities in selected accounts arose, the informed judgment of concerned ADB staff was relied upon. For example, data-splicing and data-rebasing techniques were employed to fill in breaks in time-series data. Some data breaks, however, are inevitable due to changes in definitions and methodologies.

Data from official country sources adopt as an annual reference either the calendar year or the fiscal year. For Bangladesh, Bhutan, Cook Islands, India, Maldives, Marshall Islands, Federated States of Micronesia, Myanmar, Nauru, Nepal, Pakistan, Samoa, and Tonga, all data are on a fiscal year basis. For Indonesia, balance-of-payments and money supply data are on a fiscal year basis. For the rest of the DMCs, data on national accounts, consumer price index, monetary accounts, and balance of payments are reported for the calendar year. Government finances for all countries are reported on a fiscal year basis.

Regional averages or totals for the DMCs as a whole and for each of the six subregions are incorporated in 9 of the 23 tables. These tables include those on growth rate of gross domestic product (GDP), growth rate of per capita GDP, changes in consumer prices, growth rate of merchandise exports and imports, balance of trade, current account balance in absolute level and as a percentage of GDP, and level of outstanding external debt. The groupings by region are the newly industrialized economies (NIEs), the People's Republic of China (PRC) and Mongolia, the Central Asian republics, Southeast Asia, South Asia, and the Pacific. The averages are computed as simple, weighted arithmetic means using as weights the contemporaneous GDP values in current US dollars. For the Central Asian republics, the share of 1994 GDP values in current US dollars was used in 1993, because GDP figures for Tajikistan for 1993 are not available. Because of reliability concerns, data for Myanmar are excluded in the computation of the averages or totals for the DMCs.

Tables A1, A2, A3, A4, A5, and A6: Growth and Structure of Production. The definitions used in these tables relating to national income accounts are generally based on the United Nations System of National Accounts. Table A1 shows annual growth rates of GDP valued either at constant market prices or at constant factor costs. Most countries use the constant market prices valuation. The exceptions are Bhutan, Fiji, India, Mongolia, Nepal, Pakistan, Sri Lanka, Solomon Islands, Tonga, and Tuvalu, which use GDP at constant factor cost. For Papua New Guinea the growth rate is based on GDP at constant purchaser's value.

Table A2 presents the growth rate figures for per capita real GDP. Per capita real GDP is obtained by dividing GDP at constant market prices by population. With the exception of India, countries that used constant factor costs in table A1 employ constant market prices to compute per capita real GDP. The switch, for the purpose of uniformity, creates a residual item between GDP growth, per capita GDP growth, and population growth.

Tables A3, A4, and A5 present the annual growth rates of real gross value added in agriculture, industry, and services, respectively. The agriculture sector includes agricultural crops, livestock, poultry, fisheries, and forestry. Mining and quarrying, manufacturing, construction, and utilities fall under the industry sector. The service sector comprises transportation and communications, trade, banking and finance, real estate, public administration, and other services. The sectoral growth rates are consistently defined with the reported GDP values in table A1. Adding-up restrictions are imposed where numerical discrepancies are noted or where reclassifications of the sectors are implemented.

Table A6 shows the sectoral shares of GDP based on constant market prices. For Bangladesh, Cook

Islands, Fiji, India, Lao People's Democratic Republic (Lao PDR), Mongolia, Nepal, Pakistan, Sri Lanka, and Tonga, the sectoral shares of GDP are based on constant factor costs. For Bhutan, the shares are based on gross value added at current factor cost.

Tables A7 and A8: Saving and Investment. Following the definition applied in the national accounts statistics, gross national savings, or gross domestic savings, are computed as the difference between gross national product (GNP), or GDP, and total consumption expenditure. For some countries, gross savings data are obtained from official country sources. Gross savings may differ from either gross national savings or gross domestic savings in that they are derived from the consolidated income and outlay account, and include private transfers from the balance-of-payments account. Gross domestic investment is calculated as the sum of gross fixed capital formation and increases in stocks. For the Pacific economies, except Fiji, where reliable estimates of consumption expenditures are not available, gross domestic savings are computed as the sum of gross domestic investment and current account balance minus the sum of net factor income from abroad and net transfers.

Table A7 gives the ratio of gross domestic savings to GDP as obtained from official country sources. In the cases of India, Maldives, Nepal, Pakistan, and Philippines, the ratio of gross national savings to GNP is used; for Bhutan, Thailand, and Viet Nam, the ratio of gross savings to GDP is used; and for Cambodia, the ratio of gross national savings to GDP is used. Table A8 presents the ratio of gross domestic investment to GDP, except for Maldives, Nepal, Pakistan, and Philippines, which use the ratio of gross domestic investment to GNP. All figures used in the computation of the ratios in tables A7 and A8 are in current market prices.

Table A9: Consumer Prices. This table presents the annual inflation rate based on the consumer price index as obtained from official local sources, or from the IMF for DMCs for which data are not available locally. For most of the DMCs, the reported inflation rates are period averages. For Cambodia, Mongolia, and Viet Nam, the end-of-period consumer price index is used for calculating inflation rates. For

Hong Kong, China, the inflation rate is based on the composite consumer price index. For India, the inflation rate is based on the consumer price index for industrial workers rather than on the wholesale price index.

Table A10: Growth of Money Supply. This table tracks the annual percentage change in money supply as represented by M2. M2 is defined as the sum of M1 and quasi-money, where M1 denotes currency in circulation plus demand deposits, and quasi-money means time and savings deposits plus foreign currency deposits. For India M3 is used as the measure of liquidity. All data for M2 are obtained from official country sources, except for Fiji, Indonesia, Papua New Guinea, Samoa, and Vanuatu, which are taken from the ADB's *Key Indicators of Developing Asian and Pacific Countries* (ADB 1998c) and the IMF's *International Financial Statistics* (IMF 1999a).

Tables A11 and A13: Growth Rate of Merchandise Exports and Imports. Historical data for 1993-1997 and some preliminary estimates for 1998 on merchandise exports and imports are taken from the balance-of-payments accounts, except for Cook Islands data, which are taken from the external trade account. These figures are on a free-on-board basis, except for India and the Lao PDR, for which import data are on a cost, insurance, and freight basis. Export and import statistics are reported in calendar years except for Bangladesh, India, Maldives, Marshall Islands, Federated States of Micronesia, Myanmar, Nepal, Pakistan, and Tonga, which use fiscal year figures. For Cambodia, export data refer to domestic exports only, while import data refer to retained imports only. Retained imports are total imports net of re-exports, but include project aid imports and an estimate of unrecorded imports. Data for Cambodia, PRC, Republic of Korea, Lao PDR, Malaysia, Mongolia, and Thailand are derived from IMF documents.

Table A12: Direction of Exports. For each DMC, the table indicates the percentage share of that economy's exports going to each of the economy's major trading partners (other DMCs, Australia and New Zealand, Japan, the United States, and the European Union). With the exception of Taipei,China, for which data

are obtained directly from local sources, data are from the IMF's *Direction of Trade Statistics Yearbook 1998* (IMF 1998d).

Tables A14, A15, and A16: Balance of Payments. The balance of trade is the difference between merchandise exports and merchandise imports. The current account balance is the sum of the balance of trade, net trade in services and factor income, and net unrequited transfers. In the case of Cambodia, India, Lao PDR, and Viet Nam, official transfers are excluded from the current account balance. Data reported for Indonesia, PRC, Republic of Korea, Malaysia, and Thailand are taken from the IMF's *International Financial Statistics* (IMF 1999a) or IMF staff country reports. The balance-of-payments data for the rest of the DMCs are from local sources.

Table A17: Foreign Direct Investment. The United Nations Conference on Trade and Development's *World Investment Report 1998* (UNCTAD 1998b) provides data on gross foreign direct investment flows for 1992-1997. Direct investment capital refers to equity capital, reinvested earnings, and other capital that is associated with the transactions of enterprises.

Tables A18 and A19: External Debt. For most countries, external debt outstanding includes long-term debt, short-term debt, and use of IMF credit. Principal repayments and interest payments on long-term debt and IMF credit, and interest payments on short-term debt are incorporated in the debt-service payment account. For Cambodia and Viet Nam, external debt data exclude debts in nonconvertible currencies. For Mongolia, medium- and long-term debt includes payment on Council for Mutual Economic Assistance debts, but excludes unresolved claims of former council members. Similarly, for Cambodia, total external debt outstanding from 1993 to 1996 excludes debt incurred to four former Council for Mutual Economic Assistance countries amounting to $1,346 million, but adjustments were made in 1997 to include the cited amount. The debt service ratio is defined as debt service payments as a percentage of total exports of goods and services, except for Cambodia where the debt service ratio is calculated as a percentage of domestic exports and services only. For most countries, data are collected from official local sources. World Bank data are used for PRC, Indonesia, Malaysia, Maldives, Myanmar, and Thailand.

Table A20: Foreign Exchange Rates. The foreign exchange rate quoted is the annual average of the exchange rate to the US dollar of the currency of each of the DMCs. The sources of all basic data are official country estimates, except for Bangladesh; Cambodia; India; Indonesia; Lao PDR; Mongolia; Singapore; Taipei,China; and Thailand, where the IMF's *International Financial Statistics* (IMF 1999a) is used.

Tables A21, A22, and A23: Government Finance. These tables only account for central government finance on a fiscal year basis. Government expenditure includes both current and capital expenditure. Likewise, total revenue includes current revenue and capital receipts. In most countries, the overall budget surplus or deficit is the balance between government revenue and expenditure, excluding grants. In the case of Bhutan, Republic of Korea, Kyrgyz Republic, Marshall Islands, Federated States of Micronesia, Nepal, Pakistan, Tajikistan, and Vanuatu, the overall fiscal balance includes grants. For India, the overall balance excludes borrowing and other liabilities, while for Uzbekistan it includes net lending and budgetary funds. For Kazakhstan, the fiscal balance includes grants, but excludes privatization receipts. Figures for Sri Lanka exclude not only grants, but also privatization proceeds. For Pakistan, the fiscal balance includes consolidated federal and provincial accounts. All ratios are reported as a percentage of GDP in current market prices. Data are taken from official country sources.

Net Private Capital Flows. Net private capital flow figures provided in the text are computed as the difference between the capital account and net official capital flows. Data are from the IMF and the Institute of International Finance.

Table A1 Growth Rate of GDP
(percent per annum)

Economy	1993	1994	1995	1996	1997	1998	1999	2000
Newly Industrialized Economies	6.4	7.6	7.4	6.3	6.0	-1.4	2.3	4.3
Hong Kong, China	6.1	5.4	3.9	4.5	5.3	-5.1	-0.5	2.0
Korea, Rep. of	5.8	8.6	8.9	7.1	5.5	-5.5	2.0	4.0
Singapore	10.4	10.5	8.8	6.9	7.8	1.5	1.0	4.0
Taipei,China	6.3	6.5	6.0	5.7	6.8	4.8	4.9	6.3
People's Rep. of China and Mongolia	13.6	12.7	10.5	9.6	8.7	7.8	7.0	6.5
China, People's Rep. of ·	13.6	12.7	10.5	9.6	8.8	7.8	7.0	6.5
Mongolia	-3.0	2.3	6.3	2.4	4.0	3.5	3.5	4.0
Central Asian Republics	-7.5	-11.0	-5.6	1.1	3.5	0.4	—	—
Kazakhstan	-9.2	-12.6	-8.2	0.5	2.0	-1.5	—	—
Kyrgyz Republic	-15.5	-20.1	-5.4	7.1	9.9	1.8	—	—
Tajikistan	-11.0	-18.9	-12.5	-4.4	1.7	4.0	—	—
Uzbekistan	-2.3	-5.2	-0.9	1.7	5.2	2.8	—	—
Southeast Asia	7.1	7.8	8.2	7.1	4.0	-6.9	0.8	2.8
Cambodia	4.1	4.0	7.6	7.0	2.0	0.0	4.0	6.0
Indonesia	7.3	7.5	8.2	7.8	4.9	-13.7	0.0	2.0
Lao People's Democratic Rep.	5.8	8.1	7.0	6.9	6.9	4.0	—	—
Malaysia	8.3	9.2	9.4	8.6	7.7	-6.2	0.7	2.7
Myanmar	6.0	7.5	6.9	6.4	4.6	4.0	3.0	4.0
Philippines	2.1	4.4	4.7	5.8	5.2	-0.5	2.4	4.0
Thailand	8.4	8.9	8.8	5.5	-0.4	-8.0	0.0	2.5
Viet Nam	8.1	8.8	9.5	9.3	8.2	4.0	3.7	4.5
South Asia	3.5	7.1	7.0	7.2	4.7	5.7	5.5	5.8
Bangladesh	4.5	4.2	4.4	5.4	5.9	5.7	3.6	5.5
Bhutan	6.1	6.4	7.4	6.0	5.4	5.6	7.0	—
India	—	7.8	7.6	7.8	5.0	5.8	5.9	6.0
Maldives	6.1	6.7	7.0	6.5	6.2	6.8	6.4	6.4
Nepal	3.8	8.2	3.5	5.3	4.0	1.9	2.0	2.7
Pakistan	2.3	4.5	5.2	5.2	1.3	5.4	3.4	4.6
Sri Lanka	6.9	5.6	5.5	3.8	6.4	5.3	5.0	6.2
The Pacific	12.0	4.8	-1.0	3.1	-3.4	0.1	—	—
Cook Islands	3.9	3.9	-4.4	-0.2	-0.5	-1.0	—	—
Fiji	2.6	5.1	2.6	3.4	-1.8	-3.9	—	—
Kiribati	2.1	7.7	3.4	6.3	1.5	1.5	—	—
Marshall Islands	4.1	2.8	2.7	-15.2	-5.3	-5.0	—	—
Micronesia, Federated States of	1.1	-1.8	1.6	0.7	-4.0	-3.1	—	—
Nauru	—	—	—	—	—	—	—	—
Papua New Guinea	16.6	5.2	-3.6	3.5	-4.6	2.5	—	—
Samoa	6.3	-7.8	6.5	6.9	0.8	—	—	—
Solomon Islands	2.4	5.1	6.8	0.6	-0.5	-10.0	—	—
Tonga	2.8	3.8	5.2	-1.5	-6.6	-0.3	—	—
Tuvalu	4.1	10.3	-5.0	20.4	2.5	2.0	—	—
Vanuatu	4.5	2.6	3.2	3.5	1.7	-2.0	—	—
Average for DMCs	8.8	8.6	8.1	7.4	6.2	2.6	4.4	5.1

— Not available.

Table A2 Growth Rate of Per Capita GDP
(percent per annum)

Economy	1993	1994	1995	1996	1997	1998	1999	2000	Per Capita GNP(US$) 1997
Newly Industrialized Economies	5.1	6.3	6.1	5.0	4.6	-2.8	2.1	4.1	
Hong Kong, China	4.3	3.1	1.9	1.9	2.2	-7.8	—	—	25,280
Korea, Rep. of	4.7	7.5	7.8	6.0	4.5	-6.4	1.0	3.0	10,550
Singapore	8.3	8.4	6.7	4.7	5.7	-0.9	-0.3	—	32,940
Taipei,China	5.2	5.7	5.1	4.9	5.9	4.0	4.1	5.5	—
People's Rep. of China and Mongolia	12.3	11.4	9.4	8.4	7.6	6.7	5.9	5.4	
China, People's Rep. of	12.3	11.4	9.4	8.4	7.6	6.7	5.9	5.4	860
Mongolia	-5.9	1.0	4.6	0.8	2.3	—	—	—	390
Central Asian Republics	-8.3	-11.0	-5.5	0.9	2.3	—	—	—	
Kazakhstan	-9.1	-12.2	-6.5	1.5	3.1	—	—	—	1,340
Kyrgyz Republic	-15.8	-18.9	-7.8	6.8	9.5	—	—	—	440
Tajikistan	-13.7	-19.8	-14.3	-5.9	0.1	—	—	—	330
Uzbekistan	-4.5	-6.0	-2.9	-0.4	0.4	—	—	—	1,010
Southeast Asia	5.2	6.0	6.3	4.8	2.3	-8.4	-0.8	1.2	
Cambodia	-0.4	1.8	4.0	2.1	-0.8	-1.8	1.3	—	300
Indonesia	5.5	5.8	6.5	6.0	3.3	-14.8	-1.5	0.5	1,110
Lao People's Democratic Rep.	2.6	5.0	4.0	3.5	4.3	—	—	—	400
Malaysia	5.8	6.7	7.0	3.2	5.2	-8.4	-1.6	0.5	4,680
Myanmar	4.1	5.5	5.0	4.5	2.7	2.2	1.2	2.2	—
Philippines	-0.3	2.0	2.2	3.4	2.8	-2.6	0.3	1.8	1,220
Thailand	7.0	7.6	7.6	4.5	-1.4	-9.0	-1.0	1.5	2,800
Viet Nam	5.6	6.6	7.4	7.3	6.2	2.3	1.2	2.5	320
South Asia	0.8	4.9	4.7	5.7	2.1	4.1	3.6	4.0	
Bangladesh	2.8	2.0	2.6	3.5	4.0	3.7	1.9	—	270
Bhutan	2.9	3.2	4.2	2.8	2.2	—	—	—	400
India	—	5.7	5.4	6.0	3.3	4.5	4.2	4.3	390
Maldives	2.3	5.3	5.6	3.8	3.1	3.3	—	—	1,150
Nepal	0.5	5.1	0.2	3.1	1.4	-0.2	-0.5	0.2	210
Pakistan	-1.1	0.9	2.1	6.0	-7.4	1.3	0.4	2.2	490
Sri Lanka	5.6	4.2	4.0	2.6	5.3	4.2	3.9	4.1	800
The Pacific	10.0	3.4	-2.6	1.4	-4.4	-1.0	—	—	—
Cook Islands	0.2	5.0	-3.9	-3.2	8.7	4.1	—	—	—
Fiji	1.0	5.9	1.4	2.1	-2.6	-5.1	—	—	2,470
Kiribati	0.7	6.2	1.9	6.3	1.5	1.5	—	—	910
Marshall Islands	0.0	-0.4	-0.9	-18.0	-8.1	-8.1	—	—	1,770
Micronesia, Federated States of	-0.6	-3.1	0.3	-0.6	-5.5	-4.8	—	—	1,980
Nauru	—	—	—	—	—	—	—	—	—
Papua New Guinea	14.5	3.1	-5.3	1.7	-5.5	1.4	—	—	940
Samoa	5.0	-8.3	4.6	6.2	0.2	—	—	—	1,150
Solomon Islands	-0.3	2.4	2.8	-3.1	-4.1	-12.8	—	—	900
Tonga	3.1	4.3	4.1	-2.1	-5.7	-1.5	—	—	1,830
Tuvalu	2.8	8.9	-6.2	18.9	1.3	0.8	—	—	—
Vanuatu	1.7	-0.2	0.6	0.8	-0.9	-4.5	—	—	1,310
Average for DMCs	7.3	7.0	6.6	5.9	4.6	1.3	3.4	4.2	

Table A3 Growth Rate of Value Added in Agriculture
(percent per annum)

Economy	1993	1994	1995	1996	1997	1998	1999	2000
Newly Industrialized Economies								
Hong Kong, China	—	—	—	—	—	—	—	—
Korea, Rep. of	-2.9	1.6	3.7	4.0	2.5	-6.9	2.5	2.5
Singapore	-2.4	5.4	8.1	8.8	-5.8	—	—	—
Taipei,China	5.4	-4.4	2.6	-0.6	-0.6	-5.6	0.1	2.8
People's Rep. of China and Mongolia								
China, People's Rep. of	4.7	4.0	5.0	5.1	3.5	2.5	3.5	3.5
Mongolia	-2.7	2.7	4.2	10.0	4.8	3.1	—	—
Central Asian Republics								
Kazakhstan	-6.9	-21.0	-24.4	-5.0	1.9	—	—	—
Kyrgyz Republic	-9.8	-8.6	-2.0	15.2	12.3	4.1	—	—
Tajikistan	-4.4	—	—	—	6.5	3.0	—	—
Uzbekistan	1.5	-3.4	2.0	-7.3	5.8	—	—	—
Southeast Asia								
Cambodia	-1.0	0.0	6.5	2.4	2.1	1.4	4.8	—
Indonesia	1.7	0.6	4.4	3.1	0.7	0.2	—	—
Lao People's Democratic Rep.	2.7	8.3	3.1	2.8	7.0	3.7	—	—
Malaysia	4.3	-1.0	1.1	2.2	1.3	-5.9	3.9	4.2
Myanmar	4.6	5.9	4.8	5.0	3.4	3.0	3.0	3.0
Philippines	2.1	2.6	0.8	3.8	2.9	-6.6	2.5	3.0
Thailand	-1.3	5.3	2.5	3.8	1.4	2.1	1.6	2.5
Viet Nam	3.3	3.3	4.8	4.4	4.3	2.7	—	—
South Asia								
Bangladesh	1.8	0.3	-1.0	3.7	6.0	2.9	0.0	3.2
Bhutan	3.6	3.9	4.0	6.2	3.1	3.4	2.5	—
India	—	5.4	0.2	9.4	-1.0	5.0	—	—
Maldives	0.0	2.6	1.6	1.7	1.3	2.9	—	—
Nepal	-0.6	7.6	-0.3	4.4	4.1	1.1	1.4	2.7
Pakistan	-5.3	5.2	6.6	5.8	0.1	5.9	5.0	2.6
Sri Lanka	4.9	3.3	3.3	-4.6	3.1	3.5	—	—
The Pacific								
Cook Islands	0.5	3.7	-2.5	4.3	—	—	—	—
Fiji	0.8	11.0	-3.2	1.9	-12.5	-10.4	—	—
Kiribati	-4.2	7.0	-11.9	4.7	—	—	—	—
Marshall Islands	1.8	24.2	-3.9	-20.9	1.2	—	—	—
Micronesia, Federated States of	—	—	—	—	—	—	—	—
Nauru	—	—	—	—	—	—	—	—
Papua New Guinea	9.5	4.5	2.2	6.1	-4.2	-6.4	—	—
Samoa	10.8	-22.6	15.8	-0.3	-8.2	—	—	—
Solomon Islands	-0.2	6.2	7.7	-4.3	—	—	—	—
Tonga	2.7	-0.3	6.4	-5.4	-3.0	-3.8	—	—
Tuvalu	0.9	0.6	0.6	0.8	—	—	—	—
Vanuatu	11.0	2.2	6.4	6.7	—	—	—	—

Table A4 Growth Rate of Value Added in Industry
(percent per annum)

Economy	1993	1994	1995	1996	1997	1998	1999	2000
Newly Industrialized Economies								
Hong Kong, China	—	—	—	—	—	—	—	—
Korea, Rep. of	6.2	9.0	10.0	7.4	5.6	-7.5	2.3	4.3
Singapore	9.3	13.2	9.5	6.5	6.6	—	—	—
Taipei,China	4.1	5.7	5.7	3.7	5.7	-3.6	3.5	4.8
People's Rep. of China and Mongolia								
China, People's Rep. of	19.9	18.4	13.9	12.1	10.8	8.9	7.5	7.5
Mongolia	-6.9	2.1	14.6	0.5	3.9	2.9	—	—
Central Asian Republics								
Kazakhstan	-16.7	-24.7	-14.9	-3.5	5.0	—	—	—
Kyrgyz Republic	-22.8	-37.3	-12.3	2.6	19.8	-6.6	—	—
Tajikistan	-17.8	—	—	—	-2.8	5.0	—	—
Uzbekistan	-4.2	-6.6	-5.6	1.7	6.5	—	—	—
Southeast Asia								
Cambodia	13.0	7.7	9.8	18.1	3.0	0.0	2.0	—
Indonesia	9.8	11.2	10.4	10.7	5.6	-15.6	—	—
Lao People's Democratic Rep.	10.0	10.7	13.1	17.3	8.1	8.5	—	—
Malaysia	10.1	12.4	13.7	11.2	10.5	-8.1	0.6	1.5
Myanmar	11.0	10.3	12.7	10.9	6.7	4.5	—	—
Philippines	1.6	5.8	6.7	6.4	6.1	-1.7	1.8	4.0
Thailand	10.5	10.1	10.5	7.0	-0.1	-12.1	-2.3	2.0
Viet Nam	12.6	13.4	13.6	14.5	12.6	8.5	—	—
South Asia								
Bangladesh	8.0	7.8	8.4	5.3	3.6	8.1	5.1	7.5
Bhutan	7.3	13.9	16.9	8.4	4.9	6.0	12.3	—
India	—	9.3	12.2	6.0	5.9	4.9	—	—
Maldives	8.3	6.6	8.4	9.0	9.7	12.3	—	—
Nepal	4.8	9.0	4.0	8.3	3.5	0.2	1.0	1.6
Pakistan	5.5	4.5	4.8	5.4	1.0	6.2	2.5	5.2
Sri Lanka	9.8	8.1	7.8	5.6	7.9	—	—	—
The Pacific								
Cook Islands	-13.1	5.4	-15.9	-5.0	—	—	—	—
Fiji	5.6	3.9	1.8	6.6	-1.3	-4.3	—	—
Kiribati	1.7	14.3	0.6	-4.1	—	—	—	—
Marshall Islands	-7.5	14.7	18.7	-32.6	-6.1	—	—	—
Micronesia, Federated States of	—	—	—	—	—	—	—	—
Nauru	—	—	—	—	—	—	—	—
Papua New Guinea	35.8	1.3	-9.7	3.3	-14.2	18.9	—	—
Samoa	2.2	-3.2	0.3	3.8	-3.3	—	—	—
Solomon Islands	6.1	10.2	34.1	32.0	—	—	—	—
Tonga	5.8	12.6	15.0	2.9	-28.1	1.9	—	—
Tuvalu	-13.6	4.8	-13.1	82.6	—	—	—	—
Vanuatu	1.2	7.3	6.4	2.3	—	—	—	—

Table A5 Growth Rate of Value Added in Services
(percent per annum)

Economy	1993	1994	1995	1996	1997	1998	1999	2000
Newly Industrialized Economies								
Hong Kong, China	—	—	—	—	—	—	—	—
Korea, Rep. of	6.8	9.3	8.7	7.2	5.9	-3.5	1.7	3.9
Singapore	10.7	9.5	8.3	7.3	8.8	—	—	—
Taipei,China	7.9	7.8	6.4	7.3	7.8	10.6	5.9	7.3
People's Rep. of China and Mongolia								
China, People's Rep. of	10.7	9.6	8.4	7.9	8.2	9.0	8.5	8.5
Mongolia	1.0	2.0	0.2	-4.1	3.3	4.7	—	—
Central Asian Republics								
Kazakhstan	-4.1	0.2	-1.3	3.2	0.9	—	—	—
Kyrgyz Republic	-14.1	-17.1	-4.4	-0.2	0.6	4.5	—	—
Tajikistan	—	—	—	—	—	—	—	—
Uzbekistan	-3.0	-5.4	-0.5	5.3	4.6	—	—	—
Southeast Asia								
Cambodia	7.2	7.4	7.9	7.0	1.3	-1.7	4.2	—
Indonesia	7.4	7.1	7.6	6.8	5.7	-16.6	—	—
Lao People's Democratic Rep.	7.7	5.5	10.2	8.5	7.5	4.8	—	—
Malaysia	9.7	9.5	9.2	9.5	7.7	1.2	1.6	2.5
Myanmar	6.1	8.3	7.3	6.4	5.1	5.0	—	—
Philippines	2.5	4.2	5.0	6.4	5.5	3.5	3.0	4.5
Thailand	9.3	8.9	9.0	4.6	-1.1	-6.8	1.5	3.0
Viet Nam	8.6	9.6	9.8	8.8	7.1	1.4	—	—
South Asia								
Bangladesh	5.3	5.8	6.9	6.5	6.2	6.5	5.6	6.5
Bhutan	10.1	6.2	5.9	5.2	8.8	8.0	8.5	—
India	—	8.5	9.8	8.0	8.2	—	—	—
Maldives	7.9	8.2	8.6	7.4	6.8	6.6	—	—
Nepal	7.3	7.7	6.0	5.8	4.0	4.6	3.1	3.2
Pakistan	4.6	4.2	4.8	4.8	2.1	4.8	3.0	5.3
Sri Lanka	6.2	5.1	4.9	6.0	6.7	—	—	—
The Pacific								
Cook Islands	7.0	3.8	-3.6	-0.8	—	—	—	—
Fiji	1.9	3.5	5.2	2.4	1.8	-1.8	—	—
Kiribati	1.1	11.3	0.7	8.7	—	—	—	—
Marshall Islands	4.3	-1.0	2.6	-10.7	-7.4	—	—	—
Micronesia, Federated States of	—	—	—	—	—	—	—	—
Nauru	—	—	—	—	—	—	—	—
Papua New Guinea	-8.6	9.8	-1.5	1.2	6.1	-4.9	—	—
Samoa	-1.8	11.0	6.9	11.4	6.2	—	—	—
Solomon Islands	4.7	2.9	-0.2	-2.2	—	—	—	—
Tonga	2.1	4.5	1.7	0.1	-2.4	1.6	—	—
Tuvalu	10.9	14.7	-4.8	13.4	—	—	—	—
Vanuatu	3.1	1.7	1.4	2.5	—	—	—	—

Table A6 Sectoral Share of GDP
(percent)

Economy	Agriculture			Industry			Services		
	1970	1980	1998	1970	1980	1998	1970	1980	1998
Newly Industrialized Economies									
Hong Kong, China	—	0.9	—	—	32.0	—	—	67.2	—
Korea, Rep. of	29.8	14.2	6.1	23.8	37.8	43.2	46.4	48.1	50.6
Singapore	2.2	1.1	—	36.4	38.8	—	61.4	60.0	—
Taipei,China	—	7.9	2.3	—	46.0	34.7	—	46.1	62.9
People's Rep. of China and Mongolia									
China, People's Rep. of	42.2	25.6	16.3	44.6	51.7	55.4	13.2	22.7	28.3
Mongolia	33.1	17.4	37.3	26.3	33.3	34.1	40.6	49.3	28.7
Central Asian Republics									
Kazakhstan	—	—	—	—	—	—	—	—	—
Kyrgyz Republic	—	—	52.5	—	—	18.7	—	—	28.8
Tajikistan	—	—	—	—	—	—	—	—	—
Uzbekistan	—	—	—	—	—	—	—	—	—
Southeast Asia									
Cambodia	—	—	43.4	—	—	20.8	—	—	35.8
Indonesia	35.0	24.4	17.2	28.0	41.3	42.3	37.0	34.3	40.5
Lao People's Democratic Rep.	—	—	52.6	—	—	22.0	—	—	25.4
Malaysia	—	22.9	11.3	—	35.8	45.8	—	41.3	42.9
Myanmar	49.5	47.9	43.5	12.0	12.3	16.6	38.5	39.8	39.9
Philippines	28.2	23.5	19.4	33.7	40.5	35.5	38.1	36.0	45.1
Thailand	30.2	20.2	12.0	25.7	30.1	40.4	44.1	49.7	47.6
Viet Nam	—	42.7	23.9	—	26.3	34.0	—	31.0	42.1
South Asia									
Bangladesh	—	49.4	31.6	—	14.8	19.6	—	35.8	48.8
Bhutan	—	56.7	35.6	—	12.2	29.4	—	31.1	35.0
India	44.5	38.1	26.2	23.9	25.9	26.8	31.6	36.0	47.0
Maldives	—	—	17.9	—	—	17.3	—	—	64.8
Nepal	—	61.8	40.8	—	11.9	19.4	—	26.3	39.8
Pakistan	40.1	30.6	24.6	19.6	25.6	26.8	40.3	43.8	48.6
Sri Lanka	30.7	26.6	—	27.1	27.2	—	42.2	46.2	—
The Pacific									
Cook Islands	—	—	—	—	—	—	—	—	—
Fiji	30.2	22.5	16.1	23.1	21.7	26.2	46.7	55.8	57.6
Kiribati	—	—	—	—	—	—	—	—	—
Marshall Islands	—	—	—	—	—	—	—	—	—
Micronesia, Federated States of	—	—	—	—	—	—	—	—	—
Nauru	—	—	—	—	—	—	—	—	—
Papua New Guinea	—	—	28.0	—	—	24.2	—	—	47.8
Samoa	—	—	—	—	—	—	—	—	—
Solomon Islands	—	52.5	—	—	10.0	—	—	37.4	—
Tonga	—	47.6	34.7	—	11.0	12.2	—	41.4	53.1
Tuvalu	—	—	—	—	—	—	—	—	—
Vanuatu	—	—	—	—	—	—	—	—	—

Table A7 Gross Domestic Savings
(percentage of GDP)

Economy	1993	1994	1995	1996	1997	1998	1999	2000
Newly Industrialized Economies								
Hong Kong, China	34.6	33.1	30.5	30.7	31.8	30.5	31.0	31.0
Korea, Rep. of	35.4	35.0	35.2	33.7	33.1	42.3	34.1	31.7
Singapore	46.3	48.8	50.9	51.2	51.8	52.2	50.0	49.0
Taipei,China	27.0	25.8	25.6	25.1	24.8	25.1	24.8	25.3
People's Rep. of China and Mongolia								
China, People's Rep. of	41.9	41.5	41.1	40.5	41.5	41.5	41.0	40.5
Mongolia	20.1	16.1	21.8	19.9	21.9	27.0	—	—
Central Asian Republics								
Kazakhstan	—	14.0	17.4	8.2	8.7	—	—	—
Kyrgyz Republic	4.0	2.7	5.5	-0.6	2.5	-2.0	—	—
Tajikistan	—	—	—	—	—	—	—	—
Uzbekistan	-5.4	7.8	20.4	7.9	12.0	—	—	—
Southeast Asia								
Cambodia	4.5	4.8	5.0	10.6	10.6	5.9	7.6	8.1
Indonesia	27.6	29.1	28.5	27.3	29.9	19.1	18.5	19.0
Lao People's Democratic Rep.	—	—	—	—	—	—	—	—
Malaysia	37.7	38.8	39.5	42.6	43.8	48.0	47.1	46.1
Myanmar	11.4	11.7	13.4	11.5	10.4	12.1	—	—
Philippines	15.2	17.0	16.8	18.5	20.3	20.0	20.2	20.3
Thailand	34.9	34.7	33.6	33.7	32.9	35.9	33.2	33.0
Viet Nam	16.5	17.5	16.1	17.8	21.5	24.6	22.0	23.0
South Asia								
Bangladesh	14.2	16.1	16.9	14.3	14.8	14.8	14.5	15.0
Bhutan	26.1	27.2	27.0	29.0	30.0	31.0	32.0	—
India	19.5	20.8	24.4	24.6	23.3	23.5	23.7	24.0
Maldives	21.1	33.1	41.4	43.5	—	—	—	—
Nepal	15.5	16.3	16.6	15.6	15.7	16.7	16.1	17.0
Pakistan	13.5	15.6	14.2	11.6	11.3	15.1	12.2	13.0
Sri Lanka	16.0	15.2	15.3	15.5	21.4	19.3	20.8	22.1
The Pacific								
Cook Islands	—	—	—	—	—	—		—
Fiji	10.0	12.4	12.9	14.7	13.1	7.6	—	—
Kiribati	—	—	—	—	—	—	—	—
Marshall Islands	—	—	—	—	—	—	—	—
Micronesia, Federated States of	—	—	—	—	—	—	—	—
Nauru	—	—	—	—	—	—	—	—
Papua New Guinea	31.0	25.1	28.9	32.1	23.0	28.3	—	—
Samoa	—	—	—	—	—	—	—	—
Solomon Islands	—	—	—	—	—	—	—	—
Tonga	-9.6	-10.5	-15.1	—	—	—	—	—
Tuvalu	—	—	—	—	—	—	—	—
Vanuatu	22.3	23.1	26.1	—	—	—	—	—

Table A8 Gross Domestic Investment
(percentage of GDP)

Economy	1993	1994	1995	1996	1997	1998	1999	2000
Newly Industrialized Economies								
Hong Kong, China	27.6	31.9	34.8	32.1	35.4	30.2	30.5	31.5
Korea, Rep. of	35.1	36.1	37.0	38.4	35.0	29.0	27.3	28.8
Singapore	37.7	32.7	33.1	35.3	37.4	34.0	34.5	34.5
Taipei,China	25.2	23.9	23.7	21.2	22.0	22.7	22.4	23.0
People's Rep. of China and Mongolia								
China, People's Rep. of	43.5	40.9	40.8	39.6	38.2	39.0	40.0	40.0
Mongolia	27.2	22.0	26.4	25.2	26.0	25.8	—	—
Central Asian Republics								
Kazakhstan	—	22.6	20.5	11.8	12.9	—	—	—
Kyrgyz Republic	11.7	9.0	18.3	25.2	15.8	14.7	—	—
Tajikistan	—	—	—	—	—	—	—	—
Uzbekistan	3.0	5.7	20.9	15.1	16.0	—	—	—
Southeast Asia								
Cambodia	14.1	18.5	21.8	25.9	19.0	15.0	18.4	19.0
Indonesia	29.5	31.1	31.9	30.7	31.3	18.0	17.5	20.0
Lao People's Democratic Rep.	—	—	—	—	—	—	—	—
Malaysia	37.8	40.4	43.5	41.5	42.0	33.2	34.5	35.0
Myanmar	12.4	12.4	14.2	12.3	11.1	12.8	—	—
Philippines	23.6	23.5	21.6	23.1	23.8	19.3	20.0	21.0
Thailand	39.9	40.3	41.6	41.7	35.0	24.4	24.7	27.0
Viet Nam	23.6	25.5	27.1	28.1	28.3	28.7	25.0	27.0
South Asia								
Bangladesh	14.1	13.8	16.6	17.0	17.3	16.3	17.5	17.0
Bhutan	45.8	48.2	45.7	44.4	47.0	48.0	49.0	—
India	20.8	22.9	25.8	25.7	24.8	25.2	25.2	25.3
Maldives	44.8	37.5	47.5	52.7	—	—	—	—
Nepal	23.1	22.4	25.2	27.3	25.1	25.5	25.0	25.5
Pakistan	20.5	19.4	18.3	18.7	17.5	17.4	14.8	16.2
Sri Lanka	25.6	27.0	25.7	24.2	24.4	26.6	28.6	30.0
The Pacific								
Cook Islands	—	—	—	—	—	—	—	—
Fiji	15.8	13.9	13.1	11.0	12.4	12.0	—	—
Kiribati	—	—	—	—	—	—	—	—
Marshall Islands	—	—	—	—	—	—	—	—
Micronesia, Federated States of	—	—	—	—	—	—	—	—
Nauru	—	—	—	—	—	—	—	—
Papua New Guinea	17.1	16.3	19.4	27.9	27.1	30.3	—	—
Samoa	—	—	—	—	—	—	—	—
Solomon Islands	—	—	—	—	—	—	—	—
Tonga	18.1	17.5	13.7	—	—	—	—	—
Tuvalu	25.9	67.6	68.0	48.1	—	—	—	—
Vanuatu	27.8	28.8	32.7	—	—	—	—	—

Table A9 Changes in Consumer Prices
(percent per annum)

Economy	1993	1994	1995	1996	1997	1998	1999	2000
Newly Industrialized Economies	4.7	5.7	4.7	4.3	3.5	3.8	1.1	2.3
Hong Kong, China	8.9	8.8	9.0	6.3	5.9	2.8	-1.5	1.0
Korea, Rep. of	4.8	6.2	4.5	5.0	4.5	7.5	2.0	3.0
Singapore	2.2	3.1	1.7	1.4	2.0	-1.5	0.5	2.0
Taipei,China	2.9	4.1	3.7	3.1	0.9	1.7	1.9	2.6
People's Rep. of China and Mongolia	14.8	24.3	17.1	8.4	2.8	-0.8	2.0	3.0
China, People's Rep. of	14.6	24.2	17.1	8.3	2.8	-0.8	2.0	3.0
Mongolia	183.0	66.3	53.1	58.7	17.5	6.0	9.5	5.0
Central Asian Republics	1,950.2	1,078.2	122.8	42.3	21.6	10.1	—	—
Kazakhstan	2,164.5	1,156.8	60.4	28.6	11.3	1.9	—	—
Kyrgyz Republic	1,366.0	87.2	31.9	35.0	14.7	18.4	—	—
Tajikistan	7,343.7	1.1	2,131.9	40.6	159.8	7.0	—	—
Uzbekistan	880.4	1,281.4	116.9	64.3	28.0	22.0	—	—
Southeast Asia	6.4	7.0	7.3	6.6	5.6	21.0	8.3	6.4
Cambodia	—	16.5	2.8	9.0	9.1	12.0	10.0	6.0
Indonesia	9.7	8.5	9.4	7.9	6.6	58.2	17.0	9.5
Lao People's Democratic Rep.	6.3	6.8	22.6	13.0	19.3	90.1	37.0	—
Malaysia	3.6	3.7	3.4	3.5	4.0	5.2	4.2	3.8
Myanmar	31.8	24.1	25.2	16.3	29.7	50.0	—	—
Philippines	7.6	9.0	8.1	9.1	6.0	9.7	8.5	7.0
Thailand	3.3	5.1	5.8	5.9	5.6	8.1	3.0	5.0
Viet Nam	5.2	14.4	12.7	4.5	3.6	9.2	8.0	7.0
South Asia	7.6	9.7	10.2	9.5	7.3	13.0	7.6	7.2
Bangladesh	1.3	1.8	5.2	6.6	2.6	7.0	8.0	6.0
Bhutan	11.2	7.0	9.6	8.8	7.0	9.0	10.0	—
India	7.5	10.1	10.3	9.4	6.9	14.4	7.5	7.0
Maldives	20.1	3.4	5.3	6.2	7.6	-2.2	—	—
Nepal	8.9	8.9	7.6	8.1	7.8	4.0	9.0	8.0
Pakistan	9.8	11.2	13.0	10.8	11.8	7.8	8.0	9.0
Sri Lanka	11.7	8.4	7.7	15.9	9.6	9.4	9.0	8.0
The Pacific	5.0	2.9	11.6	8.6	4.0	8.6	—	—
Cook Islands	7.3	2.7	0.9	-0.6	-0.4	1.0	—	—
Fiji	5.3	0.6	2.2	3.1	3.4	5.7	—	—
Kiribati	6.1	5.3	3.6	-1.5	2.2	2.0	—	—
Marshall Islands	5.0	5.7	8.3	9.8	4.8	4.0	—	—
Micronesia, Federated States of	6.0	4.0	4.0	4.0	3.0	3.0	—	—
Nauru	-3.6	0.0	1.7	4.0	6.1	4.0	—	—
Papua New Guinea	4.9	2.9	17.3	11.6	3.9	10.0	—	—
Samoa	1.7	12.1	-2.9	5.4	6.8	6.0	—	—
Solomon Islands	9.2	13.3	9.6	11.8	8.1	12.3	—	—
Tonga	0.9	1.1	1.4	3.0	2.1	3.0	—	—
Tuvalu	2.3	1.4	5.0	0.0	1.4	0.8	—	—
Vanuatu	3.6	2.3	2.2	0.9	2.8	3.9	—	—
Average for DMCs	8.4	19.6	10.7	7.3	4.6	6.5	3.7	4.1

Table A10 Growth Rate of Money Supply (M2)
(percent per annum)

Economy	1993	1994	1995	1996	1997	1998	1999	2000
Newly Industrialized Economies								
Hong Kong, China	16.2	12.9	14.6	10.9	8.3	11.8	8.5	9.0
Korea, Rep. of	16.6	18.7	15.6	15.8	14.1	27.9	20.0	20.0
Singapore	8.5	14.4	8.5	9.8	10.3	30.3	12.0	12.0
Taipei,China	15.4	15.1	9.4	9.1	8.0	8.4	8.6	8.9
People's Rep. of China and Mongolia								
China, People's Rep. of	37.3	34.5	29.5	25.3	17.3	15.3	17.0	17.0
Mongolia	227.6	79.5	32.9	25.8	32.5	-1.7	—	—
Central Asian Republics								
Kazakhstan	691.9	596.6	106.1	13.8	27.6	—	—	—
Kyrgyz Republic	181.5	117.8	78.2	21.3	25.3	18.2	—	—
Tajikistan	102.0	159.4	—	93.2	110.7	5.1	—	—
Uzbekistan	782.2	680.0	158.1	113.7	36.0	21.0	—	—
Southeast Asia								
Cambodia	34.4	34.9	44.3	40.4	16.6	15.7	30.0	25.0
Indonesia	20.8	22.1	28.0	26.7	52.7	62.3	25.0	22.0
Lao People's Democratic Rep.	64.6	31.9	16.4	26.7	65.8	109.7	80.0	—
Malaysia	22.1	14.7	24.0	20.9	18.5	4.7	5.4	7.0
Myanmar	25.5	33.0	31.6	29.9	25.0	—	—	—
Philippines	24.6	26.8	25.2	15.8	20.5	7.1	15.0	15.0
Thailand	18.4	12.9	17.0	12.6	16.4	9.6	11.0	13.0
Viet Nam	19.0	27.8	22.6	22.7	26.1	22.0	19.0	20.0
South Asia								
Bangladesh	10.6	15.4	16.0	8.2	10.8	10.1	10.0	8.0
Bhutan	16.2	21.5	29.9	30.4	30.9	41.7	—	—
India	18.4	22.3	13.7	16.2	17.6	19.8	18.1	17.5
Maldives	36.4	24.2	15.6	26.0	23.1	16.4	—	—
Nepal	27.7	19.6	16.1	14.4	11.9	16.9	16.0	15.0
Pakistan	18.0	16.9	16.6	14.9	12.2	14.2	9.0	12.0
Sri Lanka	23.4	19.7	19.2	10.8	13.8	13.0	13.4	11.5
The Pacific								
Cook Islands	6.5	—	—	6.9	-37.0	—	—	—
Fiji	6.7	2.7	4.3	0.9	16.0	-17.0	—	—
Kiribati	—	—	—	—	—	—	—	—
Marshall Islands	—	—	—	—	—	—	—	—
Micronesia, Federated States of	—	—	—	—	—	—	—	—
Nauru	—	—	—	—	—	—	—	—
Papua New Guinea	17.8	-1.3	13.7	30.7	7.7	1.9	—	—
Samoa	2.2	13.0	21.8	5.1	13.2	—	—	—
Solomon Islands	14.5	24.1	9.9	15.7	6.3	4.8	—	—
Tonga	4.1	8.8	17.1	2.8	14.1	2.1	—	—
Tuvalu	—	—	—	—	—	—	—	—
Vanuatu	4.9	2.9	13.3	10.1	-0.4	4.6	—	—

Table A11 Growth Rate of Merchandise Exports
(percent per annum)

Economy	1993	1994	1995	1996	1997	1998	1999	2000
Newly Industrialized Economies	10.5	15.9	21.1	4.6	3.3	-6.9	3.1	5.7
Hong Kong, China	13.2	11.9	14.8	4.0	4.0	-7.5	0.5	2.5
Korea, Rep. of	7.7	15.7	31.2	4.3	6.7	-4.9	2.0	6.0
Singapore	16.6	30.8	22.1	6.4	-3.1	-5.6	2.0	5.0
Taipei,China	4.5	9.4	20.0	3.8	5.4	-9.4	9.5	10.5
People's Rep. of China and Mongolia	8.7	35.4	24.9	17.8	21.0	0.4	-5.0	1.9
China, People's Rep. of	8.8	35.6	24.9	17.9	20.9	0.5	-5.0	1.9
Mongolia	2.8	0.3	32.3	-12.8	34.3	-17.5	8.4	9.3
Central Asian Republics	33.7	-1.9	38.8	12.5	6.4	-17.2	—	—
Kazakhstan	0.7	-8.4	57.2	21.8	7.6	—	—	—
Kyrgyz Republic	31.7	0.1	20.3	29.9	18.8	—	—	—
Tajikistan	146.5	22.6	50.1	-8.2	-3.1	-4.3	—	—
Uzbekistan	102.0	2.2	18.2	1.7	4.6	-19.8	—	—
Southeast Asia	11.7	20.9	22.7	6.7	6.5	-3.7	5.9	7.3
Cambodia	—	129.8	14.6	22.1	63.1	12.8	17.7	15.0
Indonesia	3.4	15.5	13.3	9.0	7.9	0.7	6.5	8.5
Lao People's Democratic Rep.	81.4	24.9	3.5	3.8	-1.8	22.3	—	—
Malaysia	16.1	23.1	26.1	7.3	6.0	-11.4	3.8	2.6
Myanmar	17.8	31.8	-2.8	4.6	7.5	—	—	—
Philippines	15.8	18.5	29.4	17.7	22.8	16.9	13.0	13.5
Thailand	13.4	22.1	24.8	-1.9	3.8	-6.6	5.1	8.5
Viet Nam	20.6	35.8	28.2	41.0	22.2	3.9	5.0	6.0
South Asia	15.3	13.1	20.2	6.5	3.2	-0.7	-0.4	5.2
Bangladesh	19.5	6.3	37.1	11.8	14.0	16.8	8.0	12.0
Bhutan	4.9	-4.2	11.7	9.3	1.7	12.0	—	—
India	20.2	18.4	20.3	5.6	2.1	-5.1	1.5	4.5
Maldives	-19.0	43.3	12.6	-6.0	15.8	-1.8	—	—
Nepal	18.0	3.6	-9.7	1.9	10.2	11.7	9.0	9.0
Pakistan	0.3	-1.4	16.1	7.1	-2.6	4.0	-10.1	10.2
Sri Lanka	16.4	12.0	18.6	7.6	13.3	6.7	6.0	7.0
The Pacific	28.0	7.9	1.9	-1.6	-14.1	-4.5	—	—
Cook Islands	19.2	6.8	10.4	-31.0	-10.1	—	—	—
Fiji	6.1	31.8	6.1	23.3	-18.0	-17.8	—	—
Kiribati	-28.0	50.9	43.0	-26.0	—	—	—	—
Marshall Islands	-15.6	129.6	23.1	-12.2	28.4	-16.3	—	—
Micronesia, Federated States of	33.8	135.9	-26.1	-34.7	3.1	-3.0	—	—
Nauru	—	—	—	—	—	—	—	—
Papua New Guinea	33.4	2.5	0.4	-5.6	-15.1	7.6	—	—
Samoa	10.5	-45.3	149.1	15.1	41.8	43.4	—	—
Solomon Islands	24.4	11.3	17.1	-3.5	0.2	—	—	—
Tonga	-28.3	34.7	6.4	-25.7	3.9	-9.8	—	—
Tuvalu	2.1	10.5	4.3	9.8	—	—	—	—
Vanuatu	-4.2	10.1	13.2	6.4	17.3	—	—	—
Average for DMCs	11.1	18.9	22.0	7.1	6.7	-4.5	2.0	5.1

Table A12 Direction of Exports
(percent share)

From \ To	DMCs		Japan		USA		EU		Australia/ New Zealand		Others	
	1985	1997	1985	1997	1985	1997	1985	1997	1985	1997	1985	1997
Newly Industrialized Economies												
Hong Kong, China	35.6	46.6	4.2	6.1	30.8	21.8	11.8	14.7	2.3	1.5	15.3	9.3
Korea, Rep. of	12.9	39.2	15.0	10.9	35.6	15.9	10.4	11.2	1.3	1.6	24.7	21.3
Singapore	36.7	50.1	9.4	7.1	21.2	18.5	10.1	13.9	4.4	2.7	18.1	7.8
Taipei,China	15.6	—	11.3	—	15.5	—	5.5	—	2.4	—	49.7	—
PRC and Mongolia												
China, People's Rep. of	38.2	39.4	22.3	17.4	8.5	17.9	7.8	13.0	0.8	1.3	22.5	11.0
Mongolia	3.1	41.2	11.2	23.5	5.5	9.3	20.5	7.4	0.0	—	59.6	18.6
Central Asian Republics												
Kazakhstan	—	16.6	—	1.7	—	2.2	—	26.8	0.0	—	—	52.7
Kyrgyz Republic	—	45.4	—	0.2	—	1.6	—	5.9	—	—	—	46.8
Tajikistan	—	54.4	—	0.2	—	1.4	—	14.8	—	—	—	29.2
Uzbekistan	—	19.0	—	1.1	—	1.3	—	19.9	—	—	—	58.8
Southeast Asia												
Cambodia	67.9	73.1	7.0	1.0	—	13.8	13.2	11.2	—	0.2	11.9	0.8
Indonesia	17.2	34.8	46.2	24.4	21.7	14.4	6.0	14.9	1.2	3.2	7.6	8.3
Lao People's Democratic Rep.	71.9	18.2	6.6	3.6	2.7	3.6	0.5	41.7	5.5	—	12.7	32.8
Malaysia	38.1	46.0	24.6	12.5	12.8	18.6	13.6	14.4	1.9	2.0	9.1	6.5
Myanmar	47.1	51.0	8.4	7.6	0.8	9.5	8.4	11.8	—	0.7	35.4	19.4
Philippines	19.5	23.9	19.0	16.0	35.9	34.4	13.8	16.1	2.1	1.1	9.7	8.5
Thailand	27.1	36.0	13.4	15.2	19.7	19.4	17.8	15.9	1.9	1.8	20.1	11.7
Viet Nam	50.4	22.8	17.4	22.7	—	4.3	6.2	27.4	2.2	5.2	23.8	17.5
South Asia												
Bangladesh	14.5	7.7	7.2	2.4	18.1	33.3	13.0	41.3	1.8	0.5	45.5	14.8
Bhutan	—	—	—	—	—	—	—	—	—	—	—	—
India	8.9	23.1	11.1	5.6	18.9	19.3	16.7	25.4	1.4	1.4	43.0	25.1
Maldives	50.8	37.6	10.1	18.3	24.3	20.4	4.0	22.6	—	—	10.9	1.1
Nepal	41.4	23.9	0.7	0.8	35.3	29.2	20.3	41.4	0.1	0.3	2.3	4.6
Pakistan	16.0	19.2	11.3	5.2	10.0	18.8	20.9	31.1	1.1	1.8	40.6	23.9
Sri Lanka	11.2	8.3	5.1	5.0	22.3	35.8	17.9	29.5	1.7	1.2	41.9	20.1
The Pacific												
Cook Islands	—	—	—	—	—	—	—	—	—	—	—	—
Fiji	22.5	14.0	3.0	4.9	4.9	13.6	31.0	17.5	18.2	38.0	20.4	12.0
Kiribati	7.2	—	4.3	—	—	—	44.5	—	0.5	—	43.5	—
Marshall Islands	—	—	—	—	—	—	—	—	—	—	—	—
Micronesia, Federated States of	—	—	—	—	—	—	—	—	—	—	—	—
Nauru	—	—	—	—	—	—	—	—	—	—	—	—
Papua New Guinea	9.9	15.5	22.1	17.1	4.0	2.4	46.5	15.0	12.0	26.8	5.6	23.2
Samoa	0.3	3.2	0.9	1.6	59.4	6.3	5.8	4.8	29.7	73.0	3.9	11.1
Solomon Islands	11.1	21.8	52.1	59.2	2.4	0.6	26.3	12.8	3.2	2.2	5.0	3.4
Tonga	5.9	—	0.2	52.9	3.2	17.6	0.5	5.9	83.1	11.8	7.1	11.8
Tuvalu	—	—	—	—	—	—	—	—	—	—	—	—
Vanuatu	1.4	3.8	6.7	32.1	—	3.8	25.4	45.3	1.6	1.9	65.0	13.2
Total for DMCs	25.6	40.4	16.5	11.7	26.3	18.8	10.7	14.8	2.1	1.9	18.8	12.4

Table A13 Growth Rate of Merchandise Imports
(percent per annum)

Economy	1993	1994	1995	1996	1997	1998	1999	2000
Newly Industrialized Economies	4.5	15.2	24.1	5.0	5.2	-21.3	5.7	11.0
Hong Kong, China	12.3	16.7	19.1	3.0	5.1	-11.6	-0.5	3.0
Korea, Rep. of	2.3	22.6	31.9	12.3	-2.2	-36.1	15.0	18.0
Singapore	18.0	20.4	21.3	5.4	0.1	-9.0	4.0	5.2
Taipei,China	7.1	10.4	21.2	-0.1	9.7	-5.6	6.8	11.2
People's Rep. of China and Mongolia	33.8	10.3	15.6	19.4	3.8	-1.5	5.0	6.0
China, People's Rep. of	34.1	10.4	15.5	19.5	3.8	-1.5	5.0	6.0
Mongolia	-2.7	-1.1	32.0	4.5	5.4	7.0	0.8	6.5
Central Asian Republics	37.5	-15.2	24.4	23.6	-0.4	-22.6	—	—
Kazakhstan	9.9	-18.3	28.1	22.8	8.1	—	—	—
Kyrgyz Republic	34.7	-4.6	24.6	47.5	-17.5	—	—	—
Tajikistan	175.0	7.1	24.5	-13.5	3.2	-0.3	—	—
Uzbekistan	96.3	-16.2	18.7	30.9	-11.2	-27.3	—	—
Southeast Asia	14.6	22.4	28.4	6.5	-3.1	-21.9	9.2	10.7
Cambodia	—	66.9	36.1	13.6	2.1	3.4	21.4	18.0
Indonesia	6.6	17.1	21.6	10.4	-6.8	-11.3	9.0	13.0
Lao People's Democratic Rep.	60.0	30.6	4.4	17.2	-6.1	-4.2	—	—
Malaysia	17.8	28.1	29.9	1.7	7.0	-22.5	6.6	4.1
Myanmar	28.9	14.3	2.3	8.2	7.0	—	—	—
Philippines	21.2	21.2	23.7	20.8	14.0	-18.4	13.5	16.0
Thailand	12.3	18.4	31.9	0.6	-13.4	-32.3	12.6	14.5
Viet Nam	39.3	48.5	43.8	38.9	-1.6	-2.3	4.0	6.5
South Asia	14.3	19.2	20.6	12.6	3.1	0.1	0.7	7.0
Bangladesh	15.5	2.9	39.2	19.1	3.1	5.3	10.0	8.0
Bhutan	50.4	-25.7	22.1	-8.2	18.4	3.7	—	—
India	15.1	34.3	21.6	12.1	4.4	0.9	4.5	7.7
Maldives	5.9	9.7	20.9	12.6	15.6	3.3	—	—
Nepal	14.9	21.9	21.7	5.8	21.6	-12.6	2.0	5.0
Pakistan	11.7	-13.6	18.5	16.7	-6.4	-8.2	-16.9	10.0
Sri Lanka	14.4	18.8	11.4	2.4	7.6	7.1	6.2	5.6
The Pacific	-1.8	11.4	0.4	10.4	-2.6	-17.9	—	—
Cook Islands	4.4	-14.0	-0.4	-10.7	14.9	—	—	—
Fiji	21.2	10.2	5.8	10.3	-2.5	-16.7	—	—
Kiribati	-22.4	-8.3	33.4	0.9	—	—	—	—
Marshall Islands	1.3	11.1	8.5	-0.9	-15.8	-9.3	—	—
Micronesia, Federated States of	11.2	16.6	-22.2	-26.8	-6.7	-2.4	—	—
Nauru	—	—	—	—	—	—	—	—
Papua New Guinea	-14.2	17.2	-4.5	19.3	-2.0	-6.2	—	—
Samoa	-6.7	-22.0	15.2	7.3	1.2	9.6	—	—
Solomon Islands	22.8	3.9	8.6	-1.9	23.8	—	—	—
Tonga	3.3	10.3	35.4	-9.9	-10.0	31.8	—	—
Tuvalu	26.9	11.9	6.4	9.8	—	—	—	—
Vanuatu	-2.2	13.4	6.4	2.5	-3.6	—	—	—
Average for DMCs	13.1	16.2	23.5	8.7	2.1	-15.6	6.0	9.4

Table A14 Balance of Trade
($ million)

Economy	1993	1994	1995	1996	1997	1998	1999	2000
Newly Industrialized Economies	-1,118	-7,667	-16,936	-21,032	-19,243	34,851	26,841	14,920
Hong Kong, China	-3,808	-10,923	-19,594	-18,352	-21,121	-10,946	-9,151	-10,300
Korea, Rep. of	2,318	-2,860	-4,444	-14,965	-3,179	41,165	30,205	19,508
Singapore	-11,135	-5,731	-6,132	-5,283	-9,308	-4,332	-6,803	-7,391
Taipei,China	11,508	11,847	13,235	17,568	14,365	8,963	12,590	13,102
People's Rep. of China and Mongolia	-10,663	7,287	18,047	19,463	46,250	49,073	33,209	28,064
China, People's Rep. of	-10,654	7,290	18,050	19,550	46,220	49,180	33,281	28,127
Mongolia	-9	-4	-3	-87	30	-107	-72	-63
Central Asian Republics	-2,251	-941	-149	-1,275	-511	5	—	—
Kazakhstan	-1,561	-920	-223	-326	-385	—	—	—
Kyrgyz Republic	-107	-86	-122	-252	-15	-151	—	—
Tajikistan	-204	-148	-41	9	-39	-69	—	—
Uzbekistan	-379	213	237	-706	-72	225	—	—
Southeast Asia	-5,871	-9,263	-21,126	-22,137	-1,136	40,368	36,995	33,019
Cambodia	-203	-275	-424	-459	-269	-228	-299	-352
Indonesia	7,377	8,039	6,252	6,219	13,459	18,667	18,933	18,685
Lao People's Democratic Rep.	-191	-264	-278	-368	-331	-233	—	—
Malaysia	3,037	1,577	-104	3,826	3,876	11,649	10,485	9,841
Myanmar	-606	-571	-631	-715	-760	—	—	—
Philippines	-6,222	-7,850	-8,944	-11,342	-11,127	-174	-345	-1,233
Thailand	-8,516	-8,730	-14,652	-16,148	-4,626	11,468	8,938	6,892
Viet Nam	-547	-1,190	-2,345	-3,150	-1,358	-780	-718	-813
South Asia	-10,823	-15,069	-18,877	-24,128	-24,874	-25,358	-26,443	-29,198
Bangladesh	-1,688	-1,657	-2,361	-3,063	-2,735	-2,373	-2,714	-2,707
Bhutan	-59	-30	-43	-27	-45	-40	—	—
India	-4,056	-9,049	-11,359	-14,815	-16,277	-18,514	-20,340	-22,980
Maldives	-125	-120	-151	-186	-215	-226	—	—
Nepal	-481	-656	-922	-990	-1,245	-992	-981	-1,010
Pakistan	-3,267	-2,000	-2,537	-3,704	-3,145	-1,895	-1,000	-1,085
Sri Lanka	-1,147	-1,558	-1,504	-1,344	-1,213	-1,318	-1,409	-1,415
The Pacific	761	737	793	451	41	590	—	—
Cook Islands	-53	-45	-44	-40	-47	—	—	—
Fiji	-276	-223	-235	-191	-286	-244	—	—
Kiribati	-25	-21	-28	-30	—	—	—	—
Marshall Islands	-53	-50	-51	-53	-36	-34	—	—
Micronesia, Federated States of	-109	-94	-76	-59	-52	-51	—	—
Nauru	—	—	—	—	—	—	—	—
Papua New Guinea	1,469	1,339	1,410	1,015	663	918	—	—
Western Samoa	-96	-77	-83	-89	-86	-89	—	—
Solomon Islands	-8	2	14	11	-25	—	—	—
Tonga	-38	-38	-57	-54	-47	91	—	—
Tuvalu	-6	-7	-7	-8	—	—	—	—
Vanuatu	-43	-50	-51	-51	-43	—	—	—
Total for DMCs	-29,964	-24,917	-38,248	-48,657	527	99,528	70,601	46,806

Table A15 Balance of Payments on Current Account
($ million)

Economy	1993	1994	1995	1996	1997	1998	1999	2000
Newly Industrialized Economies	3,915	7,687	4,198	2,508	14,354	60,050	32,373	19,767
Hong Kong, China	—	—	—	—	—	—	—	—
Korea, Rep. of	939	-3,868	-8,507	-23,005	-8,167	40,039	25,000	12,000
Singapore	-4,066	5,057	7,231	14,486	14,833	15,362	—	—
Taipei,China	7,042	6,498	5,474	11,027	7,688	4,649	7,373	7,767
People's Rep. of China and Mongolia	-11,943	7,617	1,565	7,180	29,733	24,876	9,910	4,917
China, People's Rep. of	-11,903	7,657	1,617	7,280	29,720	25,000	10,000	5,000
Mongolia	-40	-40	-52	-101	13	-124	-90	-83
Central Asian Republics	-1,798	-1,041	-825	-2,233	-1,690	-89	—	—
Kazakhstan	-1,072	-905	-517	-752	-909	—	—	—
Kyrgyz Republic	-88	-84	-235	-425	-139	—	—	—
Tajikistan	-209	-170	-53	-76	-60	-89	—	—
Uzbekistan	-429	118	-21	-980	-583	—	—	—
Southeast Asia	-16,692	-20,865	-33,999	-34,710	-16,751	19,810	14,471	12,047
Cambodia	-189	-329	-494	-479	-264	-262	-346	-394
Indonesia	-2,940	-3,488	-6,987	-8,069	-1,698	1,423	—	—
Lao People's Democratic Rep.	-144	-221	-235	-302	-282	-146	—	—
Malaysia	-2,991	-4,521	-8,470	-4,596	-4,791	5,113	3,671	4,282
Myanmar	-292	-195	-303	-386	-421	—	—	—
Philippines	-3,016	-2,950	-1,980	-3,953	-4,351	1,300	1,000	-100
Thailand	-6,159	-7,862	-13,248	-14,380	-3,130	13,500	11,000	9,500
Viet Nam	-961	-1,298	-2,282	-2,545	-1,814	-1,118	-854	-1,241
South Asia	-6,072	-6,725	-10,279	-11,845	-11,903	-11,377	-3,459	-2,899
Bangladesh	-255	-89	-664	-1,291	-534	-353	-1,026	-722
Bhutan	-64	-40	-33	-36	-60	-47	—	—
India	-1,526	-3,785	-6,244	-4,904	-6,824	-8,256	—	—
Maldives	-54	-11	-18	-7	-36	-36	—	—
Nepal	-295	-225	-343	-527	-460	-380	—	—
Pakistan	-3,327	-1,651	-2,163	-4,348	-3,557	-1,827	-1,600	-1,285
Sri Lanka	-551	-924	-814	-732	-432	-477	-833	-892
The Pacific	526	517	686	436	-24	-31	—	—
Cook Islands	—	—	—	—	—	—	—	—
Fiji	-75	-63	-19	61	15	-65	—	—
Kiribati	-4	1	-6	-7	—	—	—	—
Marshall Islands	-1	5	2	4	16	21	—	—
Micronesia, Federated States of	-4	13	46	62	64	67	—	—
Nauru	—	—	—	—	—	—	—	—
Papua New Guinea	646	573	673	312	-116	-45	—	—
Samoa	-31	5	8	11	17	10	—	—
Solomon Islands	-7	-2	9	5	-24	—	—	—
Tonga	4	-8	-22	-11	-2	-19	—	—
Tuvalu	1	1	1	0	—	—	—	—
Vanuatu	-2	-8	-5	-1	6	—	—	—
Total for DMCs	-32,064	-12,810	-38,654	-38,664	13,719	93,240	53,295	33,832

Table A16 Balance of Payments on Current Account
(percentage of GDP)

Economy	1993	1994	1995	1996	1997	1998	1999	2000
Newly Industrialized Economies	0.6	1.1	0.5	0.3	1.7	9.2	4.9	2.8
Hong Kong, China	—	—	—	—	—	—	—	—
Korea, Rep. of	0.3	-1.0	-1.9	-4.7	-1.8	13.2	6.8	2.9
Singapore	-7.0	7.1	8.5	15.4	15.4	18.2	15.5	14.5
Taipei,China	3.2	2.7	2.1	4.0	2.7	1.8	2.5	2.3
People's Rep. of China and Mongolia	-2.0	1.4	0.2	0.9	3.2	2.5	0.9	0.4
China, People's Rep. of	-2.0	1.4	0.2	0.9	3.2	2.5	1.0	0.5
Mongolia	-7.1	-5.9	-5.5	-10.0	1.3	-12.1	-7.6	-7.0
Central Asian Republics	-9.2	-5.7	-2.9	-6.0	-4.2	-7.2	—	—
Kazakhstan	-9.5	-8.6	-3.1	-3.6	-4.0	—	—	—
Kyrgyz Republic	-9.5	-7.6	-15.7	-23.2	-7.9	—	—	—
Tajikistan	-31.0	-21.0	-9.0	-7.4	-5.5	-7.2	—	—
Uzbekistan	-8.4	2.1	-0.2	-7.2	-4.0	—	—	—
Southeast Asia	-3.9	-4.3	-6.1	-5.5	-3.3	5.2	4.4	3.2
Cambodia	-9.4	-13.7	-16.8	-15.3	-8.4	-9.1	-10.8	-10.9
Indonesia	-1.9	-2.0	-3.4	-3.4	-1.4	1.1	1.0	-1.0
Lao People's Democratic Rep.	-10.8	-14.3	-13.2	-16.1	-16.1	-10.4	—	—
Malaysia	-4.7	-6.2	-9.7	-5.0	-5.3	8.1	5.5	4.1
Myanmar	-0.5	-0.2	-0.3	-0.3	-0.2	—	—	—
Philippines	-5.5	-4.6	-2.7	-4.7	-5.3	2.0	1.3	-0.2
Thailand	-4.9	-5.4	-7.9	-7.9	-2.0	11.5	8.5	6.0
Viet Nam	-7.1	-8.0	-11.0	-10.3	-6.8	-4.1	-3.0	-4.0
South Asia	-1.6	-1.6	-2.1	-2.3	-2.2	-2.0	-3.1	-2.5
Bangladesh	-1.1	-0.3	-2.3	-4.1	-1.7	-1.1	-3.0	-2.0
Bhutan	-27.2	-14.7	-10.7	-10.9	-15.6	-12.0	—	—
India	-0.5	-1.1	-1.7	-1.2	-1.6	-1.8	-1.6	-1.4
Maldives	-24.8	-4.6	-6.7	-2.2	-10.6	-9.9	—	—
Nepal	-7.4	-5.6	-8.1	-11.7	-9.4	-8.8	-8.9	-8.5
Pakistan	-6.4	-3.2	-3.5	-6.7	-5.8	-3.0	-2.5	-1.9
Sri Lanka	-5.3	-7.9	-6.2	-5.3	-2.9	-3.1	-5.2	-5.2
The Pacific	7.1	6.2	8.0	4.4	-1.1	-1.6	—	—
Cook Islands	—	—	—	—	—	—	—	—
Fiji	-4.6	-3.5	-0.9	2.9	0.7	-4.1	—	—
Kiribati	-13.1	2.9	-13.2	-13.6	—	—	—	—
Marshall Islands	-1.5	5.1	1.5	3.6	16.9	22.2	—	—
Micronesia, Federated States of	-1.9	6.5	22.3	28.6	30.0	31.4	—	—
Nauru	—	—	—	—	—	—	—	—
Papua New Guinea	12.8	10.6	13.6	5.9	-2.4	-1.1	—	—
Samoa	-25.3	2.6	4.2	5.1	7.3	—	—	—
Solomon Islands	-3.1	-0.8	3.0	1.4	—	—	—	—
Tonga	3.0	-5.2	-13.2	-5.9	-0.8	-11.2	—	—
Tuvalu	13.3	10.0	4.7	2.3	—	—	—	—
Vanuatu	-1.3	-3.5	-2.1	-0.6	2.2	—	—	—
Average for DMCs	-1.6	-0.6	-1.5	-1.3	0.5	3.6	2.5	1.4

Table A17 Foreign Direct Investment
($ million)

Economy	1992	1993	1994	1995	1996	1997
Newly Industrialized Economies	5,861	7,858	12,552	13,645	16,129	17,189
Hong Kong, China	2,051	1,667	2,000	2,100	2,500	2,600
Korea, Rep. of	727	588	809	1,776	2,325	2,341
Singapore	2,204	4,686	8,368	8,210	9,440	10,000
Taipei,China	879	917	1,375	1,559	1,864	2,248
People's Rep. of China and Mongolia	11,158	27,523	33,794	35,859	40,805	45,307
China, People's Rep. of	11,156	27,515	33,787	35,849	40,800	45,300
Mongolia	2	8	7	10	5	7
Central Asian Republics	140	423	764	1,172	1,255	1,492
Kazakhstan	100	150	185	941	1,137	1,320
Kyrgyz Republic	—	228	519	96	47	83
Tajikistan	—	—	10	15	16	4
Uzbekistan	40	45	50	120	55	85
Southeast Asia	9,899	10,808	10,325	14,302	17,364	15,527
Cambodia	33	54	69	151	294	200
Indonesia	1,777	2,004	2,109	4,348	6,194	5,350
Lao People's Democratic Rep.	8	30	59	95	160	90
Malaysia	5,183	5,006	4,342	4,132	4,672	3,754
Myanmar	171	149	91	115	100	80
Philippines	228	1,238	1,591	1,459	1,520	1,253
Thailand	2,114	1,804	1,322	2,002	2,268	3,600
Viet Nam	385	523	742	2,000	2,156	1,200
South Asia	717	1,137	1,581	2,753	3,313	4,379
Bangladesh	18	10	8	2	14	145
Bhutan	—	—	—	—	—	—
India	233	574	973	1,964	2,382	3,264
Maldives	7	7	9	7	8	10
Nepal	1	4	6	5	19	20
Pakistan	335	347	419	719	770	800
Sri Lanka	123	195	166	56	120	140
The Pacific	443	131	108	577	177	368
Cook Islands	—	—	—	—	—	—
Fiji	104	91	68	70	10	12
Kiribati	—	-1	—	—	1	1
Marshall Islands	—	—	—	—	—	—
Micronesia, Federated States of	—	—	—	—	—	—
Nauru	—	—	—	—	—	—
Papua New Guinea	294	-2	-5	455	111	300
Samoa	4	2	3	2	4	1
Solomon Islands	14	13	11	18	21	22
Tonga	1	2	1	1	2	2
Tuvalu	—	—	—	—	—	—
Vanuatu	26	26	30	31	28	30
Total for DMCs	28,218	47,880	59,124	68,308	79,043	84,262

Table A18 External Debt Outstanding
($ million)

Economy	1993	1994	1995	1996	1997	1998	1999	2000
Newly Industrialized Economies	—	—	—	—	—	—	—	—
Hong Kong, China	—	—	—	—	—	—	—	—
Korea, Rep. of	—	—	—	—	—	—	—	—
Singapore	—	—	—	—	—	—	—	—
Taipei,China	—	—	—	—	—	—	—	—
People's Rep. of China and Mongolia	86,294	100,931	118,594	128,557	133,674	138,686	151,834	164,803
China, People's Rep. of	85,928	100,457	118,090	128,015	133,069	138,000	151,042	163,916
Mongolia	366	474	504	542	605	686	792	887
Central Asian Republics	3,837	5,568	6,841	8,539	10,811	4,120	—	—
Kazakhstan	1,978	3,265	3,480	4,186	5,713	—	—	—
Kyrgyz Republic	311	436	762	1,154	1,368	—	—	—
Tajikistan	509	760	817	868	1,180	1,271	—	—
Uzbekistan	1,039	1,107	1,782	2,331	2,550	2,849	—	—
Southeast Asia	204,324	243,714	270,409	292,663	337,558	180,307	77,900	—
Cambodia	397	446	561	624	2,056	2,146	—	—
Indonesia	83,299	101,278	106,455	113,143	138,018	—	—	—
Lao People's Democratic Rep.	1,893	1,971	2,068	2,175	2,323	—	—	—
Malaysia	20,147	22,518	27,400	29,100	44,700	31,500	—	—
Myanmar	5,756	6,555	5,771	5,553	—	—	—	—
Philippines	35,936	39,412	37,829	41,875	45,433	46,400	—	—
Thailand	52,107	64,866	82,568	90,536	93,416	85,400	77,900	—
Viet Nam	4,788	6,670	7,756	9,657	11,612	14,861	—	—
South Asia	138,713	150,520	149,429	151,215	153,283	62,177	62,500	65,542
Bangladesh	14,100	15,700	16,500	17,600	18,700	19,800	20,800	22,004
Bhutan	137	139	135	115	119	115	—	—
India	92,695	99,008	93,730	93,470	93,908	—	—	—
Maldives	130	141	172	179	172	—	—	—
Nepal	2,004	2,320	2,399	2,349	2,370	2,544	—	—
Pakistan	22,046	24,482	27,072	28,852	29,617	31,000	32,000	33,000
Sri Lanka	7,601	8,730	9,421	8,650	8,397	8,718	9,700	10,538
The Pacific	4,443	3,786	3,478	3,244	3,124	230	—	—
Cook Islands	126	—	—	—	—	—	—	—
Fiji	330	284	250	217	213	—	—	—
Kiribati	18	—	—	—	—	—	—	—
Marshall Islands	132	158	149	133	125	117	—	—
Micronesia, Federated States of	137	129	119	110	111	113	—	—
Nauru	—	—	—	—	—	—	—	—
Papua New Guinea	3,269	2,792	2,513	2,354	2,273	—	—	—
Samoa	194	157	170	167	156	—	—	—
Solomon Islands	151	155	158	145	135	—	—	—
Tonga	44	64	70	70	61	—	—	—
Tuvalu	—	—	—	—	—	—	—	—
Vanuatu	42	47	48	47	48	—	—	—
Total for DMCs	437,610	504,518	548,750	584,218	638,450	385,520	292,234	230,344

Table A19 Debt-Service Ratio
(percentage of exports of goods and services)

Economy	1993	1994	1995	1996	1997	1998	1999	2000
Newly Industrialized Economies								
Hong Kong, China	—	—	—	—	—	—	—	—
Korea, Rep. of	—	—	—	—	—	—	—	—
Singapore	—	—	—	—	—	—	—	—
Taipei,China	—	—	—	—	—	—	—	—
People's Rep. of China and Mongolia								
China, People's Rep. of	12.6	11.9	7.3	6.7	9.8	—	—	—
Mongolia	10.6	16.3	12.1	11.8	6.3	6.2	4.3	4.6
Central Asian Republics								
Kazakhstan	—	4.7	9.5	17.9	28.5	—	—	—
Kyrgyz Republic	1.0	4.1	20.5	12.3	5.2	—	—	—
Tajikistan	5.7	9.7	25.5	32.6	13.9	11.4	—	—
Uzbekistan	0.7	10.5	17.2	8.7	15.1	14.0	—	—
Southeast Asia								
Cambodia	2.9	3.4	3.4	5.1	2.3	2.6	2.3	3.1
Indonesia	31.9	32.6	32.6	34.2	39.5	36.0	34.0	34.0
Lao People's Democratic Rep.	4.0	3.3	5.7	5.9	9.5	11.9	—	—
Malaysia	6.2	4.9	6.0	6.9	6.2	0.9	—	—
Myanmar	11.8	14.5	16.7	18.1	—	—	—	—
Philippines	25.6	18.9	16.1	12.7	11.7	11.9	12.3	12.3
Thailand	11.3	11.7	11.4	12.3	15.6	21.3	20.1	—
Viet Nam	10.7	13.4	12.2	11.0	11.4	13.4	14.0	14.5
South Asia								
Bangladesh	12.3	11.6	10.3	12.1	11.4	11.7	12.0	12.1
Bhutan	23.3	27.6	18.1	32.4	10.1	11.0	—	—
India	—	—	37.0	33.7	32.5	31.8	31.0	28.5
Maldives	4.5	4.0	3.9	3.3	6.8	—	—	—
Nepal	9.0	8.0	8.1	5.4	7.3	9.0	8.7	8.7
Pakistan	27.4	33.4	34.9	33.9	38.0	40.0	20.0	22.0
Sri Lanka	14.3	13.7	14.4	13.4	13.4	12.1	12.1	10.8
The Pacific								
Cook Islands	—	—	—	—	—	—	—	—
Fiji	8.7	8.6	6.0	3.6	3.1	—	—	—
Kiribati	27.0	—	—	—	—	—	—	—
Marshall Islands	43.7	38.6	37.9	40.1	36.9	41.1	—	—
Micronesia, Federated States of	26.2	18.8	21.4	25.3	25.8	26.8	—	—
Nauru	—	—	—	—	—	—	—	—
Papua New Guinea	28.9	30.8	20.8	12.7	15.0	—	—	—
Samoa	6.9	7.4	4.3	4.0	3.9	—	—	—
Solomon Islands	5.8	8.2	3.8	3.9	2.4	—	—	—
Tonga	3.1	4.7	5.2	5.0	7.0	—	—	—
Tuvalu	—	—	—	—	—	—	—	—
Vanuatu	1.4	1.6	1.5	1.4	1.5	—	—	—

Table A20 Exchange Rates to the Dollar
(annual average)

Economy	Currency	1993	1994	1995	1996	1997	1998
Newly Industrialized Economies							
Hong Kong, China	HK$	7.7	7.7	7.7	7.7	7.7	7.7
Korea, Rep. of	Won	802.7	803.5	771.3	804.5	951.3	1,402.1
Singapore	S$	1.6	1.5	1.4	1.4	1.5	1.7
Taipei,China	NT$	26.4	26.5	26.5	27.5	28.7	33.4
People's Rep. of China and Mongolia							
China, People's Rep. of	Yuan	5.8	8.6	8.4	8.3	8.3	8.3
Mongolia	Tugrik	294.1	412.7	448.6	584.4	790.0	854.0
Central Asian Republics							
Kazakhstan	Tenge	2.6	35.6	61.0	67.3	75.4	78.3
Kyrgyz Republic	Som	5.8	10.9	10.8	12.8	17.4	20.8
Tajikistan	Tajik rubles	—	—	135.0	298.0	564.0	—
Uzbekistan	Sum	—	11.4	30.2	41.1	67.7	94.6
Southeast Asia							
Cambodia	Riel	2,689.0	2,545.3	2,450.8	2,624.1	2,946.3	3,750.0
Indonesia	Rupiah	2,102.6	2,180.9	2,275.8	2,363.6	4,666.9	10,147.5
Lao People's Democratic Rep.	Kip	716.3	717.7	804.7	921.1	1,256.7	3,045.0
Malaysia	Ringgit	2.6	2.6	2.5	2.5	2.8	3.9
Myanmar	Kyat	6.2	6.0	5.7	5.9	6.2	6.4
Philippines	Peso	27.1	26.4	25.7	26.2	29.5	40.9
Thailand	Baht	25.3	25.1	24.9	25.3	31.3	41.3
Viet Nam	Dong	10,640.0	10,978.0	11,037.0	11,032.0	11,683.0	13,297.0
South Asia							
Bangladesh	Taka	39.6	40.2	40.3	41.8	43.9	46.9
Bhutan	Ngultrum	30.5	31.4	32.4	35.4	36.3	41.3
India	Rupee	30.5	31.4	32.4	35.4	36.3	41.3
Maldives	Rufiyaa	11.0	11.6	11.8	11.8	11.8	11.8
Nepal	Rupee	43.0	49.3	51.9	56.7	58.0	63.6
Pakistan	Rupee	26.0	30.2	30.9	33.6	39.0	46.0
Sri Lanka	Rupee	48.3	49.4	51.3	55.3	59.0	63.5
The Pacific							
Cook Islands	NZ$	1.8	1.7	1.5	1.5	1.5	1.9
Fiji	F$	1.5	1.5	1.4	1.4	1.4	2.0
Kiribati	A$	1.5	1.4	1.3	1.3	1.3	1.6
Marshall Islands	US$	1.0	1.0	1.0	1.0	1.0	1.0
Micronesia, Federated States of	US$	1.0	1.0	1.0	1.0	1.0	1.0
Nauru	A$	1.5	1.4	1.3	1.3	1.3	1.6
Papua New Guinea	Kina	1.0	1.0	1.3	1.3	1.4	1.9
Samoa	Taka	2.6	2.5	2.5	2.5	2.6	2.9
Solomon Islands	SI$	3.2	3.3	3.4	3.6	3.7	4.8
Tonga	T$	1.4	1.4	1.3	1.3	1.2	1.3
Tuvalu	A$	1.5	1.4	1.3	1.3	1.3	1.6
Vanuatu	Vatu	121.6	116.4	112.1	111.7	115.9	127.3

Table A21 Central Government Expenditure
(percentage of GDP)

Economy	1993	1994	1995	1996	1997	1998
Newly Industrialized Economies						
Hong Kong, China	16.4	16.2	17.0	15.3	14.5	19.0
Korea, Rep. of	16.8	17.6	17.4	18.3	18.8	28.0
Singapore	17.4	13.9	15.9	14.5	18.1	—
Taipei,China	30.5	30.2	29.9	28.3	29.0	28.4
People's Rep. of China and Mongolia						
China, People's Rep. of	13.4	12.4	11.7	11.7	12.1	—
Mongolia	49.9	40.5	40.4	36.0	37.9	36.2
Central Asian Republics						
Kazakhstan	25.2	18.4	20.8	18.6	20.4	18.4
Kyrgyz Republic	22.9	23.4	28.6	22.2	21.8	—
Tajikistan	—	—	—	17.9	17.0	17.2
Uzbekistan	53.4	33.3	38.1	36.2	33.0	38.1
Southeast Asia						
Cambodia	11.2	16.3	17.3	17.2	13.9	12.5
Indonesia	17.6	16.9	15.4	16.3	17.3	20.3
Lao People's Democratic Rep.	17.9	23.8	21.9	22.1	20.7	22.6
Malaysia	24.9	23.7	22.5	22.6	21.5	23.1
Myanmar	9.0	9.3	9.8	9.2	7.7	—
Philippines	17.9	17.8	18.2	18.6	19.3	18.0
Thailand	16.4	17.2	16.3	17.1	19.2	17.7
Viet Nam	27.2	25.2	24.1	23.6	22.0	19.7
South Asia						
Bangladesh	17.8	18.1	18.9	17.8	17.8	17.9
Bhutan	33.4	34.0	36.7	35.4	33.3	28.0
India	16.2	15.5	14.6	14.3	15.0	—
Maldives	58.3	48.8	52.2	47.8	45.2	—
Nepal	18.0	16.9	17.8	18.9	18.0	19.5
Pakistan	26.0	23.2	23.0	23.9	21.6	21.8
Sri Lanka	28.1	29.0	28.8	27.9	26.8	25.9
The Pacific						
Cook Islands	47.6	46.9	40.6	34.5	—	—
Fiji	29.2	27.4	26.1	30.0	33.0	34.6
Kiribati	120.2	108.7	141.4	103.4	105.3	—
Marshall Islands	97.5	88.1	90.1	62.0	62.9	62.3
Micronesia, Federated States of	88.6	85.8	82.2	75.9	72.4	75.4
Nauru	—	—	—	—	—	—
Papua New Guinea	32.6	29.7	27.9	27.0	32.2	32.0
Samoa	79.9	45.9	52.7	46.4	39.2	36.5
Solomon Islands	54.1	57.0	48.1	46.4	41.0	44.0
Tonga	29.6	26.2	47.4	35.3	41.6	42.7
Tuvalu	57.6	52.3	50.0	48.0	—	—
Vanuatu	26.9	26.5	29.4	25.3	23.7	42.2

Table A22 Central Government Revenue
(percentage of GDP)

Economy	1993	1994	1995	1996	1997	1998
Newly Industrialized Economies						
Hong Kong, China	18.6	17.3	16.7	17.5	20.9	16.5
Korea, Rep. of	19.0	20.0	20.4	21.6	21.9	22.5
Singapore	35.6	25.9	25.9	21.1	21.4	—
Taipei,China	25.3	24.5	22.5	21.7	22.7	22.4
People's Rep. of China and Mongolia						
China, People's Rep. of	12.6	11.2	10.7	10.9	11.4	—
Mongolia	32.4	29.1	33.7	27.8	29.3	26.0
Central Asian Republics						
Kazakhstan	21.2	18.4	16.9	13.2	13.3	13.6
Kyrgyz Republic	15.5	15.6	16.7	16.0	15.8	—
Tajikistan	—	—	—	12.1	13.7	14.0
Uzbekistan	35.9	29.2	34.6	34.2	30.5	35.6
Southeast Asia						
Cambodia	5.4	9.6	8.9	9.1	9.7	8.5
Indonesia	17.0	17.4	16.1	16.5	17.3	15.6
Lao People's Democratic Rep.	11.8	12.3	12.2	13.0	11.4	9.8
Malaysia	25.2	26.0	23.3	23.4	23.9	19.7
Myanmar	7.6	6.8	6.5	6.9	6.7	—
Philippines	17.7	19.9	18.9	18.9	19.4	16.6
Thailand	18.6	19.1	19.3	19.5	18.3	15.0
Viet Nam	20.5	23.6	23.3	22.9	21.1	18.8
South Asia						
Bangladesh	11.7	11.9	12.1	11.9	12.2	12.7
Bhutan	22.2	19.6	18.8	18.2	17.4	19.1
India	14.9	15.4	13.8	14.3	15.0	—
Maldives	35.1	35.9	37.3	37.9	37.0	—
Nepal	8.8	9.8	11.2	11.2	10.8	9.0
Pakistan	18.0	17.3	17.4	17.6	15.4	16.4
Sri Lanka	19.7	19.0	20.4	19.0	19.2	19.4
The Pacific						
Cook Islands	43.1	40.9	39.0	33.0	—	—
Fiji	25.9	26.1	25.7	25.1	26.5	31.2
Kiribati	166.8	125.7	145.5	97.6	114.8	—
Marshall Islands	82.5	75.0	76.0	82.4	66.8	66.5
Micronesia, Federated States of	85.3	85.3	83.8	82.7	73.8	75.7
Nauru	—	—	—	—	—	—
Papua New Guinea	26.6	26.8	27.3	27.4	32.3	30.3
Samoa	58.7	37.8	45.5	47.9	39.4	38.2
Solomon Islands	45.4	51.0	42.4	41.7	35.8	43.9
Tonga	30.6	31.1	43.8	36.1	40.4	38.4
Tuvalu	62.1	56.2	54.6	47.1	—	—
Vanuatu	23.1	24.9	26.6	23.5	23.0	28.5

Table A23 Overall Budget Surplus/Deficit of Central Government
(percentage of GDP)

Economy	1993	1994	1995	1996	1997	1998
Newly Industrialized Economies						
Hong Kong, China	2.1	1.1	-0.3	2.2	6.5	-2.5
Korea, Rep. of	0.6	0.3	0.6	0.5	-1.4	-5.0
Singapore	15.5	6.9	2.6	6.8	3.3	-0.3
Taipei,China	-5.2	-5.7	-7.4	-6.6	-6.3	-5.9
People's Rep. of China and Mongolia						
China, People's Rep. of	-0.8	-1.2	-1.0	-0.8	-0.7	-1.2
Mongolia	-17.6	-11.4	-6.7	-8.2	-8.6	-10.3
Central Asian Republics						
Kazakhstan	-4.0	-7.5	-2.7	-4.7	-6.8	-5.8
Kyrgyz Republic	-7.1	-7.7	-11.5	-5.4	-5.2	-9.9
Tajikistan	—	—	—	-5.8	-3.3	-3.3
Uzbekistan	-10.4	-6.1	-4.1	-3.3	-2.3	-2.6
Southeast Asia						
Cambodia	-5.9	-6.8	-7.8	-8.4	-4.2	-3.9
Indonesia	-0.6	0.5	0.6	0.2	0.0	-4.7
Lao People's Democratic Rep.	-7.8	-11.5	-9.7	-9.1	-9.2	-12.8
Malaysia	0.2	2.3	0.9	0.7	1.8	-3.4
Myanmar	-1.4	-2.5	-3.3	-2.2	-1.0	-4.0
Philippines	-1.5	1.0	0.5	0.3	0.1	-1.9
Thailand	2.2	1.9	3.0	2.4	-0.9	-2.5
Viet Nam	-5.2	-2.3	-1.5	-1.3	-1.7	-1.5
South Asia						
Bangladesh	-6.1	-6.2	-6.8	-5.9	-5.6	-5.4
Bhutan	4.3	-0.5	0.1	2.0	-2.4	3.3
India	-6.9	-5.6	-4.9	-4.7	-5.5	-6.5
Maldives	-17.3	-7.4	-9.4	-3.8	-4.9	-2.6
Nepal	-7.0	-5.8	-4.8	-5.7	-5.1	-6.4
Pakistan	-8.0	-5.9	-5.6	-6.3	-6.2	-5.4
Sri Lanka	-8.7	-10.5	-10.1	-9.4	-7.9	-7.7
The Pacific						
Cook Islands	-4.5	-6.0	-1.6	-1.5	—	—
Fiji	-3.3	-1.3	-0.5	-4.9	-6.5	-3.4
Kiribati	46.6	17.0	4.1	-5.9	9.5	—
Marshall Islands	-15.0	-13.1	-14.1	20.4	3.9	4.2
Micronesia, Federated States of	-3.3	-0.6	1.7	6.9	1.5	0.3
Nauru	—	—	—	—	—	—
Papua New Guinea	-6.0	-2.9	-0.5	0.5	0.1	-1.6
Samoa	-21.2	-8.1	-7.3	1.4	0.3	1.7
Solomon Islands	-8.6	-6.0	-5.7	-4.7	-5.1	-0.1
Tonga	1.1	4.9	-3.6	0.8	-1.2	-4.3
Tuvalu	4.4	3.9	4.7	-0.9	—	—
Vanuatu	-3.8	-1.6	-2.7	-1.8	-0.7	-13.6